T0358123

Something Rich
& Strange:
Sea Changes, Beaches and the
Littoral in The Antipodes

Something Rich
& Strange:
Sea Changes, Beaches and the
Littoral in The Antipodes

edited by

Susan Hosking, Rick Hosking,
Rebecca Pannell and Nena Bierbaum

Wakefield
Press

Wakefield Press
1 The Parade West
Kent Town
South Australia 5067
www.wakefieldpress.com.au

First published 2009

Designed and typeset by Michael Deves, Wakefield Press
Printed and bound by Hyde Park Press, Adelaide

National Library of Australia
Cataloguing-in-Publication entry

Title:	Something rich and strange: sea changes, beaches and the littoral in the antipodes/editor Susan Hosking … [et al.]
ISBN:	978 1 86254 870 1 (pbk.)
Subjects:	Beaches – Australia – History
	Beaches – Social aspects – Australia
	Seashore – Australia
	Australia – Social life and customs
Other Authors/ Contributors:	Hosking, Sue, 1948–
Dewey Number:	333.9170994

Contents

Introduction:
Something Rich and Strange

SUE AND RICK HOSKING

Most of these chapters began as papers presented at a Centre for Research in the New Literatures in English conference at Penneshaw on Kangaroo Island in December 2005, organised by the English, Creative Writing and Australian Studies Department at Flinders University. Drawing on Ariel's Song in William Shakespeare's *The Tempest* for its title, people attending were invited to consider the idea of the littoral, and the various kinds of sea changes.[1] It is hoped that this volume will contribute to the steadily growing archive of studies of (Australian) beach history and culture.[2]

Looking over the speakers' shoulders, delegates were able to contemplate the dramatic backdrop of Backstairs Passage, the strait separating Kangaroo Island from the Australian mainland. Matthew Flinders, the first European to chart those waters in 1802, recorded a tidal rip in these waters as he sailed eastward around Cape Jervis; he entered the phrase 'confused sea' on his charts, recording a place in the sea where tidal flows or wind shifts can create waves that interact with an existing swell, creating a hazard for sailors. While those who have sailed such waters may have vivid memories of what 'confused sea' can mean, Flinders' phrase also reminds us that beaches have long been places where the flotsam of the world beyond can wash up. The littoral is a place of encounter, where new waves must reconcile with earlier waves, where things can flow in two directions at once.

Beaches are places of contact, of confrontation and friction: first-comers always arrive on a beach. After European settlement made its tenuous beginnings at Sydney Cove, it was close on a hundred years before the inland was travelled and settled by non-Indigenous people. The continent's littoral was the first frontier to be defined: by 1803 the outline of the land mass had been drawn, the charting completed, the blank map inscribed with names that usually celebrate and codify the European discovery and conquest. Flinders' circumnavigation in 1802 had mapped 'Australia' (the word was first used by Flinders), revealing the land as 'girt by sea', as the national anthem continues to remind us.

For the next three or four decades the littoral was much studied through telescopes; in 1986 an atlas published in South Australia represents European Australia three decades after Flinders' voyage as essentially a coastline, showing incursions into the interiors in Van Diemen's Land, in Western Australia and along the eastern seaboard, mostly along what passes for Australia's major rivers.[3] These days we celebrate the bush workers as we endlessly search for popular stereotypes of Australian-ness. In the early decades after settlement, however, with the first settlements huddled along the shorelines, the beach was the place of work. Australia's first export industries were seal and whale products; the nation's economic origins were slippery with the blood of sea mammals, prompting what came close to the first extinctions of fauna as a direct consequence of the European invasion.

The chapters in this collection explore these and other related themes. Some see the littoral as a contact zone, drawing on Mary Louise Pratt's idea:

> the space of … encounters, the space in which people geographically and historically separated come into contact with each other and establish ongoing relations, usually involving conditions of coercion, radical inequality, and intractable conflict.[4]

Beaches have always been the place of edgy encounter and ambivalent contact, symbolised most powerfully in the western tradition by Robinson Crusoe's discovery of that single footprint on what he had thought of as *his* deserted beach. Crusoe remains the archetypal beachcomber: numbers of chapters in this book draw on the Crusoe story.

Since 1836, the nation has become increasingly aware that it is 'girt by sea'; its coastline stretches for 36,000 kilometres. No other nation save for Russia looks out on three of the world's great oceans. While most Australians think first of the Pacific and assume that the sun rises in the sea, others of us live with the Indian and the Southern Oceans and are used to the sun setting in the sea. Given that most of us live within an hour's drive of one of Australia's 10,685 beaches, we spend many of our days on the shore or in the water: we holiday by the beach, we walk its littoral, we fish its inshore waters, we sail, swim or surf its waters.[5] In suggesting that the coast is the 'chief spatial and symbolic focus in our culture', Philip Drew draws attention to the 'edge, expressed as a verandah … a buffer zone between inside and outside … a living edge rather than a mere physical structure'.[6] His idea has a particular potency, given real estate prices in those beachside suburbs where people can enjoy a view of the sea. Of all the places where Drew's sense of the littoral as verandah can be understood in Australia, the most dramatic is seen standing on the Bunda cliffs on the edge of the Nullarbor: it comes as no surprise that a history of the Ceduna district by Jim Faull is titled *Life on the Edge*.[7]

Robert Drewe has reminded us that many of our most significant life experiences happen on beaches:

[m]any, if not most, Australians have their first sexual experience on the coast and as a consequence see the beach in a sensual and nostalgic light. Thereafter, the beach is not only a regular summer pleasure and balm, but an *idée fixe* which fulfils an almost ceremonial need at each critical physical and emotional stage: as lovers, as honeymooners, as parents and as ... the elderly retired.[8]

While the beach may be a place of licence and freedom, a place where we disrobe and disport in each other's company, the beach can also be a sinister and threatening place, a place of violence and death, where, for example, a family of children called the Beaumonts could disappear, on Australia Day of all days, in 1966. One of the authors of this introduction was present on a South Australian beach in the early 1960s when a spearfisherman was taken by a white pointer shark a few hundred metres away.

The beach can also be a battleground, where ideas about Australianness, identity and belonging have been fought over. The Cronulla riots occurred on 11 December 2005, coincidentally in the middle of the conference, when the beach became a battleground between one group determined to patrol the boundaries of what was seen as iconic Australian space, and a second group was equally determined to test that boundary. At issue was the right to decide who can be on the beach. The infamous SMS which preceded the riots asked people to '[c]ome to Cronulla this weekend to take revenge. This Sunday every Aussie in the Shire get down to North Cronulla to support Leb and wog bashing day'. One of the delegates received one of these messages at the conference. The wearing of the Australian flag and the slogans '[w]e grew here, you flew here' and 'Aussie pride' show how significant the beach remains as a symbolic site of traditional Australianness.

In 2002 there were nation-wide celebrations to commemorate the blue water encounter between British explorer Matthew Flinders and his French counterpart Nicolas Baudin in Encounter Bay. The celebrations remind us of the enduring power of this cult of the first-comers that the Cronulla riots revealed, demonstrating the obsession with origins in (post)colonial nations and in settler colonies in particular. As part of the celebrations, the sculptor Indiana James was commissioned to build a contemplation seat out of redgum at Penneshaw on Kangaroo Island. The intention was to create a place where people could sit and reflect on the complicated early history of encounters between Indigenous and non-Indigenous people in southern Australia in the early decades of the nineteenth century, on the 'darker side of our heritage', as one webpage put it.

There were reports of some unease on Kangaroo Island about the decision: one or two islanders objected to the creation of the memorial, arguing that the island was beyond Australian cultural limits and asserting that the political issues about reconciliation that remain as 'unfinished business' on the mainland should not be ferried across the confused seas of Backstairs Passage to the holiday paradise of Kangaroo Island. All kinds of provocative ideas about the littoral, beaches, sea changes, holiday places and islands swirl around in this story.

Notes

1 'Full fathom five thy father lies,/Of his bones are coral made,/Those are pearls that were his eyes:/Nothing of him that doth fade,/But doth suffer a sea-change/ Into something rich and strange.'

2 There is a growing archive of studies of Australian beach culture. See Jack Bedson, *Don't Get Burnt! Or the Great Australian Day at the Beach* (Sydney: Collins, 1985); Greg Dening, *Islands and Beaches: Discourse on a Silent Land, Marquesas 1774–1880* (Melbourne: Melbourne University Press, 1980); Geoffrey Dutton, *Sun, Sea, Surf and Sand: The Myth of the Beach* (Melbourne: Oxford University Press, 1985); Philip Drew, *The Coast Dwellers: Australians Living on the Edge* (Ringwood, Vic.: Penguin Books, 1994); Robert Drewe ed. *Picador Book of the Beach* (Sydney: Pan Macmillan, 1993); Tim Winton, *Land's Edge* (Sydney: Macmillan, 1993); Douglas Booth, *The History of Sun, Sand and Surf* (London, Routledge 2001); Leone Huntsman, *Sand in Our Souls: the Beach in Australian History* (Melbourne: Melbourne University Press, 2001); Greg Dening, *Beach crossings: voyaging across times, cultures, and self* (Melbourne: Miegunyah Press, 2004); CA Cranston and Robert Jeffrey Zeller, eds. *The Littoral Zone: Australian contexts and their writers* (Amsterdam : Rodopi, 2007).

3 http://www.atlas.sa.gov.au/images/1settle3Aust_18362.jpg, accessed 28 September 2008.

4 Pratt goes on as follows: '"contact zone" is an attempt to invoke the spatial and temporal copresence of subjects previously separated by geographic and historical disjunctures, and whose trajectories now intersect. By using the term "contact", I aim to foreground the interactive, improvisational dimensions of … encounters so easily ignored or suppressed by diffusionist accounts of conquest and domination. A "contact" perspective emphasizes how subjects are constituted in and by their relations to each other. It treats the relations among … travellers and "travelees", not in terms of separateness and apartheid, but in terms of copresence, interaction, interlocking understandings and practices, often within radically asymmetrical relations of power'. Mary Louise Pratt, *Imperial Eyes: Travel Writing and Transculturation* (London: Routledge, 1992) 6–7.

5 Andrew Short, 'Australian Beach Systems, Nature and Distribution', *Journal of Coastal Research* 22.1 (January 2006) 11.

6 Drew 1994: 3.

7   Jim Faull, *Life on the Edge: the Far West Coast of South Australia* (Ceduna, SA: the District Council of Murat Bay, 1988).
8   Drewe 1993: 6–7.

Works cited

Atlas South Australia <http://www.atlas.sa.gov.au>

Booth, Douglas. *The History of Sun, Sand and Surf.* London: Routledge, 2001.

Bedson, Jack. *Don't Get Burnt! Or the Great Australian Day at the Beach.* Sydney: Collins, 1985.

Cranston, CA & Zeller, Robert Jeffrey, eds. *The Littoral Zone: Australian contexts and their writers.* Amsterdam: Rodopi, 2007.

Dening, Greg. *Islands and Beaches: Discourse on a Silent Land, Marquesas 1774–1880.* Melbourne: Melbourne University Press, 1980.

Dening, Greg. *Beach crossings: voyaging across times, cultures, and self.* Melbourne: Miegunyah Press, 2004.

Drew, Philip. *The Coast Dwellers: Australian Living on the Edge.* Ringwood, Vic.: Penguin Books, 1994.

Drewe, Robert, ed. *Picador Book of the Beach.* Sydney: Pan Macmillan, 1993.

Dutton, Geoffrey. *Sun, Sea, Surf and Sand: The Myth of the Beach.* Melbourne: Oxford University Press, 1985.

Faull, Jim. *Life on the Edge: the Far West Coast of South Australia.* Ceduna, SA: the District Council of Murat Bay, 1988.

Huntsman, Leone. *Sand in Our Souls: the Beach in Australian History.* Melbourne: Melbourne University Press, 2001.

Pratt, Mary Louise. *Imperial Eyes: Travel Writing and Transculturation.* London: Routledge, 1992.

Short, Andrew. 'Australian Beach Systems, Nature and Distribution', *Journal of Coastal Research* 22.1 (2006) 11–27.

Winton, Tim. *Land's Edge.* Sydney: Macmillan, 1993.

A Short History of Beach Holidays

RICHARD WHITE

We share, with reasonable unanimity, an image of the typical Australian beach holiday, marked by long lazy days of vacancy, the sounds of children and surf, the smell of barbecues and sun-screen, the exquisite sensations of sunburn and sand between the toes. It is an utterly sensual experience, a liminal time and space where things work differently, a shared experience whether in a tent, a caravan, a cabin or the San Remo Holiday Flats. There has been a shift recently in the history of tourism from John Urry's emphasis on the tourist gaze to the more fully corporeal experience, and within that historiographical shift, the Australian beach holiday stands pre-eminent.[1] It is a powerful image, not just a visual image, but something more fully and more sensually realised, something, perhaps, that relates to the simpler sensual pleasures of childhood. However, despite its power, its history was a short one; this chapter charts the long slow development of the beach holiday from the nineteenth century, its heyday in the 1950s, 60s and 70s, and its decline since.

While Australia's beach culture and its rituals have attracted scholarly attention in recent years, the beach holiday, which in significant ways stands in opposition to the essentially urbanised beach, has been somewhat overlooked.[2] Perhaps historians have tacitly accepted the valuation of its critics, who have long condemned it as conventional, predictable, mindlessly hedonistic, crudely escapist, quintessentially daggy: consider the critique of John Howard's annual holiday at Hawk's Nest. For a short time, however, it flourished as 'something rich and strange'. It deserves a valedictory.

First we should dispose of the Gold Coast—if only it were so easy. A 2001 survey of 'unAustralianness' showed widespread agreement, across a wide range of age groups and social classes, that the Gold Coast is a peculiarly unAustralian place.[3] Its power as it developed in the 1960s resided in its very atypicality: its faux sophistication, sharply defined urban skyline, high-rise apartments and attempts at a glamorous 'international' style tended to make it a unique rather than a typical holiday resort. It was the necessary 'other' that allowed the 'typical' holiday to be defined as something different: casual, unglamorous, closer to nature. The fact that Surfer's Paradise became the particular focus of

I

'schoolies week' at the end of the twentieth century suggests the importance of that atypicality: the rite of passage to adulthood at a specific site marked out as sophisticated, measured in its distance from a more typical, even if imaginary, family holiday at any generic beach.

Many of the elements of this more typical holiday had been sketched in by the end of the nineteenth century. Australians had already long been seen as having a reputation for holiday-making: alone of Anglo-Saxon populations, they had created a kind of Mediterranean attitude to work and life, working to live, rather than living to work. Both convicts and Aboriginal people had been condemned for their attitudes to work soon after the British arrived. As early as 1859, the *Sydney Morning Herald* could put a more positive spin on it:

> We are the children of the sunny south, and we borrow from the clear skies above us, and from the general clime, much of that lightness of heart and of that vivacity, which so eminently distinguish us as holiday making people.[4]

The critics remained. Beatrice Webb found Australians 'inclined to self-indulgence and disinclined for regular work'. And Marcus Clarke complained about the masses enjoying themselves in 1869:

> holiday-making, as a general rule, is the hardest work attempted by mankind, and the most weary, flat, stale, and unprofitable business into the bargain. Yet people go on the same way year after year.[5]

Clarke was talking about day trippers, spending a gazetted public holiday in the mountains or on the coast conveniently close to most of Australia's major cities. According to the authors of *Australia at Play. Suggested by 'America at Work'*, 'the Australian ideal is to do as little work and enjoy as much play as possible'. It took some time for the beach to be embraced as Australia's pre-eminent holiday destination, and for the holiday to extend to more than a day trip for the majority. But by the end of the century, the wealthy were well established in substantial holiday homes up and down the coasts from the big cities. Others could enjoy the cheap guest-houses or great tourist hotels, offering vigorous exercise or languid indulgence, which began to appear in the new coastal resorts as they earlier had in the 'hill stations' close to most colonial capitals. Even those less well off could find some time to escape, aided by cheap excursion fares, long weekends and some limited expectation of constant, fair and reasonable wages: a weekend's camping or a visit to relatives was a possibility for any worker in regular employment.

These kinds of holidays were a product of the second half of the nineteenth century, part of the massive transformations brought about by modernity and urbanisation. The technologies of steam and photography had promoted the spaces to holiday in. The possibilities of profit for entrepreneurs, and the transformation of industrial relations for workers, helped create the time. And the experience of modern life itself, of the rush and routines of modern cities, and new ways of thinking about time and space, had created the desire to get away in the first place.

The dimensions of these recognisably modern holidays were sketched in along familiar axes. The ideal holiday fell somewhere between the safety of home and the dangers of the exotic; somewhere between spontaneity and freedom, on the one hand, and planning and regulation, on the other; somewhere between indulgent luxury and invigorating exercise; and somewhere between conformity to the crowd and the expression of individuality. Along those axes new understandings of the self were being negotiated: robbed of its distinct identity by civilisation and work, the 'true' self could only be rediscovered—or was it reinvented?—by getting away on holiday.

Yet in 1914 the modern holiday was far from democratic or accessible to all. Many could only indulge in the holiday experience as a day trip on a Sunday or public holiday or at best a long weekend. They could not afford a holiday overnight, and most had no provision for a holiday within their working conditions. Single women and many men and women with families were constrained by social convention, lack of time and poverty. For vast numbers the notions of work and home, notions that helped define what a holiday was, were unstable: most work was casual, most homes were rented. The heyday of the holiday was still to come.

Nevertheless, nineteenth century holiday-makers could be found in the mountains, in the bush and in the city. There was one location of desire, however, that was attracting more than its fair share of attention from all classes in Australia at the end of the century: the beach. Coastal scenery had long had an attraction to the Romantically inclined, who enjoyed the buffeting of the wind, the drama of cliffs and the roar of the surf. Their impetus was to get away from the crowd and commune with untouched nature. At the same time the more formal European tradition of the seaside resort was well established in Australia by 1900: all the capital cities were within reach of the beach and provided the crowds to sustain a small industry of merry-go-rounds, donkey rides and food stalls. Its impetus came from the democratisation of the spa resort where the crowd was the attraction, with its socialising, promenading, observing and being observed by each other. Relatively few ventured into the water.

From 1902 prohibitions on surf bathing were abandoned. The ironic result of the new freedom was intense regulation: regulation of clothing, of behaviour, of where you could swim and who you could mix with. Very rapidly there appeared an Australian *urban* beach culture that was quite different to the seaside culture of Victorian years, though it is possible to see its contours much earlier, as Caroline Ford has shown.[6] Within a decade, it had established a new balance between freedom and propriety, culture and nature, danger and safety, the individual and the crowd. Control and surveillance came from public opinion, local councils and the new lifesaving clubs, but on the beach new freedoms were found, and new ways of connecting to the self, to nature and to each other. In particular it became acceptable to enjoy bodily sensations in public. Doug Booth has shown how advocates of surf bathing had long abandoned the claim they only bathed for their health, and simply enjoyed the sensual experience, the 'delicious rumble' of the swell, waves 'slapping the chest', the sun on the skin and the sand between the toes. Such sensations were easier to enjoy naked than in the new, heavy, regulation neck-to-knee swimming costumes, but on the beach the restraints of formal clothing were dropping off.[7] Beachgoers discarded their shoes, men their collars, women—most symbolically—their corsets. Along with them went many of the conventional markers of social distinction. The beach was a newly democratised space.

A certain formality was still to be found on the beach itself despite its assertion of casualness, but it was a democratic formality: a new etiquette regulating behaviour, a new gaze regulating body shape and new measures of social distinction relating to fitness, beauty and youth. There was still much of the eyeing each other off that had been so central to the culture of Bath: what Charles Dickens had called 'the immensity of promenading'.[8] Indeed the culture of the metropolitan beaches arguably owed more to the formal sociability of the spa and the promenade than to Romanticism; to culture more than nature.[9] But while Australians flocked to metropolitan beaches on their days off, their desire to 'get away' was not entirely satisfied by day-tripping. The urban beach had replaced one set of formalities with another. Instead, when they really set out to 'get away' on holidays, urban Australians in their thousands would begin to seek out the 'unspoilt' beach *away* from the city, where they could stay for days or weeks on end. Their definition of 'unspoilt' might vary: unscathed by the judgmental gaze, by 'the larrikin element', by development, by the paraphernalia of commerce, or by concrete promenades and other 'improvements'. But they would join together in searching for another way of balancing culture and nature, risk and safety, formality and freedom. It would be on the beach, up or down the coast, that the Australian holiday would eventually have its apotheosis. Before that could happen, two foundations needed to be put in place: mass car ownership and paid annual leave. Until the majority had access to cars and to paid leave—both achieved in the 1950s—beach holidays were more likely to demarcate social distinctions than to eliminate them.

Take the car first. Steam—boats and trains—opened up the possibility of mass holidays in the late nineteenth century. It meant almost anyone could get to the popular beach or mountain resorts that had developed by 1900. But it also meant that sort of holiday was a mass experience. The holiday crowd was its defining feature.[10] In the 1920s, however, 'mass' culture was increasingly derided by those who sought to assert their social superiority: they were individuals, impervious to the blandishments of mass culture. The arrival of the motor car suited the times perfectly, promising a new individualism in travel. Its guarantee of independence and its display of conspicuous consumption spawned new ways of signifying social status and reshaped how people holidayed. Having an 'independence', the wealth to do as one pleased, had been crucial in defining social status a century earlier; now that the working classes had sufficient means to pursue pleasure independently on their occasional days off, the fact that on holiday they all seemed to do the same thing at the same time itself became a sign of their social inferiority, their lack of true 'independence'. A stereotype developed of the Australian crowd at leisure, mindlessly demonstrating their philistinism at the beach, the races or the football. Those who sought to demonstrate their superiority to mass culture had to assert their 'independence' in new ways. Between the wars, the motor car became the greatest symbol of middle-class independence from the mob.

The new motoring classes quickly explored the new holiday opportunities that opened up. Motor camping became a popular demonstration of independence, and happy campers, setting up tent wherever the fancy took them, negotiated between spontaneity and the instruction in camping guides to plan this new form of holiday with care. Caravanning also began to be catered for, by a number of local manufacturers as well as do-it-yourself kits, though its glory days would come in the 1950s.[11] Similarly opening to a wider constituency, but still contributing to the social stratification of travel destinations and leisure, was the holiday home. While only the very wealthy could maintain substantial country houses, the middle class pursuit of property ownership was being extended to holiday shacks, which began to be called 'weekenders' in Australia in the 1920s and were seen as a new form of individual expression.[12] Shacks at popular out-of-the-way fishing spots, generally reached by car, also maintained some exclusivity, even if their amenities meant the holiday experience was comparable to the everyday lives of the very poor.

This changed in the 1950s. Where, between the wars, the car allowed a holiday away from the masses, car ownership soon became a democratic right.

In 1945, according to Queensland's statistician, car ownership was still 'a rich man's hobby', but for the new Liberal Party, promising freedom and unparalleled consumption under Menzies, '[a] car is as essential to a middle class man as a radio or a refrigerator'.[13] In 1946, there was one car for every 14 Australians, by 1960, it was one to 3.5. The vast majority of families had access to a car.[14] The result was that the 'individuality' and 'distinction' that the car promised in the 1920s disappeared in the string of holiday towns the car created around the Australian coast.

The other fundamental prop for the holiday boom of the 1950s was the provision of paid annual leave. In planning for post-war reconstruction, the federal Labor government had placed full employment at the centre of its policy-making. The job security provided by the commitment to full employment was a necessary psychological foundation for the development of a relaxed, extended holiday as a mass phenomenon. Through the 1940s and 1950s, in arbitration courts and in parliaments, a debate took place about the relative values of time and money. For all the flaws of the arbitration system—it had some, though not nearly as many as those who destroyed it claimed—it did provide a forum for a debate as to whether productivity gains should take the form of more leisure or more consumption, and workers consistently opted for more leisure. For thirty-five years from the award of a week's paid annual leave to printing workers in 1938, there was a steady move to one, then two, then three, then four weeks annual leave. And then, in the 1970s, it stopped.

In New South Wales the William McKell Labor government made leisure a centre-piece of policy, passing an *Annual Holidays Act* in 1944, providing all workers with two weeks paid leave. Legislating holidays was 'a humanitarian act':

> Those who keep the wheels of industry going and carry on domestic and other necessary work cannot be expected to go on year in and year out without a rest. Even racehorses and cart-horses are turned out for a spell from time to time.[15]

The holiday boom that followed was a defining element of the new postwar 'Australian way of life' constructed around the family, home ownership and car culture. If 'meat three times a day' had been the sign of Australia's high standard of living in 1860, then holidays three weeks a year evoked Australian life in 1960, a sign not only of prosperity but of Australianness itself. The annual beach holiday gave shape to the year's rhythms, displacing older religious meanings and creating its own social rituals. In the very repetition of going to the same place year after year, seeing the same people, doing the same things, there was something ceremonial, dependable and emotionally fulfilling, an annual marking out of special time. In a more secularised society, religious festivals, Christmas and Easter, became important for the holiday time they represented. The language changed: Christmas time had become the 'Christmas holidays'.[16] Increasingly fulfilment was to be found, for many Australians, not in church or in the workplace or in the department store, but on holiday. J D Pringle, the Scots editor of *The Sydney Morning Herald*, found Australian meaning not in any romance of hard-working bushmen, but on the beach.[17]

Pringle also stressed the egalitarianism of the beach. On the beach it was hard to see social distinctions: 'you cannot tell a man's income in a pair of swimming trunks, and the Pacific surf is a mighty leveller'.[18] The beach holiday was a symbol of an egalitarian Australia. Pringle's social antennae were acute enough to register the long-established distinctions between beaches: Rosebud was not Portsea, for example. Yet there was some truth in the egalitarian stereotype. The very emergence of a beach culture was predicated on new kinds of social distinction—body shape, beauty, depth of tan, physical prowess. The 1950s were the heyday of Mr Atlas body building advertisements around the theme of 'weaklings' not getting sand kicked in their faces. While conventional measures of social class might re-emerge at the end of a holiday at the beach, now working people's access to beach holidays obscured rather than delineated class difference. On holiday, for a time, equality was more a reality.

Part of the reason was that the stereotypical holiday did not actually cost much. A tent, a caravan or a fibro holiday cabin at the beach did not in themselves imply social distinctions. Certainly there was more expensive accommodation available but in many cases the camping area—often run on egalitarian principles by local councils—had the best location, close to the beach. When a family decided to stay in a holiday flat for a week rather than a camping area for a month, the decision was rarely an assertion of social status: it was more likely to reflect the complications of family politics, as mothers put their feet down.[19] The typical beach holiday kept expenses down: home cooking, barbecues, the occasional take away hamburger or fish and chips. There were not many extras. Hospitality services, theme park rides, restaurants and serviced resorts offering massage, beauty treatments and gym instructors would come much later.

Intriguingly, the consumer durables of the holiday bore a counter-intuitive relationship to class. As often happens, the forms of escape took on the forms of what was being escaped from.[20] While the holiday might have been an escape from the home and its consumerism, the home and consumerism insisted on coming along. The consumerism of leisure in the post-war period went more into the purchase of goods—holiday equipment—than the purchase of services.

Expenditure went into making the cheap holiday comfortable. This was the era of the holiday purchase—the beach towel, the Esky, the beach umbrella, the portable barbecue, the beach chair, the collapsible table, the ever more elaborate tent, and at the top of the ladder the caravan. Many were Christmas presents, a further sign that the meaning of Christmas was holidays. But they were peculiarly democratic purchases. While there were comparisons to be made between the biggest caravan or the latest model Esky, the comparison did not necessarily correlate to non-holiday indicators of status, the size of the home or features of the refrigerator. Holidays provided workers with an opportunity to display a superiority in the realm of possessions that their homes never could.

The car-based holiday reflected a privatisation of life in the 1950s, as a newly self-conscious tourism industry pushed towards a more private and self-contained experience—the motel over the hotel, the holiday flat over the guest house, the car over the train. Community activity seemed somehow dated, a left-over from war-time making do, and the despotic authority of the landlady could smack of the petty tyrannies of war service. Tourism was becoming a business too, increasingly big business, advertising the virtues of the commercialised and privatised experience, and painting older communal holidays as out-dated and unsophisticated. Private enterprise sought to displace state government bureaucracies such as railways and tourist bureaux, council caravan parks, community organisations such as motoring clubs, the YMCA or the Youth Hostels Association, and also the smaller scale part-time economy of those who took in lodgers, sold fish or ran souvenir stalls. The guest house all but disappeared: the older resorts of guest houses and tourist hotels clustered around railway stations fell on hard times. Victor Harbor had twenty-six in the 1930s but only one at the end of the century.[21] It could look like the victory of freedom over bureaucracy, the individual over the community, private enterprise over socialism.

Some analysts of the holiday at the end of the war had forecast a quite different future. In Britain, J.A.R. Pimlott, in his ground-breaking history, *The Englishman's Holiday*, had seen the advent of mass leisure heralding a new type of holiday experience in which communal interaction would dominate. His ideal was the Butlin's style Holiday Camp where the regulated routines of a guest house were repeated on a mass scale, with organised activities and elaborate facilities. In Australia in 1950 the *Current Affairs Bulletin* imagined something similar in its special issue on holidays. It was a kind of socialist utopia where planning produced fun for everyone—an off-shoot of the enthusiasm for the new post-war 'social order' in the planning for post-war reconstruction. In both Britain and Australia planning centred on encouraging an idealised 'community' spirit in place of self-interested individualism. Working class values of community and sociability would bring to the holiday a socialist spirit denied by the status-seeking and individualism that characterised the more bourgeois holiday of the past.[22] It has been widely assumed that the car, the motel, the holiday flat put an end to that sort of romanticised sociability in the Menzies era, as Australian workers took on bourgeois values; the new working class holiday-makers grabbed the opportunity to decide for themselves where to go and what to do and when to do it, and turned their back on each other in their holiday cocoons. The industry said they were voting with their feet for freedom, flexibility, self-expression and autonomy.

It is true that Butlin-style holiday camps never succeeded in Australia. Some of the trade union camps suggested a kind of working class solidarity and coach tours indulged in community singing; but the holiday in the private car ruled supreme. By the 1970s, as government tourism research collected more and more statistics, almost eighty-seven per cent of holiday trips within Australia were by car.[23] The privatised car and the industry it spawned seemed to dominate the democratic holiday that emerged in the 1950s as leisure was socialised and made available to workers.

But before we accept a simple embourgeoisment thesis, we should pay attention to the kind of holiday people were having. While the caravan and camping holiday boomed because of private car ownership, it was not a private affair. The camping ground holiday that emerged as a dominant form in the 1950s and 1960s can be seen as a more relaxed, more informal, more laid-back—perhaps more 'Australian'—version of the sociability of the Butlin's ideal. In the 1950s, an older ideal of the camping tour—of getting away, spontaneously choosing a site by the side of the road—was still possible but becoming harder to accomplish. Mass car ownership inevitably made camping a communal activity. Local councils began to regulate campers and provide facilities for them: necessary simply to manage the huge new influx of holiday-makers, but also a useful new source of income. By the late 1950s, camping grounds on the Mornington Peninsula were boasting that 'facilities as good as at home are provided', including television, often still not installed at home, and electric washing machines.[24] Camping holidays also became more stable and less spontaneous because cars allowed for the proliferation of equipment—camp chairs, tables, Eskys, cooking facilities, beds … there was no end to the list of what enterprising manufacturers deemed to be new holiday essentials, especially with the coming of the 'powered site'. With all that equipment, it became harder to simply pack up and go.

In its relaxed informality, this sort of holiday contributed to the idea of a unique 'Australian way of life' developing after the war. The 'Australian way of life' was presented to the influx of post-war migrants from southern Europe as both a gift and a command: it was what they were expected to conform to. Yet the communal camping holiday was surprisingly more like a 'continental' holiday than an Anglo-Saxon one. While it seems to have emerged independently in Australia, it was something that the new post-war migrants could engage in with gusto. Like other Australians, they regularly shared holidays with extended families or large groups of friends, and fishing, conversation and communal meals were high on the agenda. They had a particular appreciation of the spaciousness of Australia, and the fact that the beaches were free was a marvel. Their reputation for working hard did not interfere with their ability to enjoy leisure: indeed the very stereotype of the hard-working migrant suggested how far the Australian-born regarded their own leisurely attitude to life as a defining characteristic of Australianness.

The idea persisted that this was an escape from everyday routines of work and home, even as serious bush-walking zealots scoffed that far from these campers getting away from it all, they brought it all with them, all packed into the boot of the car. It was common for critics to satirise how the camping ground, with its neat rows of ordered tents or caravans and cars, where people put down roots, and met the same people year after year, was simply an imitation of the comfortable suburban routines a holiday was supposed to escape. Camping, they insisted, was supposed to be about adventure, testing oneself against nature, acquiring new experiences. On the other hand the new tourism entrepreneurs saw these campers as not spending enough, although the camping grounds sustained a small business economy in tourist resorts built around hamburgers and fish and chips. The couple who visited Narrabeen Caravan Park from nearby Ryde for over fifty years were simply not playing the game from the point of view of the motel chains, island resorts and hire car firms. But the attractions were in the very familiarity and enforced sociability. The ritual of returning to the same place was part of the pleasure. In 1974 almost two-thirds of visitors to Port Fairy were repeat visitors.[25] Families made friends; social interaction took place around the facilities—the barbecue, the tennis courts and swimming pools if the amenities extended to such things, even in the queues for the showers and the laundry and the fish and chips. Games and even concerts were organised but they were less competitive and more impromptu than Butlin's could manage. The special camaraderie of the holiday *was* an escape from the normal day-to-day relationships based on work or shopping or commuting. It was important that it remained a cheap holiday—three weeks at a camping ground could look better value than a few days in a motel, but it was not just an economic choice. The cheap holiday meant a special democratic connection was possible, where everyone could appreciate the sun and sand and sausages together; people who otherwise would not meet outside relationships of power and economic exchange could pretend for a time to be equal. And above all there was time to do nothing, no call of work deadlines or house repairs or cleaning. The critics were missing the point.

The victory of the casually communal, democratic holiday was evident in the instructive history of the island resort. Reg Ansett established the Royal Hayman Hotel on Hayman Island in the Whitsundays in 1950, creating a package that integrated his interests in air transport, tourism and eventually television. Royal Hayman offered cabaret, a cocktail bar, a beauty salon, sports shop, florist and swimming pool, an irresistible improvement, he imagined, on the fibro cabins and toilet blocks on nearby South Molle. But for some years the resort languished. The acquisition of the 'Royal' adjective was an appeal to status anxiety, an echo of older obsessions with royal patronage that had driven the era of the spa. But the Australian beach holiday had become, by the 1950s, insistently unglamorous, and Ansett had misjudged the power of its casualness. He explained, with the uncomprehending resentment of an overlooked tourism operator: 'Australians who could well afford to pay for luxuries had been scared lest the "continental touches" should require "socialite formality" when they wanted to relax.'[26] He had put his finger on it. Wealthy Australians too—perhaps even more than most—relished the casualness, the informality and the freedom of the beach holiday as it had emerged by the 1950s.

If the beach holiday was not entirely privatised in the 1950s, it was domesticated. In a number of ways the holiday that was institutionalised as the norm revolved around the family, as so much else did in the 1950s. The idealised nuclear family implied more than simply a retreat to security after the disruptions of war and depression: the family became the site of both civic and personal fulfilment.[27] And the family holiday was often understood as where that fulfilment was most likely to occur. The emphasis in annual leave cases before the Arbitration Court was always on 'providing ample time for the [inevitably male] breadwinner to spend in leisure with his family'.[28] This, in turn, reinforced a family holiday 'season' over Christmas. Families were taking holidays to coincide with the school break. In response, and further reinforcing this trend, industries and businesses often shut down and were literally 'closed for the holidays' over the Christmas period, giving workers no choice as to when leave could be taken. The Christmas shut-down further reinforced the choice of a beach holiday, which offered relief from the heat and cheap amusement for both children and their parents. By the 1970s the 'institutionalised seasonality' was so pronounced that government and the tourism industry were busy writing reports on how holidaying might be spread more efficiently—and profitably—through the year.

Here, in the family, was where the democratic ideal of everyone having access to time off on holiday came unstuck. The family beach holiday was profoundly gendered, structured around the leisure of the male worker and the carefree play of the children. Mothers remained homemakers even away from home as they continued to clean, cook and organise the children. The common complaint—only half in jest—was that it was a holiday for everyone but the housewife, that for her it only meant a change of kitchen sink; behind the jest was a bitterness about that unacknowledged role, and an assertion that she needed a holiday as much as anyone. Holidays for mothers were no real escape from suburbia and domesticity. The more caravans and camping grounds and holiday flats promised the home away from home, the less escape they offered women. The location may have changed but the domestic routine remained fixed.

The complaint could be overstated in the interests of holiday politics. Often others pitched in. Fathers generally provided the driving labour to get them there, and did the heavy lifting unpacking, particularly the Esky with the beer; often from that point they expected to be waited on. But just as often their 'labour', fishing and barbecuing, put at least some of the food on the folding table. The children did not have the excuse of homework to get out of the washing up. Domestic labour could be reduced. Meals were often 'scratch' meals, the ubiquitous salads of cans of beetroot and pineapple rings and, if the budget stretched, asparagus, or fish and chips from the local shop or co-op. Holidays were often the only time a family would eat take-away food.[29] Standards of cleanliness might be compromised. The washing and ironing load was cut back: no need for the effort that went into clean overalls or ironed shirts or school uniforms, with everyone sitting around in shorts or in swimming costumes all day. There was some escape from some of the housewife's labour routine, even if child-minding became more onerous. Some women imposed holiday rules: perhaps no home-made desserts for the fortnight or a regular diet of tinned spaghetti. At least one mother, wife of an Appin coalminer camping at Shoalhaven Heads, insisted that if the holiday meant camping, the family's double bed had to be accommodated too.[30]

As mothers entered the paid workforce in increasing numbers from the 1950s on, the typical beach holiday satisfied them less. They sought a holiday from their paid work which was not dominated by housework. Their paid work, especially when it was seen as providing the 'extras' of life such as holidays, gave them more authority in familial politics. It was arguably women's growing insistence that they 'should have a holiday too' that first sustained an expanding take-away food industry at beach resorts, and then increasingly created a service industry, the 'hospitality sector', to replace the labour that they had previously provided to make the family holiday possible. Eventually it would be the female wage that would provide a holiday structured around the provision of services, supported by the cheap paid labour of hospitality workers rather than the unpaid labour of the housewife. That labour was increasingly intense, providing new and more labour-intensive services, and increasingly it was out-sourced to Bali, Fiji and Vanuatu. And this would be one of the factors that contributed to the decline of the beach holiday as it had flourished in the three decades after the war.

Two other factors were crucially important. There was also the decline of job security in the name of 'flexibility', and the decline of the Arbitration Commission in setting standards. After a century and a quarter of declining standard working hours, Australians began working more from the 1980s. Casualisation, underemployment, part-time work and individual bargaining all made holidays more difficult to negotiate, and with two parents working, more difficult to organise. Declining home ownership also played a role: renters naturally resented paying twice for accommodation when they went on holidays. Economic change was making the idea of long weeks of doing nothing at the beach harder to sustain. Short breaks seemed simpler.

The intrusion of the tourist industry into the family holiday also changed it dramatically, and contributed to its decline. The industry had a clear interest in promoting the dagginess of the cheap, communal camping holiday where pleasures were free rather than paid for. First and most obviously it increased the cost, which, though increasingly affordable to middle class families, was significantly more that the average beach holiday. As different resorts were developed for different markets, it added status more explicitly as a consideration in the choice of holiday destination. The cost also meant they were marketed as short breaks. Rather than the long summer holiday stretching up to four weeks, the emphasis was on the shorter break, as in the 'Fly Away Holiday' campaign mounted by the government-owned airline, TAA, from 1963. Resort holidays were commonly for a week or less, and could be taken at any time of the year: the appeal of a week in the tropics during a Melbourne winter could be irresistible. The resort was also a more private experience, focused on the isolated nuclear family, and discouraged the more communal emphasis found in the caravan park. In the place of sociability, they emphasised facilities. This was a two-edged sword, as Jim Davidson and Peter Spearritt suggest, since it meant resorts were constantly having to update facilities.[31] Rather than returning to the same place, this new market was mobile, seeking out whichever resort offered most facilities for their particular budget. It is significant that Lena Lencek and Gideon Bosker's history of the beach from an American perspective took it for granted that 'fine accommodations, spectacular views, sensitivity to the local culture, lush gardens, and proximity to unspoiled beaches should always be part of the equation' in the search for the ideal beach holiday. Camping grounds and caravan parks did not rate. In their list of the world's eighty best beach destinations, covering 'the full spectrum of options, from hand-thatched bungalows to grand resorts', six were in Australia: three 'Resorts', one 'Wilderness Lodge', one 'Retreat' and Hayman Island, all but Cable Beach Club Resort in Queensland.[32]

At the end of the twentieth century, it was still possible to find Australians going on beach holidays that look a lot like those that were typical of the 1950s and 1960s. A proportion were doing it ironically, celebrating its retro-chic nostalgia, or retrieving their own childhood holidays as a gift to their own children. Others simply continued to do what they always had done. But these holidays were under siege. Cheap caravan parks were being targeted for more intensive development. In New South Wales, National Parks were insisting on ballots for desirable camping spots, which put an end to the possibility of groups of campers meeting up in the same place at the same time year after year. Family beach holidays were also threatened as the beach became associated with newly perceived dangers: the sun and skin cancer, strangers, drowning, the lack of surveillance. Irresponsible parents had the traditional beach holiday: the responsible middle class were measuring their responsibility by how much more they paid and how much more their children were kept under surveillance. And the alternatives to that sort of holiday proliferated both in Australia and overseas. A farmer, responding to the severity of the drought in 2005, supposed if they could not afford a skiing holiday in Switzerland that year, there was always Vanuatu.

What had once been typical, the family holiday as a shared annual event enjoyed by a mass market, had now itself become a niche packaged and marketed by the tourist industry, commodifying the nostalgia. When Ron Clarke opened Couran Cove resort in 1998 on South Stradbroke Island, he 'wanted a place that would offer an old-fashioned Australian family beach holiday'. But it also offered, among 115 activities, a gym, sprint track, lawn bowls, Olympic style pool, lifestyle counselling, yoga, tai chi, aqua aerobics, kayaking, clown school, sea plane trips, helicopter rides, bead jewellery making, fabric painting, jet skiing, wind-surfing, hydrotherapy, environmental awareness courses and complete body rejuvenation.[33] The industry has trouble conceptualising that 'old-fashioned' beach holiday because it actively resisted consumerism's fundamental assumptions. The regulars want the same holiday every year. They resist change and fashion. They want to be left alone. To just do nothing. To remember that the best things in life are still free. Their holiday remains an escape from blandishments to consume, to perform, to renew themselves. They want to block the ears and close the eyes to the cacophony of signification in the world of signs, and just indulge in the pleasures of idleness. They want to get away from it all.

This was the genius of the prime minister's holiday at Hawk's Nest. John Howard was never ironic. His persistence in having an annual summer holiday with the family at Hawk's Nest was a symbol of his connection with an 'old' Australia, to what he insisted was a set of widely shared 'mainstream' values of mateship, sociability and a desire to be 'relaxed and comfortable'.[34] A smug media sneered that this revealed a stodgy and old-fashioned perspective, in keeping with his alleged desire to retreat to the 1950s. It was precisely the sort of criticism that reinforced Howard's image of being in touch with ordinary Australians despite the derision of 'elites'. In reality, as we have seen, the holiday of 'old Australia' was based on a set of agreed principles—job security, low unemployment, a centralised industrial system, high home ownership—that John Howard, more than anyone, has sought to destroy. His genius had been to maintain a rhetoric and image so at odds with his political performance.

Notes

1   Soile Veijole and Eeva Jokinen, 'The Body in Tourism', *Theory Culture & Society* 2 (1994): 126–7; for Urry's response, see John Urry, *The Tourist Gaze: Leisure and Travel in Contemporary Societies* (London: Sage, 2002) 145–53.

2   see Douglas Booth, *Australian Beach Cultures: The History of Sun, Sand and Surf* (London: Frank Cass, 2001); Leone Huntsman, *Sand in our Souls: The Beach in Australian History* (Melbourne: Melbourne University Press, 2001); Andrea Inglis, *Beside the seaside: Victorian resorts in the nineteenth century* (Melbourne: Melbourne University Press, 1999); Ed Jaggard, 'Australian Surf Life-saving and the "Forgotten Members"', *Australian Historical Studies* 30(112) April 1999; Cameron White, Pleasure Seekers: A History of the Male Body on the Beach in Sydney 1811–1914, PhD thesis, University of Sydney, 2005; Caroline Ford, 'Gazing, Strolling, Falling in Love: Culture and Nature on the Beach in Nineteenth Century Sydney', *History Australia* 3:1 (2006). This article draws heavily on Richard White (with Sarah-Jane Ballard, Ingrid Bown, Meredith Lake, Patricia Leehy and Lila Oldmeadow), *On Holidays: a history of getting away in Australia* (Melbourne: Pluto, 2005). It too, however, gives less attention than it might have to the specificities of the beach holiday, which I hope to address here. In addition to the participants in the project, I would like to thank Caroline Ford, Laina Hall, Maria Nugent, Katarina Olaussen, Liz Todd and Cameron White.

3   Philip Smith and Tim Phillips, 'Popular Understandings of "UnAustralian": an investigation of the un-national', *Journal of Sociology* 37:4 (2001) 332.

4   *Sydney Morning Herald*, 27 December 1859.

5   *The Webbs' Australian Diary, 1898*, ed. A.G. Austin (Melbourne: Pitman, 1965) 108; Thomas Harry and V.L. Solomon, *Australia at Play. Suggested by 'America at*

Work' (Adelaide: Hussey & Gillingham, 1908) 5; Marcus Clarke, *The Peripatetic Philosopher* (Melbourne: George Robertson, 1969) 44.

6 Ford, 'Gazing, Strolling, Falling in Love'.

7 Booth, *Australian Beach Cultures* 30.

8 Charles Dickens, *The Pickwick Papers* (New York: Doubleday, 1944) 433.

9 Ford, 'Gazing, Strolling, Falling in Love'.

10 Gary Cross & John Walton, *The Playful Crowd: Pleasure Places in the Twentieth Century* (New York: Columbia University Press, 2005).

11 Rebecca Denning, Tall Pop-up Syndrome: A Cultural History of the Australian Caravan, History IV thesis, Department of History, University of Sydney, 2000.

12 Lana Wells, *Sunny Memories; Australians at the Seaside* (Melbourne: Greenhouse Publications, 1982) 134; *Australian National Dictionary*, ed. W.S. Ramson (Melbourne: Oxford University Press, 1988) 719.

13 Noel Sanders, 'Private Faces in Public Spaces: The NRMA 1921–51', *Australian Communications and the Public Sphere,* ed. Helen Wilson (Melbourne: Macmillan, 1989) 213–15; Graeme Davison, *Car Wars: How the Car Won our Hearts and Conquered our Cities* (Sydney: Allen & Unwin, 2004) 7–8.

14 Davison, *Car Wars* 15.

15 *NSW Parliamentary Debates*, Governor's Speech, Oct. 1944, 40, 14; Greg Patmore 'Legislating for Benefits – NSW 1941–1958', *Australian Bulletin of Labour* 29:1 (2003).

16 *The Courier Mail*, 24 December 1947, 3.

17 John Douglas Pringle, *Australian Accent* (London: Chatto & Windus, 1958) 198–9.

18 Pringle, *Australian Accent* 198–9.

19 I am grateful to Suzanne Gillham, Penny Russell and John Scott for discussions on this point.

20 c.f. Stanley Cohen and Laurie Taylor, *Escape Attempts: The Theory and Practice of Resistance to Everyday Life* (London: Allen Lane, 1976).

21 Jim Davidson and Peter Spearritt, *Holiday Business: Tourism in Australia since 1870* (Melbourne: Miegunyah Press, 2000) 10; Anchorage Guest House, Victor Harbor, brochure.

22 J.A.R. Pimlott, *The Englishman's Holiday: A Social History* (London: Faber, 1947); 'Holidays', *Current Affairs Bulletin*, 6:6 (1950).

23 Australian National Travel Association, *Establishing the South Australian Mid-North, Barossa Valley and Riverland as a travel region; industry appraisal* (Sydney: Australian National Travel Association, 1971) 3; Australian National Travel Association, *A plan to develop tourism in south-western Victoria and south-eastern South Australia: an industry appraisal* (Sydney: Australian National Travel Association, 1974) 3; *Sydney Morning Herald*, 28 November 1978, 11.

24 Davidson and Spearritt, *Holiday Business* 174.

25 Wells, *Sunny Memories* 132.

26 Todd Barr, *No Swank Here? The Development of the Whitsundays as a Tourist Destination to the Early 1970s* (Townsville: James Cook University, 1990) 38; Davidson and Spearritt, *Holiday Business* 300; John Richardson, *A History of Australian Travel and Tourism* (Melbourne: Hospitality Press, 1999) 155, 193.

27 John Murphy, *Imagining the Fifties: Private Sentiment and Political Culture in Menzies' Australia* (Sydney: Pluto, 2000) 16; Stella Lees and June Senyard, *The 1950s: How Australia became a modern society and everyone got a house and car* (Melbourne: Hyland House, 1987) 2.

28 *Commonwealth Arbitration Reports*, 1945, 597.

29 Helen Townsend, *Baby Boomers: growing up in Australia in the 1940s, 50s and 60s* (Sydney: Simon & Schuster, 1988) 193.

30 Townsend, *Baby Boomers* 202; conversations with Nettie Simonis and John Scott.

31 Davidson and Spearritt, *Holiday Business* 304.

32 Lena Lencek and Gideon Bosker, *The Beach: The History of Paradise on Earth* (London: Pimlico, 1999) 289–90.

33 *Sydney Morning Herald*, 21 February 2004, Travel 3; Davidson and Spearritt, *Holiday Business* 247; Couran Cove Island Resort, 'Time Well Spent' brochure, 2006.

34 James Curran, *The Power of Speech: Australian Prime Ministers Defining the National Image* (Melbourne: Melbourne University Press, 2004) 241ff; Judith Brett, *Australian Liberals and the Moral Middle Class: From Alfred Deakin to John Howard* (Cambridge: Cambridge University Press, 2003) 189–90.

Works cited

Australian National Dictionary, ed. W.S. Ramson. Melbourne: Oxford University Press, 1988.

Australian National Travel Association. *A plan to develop tourism in south-western Victoria and south-eastern South Australia: an industry appraisal.* Sydney: Australian National Travel Association, 1974.

Australian National Travel Association. *Establishing the South Australian Mid-North, Barossa Valley and Riverland as a travel region; industry appraisal.* Sydney: Australian National Travel Association, 1971.

Barr, Todd. *No Swank Here? The Development of the Whitsundays as a Tourist Destination to the Early 1970s.* Townsville: James Cook University, 1990.

Booth, Douglas. *Australian Beach Cultures: The History of Sun, Sand and Surf.* London: Frank Cass, 2001.

Brett, Judith. *Australian Liberals and the Moral Middle Class: From Alfred Deakin to John Howard.* Cambridge: Cambridge University Press, 2003.

Clarke, Marcus. *The Peripatetic Philosopher.* Melbourne: George Robertson, 1969.

Cohen, Stanley and Laurie Taylor. *Escape Attempts: The Theory and Practice of Resistance to Everyday Life.* London: Allen Lane, 1976.

Cross, Gary and John Walton. *The Playful Crowd: Pleasure Places in the Twentieth Century.* New York: Columbia University Press, 2005.

Curran, James. *The Power of Speech: Australian Prime Ministers Defining the National Image.* Melbourne: Melbourne University Press, 2004.

Davidson, Jim and Peter Spearritt. *Holiday Business: Tourism in Australia since 1870.* Melbourne: Miegunyah Press, 2000.

Davison, Graeme. *Car Wars: How the Car Won our Hearts and Conquered our Cities.* Sydney: Allen & Unwin, 2004.

Denning, Rebecca. 'Tall Pop-up Syndrome: A Cultural History of the Australian Caravan'. History IV thesis, Department of History, University of Sydney, 2000.

Dickens, Charles. *The Pickwick Papers.* New York: Doubleday, 1944.

Ford, Caroline. 'Gazing, Strolling, Falling in Love: Culture and Nature on the Beach in Nineteenth Century Sydney' *History Australia* 3:1 (2006).

Harry, Thomas and V.L. Solomon. *Australia at Play. Suggested by 'America at Work'.* Adelaide: Hussey & Gillingham, 1908.

Huntsman, Leone. *Sand in our Souls: The Beach in Australian History.* Melbourne: Melbourne University Press, 2001.

Inglis, Andrea. *Beside the seaside: Victorian resorts in the nineteenth century.* Melbourne: Melbourne University Press, 1999.

Jaggard, Ed. 'Australian Surf Life-saving and the "Forgotten Members"' *Australian Historical Studies* 30:112 (1999).

Lees, Stella and June Senyard. *The 1950s: How Australia became a modern society and everyone got a house and car.* Melbourne: Hyland House, 1987.

Lencek, Lena and Gideon Bosker. *The Beach: The History of Paradise on Earth.* London: Pimlico, 1999.

Murphy, John. *Imagining the Fifties: Private Sentiment and Political Culture in Menzies' Australia.* Sydney: Pluto, 2000.

Patmore, Greg. 'Legislating for Benefits—NSW 1941–1958' *Australian Bulletin of Labour* 29:1 (2003).

Pimlott, J.A.R. *The Englishman's Holiday: A Social History.* London: Faber, 1947.

Pringle, John Douglas. *Australian Accent.* London: Chatto & Windus, 1958.

Richardson, John. *A History of Australian Travel and Tourism.* Melbourne: Hospitality Press, 1999.

Sanders, Noel. 'Private Faces in Public Spaces: The NRMA 1921–51'. *Australian Communications and the Public Sphere* ed. Helen Wilson. Melbourne: Macmillan, 1989.

Smith, Philip and Tim Phillips. 'Popular Understandings of "UnAustralian": an investigation of the un-national' *Journal of Sociology* 37:4 (2001).

Townsend, Helen. *Baby Boomers: growing up in Australia in the 1940s, 50s and 60s.* Sydney: Simon & Schuster, 1988.

Urry, John. *The Tourist Gaze: Leisure and Travel in Contemporary Societies.* London: Sage, 2002.

Veijole, Soile and Eeva Jokinen. 'The Body in Tourism' *Theory Culture & Society* 2 (1994).

[Webb, Sidney and Beatrice]*The Webbs' Australian Diary, 1898,* ed. A.G. Austin. Melbourne: Pitman, 1965.

Wells, Lana. *Sunny Memories; Australians at the Seaside.* Melbourne: Greenhouse Publications, 1982.

White, Cameron. 'Pleasure Seekers: A History of the Male Body on the Beach in Sydney 1811-1914'. PhD thesis, University of Sydney, 2005.

White, Richard (with Sarah-Jane Ballard, Ingrid Bown, Meredith Lake, Patricia Leehy and Lila Oldmeadow). *On Holidays: a history of getting away in Australia.* Melbourne: Pluto, 2005.

'What Power What Grandeur What Sublimity!': Romanticism and the Appeal of Sydney Beaches in the Nineteenth Century

CAROLINE FORD

During the second half of the nineteenth century, the beaches on Sydney's ocean coast increasingly rivalled the parks, gardens and harbour beaches closer to town as a popular leisure destination for locals and tourists alike. In this period, there was no single, dominant way of using or understanding the beach space. A by-law which banned daytime bathing anywhere within public view was mostly effective in limiting beachgoers to the dry land, but even within this restricted space day-trippers occupied their time at the beach in a variety of ways. Some saw the beach as an ideal destination for a social outing, and spent their time there with family and friends, enjoying picnics and games while the children paddled in the shallows of the surf. Young lovers, considering themselves liberated from the norms and constraints of everyday Victorian society, used the more secluded areas which surrounded popular beaches as settings for romance, while others took the opportunity to dream about and gaze at attractive members of the opposite sex.

While the natural scenery and views of the beach were important to these groups, and certainly enhanced their experiences, the social scene of the beach was the most valued element of their day. That is, the beach primarily offered them a pleasant setting for a social day-trip, a fun time out with family and friends. But there was another group of beachgoers for whom the social side of beach activity was not important. Rather than going to the beach to spend time with other people, this group were preoccupied with the raw nature of the beach, thereby placing themselves, often quite consciously and even deliberately, within the traditions of European Romanticism. They liked to think of themselves as ardent Romantics, and they were a distinct and important group within the history of the nineteenth century beach. For these beachgoers, the natural scenery was the focus of their writings about the beach, and they drew heavily upon Romantic language and conventions.[1]

The need for a detailed analysis of Romanticism at the nineteenth century Sydney beach is highlighted by the lack of attention it has attracted until recently, in histories of the Australian beach, and of Australian Romanticism more generally. In their insightful and extensive published histories of the Australian beach, Doug Booth and Leone Huntsman each focus on aspects of the origins of Australian beach culture other than its Romantic appeal, as does Cameron White in his 2004 article.[2] Andrea Inglis alone, in her study of the Victorian seaside, identifies and discusses Romanticism within nineteenth century beach culture, describing the 'sublime' attractions of Victorian beaches of this period.[3] However, there are sufficient differences between the Sydney and Victorian coasts and beach culture, both in the nineteenth century and the twentieth, to necessitate further investigation of this topic as it relates specifically to Sydney's ocean beaches. The Romantic appeal of beach scenery, along with bathing, and other, more social uses of the beach space, played a significant role in the shaping of twentieth century Australian beach cultures. For this reason, Romanticism warrants further investigation as a crucial component of nineteenth century beach culture.

There is a range of sources in which the nineteenth century beaches of Sydney, like those of Victoria and indeed elsewhere around the Western world, are described or discussed in distinctly Romantic language. Foremost among these are the tourist guides and handbooks to the colony, which appeal to the visitor to head to the coast. The travel journals and accounts written by these visitors often drew on similar language to describe their impressions of the beach, demonstrating their Romantic sensibilities to the reader. Appreciation of the natural scenery of the beachscape was certainly not limited to visitors to the colony, however, and texts which were written both for and by Sydney locals, including newspaper and journal articles, also portrayed the beach through Romantic hyperbole.

The Romantic appeal of the beach lay in its capacity on a wild day to arouse sensations of the power and awe of God, a crucial marker of ideal scenery for European Romantics. Central to the British Romantic movement was an ideology which emphasised 'creative imagination, individual genius, and the inward self', and a new model for appreciating nature emerged through this.[4] By physically placing themselves within nature, Romantics discovered a unique forum for contemplation; alone in the wilderness, the focus could be centred on the 'self', if not on the wonders of God's world. Grand and awesome scenes, such as craggy mountains and gushing waterfalls were valued as particularly impressive, and offered all the features of the 'sublime' that Romantics craved. In this context, the ocean also became a meaningful site for nineteenth century Romantics. As

Alain Corbin writes, 'faced with the immensity of an ocean whose limits man is incapable of grasping, whose breadth he cannot conceive, the spectator experiences the emotion engendered by the sublime spectacle of nature'.[5]

By the middle of the nineteenth century a Romanticism existed in the Australian colonies that had its roots firmly entrenched in British Romanticism. Although the Australian landscape was distinctly different from that which British immigrants and tourists were used to, many nonetheless began to identify beautiful and sublime features in a variety of Australian scenes.[6] For those seeking Romantic landscapes close to Sydney, the Blue Mountains were the favourite haunt, offering grand views of mountains, rugged cliffs and deep valleys. The Romantic appeal of the Blue Mountains therefore followed in the tradition of the appeal of mountain scenery to European Romantics, although as Julia Horne explains, the distinctive features of Australian mountain scenery made up a 'local version of the sublime'.[7] Closer to Sydney, parts of the harbour were deemed picturesque by some, but they were lacking in the sublime when compared to the majestic scale of the mountains.[8] The ocean beaches, however, offered a closer, more accessible and very different alternative to the prospective Romantic; mountain views they were not, yet they offered a distinctly identifiable show of the raw power and energy of nature, a majestical and fascinating sight, especially in wild weather. They were also close enough to Sydney that a round trip could be undertaken in the course of a single morning or afternoon's travel, which was especially convenient for the time-restricted traveller.

The attraction of gazing at the sea is difficult to pinpoint. Andrew Taylor suggests that the sea '*represents* something that is not just sea … the sea is a signifier'. And whatever it signifies remains, even for poets, 'out of the reach of words'.[9] The attraction, it seems, lies not in the sea itself, but in each spectator's response to the sea. It is this that makes gazing at the sea so appealing to Romantics because 'the sight of the incommensurable forces man to experience his finite nature; it arouses passions in his soul in which the aesthetics of the sublime take root'.[10] Romantics at Sydney beaches fell short of immersing themselves in the surf. Their contemplation was instead inspired by simply looking at the sea, or by walking or trekking along the often rugged coast.

Among all of Sydney's beaches, Coogee was normally isolated as the ideal destination for Romantic tourists. Guidebooks and tourist handbooks often focussed on the wildness of the surf when describing that beach, rather than its social scene or built environment. It would seem that the presence of a group of rocks not far out from the beach, over which breakers crashed violently, added significantly to the aesthetic appeal of Coogee, although commercial interests were no doubt paramount to the relentless promotion of the region. Sydney guidebooks consistently urged the visitor to see Coogee purely on account of its physical appeal. It is 'wild and grand in the extreme', claimed one guide, and should 'on no account be missed', asserted another.[11] It was especially worth seeing 'when the fierce winds "blow" and whine, (and) the spray rises in white sheets above the rocky reef', insisted the *Grosvenor Hotel Visitor's Guide* in around 1888. At such times, it continued, 'words and pictures fail to describe its awful grandeur'.[12]

And so, visitors to Sydney dutifully went to Coogee to admire its natural scenery, although just as many seem to have gone to Bondi and Manly for the same purpose. They did not spend too much time there; sometimes just long enough to note the 'crashing' and 'dashing' waves, with the beach inviting less discussion in some journals and published travel accounts than the journey there. Occasionally though, enough time was spent at the beach to really appreciate the view of the sea, and even to contemplate broader questions, the mind invigorated by the 'sublimity' of the scene. Josiah Hughes, an elderly British man holidaying in the Antipodes, was more moved than most by the display of surf at Coogee beach:

> the continuous roar and boom, and far distant murmuring sound of these mighty waves as they broke on the shingly and rock-strewn beach, was very impressive, and filled my mind with a singular sadness and reverence. What power, what grandeur, what sublimity![13]

Few other travellers reacted so emotively or dramatically to Sydney's beach scenes. The view of the surf nonetheless remained a key motivation for making the trip to Sydney's coast for visitors to Sydney.

The natural beauties of Sydney's ocean beaches were not purely a tourist attraction for visiting parties in the nineteenth century though; as in the twentieth, Sydney beaches were hugely popular leisure destinations among locals, and the scenery invited just as many local day trippers as it did tourists, if not more. Contributors to Sydney newspapers and journals, when describing the ocean beaches and coastal cliffs, often drew on Romantic hyperbole to engage the reader. A remarkable example of this can be found in an article about Bondi which was published in the *Town and Country Journal* in 1876.[14] The author, RA, is unashamedly moved by the beach scene, declaring that 'whomsoever "can find sermons in stones and tongues in running brooks"', would find the 'grand chance of fully enjoying that "lonely talk with Heaven"' at Bondi. He continues, 'in the presence of the far stretching purple ocean, untamed and untamable … he feels his own littleness, and the awe of the majesty of nature and the might of God'. An article written about Bronte in the same newspaper at the close of

1876 evokes a similar image. At Bronte, the anonymous author relates, 'the earth seems to suddenly grow more lovely and heaven seems to come nearer, and the yearning spirit within us seems striving to interpret … the whisperings of the hidden voices of nature'.[15]

This is powerful language, clearly conveying the potent effect the beachscape had on these beachgoers. Various writers represent the extreme in nineteenth century responses to Sydney's ocean beaches through powerful language. Many other contemporary newspaper and journal correspondents described the attractions of beach scenes in Romantic prose, but few were moved to such powerful, soulful and religious responses. The most that could be managed within these other accounts were descriptions of 'perfectly appalling' wash, the 'ever dashing' sea, and the 'terribly grand' scene of the coast during a storm.[16] These were all Romantic responses, but the writers seem to have been less moved to express themselves with commanding hyperbole than those contributors discussed above.

Such accounts can be found in many of the brief descriptions of beach scenes that were published in late nineteenth century newspapers. Several narratives of coastal walks which offer lengthy and detailed accounts of time spent in the beach environment can be particularly revealing of Romantic sentiment and the beach. Around the middle of the nineteenth century, before the beaches of Sydney's Eastern Suburbs were made accessible by roads, and pathways along the beaches had been cleared, walking to or along Sydney's coastline was a considerably arduous task. It took one group of walkers over seven hours to walk from Bondi beach to South Head in 1857, as recorded in *The Month* magazine:

> At 9 o'clock at night, with just a few pale stars overhead, we found ourselves still fighting our way through the dense scrub about a mile from the lighthouse. We were up to our hips in water; our precious face and fingers were most gloriously lacerated with the burrs and brambles; our nether integuments were thickly perforated with the rigid barbs of the grass tree.[17]

This unidentified writer apparently derived no pleasure from negotiating the coastal walk, finding it 'so fraught with fears and dangers that no-one but a Borrow or a Livingstone would care to take it more than once in a lifetime'. Rather than describing the walk or scenery in depth, they spent most of the article reflecting on the demonic nature of the sea, which fed 'her "white flames" on the souls of men'. At night, they continued, 'the waves shoot up like flame, and seethe and smoke in the wild vortex of the inferno', and the pebbles which are caught in the surf 'shriek demonically, or seem to be borne down with a low despairing wail'.[18]

Such descriptions reflect public sentiment in the period immediately following the tragic wreck of the *Dunbar* against The Gap in 1857, from which there was only one survivor. They also reflect ancient Western attitudes towards the ocean, an alien environment which traditionally evoked incessant fear among all.[19] By the nineteenth century, such attitudes were beginning to be influenced by Romantic ideas about the beauty and wonder of nature; the ocean remained a feared entity on an individual level, but such negative descriptions soon became a relic of medieval thought.[20] This writer was most certainly aware of the possibility of enjoying such a walk, as the reference to the Romantics Borrow and Livingstone demonstrates. Their refusal to do so perhaps reflects as much a personal reaction to the tragedy of the *Dunbar* as it does the difficulty of the terrain. Yet the writer seems almost to revel in the sublime horror of the sea, adding a hint of Romantic contemplation to their account of an extremely difficult walk, and the 'glorious lacerations' that were suffered signify a Romantic endurance of the elements, even if this was not overtly celebrated in the writing.

A decade later, F.S. Wilson strode out for Bondi from South Head, and wrote about his experiences on this same, still very rough track. He, too, spent several pages dwelling on the 'wild night at sea' when the *Dunbar* 'lay gashed and grinding in the frightful turmoil; and the shrieks of the dying, the wild scream of the sea birds, and the roar of the tempest, mingled in one direful midnight medley!'[21] But the decade which had passed allowed this writer to quickly abandon contemplation of the wreck, and enjoy elements of the walk and cliff-scenery. Although Wilson also found the walk to be 'toilsome', and more a 'scramble' than a ramble, unlike his predecessor his experience of the track was 'rendered pleasant by the bright sky overhead, the healthy salt wind blowing lusty and strong from the ocean, and the sonorous boom of the breakers beneath the cliffs'.[22]

This pleasure found in the beach and coastal environment at first appears less emotional than the account of Josiah Hughes and the *Town and Country* correspondents, which were to be written much later in the century, with Wilson describing Bondi quite simply as a 'place of pleasant nooks and picnic parties, with its milk-white beach'. He was soon moved to contemplation, however, declaring that the white of the foamy surf 'challenge[s] art to compare with it for purity'. Later he described the way 'our feelings for the beautiful have been stirred by the grandeur around us'. Here on Bondi beach, Wilson was moved to contemplation of the whereabouts of lost loves who were the 'bright-eyed, warm-lipped partners' of his boyish rambles, hinting at an interesting link between Romantic landscape and 'romance'.[23]

The sum of Wilson's account is fairly similar in language and general appreciation of nature to Hughes, and yet the former encompasses a further element of Romanticism which Hughes' does not. That is, Romantic liaisons aside, rather than merely *gazing at* nature, Wilson physically experienced it. By walking along the rough track which followed the coast, Wilson—as with the writer for *The Month* in 1857 and another for the same publication a year later—immersed himself in nature in the tradition of such European Romantics as Byron, the Wordsworths and the Shelleys, among others.[24] For these Romantics, it was necessary to become a part of nature in order to truly appreciate it, and often this took the form of swimming or walking, ideally in challenging conditions. As Miles Jebb wrote, 'walking was the best means of comprehending for oneself the cult of nature … Effort, attention and sensory experience were all desirable ingredients, and walking provided them all'.[25] Walking along Sydney's coast, whether experiencing the coastal winds on the sand of the beaches or fighting through scrubs and traversing cliffs, beachgoers enjoyed a more physical experience of the beach environment than that which could be gained by merely picnicking.[26]

Wilson was an advocate of the Romantic walk, asking 'who that is fond of the ocean can cavil at the occasional clamber of rude headlands, the involuntary slides over raspy rocks, and the splash of scattering sea-spray which such an expedition entails? Few, if any'.[27] For him, the difficult walk to the beach was 'an interesting ramble'; while not necessarily enjoyable on its own, such obstacles as the slippery rocks gave the journey a hint of fun, and it was an effective way to truly experience Sydney's coastal environment, the walk being enhanced by the smells and sounds of the surf.

Another walker around the mid-nineteenth century who deemed a coastal hike a worthwhile experience despite the hardships of the track interpreted the journey in a slightly different way. This anonymous rambler walked from Bondi's south head to Nelson Bay (now Bronte), and subsequently described a similar mixture of emotional satisfaction and physical hardship in this journey in *The Month* in 1858.[28] The first few miles were described as 'invigorating', but soon the 'rugged rocks, the tangled masses of scrub, the numerous ups and downs … drive the poetry—for a while, at least—out of the traveller's mind'. Fortunately, however, 'repose is near', and the writer's brain was 'soothed' at the sight of the beach and sea.[29]

For this writer, the chief pleasure of the day lay in the destination; the walk itself was tiresome and difficult, and only allayed when, in sight of beach, he allowed himself to rest and gaze at the view. Wilson, too, had enjoyed the destination far more than the walk, but he also valued the walk as part of the overall experience.

These writers all shared the perspective that walking was more than just a way of getting to the beach; the fact that Wilson and his companions walked only one leg of their journey, and returned to Sydney by 'bus, demonstrates that walking was specifically chosen, at least on this occasion, for its own distinct experience. The same is implied for *The Month* correspondent of 1857. All three writer-walkers were distinctly aware of, and drew on, their identity as walkers in the coastal landscape. Regardless of whether they actually enjoyed their walks, the difficulty of the terrain, and its status as pure wilderness made the ramble inherently 'Romantic'. The even wilder backdrop of ocean and cliffs only served to enhance this. By using this environment as a setting for contemplation, whether of the terror of the ocean or the beauty of Bronte Bay, these walkers consciously placed themselves within the tradition of Romantic writing.

It is telling, however, that these writers stopped short of immersing themselves in the surf in their attempts to fully experience the beach environment. The British Romantics Lord Byron and Shelley would have unflinchingly flouted the local by-laws in order to experience the wonders of the surf.[30] But while Wilson and the other walkers certainly went further than many beachgoers in their attempts to sense the beach scenery, their inability or unwillingness to enter the water left one important realm of the beach environment largely untouched and unfelt. While their walking clearly situated them within the Romantic tradition, they remained removed from its original and in some ways most dedicated devotees.

Corbin argues that in Europe, this new 'intimacy between the walker and the elements' followed the era in which the ocean was purely spectacle, only to be gazed at, and roughly coincided with the period which saw some Romantics dive into the sea.[31] However, since all this occurred in Europe before Sydney's beaches were popularised, there was no such chronological distinction in Australia. If anything, the 'sensual' walk preceded mass gazing at the sea, as it was all that was possible at the popular beaches before they were transformed by benches and cleared walkways.

Walking to the beach merely as a cheap way of accessing it was quite possibly as common, if not more common, than the 'Romantic' coastal walk, and it is crucial to bear this in mind when analysing nineteenth century beach experiences. Clearly, different beachgoers valued the environment and beach scenery in different ways, and to differing degrees.[32] As Melissa Harper points out, for example, walking offered advocates an opportunity for escape, and for 'physical, moral and spiritual renewal', a Romantic notion in itself, even if it was perhaps only subconscious among many of its proponents.[33] On another level, the practice of holding open-air Christmas Church services at Coogee beach, which had 'long since been an institution of Coogee' by the mid 1890s, allowed and perhaps even encouraged local Christians to find God in nature.[34] And even those who did not write in the language of the Romantics, or find themselves contemplating the power of God while gazing at the sea, nonetheless still enjoyed looking outwards from the beach, and gazing was a normal part of any time spent at or near the beach.

Furthermore, a battering by strong sea-winds could allow the non-walking non-swimming beachgoer to experience the elements in a physical way. This perhaps explains the disappointment of a traveller by the name of WF, who travelled to Coogee but 'owing to the day being beautifully fine and sea calm … did not see it to perfection'.[35] Although this traveller seems to have made no effort to walk through the landscape or dive into the surf, the writer nonetheless believed it possible to experience the pure wildness of the ocean from the shore, and was eager to do so.

We can see then, through one strand of Australian attitudes to the beach, a familiarity with the ideas and language of Romanticism as it had been practised in Europe up to a century earlier. This is not surprising given that Romanticism had become part of the common discourse regarding the viewing of nature by the Victorian era. And this is also not unique to the Australian colonies. By the late nineteenth century, Romantic ways of viewing and valuing landscape and seascapes had become the norm for many western travellers. Anne Wallace writes that the suffusion of 'Wordsworthianism' into Victorian culture was necessarily an unconscious process, and that 'his representations and precepts now seemed "natural", obvious, not constructed by Wordsworth but fundamental to human experience'.[36] While they have differing opinions as to exactly how conscious or unconscious this really was, many scholars agree that nineteenth century tourists were 'schooled to appreciate' the sublime and the beautiful, just as non-travellers 'learned' a taste for landscape.[37] Indeed, according to Solnit, 'to display a correct taste in landscape was a valuable social accomplishment quite as much as to sing well, or to compose a polite letter'.[38] But it became more than simply a middle-class attribute as aesthetic appreciation of a range of sceneries became part of the norm for many in late Victorian Sydney.

It is in this context that most visitors to Sydney beaches spent time gazing at the sea and cliffs, and some later wrote about them. Perhaps the majority of beachgoers during this period were completely unselfconscious in their appreciation of the scenery. However, there is evidence in some of the more flagrantly Romantic beach descriptions of writers who were consciously and deliberately situating themselves within the conventions of Romanticism. Indeed, there is sometimes quite significant overlap with some of the more prominent poems of the Romantic era.

Josiah Hughes, for example, in observing the 'shingly and rock strewn beach' at Coogee, which is in fact not a particularly shingly beach, draws a clear comparison with the 'naked shingles' described in Matthew Arnold's *Dover Beach*.[39] This poem, an emblematic piece of mid-nineteenth century coastal Romantic poetry, is also echoed in a *Town and Country* article about Coogee, where the 'battle array' of the surf reflects the 'ignorant armies' at Dover.[40]

Yet Arnold was not the only late Romantic poet whose words and images were echoed and even borrowed by colonial writers and travellers who wrote about Sydney beach scenes. The articles about Bondi and Bronte which were published in the *Australian Town and Country Journal* in 1876 go beyond merely echoing the sentiments of Britain's best known Romantic poets, and interweave sometimes quite extensive quotations throughout the text. While reflecting on Bondi, RA quoted the poetry of Lord Byron several times, as well as Tennyson and Keats, and he also included some slight misquotations from Shakespeare and the book of Nehemia from the Old Testament. Although he named the author of some of these quotations, most went uncited, only the inverted comers suggesting the true source of his words. Likewise, the meditations over Bronte that were published in December of the same year, and which appear to have been penned by the same author, included lines taken from Tennyson, Byron and Shelley, among others, and a misquotation from Wordsworth. In addition, the numerous mentions of the 'purple sea' at Bronte quite likely reflect the author's knowledge of Shelley's *The Cloud* more than his own interpretation of the beach.

It is revealing that the sentiments of these poets, among the most well known of the Romantic authors, should be so closely evoked in these descriptions of Sydney's beaches. The *Town and Country* authors of 1876, in particular, appear to have been more intent on demonstrating their extensive knowledge of Romantic poetry, than describing the particular beach scenes they visited, and importantly demanded at least a basic knowledge of the same from their readers. Like Hughes, Wilson and several others, they demonstrated to the reader that they were capable of 'feeling the finest sentiments of the poet', consciously, but ironically falsely, situating themselves within the Romantic genre.[41] It is possible only to speculate whether even the misquotations were intentional, but in this context it would not be entirely surprising. If contrived, these misquotations suggest to the reader that these writers are relying solely on their extensive although naturally imperfect knowledge of Romantic poetry, rather than merely referring to books.

Most descriptions of Sydney beaches were far less pretentious, but no less artificial. Writing about the scenery with rather less originality, many of the accounts of Bondi, Coogee and Manly incorporated terms which had by then become part of the everyday discourse of admiring scenery, rather than directly quoting or appropriating from specific poems. Beach scenes were 'grand', 'picturesque', 'wild', 'rugged' and 'beautiful', and the waves 'dashed' violently, were 'lashed' by winds and 'crashed' against the shore. Hipple argues that through increased usage, the original meanings of the word 'picturesque' inevitably became vaguer, and the word accordingly came to represent a variety of meanings.[42] This is certainly evident in the context of late nineteenth century beach descriptions, where 'picturesque' was frequently deployed to describe both wild and calm scenes, and the same could be said for the initially specific connotations of 'sublime'.

The widespread adoption of these sorts of terms and images when describing Sydney ocean beaches demonstrates the extent to which the ideals of Romanticism were by now understood among general audiences. People not only looked at and admired the scenery, but many knew which specific features to value over others. There was a distinction among beach writers between those who valued dramatic scenes in particular, and those who found the view of an ordinary beach on a fine day to be 'picturesque' or worth looking at. Perhaps this is where the distinction lies between those who were consciously treading in the steps of the Romantics and those who were simply appreciating the scenery according to the customs of the period.

While modern Australian beach culture owes much to the lifting of the daylight bathing bans in the opening years of the twentieth century, too much emphasis should not be placed on this single event. For we can see within this culture a continuation of the Romantic appeal of beach and sea-scapes. The sight of humans submitting themselves to the will of mother nature by entering and taking on the surf, which itself aroused awe and wonder among many spectators for several decades, only served to enhance the Romantic sense of the beach scene beyond the nineteenth century.

Notes

1   For a more detailed examination of the culture/nature distinction of nineteenth century Sydney beach culture, see Caroline Ford, 'Walking, gazing, falling in love: Culture and nature on the beach in nineteenth century Sydney', *History Australia*, June 2006.

2   Douglas Booth, *Australian Beach Cultures: A History of Sun, Sand and Surf* (London: Frank Cass, 2001); Leone Huntsman, *Sand in Our Souls: The Beach in Australian History* (Melbourne: Melbourne University Press, 2001); Cameron White, 'Picnicking, Surf-Bathing and Middle-Class Morality on the Beach in the Eastern Suburbs of Sydney, 1811–1912', *Journal of Australian Studies, New Talents*, 2004.

3 Andrea Inglis, *Beside the Seaside: Victorian Resorts in the Nineteenth Century* (Melbourne: Melbourne University Press, 1999).

4 Iain McCalman (ed.), *An Oxford Companion to the Romantic Age: British Culture 1776-1832* (Oxford: Oxford University Press, 1999) 2.

5 Alain Corbin, *The Lure of the Sea: the Discovery of the Seaside in the Western World 1750–1840* (Los Angeles: University of California Press, 1994) 126. See also Sarah Howell, *The Seaside* (London: Cassell and Collier Macmillan, 1974) 43; and John Urry, *The Tourist Gaze: Leisure and Travel in Contemporary Societies* (London: Sage, 1990) 20.

6 David Denholm, *The Colonial Australians* (Ringwood: Penguin, 1979) 137–59.

7 Julia Horne, *The Pursuit of Wonder: How Australia's landscape was explored, nature discovered and tourism unleashed* (Melbourne: Miegunyah, 2005).

8 Helen Baker Proudfoot, 'Botany Bay, Kew and the Picturesque: Early Conceptions of the Australian Landscape', *Journal of the Royal Australian Historical Society*, June 1979, 42–4.

9 Andrew Taylor, 'What do we see when we look at the sea? The sea in post-Romantic Australian, British and American writing', paper presented at *On the Beach: Interdisciplinary Encounters* Conference, Fremantle, February 2004.

10 Corbin, *The Lure of the Sea* 127.

11 William Maddock, *Visitor's Guide to Sydney, Comprising Description of the City, its Institutions, Parks, Excursions, and Other Information* (Sydney: Maddock, 1872); William Woolcott (ed.), *Cook's Guide to Sydney, The Blue Mountains, Jenolan Caves, Hawkesbury River, and Scenic Resorts of New South Wales* (Sydney: Thomas Cook and Sons, c.1890s) 43.

12 *The Grosvenor Hotel Visitor's Guide to Sydney and Suburbs* (Sydney: Grosvenor Hotel Company, c.1888) 85.

13 Josiah Hughes, *Australia Revisited in 1890 and Excursions in Egypt, Tasmania and New Zealand* (London: Simpkin, Marshall, Hamilton, Kent & Co., 1891) 237.

14 RA, 'Bondi', *Australian Town and County Journal*, March 11, 1876 .

15 'Bronte – Nelson's Bay', *Australian Town and County Journal*, Dec 16, 1876.

16 *Illustrated Sydney News,* 20 January 1883; *Town and Country Journal*, 11 May 1889; *Town and Country Journal*, 8 June 1889.

17 'Sydney and its Suburbs: Bondi', *The Month* 1857, vol.1, no.2, 162.

18 'Sydney and its Suburbs: Bondi', *The Month* 1857, vol.1, no.2, 161.

19 see Caroline Ford, 'Squads of brown men in defiance of the undertow and lurking sharks': the rhetoric of fear and danger on Sydney beaches', unpublished chapter of PhD thesis (2002).

20 Corbin, *The Lure of the Sea.*

21 F.S. Wilson, 'Loose Leaves from an Australian's Portfolio: Along the Coast', *Colonial Monthly,* September 1867, 20.

22 Wilson, 'Loose Leaves from an Australian's Portfolio' 23.

23 Wilson, 'Loose Leaves from an Australian's Portfolio' 24. For a more detailed discussion of the connection between Romanticism and 'romance', see Ford, 'Walking, Gazing, Falling in Love'.

24 'Sydney and its Suburbs: Fairlight Glen', *The Month*, vol. 3, no. 5, 1858, 240–2.

25 Miles Jebb, *Walkers* (London: Constable, 1986) 65. See also Melissa Harper, *The Ways of the Bushwalker: Bushwalking in Australia, 1788–1940*, Phd Thesis, University of Sydney (2002) 37.

26 For a detailed discussion of picnicking on Sydney's beaches in the nineteenth century, see Cameron White 'Picnicking, Surf-Bathing and Middle-Class Morality'.

27 Wilson, 'Loose Leaves from an Australian's Portfolio' 19.

28 It is entirely possible that this was the same contributor who walked from Bondi to South head in 1857, but difficult to be certain.

29 'Sydney and its Suburbs: Fairlight Glen'.

30 Maxine Feifer argues that while travelling, 'the Romantic was prone to the kind of unconventional behaviour that could lead to scandal'. Maxine Feifer, *Tourism in History: From Imperial Rome to the Present* (New York: Stein & Day, 1985) 140. From early in the twentieth century, body surfers were attracted by the prospect of being at one with the sea, Ed Jaggard, 'Body Surfers and Australian Beach Culture', paper presented to *On the Beach* Conference, Fremantle, February 2004.

31 Corbin, *The Lure of the Sea* 172.

32 As RA pointed out, most of Sydney's beaches were within distance of 'a healthy walk for a healthy man', RA, 'Bondi' 1876.

33 Harper, *The Ways of the Bushwalker* 10.

34 *Sydney Morning Herald,* 27 December 1894, 6.

35 W.F., *Notes of a Trip to Tasmania and Australia* (Lahore: Civil & Military Gazette Press, 1884).

36 Anne Wallace, *Walking, Literature and English Culture: The Origins and Uses of Peripatetic in the Nineteenth Century* (Oxford: Clarendon Press, 1993), 200–01.

37 Robin Jarvis, *Romantic Writing and Pedestrian Travel* (London: MacMillan 1997) 40. See also James Buzard, *The Beaten Track: European tourism, literature and the ways to culture, 1800–1918* (Oxford: Clarendon Press, 1993) 21–2; Peter Bicknell, *Beauty, Horror and Immensity: Picturesque Landscape in Britain, 1750–1850* (Cambridge: Cambridge University Press, 1981) xi; Howell, *The Seaside* 44–5; Corbin, *The Lure of the Sea* 148; Matthew Brennan, *Wordsworth, Turner and Romantic Landscape: A Study of the Traditions of the Picturesque and the Sublime* (Columbia Camden House, 1987) 23; Lena Lencek and Gideon Bosker, *The Beach: The History of Paradise on Earth* (London: Pimlico, 1999) 99; Rebecca Solnit, *Wanderlust: A History of Walking* (New York: Viking, 2000) 95.

38 Solnit, *Wanderlust* 95. Julia Horne also discusses the transition of once powerful terms into 'travel clichés' by the end of the nineteenth century. Horne, *The Pursuit of Wonder* 225.

39 I would like to thank Richard White for suggesting this point of comparison.

40 'Sydney Holiday resorts: Beautiful Coogee', *Australian Town and Country Journal*, 11 May 1889.

41 *Teggs Almanac*, 1842, quoted in George Blackmore Philip, *Sixty Years Recollections of Swimming and Surfing in the Eastern Suburbs* (Sydney: George B Philip and Son, 1940).

42 Walter John Hipple, *The Beautiful, the Sublime and the Picturesque in eighteenth Century British Aesthetic Theory* (Carbondale: Southern Illinois University Press, 1957) 188.

Works cited

Baker Proudfoot, Helen. 'Botany Bay, Kew and the Picturesque: Early Conceptions of the Australian Landscape'. *Journal of the Royal Australian Historical Society*, June 1979.

Bicknell, Peter. *Beauty, Horror and Immensity: Picturesque Landscape in Britain, 1750–1850*. Cambridge: Cambridge University Press, 1981.

Blackmore Philip, George. *Sixty Years Recollections of Swimming and Surfing in the Eastern Suburbs*. Sydney: George B Philip and Son, 1940.

Booth, Douglas. *Australian Beach Cultures: A History of Sun, Sand and Surf*. London: Frank Cass, 2001.

Brennan, Matthew. *Wordsworth, Turner and Romantic Landscape: A Study of the Traditions of the Picturesque and the Sublime*. Columbia Camden House, 1987.

Buzard, James. *The Beaten Track: European tourism, literature and the ways to culture, 1800–1918*. Oxford: Clarendon Press, 1993.

Corbin, Alain. *The Lure of the Sea: the Discovery of the Seaside in the Western World 1750–1840*. Los Angeles: University of California Press, 1994.

Denholm, David. *The Colonial Australians*. Ringwood: Penguin, 1979.

Feifer, Maxine. *Tourism in History: From Imperial Rome to the Present*. New York: Stein & Day, 1985.

Ford, Caroline. 'Walking, gazing, falling in love: Culture and nature on the beach in nineteenth century Sydney', *History Australia*, June 2006.

Ford, Caroline. 'Squads of brown men in defiance of the undertow and lurking sharks: the rhetoric of fear and danger on Sydney beaches', unpublished chapter of Phd thesis (2002).

Harper, Melissa. *The Ways of the Bushwalker: Bushwalking in Australia, 1788-1940*. Phd Thesis, University of Sydney (2002).

Hipple, Walter John. *The Beautiful, the Sublime and the Picturesque in eighteenth Century British Aesthetic Theory*. Carbondale: Southern Illinois University Press, 1957.

Horne, Julia. *The Pursuit of Wonder: How Australia's landscape was explored, nature discovered and tourism unleashed*. Melbourne: Miegunyah, 2005.

Howell, Sarah. *The Seaside*. London: Cassell and Collier Macmillan, 1974.

Hughes, Josiah. *Australia Revisited in 1890 and Excursions in Egypt, Tasmania and New Zealand*. London: Simpkin, Marshall, Hamilton, Kent & Co., 1891.

Huntsman, Leone. *Sand in Our Souls: The Beach in Australian History.* Melbourne: Melbourne University Press, 2001.

Inglis, Andrea. *Beside the Seaside: Victorian Resorts in the Nineteenth Century.* Melbourne: Melbourne University Press, 1999.

Jarvis, Robin. *Romantic Writing and Pedestrian Travel.* London: MacMillan 1997.

Jebb, Miles. *Walkers.* London: Constable, 1986.

Lencek, Lena and Bosker, Gideon. *The Beach: The History of Paradise on Earth.* London: Pimlico, 1999.

Maddock, William. *Visitor's Guide to Sydney, Comprising Description of the City, its Institutions, Parks, Excursions, and Other Information.* Sydney: Maddock, 1872.

McCalman, Iain (ed.). *An Oxford Companion to the Romantic Age: British Culture 1776-1832.* Oxford: Oxford University Press, 1999.

Solnit, Rebecca. *Wanderlust: A History of Walking.* New York: Viking, 2000.

Taylor, Andrew. 'What do we see when we look at the sea? The sea in post-Romantic Australian, British and American writing', paper presented at *On the Beach: Interdisciplinary Encounters* Conference, Fremantle, February 2004.

Urry, John. *The Tourist Gaze Leisure and Travel in Contemporary Societies.* London: Sage, 1990.

Wallace, Anne. *Walking, Literature and English Culture: The Origins and Uses of Peripatetic in the Nineteenth Century.* Oxford: Clarendon Press, 1993.

White, Cameron. 'Picnicking, Surf-Bathing and Middle-Class Morality on the Beach in the Eastern Suburbs of Sydney, 1811–1912', *Journal of Australian Studies, New Talents,* 2004.

Wilson, F.S. 'Loose Leaves from an Australian's Portfolio: Along the Coast', *Colonial Monthly,* September 1867.

Woolcott, William (ed.). *Cook's Guide to Sydney, The Blue Mountains, Jenolan Caves, Hawkesbury River, and Scenic Resorts of New South Wales.* Sydney: Thomas Cook and Sons, c.1890s.

W.F. *Notes of a Trip to Tasmania and Australia.* Lahore: Civil & Military Gazette Press, 1884.

The Grosvenor Hotel Visitor's Guide to Sydney and Suburbs. Sydney: Grosvenor Hotel Company, c.1888.

The Australian Midsummer Dream:
From Beach Shack to Titania's Palace

SUSAN HOSKING

We're all going on a summer holiday
no more working for a week or two
fun and laughter on our summer holiday
no more worries for me and you
for a week or two

We're going where the sun shines brightly
we're going where the sea is blue
we've all seen it in the movies
now let's see if it's true[1]

Memories of the family beach shack (or staying at someone else's family beach shack) are strongly tied to perceptions of traditional Australian values. As the shack becomes an 'endangered' species, nostalgia for shack culture is increasing.[2] Matthew Newton's photographic record of Tasmanian shacks titled *Shack Life: Tasmanian Shacks and Shack Culture* has proven to be a popular 'souvenir' for visitors to Tasmania. First published in 2003, the photographs are introduced by Richard Flanagan, who describes shack culture as 'ingenious, warm, colourful, peripheral, eccentric, often rough, sometimes funny and occasionally brilliant'. Although he sees this way of life as having 'all but disappeared for the majority of Australians', Flanagan identifies Tasmanian shacks and shackies as 'the perfect symbol for Tasmania itself'.[3] He might just as well have claimed beach shacks more generally as Australian icons. The association between shacks and nostalgia about Australian identity is confirmed by the continuing popularity of Matthew Newton's photography, showcased not only in his booklet *Shack Life*, but also in the documentary film *Titania's Palace*, by Roar Film Pty Ltd, written and directed by Stephen Thomas. *Titania's Palace* was shown twice on the Australian Broadcasting Commission (ABC) in 2005. The first of four documentaries on shacks made in 2003, *Titania's Palace* was promoted as a celebration of the 'eccentric and, at times, bizarre, shack culture of Tasmania'.[4] Newton's booklet is obviously a spin-off from the series.

Nostalgia for shack culture also permeates the contemporary Australian summer holiday industry. 'The Beach Shacks' at 1770, on the southern tip of the Great Barrier Reef, offer a typical 'shack pack' of 'tranquil … beaches … with numerous great fishing spots. Ideal for families or a romantic getaway for two … and endless amounts of fun'. The 'shacks' overlook Bustard Bay and Round Hill Creek and are promoted as having 'historical significance'. The site of 'The Beach Shacks' is advertised as 'the second place in Australia, after Botany Bay, where Lieutenant Cook took the Endeavour'. From the 'shacks' on the headland, paying visitors can indulge their nostalgia for 'Australianness' in luxury, admiring magnificent sunsets from their private decks or retiring inside to enjoy their facilities which include: air conditioning, bathroom, laundry facilities, television, video player, mini-bar, ceiling fans, microwave oven, large refrigerator and cook top.[5]

The shack holiday, originally, was the working-class man's celebration of freedom, family and place. The shack was an expression of ingenuity and inventiveness: a means to an end rather than an end in itself. In the age of consumerism the shack holiday is categorised by its architecture and infrastructure. Atmosphere ('an exotic castaway feel') is part of the packaging; tickets are required for activities such as sunset cruises, supervised scuba diving, marine animal viewing, visits to water museums and art galleries, classes in meditation or crafts. And for those who miss the boat, there will always be a gym nearby.

Shacks, or weekenders as they are more commonly called in the Eastern states, are now retreats for the moderately wealthy. In November 2006, the lifestyle magazine *House and Garden* featured what is captioned a 'Slice of heaven':

> This distinctive weekender on Victoria's Mornington Peninsula—nicknamed 'Wedge House'—may appear diminutive and spartan at first glance, but the family who own it wouldn't have it any other way.[6]

This particular weekender is architecturally designed to capture 'all the quintessential values of the classic Australian weekender'.[7] The materials have been 'chosen' for their economy, function and environmental credentials. The weekender is clad and bedecked in silvertop ash, which will 'weather to a driftwood grey, perfect for a seaside location'.[8] Not everyone who wants to join the 'eight per cent of contemporary Australian households who escape regularly to their own holiday home'[9] has the good fortune to have an architect as a friend.[10] The not-so-moderately wealthy are advised in the same issue of *House and Garden* that prefabricated options exist 'that are affordable and beautifully designed—some even developed by leading Australian architects'.[11] Such 'options' cost about $140,000 for a two-bedroom weekender. And for the even-less-moderately-wealthy there is always the 'Takeaway', an 'affordable, factory-built house' manufactured in Cairns and transportable to 'anywhere in Australia' for about $65,000.[12]

In the late 1930s and 1940s, shacks were built from scrounge. Helen Voysey continues to care and fight for the shack her father built in 1937 at Era Beach, near Wollongong in New South Wales. She describes how the family shack was built. With four mates, Helen's father

> carried all the materials down the escarpment. Down two and a half kilometres of track—every windowsill, every piece of iron, the water tank, bedding—everything. That goes for all the shacks here. That long, steep track is still the only way to get to Era Beach. Doesn't matter who you are or what you do for a living. There's no electricity either. We still use kero stoves and fridges.[13]

By the 1950s, the new way of life in Australia was overtaking the old. The developers had arrived and shackies had to fight to preserve what they had established. Helen Voysey's father joined a shackowner's delegation to the Lands' Minister when the government decided to auction off coastal land to developers in 1950. Era Beach subsequently became part of the Royal National Park and the shacks were saved, at least in the short term. But around Australia, descendents of the original shack builders are now fighting for what the shacks represent:

> Shacks are a great leveller. Life here harks back to former times. We only bring what we need. We recycle whatever we can … The beach is open to anybody prepared to walk down the track … Dad's ashes were scattered off Era Point, his last wish to have his children inherit the shack. That is why we can't leave, why we strive to retain control over this place we love and care for.[14]

Originally shacks were built along favourite stretches of Australian beach by families and groups of friends on government land that appeared to 'belong' to no one, and therefore seemed to be available to anyone who, with a few sheets of tin or asbestos, was prepared to create a shelter for a summer holiday. Communities of (especially summer) holiday makers were established. This happened at countless now developed or developing coastal places: Normanville, Port Elliot and Kangaroo Island in South Australia, Era Beach in New South Wales, Grey Beach in Western Australia and nowhere more distinctively than around the coast of Tasmania.

Notions of Australian identity are of course themselves owner-built. Richard White offers insight into the evolution of shack culture and the holiday home in his fascinating study, *On Holidays: a history of getting away in Australia*.[15] Clearly, the annual holiday became a reality in Australia with the passing of the *Annual Holidays Act* in 1944. Those who worked towards legislation of the summer holiday constructed it as beneficial to the health of families, especially the 'physical and mental health' of 'breadwinners'—men, of course. Healthy workers would create a healthy economy. The consolidation of holiday weeks around Christmas was common sense. To shut everything down at the same time was economically rational.

Working class people, obviously unable to fund expensive trips or pay for accommodation, headed in the summer heat for water: inland lakes, rivers, or the coast—most significantly the beach. As the family holiday became a ritualised escape in a 'designated holiday season', shacks were built to enable families and/or friends to holiday together, generally in the same places, year after year.[16] In these extended 'other' communities, the conventions and demands of work and suburban protocol could be left behind. But by the sixties, the 'new way of life' had left the old values behind.[17] Ownership, not just of one home but two, became a significant mark of prosperity. Dinky-di shackies or their grown up children refused or were simply financially unable to move on or upwards. Rejecting the culture of consumerism, they became an endangered species, to which public attention is now returning in paradoxical ways.

Two Australian short stories testify particularly well to the passing of shack culture, contesting the romance of the holiday home in particularly interesting ways. Both Patrick White's 'Dead Roses' and Elizabeth Harrower's 'A Beautiful Climate', written in the 1960s, highlight the old-fashioned values that were jettisoned as Australians embraced the culture of ownership and the display of wealth.[18]

The substantial holiday home represented in 'Dead Roses' is based on Rocky Point, formerly owned by Geoffrey and Ninette Dutton on Kangaroo Island at American Beach. David Marr reveals in White's biography that White refused a couple of invitations to join the Duttons' summer party on the Island, but finally succumbed in 1962.[19] Marr describes holiday life at Rocky Point as 'simple and generous in an old house perched above a deserted bay'.[20] On holiday, the Duttons maintained a way of holiday life that deferred to shack culture, although their holiday house was far from a shack; they had a rule that no work was to be done while on holiday, so White did not write while he was there.[21] Guests and their hosts fished, ate, drank and read books. Children, adults and carefully chosen invited guests mingled under one roof, like an extended family. Breakfasts were long and leisurely. The rooms were lit at night by kerosene lamps and precious water was drawn from deep tanks.[22] Back in Sydney, White wrote 'Dead Roses', drawing upon what he knew of Rocky Point and the holiday party he had joined there. Val and Gil Tulloch were immediately recognisable as the Duttons and other members of the holiday party recognised themselves as well and were 'outraged'.[23]

In White's 'Dead Roses', the Tullochs certainly espouse notions of community and egalitarianism, but the spectre of class hovers over the holiday party. Val Tulloch 'arranges' summer holidays like bunches of flowers. She selects her guests carefully, balancing positive human traits against faults, anticipating peace and harmony, imposing her own formula for happiness. She uses her skills to create, as White puts it, one of those 'temporary communities far closer knit that most of the lifelong relationships'.[24]

Val Tulloch creates a holiday environment that is typically 'Australian', consciously reproducing the values that shack communities represent, but in a parallel world. The Tullochs are regarded by the more obviously class-conscious amongst their acquaintances as 'lax … and in appearance often downright shabby'.[25] They are 'jolly' and 'informal' and rumour has it that Gilbert is 'red'. But they wear the 'aura which only inherited wealth and station can give', so when Anthea Scudamore is invited to the Island for the Christmas season, her socially conformist mother is pleased. The fact that the Tullochs have 'property' reconciles her to 'their aberrations of the mind'.[26]

Val has clearly adopted Anthea, the 'spotless girl from the city', as a 'project': she's a girl who has been 'brought-up' rather too strictly within social conventions; she's a girl who needs to be 'brought-out'.[27] Val arranges for Anthea to be met by the local mail-man, 'sandy' Ossie Ryan, who runs 'one of those loosely connected bombs which rattle between fixed points in the remoter parts of Australia'.[28] She sits beside him, 'lush, white' and 'imported beside her red, skinny, indigenous companion'.[29] She has few words for him, but Ossie attempts to 'widen her experience by telling her what was happening in the stone cottages they pass'.[30] She has few words for her driver, but does tell him that she is fascinated. Her expression carries such sincerity that Ossie wonders whether it means anything. Ossie's own view, as a working class rural Australian, is that 'people are about the same … wherever they happen to be'.[31] But this is clearly not the case.

The space of the Tullochs' holiday home enables Anthea to enjoy a degree of self-expression and intimacy with others that she has never been allowed to experience. She sprawls on the faded Indian counterpane. She slops washing up water on her raw silk dress. She accepts the disorder of the living room. And yet, she cannot quite lose herself. She cannot abandon herself to the generalised love of people, such as she has heard expressed by her mother's cleaning lady.

> *I love people*, Mrs Meadling used to say, several times every Thursday, as she turned out the house for Mummy. *Oh, but Mrs Meadling, how can you be so general?* the irritated Anthea had once exclaimed. *Eh? I was never a general, only ever went out daily.* Anthea murmured: *What I mean, Mrs Meadling, is, there are reservations in everything.*[32]

On the Island, fishing, rowing, feeding possums, shooting at wallaby, driving to fetch provisions, Anthea Scudamore feels herself 'becoming a Different Person'.[33] Her white arms become 'red and ugly'. She doesn't care. She lets herself go. Her will slackens, her voice flaps 'uncontrolled', her shirt unbuttons 'lower because of summer and the beach' and before she knows it, she's lying next to coarse Barry Flegg on the beach.[34] He is a university man, but with common origins: his father was a stationmaster at Buckleboo and his mother a cleaner of toilets before her marriage.

As befits her upbringing, Anthea extricates herself from a difficult situation. Val's plan to undermine social rigidity and convention fails, perhaps because, after all, it is merely an amusement for the hostess: a genteel arrangement by someone who does not have to think about class. Anthea Scudamore goes on to live the life her mother wants for her: the achievable Australian dream, where happiness is being 'well provided for, and of a happy social level'.[35] Harry Heseltine famously summed up 'Dead Roses' as 'how Anthea Scudamore turns into her mother'.[36] But that one moment of connection on the beach, in the liminal zone where anything is possible, where Anthea might have become someone else, is clearly represented as the only moment Anthea truly lived. Only on the beach, on summer holiday, might the coarse and the refined mingle. Nevertheless, for the class conscious, life cannot be lived on the beach, at least not in White's fiction. The holiday-makers in 'Dead Roses' are neither family nor community, but 'invited guests', temporarily and artificially arranged (with some daring) to decorate the house for a short season. The myth that class can be permanently transcended or rearranged is clearly contested. In the end it is property that matters and material wealth that must be pursued.

Elizabeth Harrower's short story, 'A Beautiful Climate', undermines another myth: that of the happy holiday family, having fun while building future wealth. Harrower's story centres around a weekender: a cottage on Scotland Island, about an hour's drive and a short ferry trip away from Sydney. The cottage, owned originally by someone who built it himself, has changed hands a number of times and its history is lost. The cottage is bought by Hector Shaw, from 'some hotel-keeper he knew' in a deal that Hector's wife and daughter are not party to.[37] In fact, Hector's intention to buy a weekender is never discussed with his family until the contract is signed, at which time he announces his ownership of a second home, tells his wife and daughter where it is, and establishes as fact 'that they would all go down every Friday night to put it in order'.[38]

What Hector Shaw inflicts on his little family is a travesty of the intangible values that characterise the family holiday: relationships, friendship, community and freedom in an undeveloped environment. Hector is a man of 'silent, smouldering violence'.[39] His every action draws attention to the incongruity of such a personality in the 'land of the long weekend'.[40] The values at the heart of shack culture are glaringly absent. Hector Shaw buys a dilapidated cottage amongst holiday homes with handsomely constructed jetties 'equipped with special flags and lights to summon the ferryman when it was time to return to civilization'.[41] Described as a 'camp commandant', Hector Shaw commits his wife and daughter to heavy labour in order to improve his investment. They scrub, sand and paint furniture, floors and walls. Hector clears away the eucalyptus gums in which the cottage nestles and installs a generating plant so that they can 'have electric light instead of relying on kerosene lamps at night'.[42]

The shift in emphasis from 'holiday' to 'house' enables exploration of the kind of dreadful oppression that is central to Gothic fiction—something that Harrower develops much more pointedly in her novel *The Watch Tower*.[43] In 'The Beautiful Climate', although Harrower does not use obviously Gothic machinery, she nevertheless exposes her male protagonist, Hector Shaw, as a misogynist and psychological torturer, much like his counterpart Felix in *The Watch Tower*. Hector exploits the perceived togetherness of the traditional Australian family holiday or holiday weekend to a terrible degree, binding his women to him and denying them the freedom of holiday space, even when they are outside the house. Del, his eighteen-year-old daughter, wishes she could stay in town, working seven days a week. She never wants to go on the rare excursions down the steep bushy track to the spindly jetty, where the rowboat is tied. But Del is trapped. If she does not go, her absence will be used against her mother. So her protests are silent, battering nothing but the air about her.

> They were not free. Either the hostage, or the one over whom a hostage was held, they seemed destined to play for ever if they meant to preserve the peace.[44]

In shack culture, as represented in the contemporary photographs of Matthew Newton, notions of family are relatively flexible within any given community: a shack might be occupied by a man or woman alone, women together, marital couples, combined families, blokes together, groups of friends and or relatives, and so forth. Harrower, however, represents and critiques a rigid definition of family in her male protagonist. Hector Shaw is defined not as a member of a community but as 'the man of the family'.[45] The point of family, for Hector, is to be head of a household, and the point of being head of a household is to exercise power. His family is 'clamped together'.[46] His fishing expeditions take place not to experience the environment or to catch a meal, but whenever he feels the 'desire for some sport'.[47] And the sport he enjoys most is tormenting his captive wife and daughter:

> Stationed in the dead centre of the glittering bay, within sight of their empty house, they sat in the open boat, grasping cork rollers, feeling minute and interesting tugs on their lines from time to time, losing bait and catching three inch fish …
>
> As the inevitable pain began to saturate Mrs Shaw's head, she turned gradually paler. She leaned against the side of the boat with her eyes closed, her hands obediently clasping the fishing-line she had been told to hold.
>
> The dazzle of the heavy summer sun sucked up colour till the scene looked black. Her light skin began to burn. The straw sun-hat was like a neat little oven in which her hair, her head and all its contents, were being cooked …
>
> The wooden interior of the boat was dry and burning. The three fishers were seared, beaten down by the sun. The bait smelled. The water lapped and twinkled blackly but could not be approached: sharks abounded in the bay.[48]

Community is something that Hector Shaw and his tragically passive wife do not seem to understand. Eight months pass before the Shaws strike up a friendship with a family who have just bought the cottage next door. The Rivers are easy-going people and a routine of reciprocal visits is established. For the Shaws, this routine is considered as 'a sort of rest-cure ordered by a specialist, from which they might pick up some health'.[49] But that too goes wrong, when the Rivers' son Martin dares to ask Del to accompany him to a party on the other side of the bay. Del makes her excuse:

> 'I have to paint those chairs this afternoon.'
> '*Have* to?'[50]

Martin, '[o]ne of the new generation', dares to question the authority of the father, who is ever vigilant against any perceived threat to his prison security. Later, adopting the stance of a Victorian patriarch, 'back to the fire, hands clasped behind him', Hector ruminates: 'He had a nerve … I mean—he's a complete stranger.'[51]

When the restoration of the cottage is finished, Hector Shaw's weekender is put up for sale, as it was bought, without consultation. 'Life's short' says Hector to his incredulous wife. 'I've earned a holiday'. He plans a trip overseas: a cruise, up the coast of Australia, 'to Colombo, Bombay, Aden, through the Suez, then up through the Mediterranean, through the Straits of Gibralta to Marseilles, then London.'[52]

This little story brings into stark relief the significance of the shack or holiday home in the evolution of a distinctively Australian 'way of life'. The Shaws do not belong: not even to the 'new' way of life that embraces materialism. The island, where they have laboured on Hector Shaw's investment, remains indifferent to them, as they remain indifferent to what it has to offer:

> The hillside sat there, quietly, rustling quietly, a smug curving hillside that had existed for a long time. The water was blue and sparkled with meaningless beauty. Smoke stood in the sunny sky above the bush here and there across the bay, where other weekend visitors were cooking chops, or making coffee on fuel stoves.[53]

As for the daughter, Del, she looks forward to what seems like a 'reprieve' from dullness and confinement. Having rejected Martin, the 'open, slightly freckle-faced' Australian boy, she sees departure from the shores of Australia as an opportunity in a wider world to escape.[54] Her conflation of the prison of family with the prison of an Australian island holiday home underlines her inability to identify as Australian.

It is not difficult to come to conclusions about the resurgence of shack nostalgia in the last few years. Who would not understand the longing to return to simpler times, before coastal views could be bought for well over half a million dollars; when it was possible to squat on Crown Land and really experience the weather, before people talked about the ozone layer, let alone the hole in it; when water could be accessed through wells and stored on a roof in an old beer keg: just enough for basic needs, including an occasional shower; when 'biscuits were only sold in tins' and 'fishing mates rode pushbikes along a bush track to the beach'.[55]

Shackies have described and often named their shacks and shack communities in terms of little Utopias or Edens. Stubby in hand, cigarette drooping from his lips, one of Matthew Newton's photographic subjects describes the nondescript shacks at Saltwater River, Tasman Peninsula, as 'Paradise, absolutely paradise. That's what we think anyway'.[56]

Looking back on their childhood and adolescence in the 1930s, 40s and 50s, descendents of shack builders describe these places as magical. The Thompsons' shack at Clifton Beach Estate, South Coast Tasmania, was named 'Titania's Palace'. Helen Thompson had been much impressed by an 'intricately constructed fairy house', exhibited throughout Australia in the mid 1930s to raise funds for crippled children.[57] The little house had been created by British peer Sir Neville Wilkinson, as 'a dwelling place for the fairies of his small daughter's imagination'. It included '4,000 pieces of miniature furniture' arranged throughout 'sixteen glass-enclosed rooms facing a central courtyard into which visitors could peer' and 'featured botanical specimens realistically moulded in brass'.[58]

In Stephen Thomas's film, *Titania's Palace,* the elderly daughters of Margaret Thompson talk about their parents who were surfers in the 1930s, attracted to Clifton Beach by the waves. Margaret Thompson used the middle plank of a cedar dining table as her board for over thirty years, and her husband was reputed to have surfed on a plank from a fence. The daughters, who were still using the shack in 2005, vaguely remembered that 'some man in England' had exhibited a miniature palace in Hobart. What they clearly remembered was how amused their mother had been by the contrast between the opulent fairy house and their own basic dwelling. Would Margaret Thomson have been equally amused by the designer shacks of the early twenty-first century? Would she have laughed at the assumption that the essence of a poor family's holiday can be bought? Did she think of 'Titania's Palace' as a magical zone? Or was her humble family beach shack simply 'an excuse to live in a place'?[59]

Notes

1 Cliff Richard, 'Summer Holiday'. Lyrics courtesy of Cliff Richard, accessed 20 October 2006, http://www.singulartists.com/artist_c/cliff_richard_lyrics/summer_holiday_lyrics.html

2 Heritage WA, 'Western Australian Endangered Places: Grey Beach Shack Community' nominated by Grey Community and Conservation Association, accessed 20 October 2006, <http://www.heritagewa.org.au/places/shacks/>

3 Matthew Newton, *Shack Life. Tasmanian Shacks and Shack Culture* (Hobart: Matthew Newton, 2003) unpaginated [i].

4 Accessed 20 October 2006, <http://www.roarfilm.com.au/film_television/titianas_palace.shtml>.

5 Accessed 20 October 2006, <http://www.qldtravel.com.au/accommodation/the-beach-shacks/>.

6 *House and Garden*, November 2006, 47.

7 *House and Garden*, November 2006, 48.

8 *House and Garden*, November 2006, 46.

9 *House and Garden*, November 2006, 52.

10 *House and Garden*, November 2006, 52.

11 *House and Garden*, November 2006, 52.

12 *House and Garden*, November 2006, 52.

13 Voysey, 'Era Beach Shacks', accessed 20 October 2006, <http://www.sbs.com.au/myspace/index.php3?action=show&id=18>.

14 Voysey, 'Era Beach Shacks' 18.

15 Richard White, *On Holidays: a history of getting away in Australia* (North Melbourne: Pluto Press, 2005).

16 White, *On Holidays* 124.

17 White, *On Holidays* 129.

18 Patrick White, 'Dead Roses' in *The Burnt Ones* (London: Eyre and Spottiswoode, 1964) 11–75; Elizabeth Harrower, 'A Beautiful Climate', first published in *Modern Australian Stories*, ed. Geoffrey Dutton (London: Collins, 1966) 217–30. Quotations here taken from 'The Beautiful Climate' in the anthology *Contemporary Australian Short Stories*, edited by Santosh K. Sareen (New Delhi: Affiliated East-West Press, 2001) 44–57.

19 David Marr, *Patrick White, A Life* (Sydney: Random House [Vintage edition], 1992).

20 Marr, *Patrick White* 409.

21 Marr, *Patrick White* 410.

22 Marr, *Patrick White* 409.

23 Marr, *Patrick White* 410.

24 White, 'Dead Roses' 15.

25 White, 'Dead Roses' 10.

26 White, 'Dead Roses' 15.

27 White, 'Dead Roses' 11.

28 White, 'Dead Roses' 15.

29 White, 'Dead Roses' 16.

30 White, 'Dead Roses' 16.

31 White, 'Dead Roses' 17.

32 White, 'Dead Roses' 20.

33 White, 'Dead Roses' 25.

34 White, 'Dead Roses' 27.

35 White, 'Dead Roses' 12.

36 HP Heseltine, Review of *The Burnt Ones*, *Southerly*, XXV (1965) 71.

37 Harrower, 'A Beautiful Climate' 44.

38 Harrower, 'A Beautiful Climate' 44.

39 Harrower, 'A Beautiful Climate' 44.

40 White, *On Holidays* 129.

41 Harrower, 'A Beautiful Climate' 44.

42 Harrower, 'A Beautiful Climate' 46, 48.

43 Elizabeth Harrower, *The Watch Tower* (London, New York and Melbourne: Macmillan and St Martin's Press, 1966.

44 Harrower, 'A Beautiful Climate' 45.

45 Harrower, 'A Beautiful Climate' 46.

46 Harrower, 'A Beautiful Climate' 45.

47 Harrower, 'A Beautiful Climate' 46.

48 Harrower, 'A Beautiful Climate' 46–7.

49 Harrower, 'A Beautiful Climate' 49.

50 Harrower, 'A Beautiful Climate' 49.

51 Harrower, 'A Beautiful Climate' 50, 51.
52 Harrower, 'A Beautiful Climate' 55, 54.
53 Harrower, 'A Beautiful Climate' 56.
54 Harrower, 'A Beautiful Climate' 56, 49.
55 Les Peters, 'Mayor' of 'Tin City', Port Stephens, New South Wales, accessed 20 October 2006, <http://www.portstephens4wd.com/port_stephens. php?Name=Tin%20City>.
56 Newton, unpaginated [plate 11].
57 *Titania's Palace*, by Roar Film Pty Ltd, 2003.
58 Extract from 'Rocky Bay: A Short History 1938–2000', compiled by Beth Evans, accessed 20 October 2006, <http://www.rockybay.org.au/about/history.cfm>.
59 Newton, *Shack Life*, unpaginated [plate 46].

Works cited

Harrower, Elizabeth. 'A Beautiful Climate', in *Modern Australian Stories*. Ed. Geoffrey Dutton. London: Collins, 1966.

Harrower, Elizabeth. *The Watch Tower*. London, New York and Melbourne: Macmillan and St Martin's Press, 1966.

Marr, David. *Patrick White, A Life*. Sydney: Random House [Vintage edition], 1992.

Newton, Matthew. *Shack Life. Tasmanian Shacks and Shack Culture*. Hobart: Matthew Newton, 2003.

Sareen, Santosh K. (ed.). 'The Beautiful Climate', in *Contemporary Australian Short Stories*. New Delhi: Affiliated East-West Press, 2001.

White, Patrick . 'Dead Roses', in *The Burnt Ones*. London: Eyre and Spottiswoode, 1964.

White, Richard. *On Holidays: A history of getting away in Australia*. North Melbourne: Pluto Press, 2005.

SeaChange, Where Fish Fly

REBECCA PANNELL

Don't wanna live in the city, my friends tell me I'm changin',
The smell of salty air, is what I'm chasin',
You probably think I'm mad, but it feels good to me,
Cos from now on I'll live as close as I can to the sea.
I don't know why I'm going through the seachange
I'm reaching out to the sky for a seachange.[1]

In 2006 Channel Seven Australia aired their new reality television series *The Real SeaChange,* hosted by none other than 'Bob Jelly' himself, actor John Howard.[2] This is Howard's third 'seachange' genre series. Best known for his Logie-winning role as Jelly in ABC TV's *SeaChange,* Howard is also remembered for his work in Channel Seven's *Always Greene*—the 'treechange' equivalent. In *The Real SeaChange* Howard is supposedly at the helm of a 'new exciting program' where 'families, couples and singles' leave the 'big smoke … in search of a better life'. The challenge is to see if 'they have what it takes to make a go of it in paradise. Or will their dream become a nightmare?'[3]

Seven claim in the promotional blurb for this show that the term 'seachange' became part of Australian vernacular due to the ABC TV series of the same name. They assume that this makes Howard 'a fitting choice as host'.[4] Not only does he bring with him the kudos of the Logies and the public face of Channel Seven, most importantly Howard brings the cultural memory for viewers of their beloved *SeaChange.* Seven's *The Real SeaChange* forms part of the growing conversation between Australians, geography, place and lifestyle. But what of the original—where does the series *SeaChange* belong in our 'popculture' memory: is it saccharine or salty? [5]

Sea Change has a SeaChange

Full fathom five thy father lies;
Of his bones are coral made;
Those are pearls that were his eyes;
Nothing of him that doth fade

> *But doth suffer a sea-change*
> *Into something rich and strange.*[6]

There is no mistaking *SeaChange's* literary relationship to *The Tempest*: from its title to episodes entitled 'Something Rich and Strange' and 'Full Fathom Five; a character named Miranda; and narrative turns of storms and freak weather patterns the connection is obvious to those with any high school Shakespeare. The idea of what a 'sea change' means is uppermost in our minds forming part of the charm and desire associated with the show. This is a series about significant changes: metaphorical, literal, littoral.

In the traditional sense of *The Tempest*, a sea change is a *physical* change—from human form into forms of the seabed—coral, pearls, sand, and weeds. We could argue, however, that since the airing of *SeaChange*, the idea of a sea change is now taken primarily to mean a geographical one, usually from the city to the coast. More distinctly, it signals a move to a coastal town, such as the ironically named Pearl Bay. But more than geography is at stake in *SeaChange*; for Laura Gibson (played by Sigrid Thornton) and her family we are talking about a paradigm shift. In this sense, we could argue that the sea change that occurs here is 'a radical, and apparently mystical, change' in the traditional sense.[7] However, this is not simply a change brought about by the sea once they get there, it is also a generic major change brought about in the first instance by Laura's *decision* to move to the sea. Laura's sea change is traditional too in the sense that she is irreversibly altered—there is no going back. We know this because her ex-husband Jack tries to re-form their marital relationship. Laura, however, is unable to go back to the way they were—in fact, she is even unable to contemplate a different life together; this is because Laura herself has metamorphosed into a creature of the coast, a creature who is no longer partner-to-Jack. And at the end of the series, her old legal firm senior partner makes it clear that Laura is no longer one of 'them'; her old job is simply no longer available to her.

SeaChange is also metamorphic in terms of genre; it takes one of our 'compulsory' television genres—crime and the law—and turns it on its head. Yes, Laura Gibson is a lawyer who becomes a magistrate: many of the scenes are set around or in the police station or the courthouse, many crimes are committed. But the series does not revolve around 'catching murderers' or protecting citizens from rapists, frauds, thieves and 'psychos'. In fact, the twist is that several Pearl Bay citizens, for various reasons, try to put themselves *in* jail, and if they have committed crimes, their crimes are subsidiary to the plot. For example, in the same episode, Diver Dan attempts to get out of a date with Laura by admitting to multiple parking offences, Harold, in his attempt to get sober tries to spend as much time in jail as possible and Karen's father admits to a crime from long ago. But these are merely 'backstory' or plot devices that expose the characters' relationships and histories: the crime always leads us back to the idea of community, to our foundation myths and to our social issues.[8] In the episode 'Blowing in the Wind', when Tama destroys Sergeant Grey's trumpet, the investigation is not about the crime, it is an investigation into the motivation of the inner self. The end result is not a 'conviction' but friendship through acts of courage.

Paradox in Paradise

As Betsy Williams observes, the show that *SeaChange* is often compared to, *Northern Exposure*, had that great divide 'between East and West, frontier versus civilisation, science versus mysticism and male versus female' to explore.[9] *Sea-Change* too highlights the paradoxes and divides in life. A move to the seaside prompted by nostalgia, stress, and a yearning for simple times and simple people, exposes the complexity of human beings and life everywhere. Instead of simplicity Laura and others find personal complications and emotional turmoil. Rather than the idyllic life of beach culture, Pearl Bay is wracked by storms—tempests if you like—that signify disruption in the community. Its beaches have problems dumped upon them and strange cargo delivered up from the deep that force the inhabitants to re-evaluate their lives and their pasts; despite its nod towards rural idyll, it is not a beach paradise peopled by simple country 'hicks' untouched by the world.

In episode one, Miranda Gibson asks her video-camera diary: 'is this paradise'? As Miranda discovers, the answer is yes *and* no. Utopia, it seems, is both paradise lost and paradise gained. Life is cyclical not linear, scenes repeat themselves—sometimes from different perspectives, in different guises. The sea regurgitates memories and people that we had hoped were drowned: Tensing (formerly Mabel), Prahni's husband, Max's father. Others, such as Max's wife Elena, Diver Dan, Griff and Madi, even Trevor and Kevin, are cast adrift upon the sea—only Trevor and Kevin return. Utopia, an Australian ideal, is necessarily the dystopia of Pearl Bay. We know this to be so because of the homily delivered at the end of each episode.[10]

Spiritual Change

In the opening credits we are exposed to all that Laura is leaving behind: soulless concrete towers with windows that imprison you rather than let you breathe; claustrophobic traffic and polluted air; a fast-paced lifestyle that has no space for thinking; and a world in which the material outruns the spiritual in the race to partnership in the firm. Juxtaposed to this is the driving narrative force behind

SeaChange: care of the soul. This is not necessarily a Christian soul, but 'soul' in the sense that there is something more fulfilling than life in the fast lane, than mindless television about crime or hospital drama. Beyond these is community; in community are individuals who matter. These individuals are not saints, they are not perfect, they are human. The sea and seaside towns, as much if not more so than desert spaces (precisely because they contain larger human communities), can be sacred, life-changing and spiritual zones too. In some ways this 'theology' links to Elaine Lindsay's observation in *Rewriting God*, that:

> While male theologians are tracking around the desert in ever-decreasing circles women are making sacred the coastal cities, the cultivated areas, the places where most of us live and where the fruitfulness of nature runs rampant.[11]

While Pearl Bay is not a highly populated area, it is also not 'woop woop'. In-between 'urbania' and isolation, it is to a degree a littoral space between the coastal cities and the desert spaces. *SeaChange* also reflects this feminine response to the sacred, for while there are also men on spiritual journeys in Pearl Bay, this is primarily Laura's quest. Laura, in order to restore her soul and reset her moral compass, travels to the 'other'—in this sense she is a classic 'seeker'. Other than a faint memory of a seaside holiday, she is not quite sure of what she is after but is certain of what she can no longer live with. Drawn to past rituals, she heads to the cleansing coast. Laura of course is not the only sea-side ascetic; Prahni has travelled away from life in India and an abusive husband. In series two, Max Connors is also waiting for a renewal in Pearl Bay; he is biding his time in the belief that he will once more be able to face the horror of being a foreign correspondent in Middle-Eastern war zones. Even the Buddhist nun Tensing, who travelled from Pearl Bay across the water to Tibet to 'find herself' and 'escape people', is drawn back across the water to Pearl Bay.[12] Tensing comes to realise that her spirituality is linked, ultimately, to people not to ideas. She learns that backstory and memory are as important to her as 'enlightenment'. In fact, Tensing learns that enlightenment cannot be achieved without them.

SeaChange represents a sacred and mystical perspective about the beach and the coastal; the beach is where life ends and where it began. In *Seachange* the beach embodies more than a leisure spot, or a place to take the waters and heal the body; it is somewhere to find yourself—a spiritual awakening usually reserved in the Australian imagination for the desert. However, the self that is found is not necessarily a profoundly charismatic or spiritual one—it may very well be a conflicted and flawed changeling. Precisely because it is liminal, unpredictable and at times dangerous, the beach opens us to new possibilities of self. Here, beyond the 'rat race', the spirit is capable of engaging with community and family. Ironically, as Karen Ford has noted, it is that false 'prophet' Bob Jelly who advises Laura when she first moves to town that community is like family:

> You're not in the city now; you're joining a community. There's a sense of fellow-ship in the town. We're family, family. We have our arguments and our differences. In the end we're there for each other, I help you in times of difficulty and you help me.[13]

Family is integral to who we are, and it is integral to co-creator Andrew Knight's vision of story in *SeaChange*.

According to Knight, Tim Winton criticised the show for being 'unreal'. Winton 'really hated the series because he said it wasn't true' and it did not paint a truthful (whatever that is) picture of the seaside in the Australian life and imagination.[14] However, as Knight says, this is primarily a story about community and 'the need for a connection'. As we can observe, it is also a fable, determinedly unrealistic and realistic: an intertextual fable at that. Winton's observations seem to miss the mark; *SeaChange* is about possibility, change and escape. And this misfire is ironic considering that in his memoir *Land's Edge* Winton claims that:

> Australians are surrounded by ocean and ambushed from behind by desert—a war of mystery on two fronts … Of the two mysteries, the sea is more forthcoming; its miracles and wonders are occasionally more palpable, however inexplicable they be. There is more bounty, more possibility for us in a vista that moves, rolls, surges, twists, rears up and changes from minute to minute … The sea is the supreme metaphor for change.[15]

If we read the visual and verbal text closely, *SeaChange* plays with a number of binaries and dualities: escape/ism and capture, order and chaos, freedom and control, truth and false/hood, real and unreal, lost and found. There is a lot of subtext regarding vistas and horizons in *SeaChange*. Throughout the progression of the series Laura's perspective changes as she becomes more in tune with the sea and less in tune with the interior of city skyscrapers. As she leaves behind the certainty of the city Law Courts she opens herself to the mysteries of the sea and makes herself vulnerable enough for significant, even magical, change to enter. Karen Ford makes this point about perspective, especially in relation to windows, doorways, and reflections.[16]

Pearl Bay is a world in which the real and the magical meet. *SeaChange* privileges the importance of stories and memories—real and imagined—in our lives. The homilies delivered by Kevin and Trevor re-connect us as viewers to the beauty of human frailty through humour, observation and simple interpretations of events. They are gentle reminders, for want of a less saccharine phrase, that we are all earth's children—and it is earth, Gaia, who hovers as the supreme being here—care of the soul also means stewardship of the earth and of each other. There is no one theology, 'ism', or deity in *Seachange*; Catholicism, Hinduism, Buddhism, mysticism, idealism, even cynicism, all inform the text and are encountered by the characters. One could even argue that Indigenous spiritualities about belonging and ownership underpin the whole if we acknowledge the soundtrack as a key character in the series, as it works as a counterpoint to the ideas and the assumptions that we carry with us about 'the sea' in the 'Australian imagination'. [17]

Magical Realism

Many of the characters in Pearl Bay are operating across what could be termed different spiritual planes. While *SeaChange* is disguised as a rational law-and-order enforcement genre, miracles, mystery and enchantment all happen in the 'real world' of Pearl Bay—they are the antithesis of the crime genre. It is not so much that things are not as they seem, as in *The Tempest*, but rather things *are* what they seem; both the real and the magical-real exist side by side in Pearl Bay, never to be fully connected to the outside world by the infamous bridge or the contentious tunnel. In Pearl Bay the ordinary and the extraordinary are accepted by the residents.

Laura herself operates on several levels: between revenge and bitterness on the one hand, like Prospero; and forgiveness and reconciliation on the other. In the end, her lawyer's cynicism does not give way to idealism and love, but rather, in the spirit of magical realism, two things that seemingly shouldn't coexist harmoniously in one human being or one world, do. For Laura, order has brought chaos, and chaos has brought her happiness—another of life's paradoxes. Pearl Bay enables her to discover how closely and naturally linked these effects are. In essence, *SeaChange* embodies Uslar Pietri's idea that we are 'a mystery surrounded by realistic data'—despite the rational disciplines of law, science and finance the unexplainable happens.[18] We could argue that magic happens: Meredith lives, the tunnel collapses, the town is saved, Laura and Max create a new life together. This is not to say that the outside world cannot enter Pearl Bay, this is no Brigadoon; the outside world very much enters in to Pearl Bay and changes it and its inhabitants.

The Tempest is full of the unreal that seems real, and things rich and strange. We find out though that this is all due to Prospero's artistry and magic. In Pearl Bay, the coincidences, miracles and happenings are not the work of one individual. There are times when there is a clear relationship of cause and effect between the hearts and minds of the residents of Pearl Bay and the natural world around them—but even Bob Jelly and Morton Tregonning don't have the power of Prospero. There are bigger forces at work: God, Karma, Gaia, Fate, Coincidence, the Sea.

The Sea and the littoral

John MacLaren has referred to *SeaChange* as a rural idyll or a pastoral rather than a coastal.[19] While much of the action takes place in the pub and the courts and Kevin even refers to their home as 'the country' in 'Full Fathom Five'—it is difficult to imagine *SeaChange* without one of its central protagonists and characters: the sea. The sea is an integral part of plot development in the series: cargo washes up on its shores in that littoral space; it delivers to and takes life from the bay; it provides the vista for Kevin and Trevor's 'everyman' homilies; it is the memory of a seaside holiday that prompts Laura to choose Pearl Bay as her refuge; the sea is even partly responsible for the freak weather patterns at the end of series one. Most importantly the sea enables perspective and horizon. Water, especially sea-water, is the medium through which change is instigated and executed. The estuaries, tides, river and sea life make important contributions to the storylines of *SeaChange* – they are not peripheral to it. *SeaChange* is littoral in the sense that the littoral supports a microclimate enabling unique life forms and weather patterns.

Changes in the sea affect the townsfolk: Angus's sandbar, the flying fish, the king tides, the storm, and the flood. While Australian soap operas such as *Water Rats*, *Home and Away*, *Breakers* or the ill-fated *Echo Point* might use the beach as a setting, in *SeaChange*, the sea is embedded in the characters' and the town's personalities.[20] The narrative line of the series is often guided by the events of the ocean. While the sea enables transport in *Water Rats*, the characters are 'transported' and metamorphosed by what the sea brings in *SeaChange*. The sea here is a fully integrated character that often enables the magic of the show to co-exist with the 'real' of the show—the sea itself has backstory and memory. The ocean brings danger and it brings calm; it takes and it gives. In Pearl Bay, the sea speaks to different 'souls' in different ways. To Diver Dan, the former squid wrangler, it is about fishing, the natural world, and adventure; for Max Connors, it is a therapeutic place to swim away his wife's death and memories of the war zones. For Meredith and Harold, it is where they talk about their past, for them the sea holds memories of their love and the conception of their daughter. For Angus Kabiri, it is a temple, a place to worship—Angus after all has given up that other great Australian religion, football, in order to become a surfing champion; Karen realises that in order to keep Angus she has to 'learn to surf', physically and metaphorically. For Laura, ultimately the sea is her saviour. She emerges at the end of the series a mother-to-be, an engaged and fully present mother to Rupert and Miranda, a partner to Max, and a magistrate without a job. At the beginning of the series in 'Full Fathom Five', we see Laura take her first steps into the ocean, an act that Karen Ford refers to as her 'baptism'.[21] By the end of the series the sea has enabled for Laura the spiritual act that Carol Christ calls 'diving deep and surfacing'.[22]

The sea, as John Grech has noted, is also symbolic of the impermanence of human existence. In analysing the episode entitled 'Head for Water' from Series Two, Grech has observed that:

> In [the] opening sequence, water is presented as a symbolic motif through which to reflect on the ever changing realities of life, its impermanence and the constant presence of death. The 'beach' and the 'surfer'—two icons synonymous with Australian culture—form the central contextual 'terrain' and 'motor' through which the exploration of these themes take place.[23]

In this episode grief and loss are paramount: Angus grieves for the sandbar that has disappeared altering his spiritual terrain by changing the waves; Max is mourning the loss of Elena; and Bucket is inconsolable over the death of his beloved dog, Alphonso Dominico Jones. The sea and the beach enable the encounters between humans who would normally be unable to communicate their grief and discomfort in an 'impermanent' world. Almost anything, it seems, can be said to each other, whilst staring ahead to the vista that 'rolls and surges'. The sandbar provides the backstory and the lesson of the parable. Meredith, the town's repository for its memories, tells Angus

> how she remembers the changing states of his beloved sandbar over the many years she has lived in the town. Angus learns that the sandbar was always 'at the mercy of the currents', something that comes and goes; there is never anything permanent or solid, either in water or on dry land.[24]

Elena, Max's late wife, in her farewell letter to Laura voices her concern that one day Max will 'swim out to sea and not come back'—she knows that he is 'adrift' in Pearl Bay and in life. She was his anchor; now she is gone there is nothing to stop the currents from taking him. This, of course, is a lesson to us all. We are all at the mercy of the currents; the ocean points to something more momentous than the self. And in the patterns of nature we see order and chaos, control and abandonment. This is very evident in the first episode of Series Two, 'If Fish Could Fly'.

If Fish Could Fly

At the end of Series One, we are left with the beginnings of a massive storm. Kevin and Trevor, the father and son, have headed out to sea on their adventure. At the beginning of Series Two they return, carrying in a wheelbarrow what is left of their belongings from the boat, to find the caravan park in ruins with their prized caravan, the Deluxe Continental washed out to sea. The bridge is closed, and the town is in chaos. Laura is swamped with sixty-three civil actions to hear as a result of the storm. One has been brought against Kevin by foreign backpacker Krystov who is claiming that his work about chaos theory, *Chaos Analysis, A Reappraisal*, has been swept out to sea by the 'predictable storm'.

This episode turns on the conflicting ideas of control and abandonment, order and chaos. Krystov's position is that 'everything is predictable', nothing is 'an accident', 'there is no such thing as a random event'; Diver Dan's claim is that a 'little chaos is a good thing' and that the weather patterns that led to the storm were completely unpredictable. Teenagers Rupert and Trevor are simply bored by the whole thing. For them, the irony of the dog swept out to sea in a storm-water drain that ends up outside the vet's is merely another of Pearl Bay's 'boring coincidences'. But for Angus, Krystov's theory holds the possibility that, as Dan puts it, 'there's someone at the wheel'. He begins to think about the master plan and whether or not it can be manipulated. Even Prahni believes that she knew in advance about the caravan's demise through her visions; for her there is a plan, and she failed to interpret it, too distracted by other things to follow her path.

This is not your average storm, nor is this the first or the last time that Pearl Bay will be portrayed as a nexus for the weird and the bizarre. In court, Laura is exposed to the locals' belief that the freak weather patterns, while not predictable, are usual. Evidence is presented to her of the various ways in which this bizarre nexus has manifested itself over the years—flying fish are the least of it. There appears to be a very strong connection between the tides, the lunar cycles, the currents and the bay. There are also strange behaviours that come with the cycles; all this chaos seems to run parallel with the relationships of the townsfolk. The tempest is reflective of the tempestuous relationships: Heather has left Robert; Dan and Laura have begun a relationship; Angus is questioning his relationship with Karen; and Jack Gibson is trying to restore his relationship with Laura. This is to say nothing of the tidal wave that will hit the bay if Heather reveals she is Harold and Meredith's daughter. Diver is caught in a relationship with a woman who needs order, predictability and forewarning. So is Angus, who attempts to get Karen to reveal her 'dark side' and be unpredictable. The sea and its tempests act as a catalyst for the townsfolk to ponder the meaning of life, especially their place in the world, for the sea and the tempestuous oceans make us all seem small and insignificant—that we have survived at all appears to be a miracle. How much control do we have over our lives and the events that shape them? The churning in the bay symbolically mirrors the townsfolk's churning emotions.

The miracles seem to have followed Kevin and Trevor who have remarkably travelled over fifty-eight nautical miles in little more than a tinnie, encountering all sorts of astounding natural phenomena such as enormous whales and strangely behaving sharks, bizarre star patterns and odd schools of fish. Yet, they take this all in their stride. Back home in Pearl Bay, however, it becomes apparent that the town is a vortex for even more odd and dangerous natural phenomena, including storms strong enough to wash away a bridge. Krystov attempts to argue, in line with his book, that even the storm could have been predicted and therefore his work saved. However, it is clear that the only 'predictable' thing in Pearl Bay is the randomness of the phenomena that occur. Laura is unconvinced of the importance of these random weather patterns, but ironically is forced to adjourn the Kevin/Krystov case because of a freakish downpour in the afternoon that is so loud she can barely be heard above the rain on the roof of the court. This adjournment enables Diver Dan to gather his proof about the weather that finally convinces Laura to dismiss the case against Kevin.

As Diver Dan explains through his study of fish patterns and king tides, there are events that not even expert weathermen such as 'Cyclone Ted Devondale' could predict, including the flying fish caught in those unpredictable currents. These events are all aligned in readiness for what Diver refers to in court as 'a classic storm scenario'. Of course, he is obliquely paralleling his relationship with Laura to the tempestuous and unusual weather. For Diver, to be amongst the elements, to feed your love a flying mullet, and to climb to the top of a hill to watch the meteor shower after a storm are all romantic gestures; the natural cycle should enhance the romantic one. To do the everyday, the usual, is not his idea of an extraordinary love. He sees unpredictability as the key to romance, while Laura sees the familiar and the comfortable as essential to it. For Diver, the storm and the unusual weather patterns in the bay are his signal to woo Laura into his world. Laura, of course, is stuck in her predictable and safe world of law and order and she is not yet ready for the chaotic spontaneity that Dan is so comfortable with. But Laura learns that fish can fly, and that there is nothing more romantic than a mullet (confused by the currents) that jumps onto your lover's roof. The sea offers up the opportunity for new experiences, and by the end of the episode, Laura is ready to at least give them a go, even if she retains some of her cynicism.

Karen, however, retains all of her cynicism. She returns Krystov's 'drowned' book to him. He asks how this 'miracle' occurred. Karen offers a tale of strange coincidences, complicated connections and good luck. Krystov feeling completely dejected because his theory about cause effect and chaos has been disproved, says, 'and so we create order from chaos'. Karen, forever the 'realist', divulges to Angus: 'he left his stupid book on Prahni's bus'. But of course, this doesn't explain away all of the other coincidences such as the dog swept out to sea. It seems that in Pearl Bay everything is connected—there is order even in the chaos.

Manna From Heaven

This sense of connectivity via the oceans is echoed in a later episode entitled 'Manna From Heaven'.[25] While earlier titles have played on themes from *The Tempest*, this episode also plays directly on the Biblical themes of exodus, exile and return. It is also an exploration of the etymological similarities and differences between salvage, salvation and salvaging relationships. We have the parting of the seas, the sea as a carrier and, ironically, bridge building in both the symbolic and the actual sense. In 'Manna From Heaven' we revisit Pearl Bay as an area that attracts more than its fair share of disasters, and we explore the idea of Karma—is Pearl Bay 'cursed' because of an act that happened several years ago on the beach when the town celebrated its grand final win against Port Deacon? Of course, those of us who have been listening closely to earlier episodes will know that the natural disasters go at least as far back as the early life of Cyclone Ted Devondale and the 1979 flood.

Like *The Tempest*, the trouble appears to have begun with a shipwreck, and like *The Tempest*, it is merely the catalyst not the cause; it is not *human* castaways that cause trouble for Pearl Bay. There is one date, five years ago, that Meredith seems unable to remember anything about: the 26th September. Five years earlier a squall had deposited a containership load of timber, farm machinery and foodstuffs onto the beach. The townsfolk, drunk and celebrating a football victory, had taken the produce and distributed it throughout the town, including the timber. They have been uneasy since then, aware that the laws of beachcombing may have ambiguous moral grounds. Coinciding with Tensing's return, the town is being ravaged by a rare form of borer. All methods of pest control have been tried to no avail. It transpires that furniture in the container-load belonged to Tensing who was delivering it to a Philippine temple. So, the arrival on the beach of the container and the town's pillage of it has resulted in guilt, Meredith's amnesia—and borers. The arrival of Tensing makes memories resurface from the deep. It is clear that many of the townsfolk are out of their spiritual depth and that others are spiritually drifting. Many begin to question their 'moral compass' and to seek something beyond the values they have been operating under. The conversations drift between spiritual hunger and Max's cynicism ('Swimming … that's what I believe in'), Prahni's inherent Eastern spirituality, the Western search for Eastern mysticism, and the nature of truth and belief. For Laura, truth and 'the pursuit of justice' is the ultimate moral guide ('Please learn to tell the truth—it makes life so much simpler in the end') in contrast to Karen's steadfast Catholicism ('I'm Catholic, I'm lucky, I don't have to think about it' 'there's not much point in believing in something if you question it all the time'). Tensing too believes in 'the truth'—after all that is why she has returned to Pearl Bay. 'I'm on the path to truth' she tells Prahni. 'Westerners!' responds Prahni under her breath.

Tensing had travelled to Tibet in order to find 'some calm away from the crass commercial world'. However, she needed to return to Pearl Bay in order to explain her actions to Harold and Meredith, whom she 'abandoned' in the aftermath of Heather's birth. In Tensing's pressing need to come back from her self-imposed exile before she can go forward there are lessons for Laura Gibson: deal with the difficult truths from your past or the 'seachange' won't be complete; memories will resurface and you will not attain the 'release that truth brings'.[26] The cargo had been seen as 'manna from heaven' by the town, but instead of physical 'bounty' it is really a cargo of spiritual nourishment. The nourishment takes a while to come to the fore and is instigated by the insertion of the 'other'—the prodigal return of Tensing-Mabel who comes back across the water dredging up memories and sorting out her own. Kevin has believed that with the advent of the borer, to say nothing of the natural disaster matrix they seem to inhabit, 'the day of Judgement' is upon them. In the long run though, after all their complex methods and chemicals, Tensing reveals that the control of the 'pest' is something as simple as vinegar. She returns back across the sea to Tibet and the town learns from Tensing that 'everything passes, even great pain'.

SeaChange: Saccharine or Salty?

> A real charmer, full of whimsy and the sort of humanity that you won't find in most saccharine imports.[27]

Jonathan Bollen has asked serious questions about the politics and influence of *SeaChange*. How does it sit within a circle of influence? Are we mesmerised and therefore blind to its inadequacies as an Australian story? Is it simply saccharine pap? Does it merely perpetuate dangerous stereotypes and soft politics? Yes, it can be read on a very simple level where subtle politics and jibes about the way we treat people are not obvious, where love story would subvert all other commentary within the series on issues such as corruption, tolerance, greed, acceptance, cultural diversity, the spiritual in our 'secular' nation, and the dichotomy of Australian culture—city versus elsewhere—Bush/sea/pastoral.

But each episode turns on significant moral questions. The sea, with its moving vista, makes us wonder what will wash up on the shores of Pearl Bay that will shake the needle of our own moral compass. Like Kevin and Trevor, our everyman lay preachers, we wait patiently on the littoral, gazing into the horizon, receiving salty and sweet pearls of wisdom.

Notes

1 Richard Pleasance, (vocalist Wendy Morrison). *SeaChange* Theme Song. n.d. *The Very Best of SeaChange*, producer, record label not known.
2 Interestingly, the distinction is nearly always made in website references to 'John Howard (*the actor*)' as of course opposed to Howard, the former Prime Minister, a reference that partly comes from John Howard the actor's appearance on ABC TV's *The Games* where he apologised to the Indigenous People of Australia, an apology that the Prime Minister has declined to give.
3 Channel 7, 'Real people, real stories, real risks—this is THE REAL SEA CHANGE' online accessed 2/2/06. http://seven.com.au/seven/realseachange The series involves RMIT, who were purportedly working on a similar series with ABC TV in 2003.
4 Channel 7, http://seven.com.au/seven/realseachange, online accessed 2/2/06.
5 Thanks to Peter Manthorpe for these adjectives. Regarding viewer memory, *SeaChange* made it into the top ten television shows remembered by South Australian viewers in *The Advertiser's* '50 years of television' poll, published on Saturday 16th Sept. 2006, 3.
6 William Shakespeare, *The Tempest*, I.ii. *The Complete Works of Shakespeare The Cambridge Text*, (Glasgow: Collins, 1985) 16.
7 Gary Martin. The Phrase Finder. 'Sea change'. Online accessed 2/12/05 http://www.phrases.org.uk/meanings/312800.html,
8 The episode is entitled 'My Own Sweetheart', *SeaChange* Series 1.08.
9 Betsy Williams, ' "North to the Future": *Northern Exposure* and Quality Television' *Television, the Critical View*, fifth edition ed. by Horace Newcombe, (OUP, New York, 1994) 142.
10 Episode 1, Series One is the only *SeaChange* episode missing the 'homily'.
11 Elaine Lindsay 'Marginalizing the Centre (or centering the margin)' in *Dangerous Memory: Feminist Theology Through Story,* proceedings of the Fourth National Feminist Theology Conference, Canberra, Sept. 1995, Clovelly West, Australian Feminist Theology Foundation, 75, quoted in Nancy M. Victorin-Vangerud, 'The Sacred Edge: Women, Sea and Spirit'. Online accessed 8.12.05. http://www.wsrt.com.au/seachanges/volume1/html/victorinframes.html
12 'Manna from Heaven', *SeaChange* Series 2.21.

13 Bob Jelly to Laura Gibson, 'Something Rich and Strange', *SeaChange* 1.01. And Karen Ford, 'Such Stuff as Dreams are Made on', *ASE* 335 Winter (2004): 115

14 Tim Winton paraphrased by Andrew Knight, 'Getting to the Heart of the Matter', interview with Paul Davies. *Metro*, 139 (Feb 2004): 120.

15 Tim Winton, *The Land's Edge*, (Sydney: Pan Macmillan, 1993) 36, 85.

16 Karen Ford, 'Such Stuff as Dreams are Made on', *ASE* 335 Winter (2004).

17 The soundtracks (there are 3 soundtracks and a best of) to each of the series feature a plethora of artists with an emphasis on Indigenous artists, social commentators and political writers such as Ruby Hunter, Archie Roach, Tiddas, Paul Kelly, Christine Anu, Jimmy Little, Vika and Linda Bull, Kavisha Mazzella. They also feature music that has the ocean or the seaside in its title or lyrics. Making notable repeat appearances are The Backsliders and Felt. Most of the featured artists are Australian, many are iconic.

18 Taken from Uslar Pietri's 1948 definition of magical realism, cited in Texas A&M University English Home Page. Online accessed 18/9/06. http://www-english. tamu.edu/pers/fac/andreadis/474H_ahapw/Definition_Magic.Realism.html.

19 CRNLE conference 'Something Rich and Strange' December 2005, Kangaroo Island.

20 I want to distinguish here between *SeaChange*, which is classified as a drama series, or in today's terms, a 'dramedy', and the other shows which are classified as soap operas.

21 Karen Ford, 'Such Stuff as Dreams are Made on', *ASE* 335 Winter (2004) 114.

22 Carol Christ, *Diving Deep and Surfacing, women writers on spiritual quest*, second edition, (Boston: Beacon Press, 1980). Christ is here referring to Adrienne Rich's poem 'Diving into the Wreck'; she extends the metaphor to enable the woman to surface from her quest in her exposition on women's spiritual questing.

23 John Grech, 'Seachanges in Imaginary Communities', *Australian Screen Education*, Summer 2001: 68. The episode 'Head for Water', Series 2.18, *SeaChange*.

24 Grech, 'Seachanges in Imaginary Communities', 69.

25 'Manna from Heaven', *SeaChange*, Series 2.21.

26 'Manna', Tensing to Meredith.

27 Law For You.Com: plain English legal information Australia. 'TV, Movies, Books' section, '*SeaChange*' Online accessed 18/9/06 http://www.law4u.com.au/ lil/lil_tv_books_movies.asp

Works cited

Channel 7 website, 'Real people, real stories, real risks—this is THE REAL SEACHANGE.' Online accessed 2/2/06. http://seven.com.au/seven/ realseachange

Christ, Carol. *Diving Deep and Surfacing, women writers on spiritual quest*, 2nd edn. Boston: Beacon Press, 1980.

Davies, Paul. 'Getting to the Heart of the Matter' interview with Andrew Knight. *Metro* 139 (Feb 2004): 118-121.

Ford, Karen. 'Such Stuff as Dreams are Made on.' *Australian Screen Education* 335 (Winter 2004): 113-116.

Grech, John. 'Seachanges in Imaginary Communities', *Australian Screen Education*, 28 (Summer 2001) : 1443-1629

Law For You.Com: plain English legal information Australia. 'TV, Movies, Books' section, '*SeaChange*' Online accessed 18/9/06 http://www.law4u.com. au/lil/lil_tv_books_movies.asp

Lindsay, Elaine. 'Marginalizing the Centre (or centering the margin)' in *Dangerous Memory: Feminist Theology through Story,* proceedings of the Fourth National Feminist Theology Conference, (Canberra: Australian Feminist Theology Foundation, Sept. 1995) quoted in Nancy M. Victorin-Vangerud, *The Sacred Edge: Women, Sea and Spirit.* Online accessed 8.12.05. http://www.wsrt.com.au/ seachanges/volume1/html/victorinframes.html

Martin, Gary. The Phrase Finder. 'Sea change.' Online accessed 2/12/05 http:// www.phrases.org.uk/meanings/312800.html,

Pleasance, Richard comp. *The Very Best of SeaChange*, n.d. producer, record label not known.

SeaChange the Complete Series 1-3. Creators Sue Masters, Deborah Cox and Andrew Knight. Dir. Michael Carson, Ali Ali, Sue Brooks, Mandy Smith, Paul Maloney, Ray Argall. Perf. Sigrid Thornton, John Howard, Kerry Armstrong, David Wenham, William McInnes. ABC Television 1998-2001.

William Shakespeare, *The Tempest*, I.ii. *The Complete Works of Shakespeare The Cambridge Text*. Glasgow: Collins, 1985. 11-32.

Williams, Betsy. ' "North to the Future": *Northern Exposure* and Quality Television' *Television, the Critical View*, fifth edition. Ed. Horace Newcombe. OUP: New York, 1994. 141-154.

Texas A&M University English Home Page. Definitions: 'Magic realism.' Online accessed 18/9/06. http://www-english.tamu.edu/pers/fac/andreadis/474H_ ahapw/Definition_Magic.Realism.html

Victorin-Vangerud, Nancy M. *The Sacred Edge: Women, Sea and Spirit.* Online accessed 8.12.05. http://www.wsrt.com.au/seachanges/volume1/html/ victorinframes.html

Winton, Tim. *The Land's Edge.* (Sydney: Pan Macmillan, 1993)

White Men, Wet Dreams:
Fishing, Fatherhood and Finitude in
Australian Theatre, 1955–2004[1]

JONATHAN BOLLEN

In the Australian literary tradition, the Bush was long the distinctive setting for dramatising the actions of white men in this land. Representing the expanse of the Bush on stage was once regarded as a necessary challenge for the playwrights and producers of an emerging national drama. The Bush continues to figure in Australian theatre, but it is no longer the primary locale for dramatising the actions of white men. Rather, to countenance and critique contemporary projections of white masculinity into the future, we must look to the beach, to horizons of sea and sky, and to elemental exposures of masculinity in such practices as swimming, surfing, fishing, boating and flying. Surveying Australian theatre since the 1950s, though with a view to plays which premiered since the mid-1980s, this chapter describes three kinds of scenes wherein the actions of white men are exposed between the sea and the sky.

On the beach

The sites of Australianness, those representational spaces wherein our culture has imagined the unfolding of Australian life—the Bush, for instance, the backyard and the beach—are not evenly distributed across the history of Australian cultural production. There was a time, in the first half of the twentieth century, when Australian drama turned to the Bush, when Australian dramatists Louis Esson and Katharine Susannah Prichard addressed themselves to the task of framing the landscape of the Bush as a setting upon which and against which to stage the actions of white men and women in colonising the land.[2] By the 1950s and 1960s, however, attention had turned elsewhere. Plays such as Ray Lawler's *Summer of the Seventeenth Doll* from 1955, Richard Beynon's *The Shifting Heart* and Barbara Vernon's *The Multi-Coloured Umbrella* from 1957, Peter Kenna's *The Slaughter of St Teresa's Day* and John Hepworth's *The Beast In View* from 1959, and Alan Seymour's *The One Day of the Year* from 1960, were described at the time by director Hugh Hunt as belonging to a 'slice-of-life school' and as 'backyard' realism.[3] That the backyard is only represented on stage in just one of these plays, in Beynon's *The Shifting Heart*, or that its significance would soon be satirised in Patrick White's *The Season at Sarsaparilla* in 1962, only serves to underscore its imaginary status, indicative if not always apparent, as a site of Australian everyday life at that particular moment.

At the same time—that is, across the middle decades of the twentieth century—creators working in other areas of cultural production, in the visual arts and advertising, in television and film, were turning their attention to the beach. This turn to the beach is evident in the photography of Max Dupain, for instance, or in tourism advertising and campaigns to encourage migration to Australia.[4] It is also apparent in Stanley Kramer's feature film *On The Beach* from 1959, based on Neville Shute's 1957 novel of the same name. Indeed, the legacy of Australian cultural production and critique has itself been structured by such a turn to the beach; we may associate the Bush, for instance, with the literary nationalism of Andrew 'Banjo' Patterson and Henry Lawson and with the high-art romanticism of the Heidelberg school of landscape painting; whereas our apprehension of the beach has evolved through more popular, more realist, more widely mediated modes such as photography, television and film and through the critical understandings of contemporary cultural studies.[5] For this reason, it is interesting to consider how the beach comes to figure when two of those backyard realist plays from the 1950s transitioned from the stage to the screen.

Leslie Norman's feature film of *Summer of the Seventeenth Doll* from 1959 was retitled *Season of Passion* for distribution overseas. The film relocates the story from Melbourne to the city of Sydney and key sequences were shot on location. When Barney and Roo arrive in Sydney from up north, the first thing they do with Olive and Pearl is head off for a day at the beach. We see them embark on a ferry from Circular Quay, heading out into the harbour, under the harbour bridge, to arrive at Bondi Beach for a scene in a licensed club, with panoramic views overlooking the beach. The imaginary geography of this ferry trip may indicate something of the attitude of the film's producers to its local consumption: whereas the play had been celebrated for representing Australians to themselves, the film's representational vector, with its Hollywood actors and tourist-brochure cinematography made appeal to a broader, pan-Pacific audience.[6] The screenplay's elaboration of the romance between the young lovers Bubba and Johnnie Dowd, depicted on a lobby card for the film, clearly rendered the beach a site for heterosexual passion.

Barbara Vernon's play *The Multi-Coloured Umbrella* also transitioned from the stage to the screen. The play was first presented in the New South Wales country towns of Inverell and Glen Innes in 1957, then at Melbourne's Little

Theatre, before being presented by J.C. Williamson at the Theatre Royal in Sydney and the Comedy Theatre, Melbourne, later that year. In the case of this play, the transition was from the stage to the small screen; a studio production of *The Multi-Coloured Umbrella* was broadcast live by ABC Television in Sydney on 29 January 1958. The setting for the play is the rooftop sun-deck of a house at Bondi Beach: 'Beyond the parapet', instructs Vernon, 'we see a headland, closely built over, and below the curve of the sand, where the creaming waves ignore the many sunbathers'.[7] John Truscott's meticulous set for the Melbourne Little Theatre production depicted a stylish outdoor living area referencing elements from both the backyard and the beach—notably a large, fringed, multi-coloured beach umbrella shelters the drinks table upstage centre.

Vernon's play is about the Donnellys, an upwardly mobile family who run a successful bookmaking business at Randwick Racecourse. The main action concerns the Donnelly's two sons, Joe and Ben, and Joe's middle-class wife, Kate. Inflamed by money concerns, alcohol and sexual jealousies over Kate, Joe and Ben fight in the climactic scene, one brandishing a broken bottle as a weapon, the other falling from the rooftop in his attempt to retreat. As an off-stage locale, the beach really only figures at the end of the play; although the ABC production for television may have given the beach a more prominent role. While the play's scripted action on the rooftop sun-deck was broadcast live from the ABC's television studio and was not recorded, the broadcast also incorporated some film inserts, shot on location at Bondi Beach, and these inserts have survived. One shot depicts a man and woman, presumably Joe and Kate, walking hand-in-hand along the beach. In a subsequent shot, a tussle breaks out between the couple: the woman runs into the waves and the man chases after her, with much playful splashing about. The action in this insert is not actually staged in the play; it was specifically created for the television adaptation. It may have been preceded by the following dialogue from the final scene of the play.

> JOE: … Katey, I don't want to worship you like a saint in a church. I want you out in the sun and air with me.
>
> KATE: But you—if you don't respect me—if I can't rouse you—
>
> JOE: Respect you? Rouse me? I was so jealous you nearly killed me—and Ben. I can't kiss you with Ben here looking on. Come down on the beach with me.
>
> KATE: It's going to rain—my dr—my h—I'll look terrible if my hair—
>
> JOE: Katey, your hair don't matter, and if you wear that Goddam dress again I'll tear it off you …
>
> KATE: I don't know if I can. I'm not like you … I can't let go all of a minute, I can't—

JOE: It's now or never.

(He goes to the steps, waits a moment then turns to go)

KATE: Joe— don't leave me— Joe— wait for me Joe …

(She runs after him and trips on the steps falling into his arms. JOE sweeps her up triumphantly, and they go together into the darkness.)[8]

In the play script, a summer storm is breaking as Joe and Kate head down on to the beach at the end of the play. Joe's mother Gloria is concerned: 'Those kids'll get soaked. Did they take coats or umbrellas or anything?' she asks her other son, Ben. 'No coats. No umbrellas', observes Ben in the final speech of the play, 'But don't worry—maybe that's what this marriage needed. A little bit of sun and rain on it'.[9] The beach, in Vernon's play, is an off-stage location where the elements—the sun, the wind and the rain—restore passion to everyday life and reinvigorate sexual relations between a man and his wife.

Ray Lawler's second play, *The Piccadilly Bushman*, did not make the transition to the big screen or small, although it was afforded a panoramic photo-spread in *Australian Theatre Year 1959/1960*. Desmonde Downing's set for the J.C. Williamson production depicts the interior of an eastern-suburbs mansion in Sydney with views of the harbour and the bridge which recall the locations featured in the film of *Summer of the Seventeenth Doll*. Perhaps Lawler's second play, which underwhelmed critics in its 1959 theatre production, might have worked better on film; certainly, the play marked Lawler's transition from the concerns of 'backyard realism' towards a more affluent, leisure-class milieu. Like Vernon's *The Multi-Coloured Umbrella*, Lawler's play features sunshine, fresh air and a beach off-stage, which provides for some leisurely distraction and dishevelment—although, somewhat sadly, fails to restore vigour to those jaded by married life.

The beach in *The Piccadilly Bushman* is associated with Meg, the wife of expatriate actor Alec Ritchie, the 'Piccadilly Bushman' of the title. Meg's life is described in one review as 'further complicated by drink, nymphomania and a son in the bush'.[10] When Meg first enters, she's been down 'watching the sea with the sun on it', she's suffering somewhat from 'a touch of the sun' and, as the playwright informs us, 'her present mood of strained gaiety is a cover up for the fact that she is rather drunk, nervous and very much on the defensive'.[11] Alone with her husband, she recalls how on 'a little beach' by the harbour she asked Alec to marry her, 'with my shoes full of sand and a broken brassiere strap'.[12] Later, when Meg and the rugged Douglas O'Shea ('a forty-year-old lump of a man' with 'a larrikin grin') are missing and her husband is waiting at home for her return and making references to his wife's 'casual sort of lust', perhaps we're meant to assume that she and O'Shea are lying, romantically entwined, on some beach—although, as it turns out, they just went for a drive to the Blue Mountains where, according to Meg, 'it was talk and nothing else'.[13]

The beach has not figured prominently in Australian theatrical representation. There may be no genre of beach plays to compare with those of the Bush and the backyard. Still this passionately sexualised, potentially violent, yet somehow restorative characterisation of the beach—evident in *The Multi-Coloured Umbrella* and *The Piccadilly Bushman*—would be later deployed in such recent plays as Janis Balodis's *Wet And Dry* and Michael Gow's *Away* from 1986 and Nick Enright's *Blackrock* from 1995. In a scene set on a beach up north in *Wet and Dry*, sex between a woman, Pam, and her husband's brother, Troppo, complicates their relationships but restores fertility to life—for by the end of the play, Pam has given birth to Alex, her brother-in-law's child, while her infertile husband George struggles with being a father to Alex, his brother's son. After the storm scene in *Away*, the sickly teenager Tom is walking with his school friend Meg on the beach and wants to have sex with her, but Meg refuses, finding him too skinny; instead, Tom fronts up for the holidaymakers' amateur night, performing an imaginative mermaid romance with the creative Coral, entitled *Stranger on the Shore*. More bleakly in *Blackrock*, the beach is the scene for the off-stage rape and murder of a teenage girl, yet it is also the scene for the play's reconstruction of gender relations as seventeen-year-old Jared allows his younger cousin Cherie to borrow his surfboard and learn how to surf.

Gone fishing

A second scene is the masculine world men create when they go fishing—a scene prefigured in *The Piccadilly Bushman* when a fishing trip on the harbour disrupts plans for a film production meeting, the outdoor 'exhilaration of sun, sea and air', as Lawler puts it, intruding upon the indoor business of cultural production.[14] In more recent plays, fishing—or a failure to go fishing together—is indicative of the communicative capacity of relations between a father and his son, as it is between mates. For instance, in Stephen Sewell's *The Father we Loved on a Beach by the Sea* from 1978, Joe, a father of two sons, tells his wife: 'I'm gonna be a better man for you, Mary, I promise you. I'll make you happy. And I'll be a good father. We'll all go fishin' together or somethin', ay?'[15] But at the end of the play we see Joe in the scene from which the play is named: dressed in bathing trunks and carrying a plastic bucket, he simply looks blankly out to sea; there is the sound of the surf and of children playing, but the father is immobile and unresponsive.

Immobile and unresponsive fathers who, having failed to go fishing, are all but incapable of communicating with their sons, feature in a number of Australian plays from the 1990s.[16] In Tony McNamara's *The John Wayne Principle* from 1996, we learn early on in the play that Robbie likes to take his young son fishing and to cook what they catch for dinner. As the wayward son of a corporate patriarch, Robbie lives in remote far north Queensland and his fishing is indicative of a new kind of communicative relationship with his son, one which differs markedly from the kind of relationship he has had with his father. In a hospital scene at the end of the play, with his father unconscious and Robbie just about to pull the plug, he has this to say:

> But I have no hard feelings, I guess that's what I'm here to say. And that I've got a problem only you can help me with. Think of it as working together, a new experience, our first father-son thing. We probably should've done some fishing, Dad, might have helped.[17]

In Tim Conigrave's *Thieving Boy* from 1997, the twenty-two-year-old homosexual Moxy, also visits his father in hospital. His father is almost comatose and Moxy's speech is all but incoherent. Putting his head in his hands and trying not to cry, Moxy stammers in a final attempt to communicate with his father:

> You're my Dad … I been readin' this thing … it says somethin' like … In it there's all this stuff about fishin' and that … I can't explain it … you'd know what I mean if you read it. It's when … well, it's from a while ago … You'd understand. You'd … I wanted you to be my friend.[18]

The dramatic possibilities of putting men in a boat to go fishing are literally staged in Noel Hodda's *Half Safe* (1990), in Glynn Nicholas and Scott Rankin's *Certified Male* (1999), and in Margery and Michael Forde's *James and Johnno* (2004). In Nicholas and Rankin's *Certified Male*, three businessmen are away with their boss for a weekend retreat. When they go out fishing for marlin, one of them falls overboard and almost drowns. The fishing and near drowning are mimed by Nicholas and his fellow actors with much hilarity. But what renders serious the sentiments that resonate within these images of men fishing in boats is the story of the raft of the Medusa, the subject of a nineteenth-century painting by French artist Théodore Géricault depicting a scandalous French shipwreck off the west coast of Africa in 1816. The Medusa story is episodically retold in *Certified Male* as a myth about masculinity in crisis, about men cut adrift from relationships with women, children and the world, their raft drifting aimlessly and endlessly on.

In the other two plays, fishing and boating enable communicative encounters between men and narrative reckonings with life and death which are seemingly only possible under conditions of remove from women, family and work. Ken and Les, two mates in their sixties, are set adrift on a lake when their motor fails in Hodda's *Half Safe*. Adrift in their boat overnight, their casual banter about fishing, smoking, drinking and sex soon turns to more sombre concerns: to the death of Les's wife, the suicide of Ken's son, to a group of teenagers who drowned in the lake when their canoe capsized. As they drift on into the night, Ken is tormented by nightmares and angry voices from his past; while Les quietly dies in his sleep of exposure, sadness or both. The final moving image, as Bob Evans recalled in a review for the *Sydney Morning Herald*, is of Ken 'praying tearfully for the dawn breeze to blow the boat and Les's dead body to shore'.[19]

A similar scenario develops in Michael and Margery Forde's *James and Johnno*, when two middle-aged brothers set out to scatter their father's ashes on Moreton Bay, where the three once used to fish. Johnno has rediscovered their father's old boat and convinces James to come with him on one last trip. Johnno has also found their father's diary in the boat's hold and reads of their last fishing trip with their father in 1962 at the time of the Cuban Missile Crisis. 'World War Three could begin any old tick of the clock', wrote their father. 'If it's the end—this is where I want to be. Out on the bay with my sons'.[20] With the world in crisis, Dad had given up hope: with the boys asleep in the hold he planned to set the boat adrift and send them 'over the bar'—but James woke up to discover Dad in tears and the boat drifting dangerously. He restarted the boat's engine and turned them around, saving the boat from wreckage and the three of them from drowning. 'Don't tell Johnno. Promise you'll never tell Johnno', his father implored and James kept the secret from Johnno until now.[21] At the end of the play, having scattered their father's ashes, James tries to start the boat but the ignition lock breaks. The two brothers drift again, without an anchor or engine, towards the bar.

JOHNNO: We're going to go over, aren't we, James.
JAMES: Looks like it.
JOHNNO: We're gone, aren't we?
JAMES: We're gone.
The roar of Jumpinpin swells. They shout above the din.
JOHNNO: Hey, James? When you go to Anakie!
JAMES: What?
JOHNNO: When you find your first sapphire!
JAMES: It's yours! (*Brief pause*) Hey Johnno!
JOHNNO: What?
JAMES: Magic night, isn't it?

JOHNNO: An absolute piss cutter! (*Brief pause*) Hey, this is not too bad. I've had worse than this at 'Wet and Wild.'

JAMES and JOHNNO scream as Jumpinpin thunders down on them. Change of lighting state. They are floating in calm waters. The boat is like a little planet … floating in space. JAMES and JOHNNO are solitary figures—suspended between the sea and stars.[22]

Between the sea and the sky

Men in boats, fishing and talking (or not), set adrift on the water, beyond reach of land and relations, exposed to the elements, to the sun, sea and sky—perhaps the most widely disseminated, most recognisable and appealing images of this kind of scene were those from Nick Enright and Justin Monjo's adaptation of Tim Winton's *Cloudstreet*, where dreams about water, sky and stars and images of boats, beds and bathtubs create a richly fluid and immersive world for brothers Quick and Fish Lamb. *Cloudstreet* may also serve to introduce a third scene: one where masculinity is exposed between sea and sky under conditions of incapacity, disability and loss. In the opening scene of *Cloudstreet*, the Lamb family is prawning in the river at night, when Fish gets tangled in a net and almost drowns in the dark. His mother Oriel revives him, but as 'Quick holds his brother's head in his hands, he knows it isn't quite right [b]ecause not all of Fish Lamb has come back'.[23] In the end, it is to the water that Fish Lamb returns.

> FISH: I know my story for just long enough to see how we've come, how we've all battled in the same corridor that time makes for us, and I'm Fish Lamb for those seconds it takes to die, as long as it takes to drink the river, as long as it took to tell you all this, and then my walls are tipping and I burst into the moon, sun and stars of who I truly am. Being Fish Lamb. Perfectly. Always. Everyplace. Me.
>
> *He's gone into the water. QUICK lets him go.*[24]

A similar sense of dissolution, of masculinity dissolving between the sea and the sky, is evident in other recent plays. In John Misto's monodrama *Sky* from 1992, for instance, a father mourns the loss of his son who disappeared while flying solo over the sea. One explanation for the disappearance is that the pilot suffered from 'the twilight syndrome' where sea and sky look so alike that a pilot becomes disorientated and loses control of the plane. The play begins with Rocco Betoni, the father, standing on top of a cliff, staring into the wind and holding a red rose. The sounds of the sea are crashing on rocks below and the sound of a light plane flying overhead. Rocco recalls taking his son Frankie on a joy flight as a surprise present for his twelfth birthday. Frankie had shocked Rocco with a precocious knowledge of sex. 'If you're old enough to know about sex, [then] you're old enough to fly'.[25] 'Five years later,' Rocco recalls:

> Frankie raced home from Bankstown airport. 'Look, Dad. Look!' And he held out a pamphlet … (with) three words which chilled my heart. *Learn To Fly.* 'I belong up there, Dad! I want to be a pilot'—that's what he said … and he had that look and I knew he was a man … My little son.[26]

The sky and the sea, fishing and flying, mourning and melancholia, disability and death—similar elements as these are arranged in Robert Hewett's *Gulls* from 1983, where a brain-damaged man lives by the beach; cared for by his sister and unable to converse, he seeks solace amongst the company of seagulls. More recently, Hannie Rayson's title character in *Life After George* (2000), is an academic, a professor of Australian history, but also a keen fisherman and an amateur pilot. George dies, spectacularly, in a plane crash, in the very first scene of the play, while flying his plane to Flinders Island. Later his best mate Duffy recalls their trips away fishing and flying and his ex-wives Beatrix and Lindsay recite his favourite poem 'High Flight' ('Oh! I have slipped the surly bonds of earth / And danced the skies on laughter-silvered wings') by John Gillespie Magee, the Second World War fighter pilot.[27]

In other recent plays, fathers and sons are exposed between the sea and the sky in an encounter with finitude. In Neil Cole's *Alive at Williamstown Pier* from 1999, Dave, a politician and father of two boys, suffers throughout the play from manic-depression, but returns repeatedly to the pier, to a place on the edge of the land, between the sea and the sky, where he feels a kind of distanced at-one-ness with the world:

> Can I say that I'm standing at the end of the pier looking out over the water with yachts moored on the left and right of me, cargo ships sailing slowly in front of me. [...] I know I see all this, it feels like my two young boys alongside of me, and that I am alive. [...] Two boys who stand between me, and the call of death's inevitability. As I stand here aware of them, and without depression, I finally know I am Alive, At Williamstown Pier.[28]

And, in a scene from Daniel Keene's *To Whom It May Concern* from 1998, a sixty-year-old father, at a loss what to do with his mentally disabled 40-year-old son, takes him to the beach. With his son standing naked and shivering, the father encourages him to go swimming:

> I want you to go in the water you'll feel good it's peaceful in the water you'll feel the tide pulling you all that blue so big it's all so big you'll feel safe Leo out there in something so big it covers the earth just floating you know how to float don't be scared put your trunks on don't stand there naked like that you look so Leo you look so please Leo go in the water let the water take you please Leo.[29]

Cumulatively, speculatively, the plays discussed in this chapter envisage a different relation between masculinity and environment from that of the Bush realist plays. This new relation is one in which an exposure to the sea and the sky has a resolutive effect on men who are somehow incapacitated or incomplete. One might be tempted to see something feminine in this oceanic immersion in the sea and the sky, but there is no need to resort to archetypal modes of gender analysis where more particular meanings are there to be had. Firstly, these are plays which, in various ways, worry about the future: they worry that the past is somehow insufficient or inadequate, somehow not up to the task of encountering the future. Anxieties, inadequacies and incapacities structure relations between fathers and their sons, as fathers face or fear an uneasy future for their sons. Secondly, these are white Australian fathers and white Australian sons, so these scenes of dissolution are, if you like, white men's wet dreams. As I argue elsewhere, relations between fathers and sons are also relations of race, of racial transmission, inheritance and succession.[30] In looking to horizons of sea and sky to imagine a watery future for white masculinity, the men in these plays inevitably turn their back on the land, thereby eliding their involvement, their implication in the inter-race relations that now indelibly score the land.

Notes

1   This paper was written as part of 'Marking masculinity in Australian theatre, 1955–1970 and 1985–2000', an ARC Discovery project undertaken in collaboration with Adrian Kiernander and Bruce Parr whose contributions I acknowledge. I also acknowledge playwrights Margery Forde, Michael Forde, Noel Hodda, John Misto, Glynn Nicholas and Scott Rankin for providing the project with unpublished typescripts of their plays.
2   Paul Makeham, 'Framing the landscape: Prichard's Pioneers and Esson's The Drovers', *Australasian Drama Studies* 23: 121–34.
3   Hugh Hunt, *The Making of Australian Theatre* (Melbourne: Cheshire, 1960) 17.
4   Max Dupain, *Max Dupain Photographs* (Sydney: Ure Smith, 1948); *Follow the Sun: Australian Travel Posters, 1930s-1950s* (Canberra: National Library of Australia, 2000; accessed on 20 August 2006 at http://www.nla.gov.au/exhibitions/sun/index.html).
5   John Fiske, Bob Hodge and Graeme Turner, *Myths of Oz: Reading Australian Popular Culture* (Sydney: Allen & Unwin, 1987); Mark Gibson, 'Myths of Oz Cultural Studies: the Australian beach and 'English' ordinariness', *Continuum: Journal of Media & Cultural Studies*, 15.3 (2001): 275–88; Helen Grace, 'The persistence of culture: recovering *On the Beach*', *Continuum: Journal of Media & Cultural Studies*, 15.3 (2001): 289–301.
6   John McCallum, 'The Doll and the Legend', *Australasian Drama Studies*, 3.2 (1985): 34–5.
7   Barbara Vernon, *The Multi-Coloured Umbrella* in *Theatregoer*, 1.3 (1961): 27.

8   Vernon, *The Multi-Coloured Umbrella* 42.

9   Vernon, *The Multi-Coloured Umbrella* 42.

10 Colin Bennett, 'New play by Ray Lawler brilliant—but fails in its high endeavor', *The Age*, 14 September 1959, 5.

11 Ray Lawler, *The Piccadilly Bushman* (Sydney: Angus & Robertson, 1961), 17-18

12 Lawler, *Piccadilly* 48.

13 Lawler, *Piccadilly* 90, 101.

14 Lawler, *Piccadilly* 67.

15 Stephen Sewell, *The Father We Loved On A Beach By The Sea* in *Three Political Plays*, ed. Alrene Sykes (St Lucia: University of Queensland Press, 1980) 63.

16 Other Australian plays from the 1990s with incapacitated fathers who are uncommunicative with their sons include Richard Barrett's *Words of One Syllable* from 1990, David Stevens' *The Sum Of Us* from 1992 and Elizabeth Coleman's *It's My Party (And I'll Die If I Want To)* from 1993.

17 Tony McNamara, *The John Wayne Principle* (Sydney: Currency Press, 1997) 53; David Stevens, *The Sum Of Us* (New York: Samuel French, Inc., 1990).

18 Tim Conigrave, *Thieving Boy / Like Stars In My Hands* (Sydney: Currency Press, 1997) 30.

19 Bob Evans, 'The grip of the past's dead hand', *Sydney Morning Herald*, 13 October 1990, 81.

20 Margery Forde and Michael Forde, *James and Johnno* (unpublished typescript, 2004) 7.

21 Forde and Forde, *James and Johnno* 47.

22 Forde and Forde, *James and Johnno* 51–2.

23 Nick Enright and Justin Monjo, *Cloudstreet* (Sydney: Currency Press, 1998) 5.

24 Enright and Monjo, *Cloudstreet* 122.

25 John Misto, *Sky* (unpublished typescript, 1992) 2.

26 Misto, *Sky* 3.

27 Hannie Rayson, *Life After George* (Sydney: Currency Press, 2000) 23–5, 41.

28 Neil Cole, *Alive At Williamstown Pier* (Haymarket, N.S.W.: Esson Press, 1999) 55.

29 Daniel Keene, *To Whom It May Concern and Other Plays* (North Fitzroy, Vic.: Blackpepper, 2000) 19.

30 Jonathan Bollen, 'Boxing the man: fighting the choreography of race and generation in Australian theatre from the 1990s', in *What a Man's Gotta Do?* eds Adrian Kiernander, Jonathan Bollen and Bruce Parr (Armidale: CALLTS, in press

Works cited

Balodis, Janis. *Wet And Dry*. Paddington, N.S.W.: Currency Press, 1991.

Barrett, Richard. *Words of One Syllable*. Unpublished typescript, author's collection, 1990.

Bennett, Colin. 'New play by Ray Lawler brilliant—but fails in its high endeavor', *The Age*, 14 September 1959, 5.

Beynon, Richard. *The Shifting Heart: A Play*. London: Faber & Faber, 1958.

Bollen, Jonathan. 'Boxing the man: fighting the choreography of race and generation in Australian theatre from the 1990s', in *What a Man's Gotta Do?* eds. Adrian Kiernander, Jonathan Bollen and Bruce Parr. Armidale: CALLTS, in press.

Cole, Neil. *Alive At Williamstown Pier*. Haymarket, N.S.W.: Esson Press, 1999.

Coleman, Elizabeth. *It's My Party (And I'll Die If I Want To)* in *The La Mama Collection: Six Plays For The 1990s*. Sydney: Currency Press, 1997.

Conigrave, Tim. *Thieving Boy / Like Stars In My Hands*. Sydney: Currency Press, 1997.

Dupain, Max. *Max Dupain Photographs*. Sydney: Ure Smith, 1948.

Enright, Nick. *Blackrock*. Sydney: Currency Press, 1996.

Enright, Nick and Justin Monjo. *Cloudstreet*. Sydney: Currency Press, 1997.

Evans, Bob. 'The grip of the past's dead hand', *Sydney Morning Herald*, 13 October 1990, 81.

Fiske, John, Bob Hodge and Graeme Turner. *Myths of Oz: Reading Australian Popular Culture*. Sydney: Allen & Unwin, 1987.

Follow the Sun: Australian Travel Posters, 1930s-1950s. Canberra: National Library of Australia, *2000. Accessed on 20 August 2006 at http://www.nla.gov.au/exhibitions/sun/index.html*

Forde, Margery and Michael Forde. *James and Johnno*. Unpublished typescript, author's collection, 2004.

Gibson, Mark. 'Myths of Oz Cultural Studies: the Australian beach and "English" ordinariness', *Continuum: Journal of Media & Cultural Studies*, 15.3 (2001): 275–88.

Gow, Michael. *Away*. Sydney: Currency Press in association with Playbox Theatre Company, 1986.

Grace, Helen. 'The persistence of culture: recovering *On the Beach*', *Continuum: Journal of Media & Cultural Studies*, 15.3 (2001): 289–301.

Harvey, F.R., ed. *Australian Theatre Year 1959/1960*. Sydney: F.P. Publications.

Hepworth, John. *The Beast In View*. Adelaide University Theatre Guild collection, University of Adelaide Archives, 1959.

Hewett, Robert. *Gulls*. Sydney: Currency Press, 1984.

Hodda, Noel. *Half Safe*. Unpublished typescript, author's collection, 1990.

Hunt, Hugh. *The Making of Australian Theatre*. Melbourne: Cheshire, 1960.

Keene, Daniel. *To Whom It May Concern and Other Plays*. North Fitzroy, Vic.: Blackpepper, 2000.

Kenna, Peter. *The Slaughter of St Teresa's Day*. Sydney: Currency Press, 1972.

Lawler, Ray. *Summer of the Seventeenth Doll*. London: Angus & Robertson, 1957.

Lawler, Ray. *The Piccadilly Bushman*. Sydney: Angus & Robertson, 1961.

Makeham, Paul. 'Framing the landscape: Prichard's Pioneers and Esson's The Drovers', *Australasian Drama Studies*, 23 (1993): 121–34.

McCallum, John. 'The Doll and the Legend', *Australasian Drama Studies*, 3.2 (1985): 33-44.

McNamara, Tony. *The John Wayne Principle*. Sydney: Currency Press, 1997.

Misto, John. *Sky*. Unpublished typescript, author's collection, 1992.

On the Beach [film], dir. Stanley Kramer. United Artists, U.S.A., 1959.

Rankin, Scott & Nicholas, Glynn. *Certified Male*. Unpublished typescript, author's collection, 2003.

Rayson, Hannie. *Life After George*. Sydney: Currency Press, 2000.

Sewell, Stephen. *The Father We Loved On A Beach By The Sea* in *Three Political Plays*, ed. Alrene Sykes. St Lucia: University of Queensland Press, 1980.

Seymour, Alan. *The One Day of the Year* in *Theatregoer*, 1.4 (May-Jul 1961): 25–44.

Shute, Nevil. *On the Beach*. London: Heineman, 1957.

Stevens, David. *The Sum Of Us*. New York: Samuel French, Inc., 1990.

Summer of the Seventeenth Doll [film], alt. title *Season of Passion*, dir. Leslie Norman. Metro-Goldwyn-Mayer & United Artists Pictures Inc., 1957.

Vernon, Barbara. *The Multi-Coloured Umbrella* in *Theatregoer*, 1.3 (Feb-Apr 1961): 27–42.

White, Patrick. *The Season at Sarsaparilla* in *Four Plays*. London: Eyre & Spottiswoode, 1965.

Sharks and the Australian Imaginary

HELEN TIFFIN

As scientists increasingly acknowledge, public perceptions and opinions are crucial to the success or failure of conservation measures. From the preservation of whole river systems, forests and bushland, mangroves and wetlands to individual animal and plant species, the (enforceable) legislation required depends on public support, and thus, whatever the importance and authority of scientific data available, on popular understanding and beliefs. Not surprisingly, therefore, while the conservation of charismatic mega fauna attracts sympathy and support, it is much more difficult to win campaigns for the long-term preservation of habitats (such as eel-grass beds or plankton nurseries) on which the survival of endangered species often depends.

Sharks are certainly seen as mega fauna, but they are charismatic in a very different sense from that of whales, dolphins or even tigers, and particular species such as the 'Grey Nurse' (*Eugomphodus taurus*) and the 'Great White' (*Carchardon carcharias*) are now doubly imperilled by pollution, habitat encroachment and because of popular beliefs about the dangers they pose.[1] Humans worldwide may certainly be in awe of some sharks, admiring their persistence in time, their power, speed and streamlined 'design'; but more usually sharks are feared, vilified and slaughtered in almost unimaginable numbers.[2] Moreover, while the clubbing of juvenile seals to feed the fur trade has been widely (and rightly) condemned, few voices are (or have ever been) raised against the ill-treatment and killing of sharks for profit, 'vengeance' and sheer amusement. Since earliest times records of voyages describe horrific tortures of sharks by sailors. Contemporary practices in both the Australian and Asian fishing industries perpetuate such behaviours, albeit in the name of commerce rather than as 'vengeance' or as a panacea for human boredom during long voyages. Even where protective legislation for shark conservation *has* been initiated, it is often difficult to enforce, and highly susceptible to revocation at public behest when even an isolated 'attack' on humans occurs.[3] In spite of statistics (both in Australia and worldwide) which clearly demonstrate that human fatalities due to shark attacks are very rare and that more people die of dog bites, are stung to death by bees or kicked to death by donkeys each year; or that road tolls so far exceed shark-caused injury or death as to be genuinely incomparable, sharks generate greater fear in humans (even those of non-maritime cultures) than virtually any other animal species, and are often referred to as *the* primary human fear.

In response to three Australian fatalities in 2000, *The Weekend Australian* ran an article entitled 'A Monster of Our Own Making', subtitled, after Robert Hughes' classic history of white Australian settlement, 'The Fatal Shore(s)'. The article raised issues of conservation versus human safety, and opened provocatively with a false binary proposition drawing on stereotypical images: 'White Pointers are circling. There's blood in the water—and on some people's hands. Do we save the sharks or safeguard our beaches? Frank Robson enters the jaws of a dilemma.'[4] The phrase should be 'horns of a dilemma', but its transfer forcefully captures the popular idea of the ultimate end of a shark's circling; the blood in the water and the lunging animal. Such images are necessarily related to those other pandemic shark representations: the calm surface of the ocean cut by the dark fin; the placid blue water under which can be seen lurking the dark torpedo mass or bloodied jaws and teeth of the shark. Why are these tropes so pervasive, influential, and so frequently invoked by urban cultures whose sense of individual or collective safety is, quite unrealistically, so profoundly disturbed by the image of sharks and shark attack?

An eyewitness to the Cottesloe (West Australia) shark death in 2000 described her feelings in this way:

> I tried to swim and I kept wanting to move, but just nothing. It was just terror, pure unadulterated terror as you never experience. And I defy anybody to experience that because we're bred to be terrified of sharks. What brings most terror to your heart? It's a shark.[5]

One of the key words here is 'bred' and its meaning remains unclear. In using the term, the witness may have meant 'brought up to', that is, a learned response; or she may have intended something deeper, atavistic. Or both. Whatever the case, her account pinpoints the problem addressed here. In the face of these entrenched beliefs and apparently immutable stereotypes, how can conservationists hope to alter traditional attitudes to sharks or even the marine environment generally? The case of the shark is extreme, but like all limit cases, it is a particularly suggestive one. While scientific experiment and scientific facts are obviously crucially important, alteration of public perception requires less a detailed knowledge of shark behaviour than an understanding of why sharks embody human fears to such an extreme degree.

Duncan Richards observes that sharks have 'Teeth that cut, just by suggestion, especially in dreams'.[6] The shadow of the shark is the shadow of danger and death; the image of an ultimate evil; or, like that of Moby Dick, of the inscrutability of a malign universe. This is one reason why shark fatalities attract the kinds of headlines they do, even though such incidents are rare; even though experiments have shown sharks do not like the taste of human flesh, preferring seals or fish; even though great whites are known to frequent the South Australian coast especially in the seal pupping season, and that surf-board riders in flippers and wet suits look very like seals; even though, from 1997 to 1999, wet suits filled with offal had been towed behind tourist boats off South Africa and South Australia to attract Great Whites; even though it was well known that in 2000 there was a significant plankton deficiency due to a water temperature rise in the north Pacific with consequent Pacific-wide fish die off; even though it has been known for decades that most sharks are (not surprisingly) territorial.[7] Though all these things are generally known outside the scientific community, single deaths by 'shark attack' still provoke disproportionately widespread fear and sensationalist media coverage.

Steve Baker notes that stereotypical animal images are usually accepted as the reality without our ever considering their historical and psycho-cultural production, their bases being found in human fears and human self-definition rather than in scientific or observational accounts. This is especially the case with sharks; scientific knowledge rarely influences our expectations of sharks in the ways in which it can inform our perceptions of, for instance, wombats or lions. Given that the actual danger to humans from shark attack is miniscule (on average nine fatalities per year worldwide), it is clear that it is the shark's *symbolic* freight, rather than its real depredations on humans, which most strongly influences popular imagery, (re)contributing in turn to the (re)formation of popular perceptions. What lies behind this psycho-cultural complex of shark images, metaphors and symbols thus demands investigation if public attitudes are to be challenged in the interests of conservation of sharks (and the ecosystems of which they are an intrinsic and essential part) and indeed, of those other animal species whose symbolic history and usage in contemporary cultures far outweighs their actual presence and impact.

'Attitudes to living animals are in large part the result of the symbolic uses to which the concept of the animal is put in popular culture', and sharks again offer an extreme example in a number of ways.[8] First, although there are over 340 species of shark, some small enough (as adults) to fit in the palm of a human hand, there is only one popularly accepted image, or rather, series of related images. The pointed fin cutting the surface of the water; the shark—a large dark, indeterminate object—lurking under the clear calm waters while human families play on the beach and swim unsuspectingly; the water surface savagely broken by the emerging teeth and jaws, frequently bloodied, and, accompanying these, the 'cold eye' of the 'merciless' predator as it lunges at its prey, a grey 'torpedo' of death.[9] For present day humans, as Baker observes, 'animals exist more in representation than the real', as part of a 'multiplicity of animal signs circulating in an only randomly historical space of representation, that of the city'.[10] In this space of representation to which Baker refers, these dominant animal images lend themselves to a 'vicious circularity' wherein 'only that which is already known will be readily recognised as having meaning'.[11] Peter Benchley's novel *Jaws* (and the even more influential film based on it) deliberately exploited the shark stereotypes referred to above.[12] Operating 'largely independently of the living animal even if they once derived from it or now even apply to it', such images continue to accord with popular expectations as they simultaneously (re) produce them.[13]

It is not then difficult to argue that one of the major problems, if not *the* major problem for shark conservation today, is in large part one of representation, particularly the ways in which sharks have been depicted throughout the Western world in a wide range of genres from cartoons to even scientific treatises. Perhaps nothing more clearly demonstrates the destructive effects of the historical and symbolic freight sharks carry than the decline of shark conservation and thus shark populations worldwide after the release of Stephen Spielberg's 1975 film of Benchley's novel. Disconcerted, even horrified by his role in that 'vicious circularity' of animal imaging to which Baker draws our attention, Benchley has since spent some of the money he made from *Jaws* on shark conservation. His public recognition of the catastrophic effect of these two imaginative works on shark numbers was not a singular one. There has been a general recognition of this impact, and in a number of quarters, deliberate moves to counteract it. (A project questionnaire designed for children in Australia, for instance, draws attention to the significance of the film in asking 'What happened in 1975 to make the Great White one of the most feared animals in the world?') But long before 1975 large sharks had, to a substantial degree, occupied that position in the lives of people never likely to swim in the ocean, let alone encounter a shark at close range.

There are a number of reasons why sharks conjure fear in humans, and these continue to operate through that 'vicious circularity' referred to by Baker. Images which both reflect and energise these fears include general (and by no means irrational) responses to large carnivorous animals (such as wolves, lions, crocodiles or bears); those provoked by narratives of marine giants such as the grouper, giant squid and the whale (the fates of Jonah and Ahab, for instance) and those referred to above which are specific to large shark species. Such images help draw the binary bases of human self-definition, and include those once also applied to non-European peoples: savagery versus domesticity or 'civilisation'; 'cannibalism' as the extreme marker of barbarism and the not-human; inanimate, mechanistic behaviour as against an affective human way of being; and the extreme 'Other', the 'alien' versus the terrestrial.

The continual invocation of such Western anthropocentric binaries in shark representation also contributes to our eagerness to distinguish ourselves, as top predators of the terrestrial food chain, from sharks, the top predators of the marine food chain. The language we use for our similar activities reinforces this distinction. Sharks guard their territories jealously, and they kill members of their own and other species in competition over food and to obtain food, just as we do. But they do so 'mercilessly'; 'mauling' or 'chomping' their prey in a 'feeding frenzy'. We, by contrast, go to all-you-can-eat restaurants to consume shark and other animal flesh, but this is not generally described as a 'feeding frenzy'. We 'raise' animal species for the sole purpose of 'processing' (rather than 'mauling' or dismembering) them as food, but this is not regarded as 'merciless'.

Humans thus distinguish between their own killing and feeding habits and those of sharks by applying different vocabularies to similar activities; while sharks kill, attack, maul and dismember their 'prey', we raise, produce and 'process' our 'food'. Descriptions of feeding sharks stress blood, horror, and pain while we euphemise these as simply part of 'meat production'. The classic 'feeding frenzy' of sharks suggests a mechanistic, automatic set of 'savage' responses, bolstering the idea of sharks as biologically and emotionally alien, lacking any vestige of 'human' compassion. Kim Gamble, an eyewitness to the death of Ken Crow at Cottesloe in 2000, reported a description of the attack he had found particularly apposite. It was, he said, like 'sitting around watching a cricket match, enjoying your day when suddenly this alien comes over the top of the grandstand, chomps the slips fieldsman in half and goes away, leaving him bleeding on the pitch'.[14] Once again the shark is pictured as the inhuman, abrupt disturber of 'domestic' bliss and holiday relaxation; the 'devil' of the paradisial Australian summer of beaches and cricket.

Just as these distinctions are insisted on and thus reflected in our language usage, so our particular alarm at shark attacks on humans (as against, for instance, deaths caused by cars or even wasp stings) suggests their imbrication in what has sometimes been described as the 'cannibal complex': our acute sensitivity to *what* and whom we eat and our taboos in relation to 'edibility' as well as our own fears of being eaten. The latter psycho-cultural complex is connected to both food chain placement and issues of ingestion, the abject and dismemberment; and to the notion of alien, apparently uncontactable and uncontrollable non-human 'Others' who do not share our proclivities and prohibitions.

Such image clusters circulate within textual material such as novels, films, popular magazine accounts of near-death escape, travellers' tales and cartoons whose frequent underlying (human-centred) assumption is that sharks lie in wait for people to enter their domain—that our fetishisation of their (unwanted) attention to us is in response to their own human-directed malevolence. Sharks always 'lurk'; they never simply go about their own business until we intrude into *their* territory. In Australian and American cartoons they are often depicted as surrounding the continent, sometimes 'holding fins'. Even serious statistical publications echo this format in geographically mapping all recorded 'shark attacks' around coasts. And the reputation of particular areas as shark-prone (such as certain surfing beaches) is not confined to Australia nor to twentieth-century accounts. Henry David Thoreau, writing of the United States in the nineteenth century, commented that: 'I have no doubt that one shark in a dozen years is enough to keep up the reputation of a beach one hundred miles long'.[15]

Paradoxically it is actually *because* shark deaths *are* so rare that the image of the shark as a malign, inscrutable force, metonymic of the universe itself, persists. Like death, the shark's unheralded attack can occur at any time, and like death itself, the shark seems cold and remote, erupting into life from 'nowhere' to carry the victim off. The 'shadow of sharks' as writer Peter Matthiessen notes, 'is the shadow of death' and it calls forth 'ultimate fears'. There is, he comments, 'something unholy in their silence'.[16] But as well as symbolising the forces of a malign universe and/or death, the shark is also figuratively represented as a savage disruption to domestic calm. The ubiquitous images of the calm surface of the sea with the dark torpedo-shaped body 'lurking' below or the fatal fin, a 'dead giveaway' on a flat ocean surface is often imaged from the perspective of an observer on a white sandy beach on which children are playing, or more usually from out at sea (and under water); that is, a shark's pseudo-perspective of happy humans on the beach or unsuspectingly frolicking in the water. The second image, that of a calm sea surface cut by the telltale fin, relies, like the first, on the trope of 'savagery' disrupting (human) domesticity/civilisation; and though sharks in such images are represented as distinctly 'other', their presence at the heart of our holiday world, precisely where we feel most relaxed and 'safe', evokes the dangerous, unstable basis of life itself. It is also a reminder that the ocean depths represent one of the very few realms we have not yet totally 'conquered'.

Writing of growing up on the coast of Western Australia, novelist Tim Winton succinctly expresses the way in which 'the shark' has come to symbolise much more than simply a large marine predator. 'While the sea was benign', Winton writes:

> at the blurring perimeter of that boyhood, beyond the reach of conscious thought, there was an unacknowledged moving shadow. It was what the eye searched for when you weren't even looking. It was the reflex that made you swivel now and then as you trod water off the back of the boat, the thing that made your skin tingle as you snorkeled in a murky surge.[17]

Sharks do injure and kill humans, and exercising caution in the ocean is common sense. But although we practise a similar caution in relation to box jellyfish in our northern waters (box jellyfish, which, like the shark, can injure or kill us) and in relation to other species dangerous to humans, these are not feared in the ways in which sharks are. Though box jellyfish can kill as unexpectedly and quickly, they are not imaged as evil or inscrutable, or even 'inhuman'; nor are they theriomorphised in the ways in which the shark so pervasively is in our societies.

In the marine environment we are direct competitors for food resources, although once again the actual 'competition' involved is dismissably slight— we humans win that contest 'hands down'. But the crux of this competition is again less a physical than a psychical one, and turns less on real competition for fish resources than on an apparently atavistic fear. Our symbolic relationship with sharks is much more important and more complex than that involved in purely commercial competition and a major part of our fear has to do with the fact while we eat their flesh routinely (and kill and process them for soup, oil and cartilage, all of which we consume) they also very occasionally eat us. This fear of being eaten, an affront to our status as top predator, is also redolent of Christian prohibitions against dismemberment (and reabsorption into non-human [or 'inhuman'] being), a biological and religious complex which thus energises so many of our responses. In one sense there can be no closer material relation between beings than that which clusters around the fetishised issue of consumption. At the heart of Christianity lies the sacramental ingestion of the host, while perhaps paradoxically, Western cultures have always used cannibalism—the consumption of one's own kind—as *the* marker of obdurate difference between civilisation (as we choose to construct it) and 'savagery'; that which lies beyond the 'pale'.[18] Humans eating shark, or sharks 'eating' a human are not generally described as 'cannibalistic' acts, although as Nick Fiddes has shown, our attitudes to other top predators are at best ambivalent, combining awe and admiration with loathing, tacitly (or subconsciously) acknowledging their psychically threatening similarity to us, a similarity which requires firm rejection of them as the 'not-us' (the alien, malign, inhuman).[19] It is precisely by such strategies of exclusion that we maintain our human self-definition and our claims to special ontological status.

Settlers and whalers arriving in Australia after 1788 brought European (and with the whaling industry, also American) attitudes to sharks. Nevertheless, the earliest written newspaper accounts of contact with sharks in Sydney Harbour are not of 'attacks' on humans but of the killing of sharks for eating and trading in shark fins. Colonists were, however, aware that sharks were prevalent and relied on their presence as a deterrent to convict escape attempts from, for instance, Fort Dennison (Pinchgut). With the increasing dumping of offal and human waste into the water, shark presence in the vicinity no doubt increased. During the nineteenth and twentieth centuries a caught shark was always a spectacle, whether in terms of size or, in an even more popular display, its stomach contents; while jaw trophies and even shark tooth 'jewellery' accorded with a male triumphalism that has always been a component of shark catching and characteristic of so many photographs where the proud (and frequently tattooed) fisherman stand by a dead shark hung ignominiously by its tail, blood dribbling from its mouth.

A particularly bizarre incident involving a tattoo and the catching of two sharks occurred at Coogee Beach (Sydney) in 1935 and was still the subject of popular magazine accounts sixty years later. The 'Shark Arm Affair' as it soon came to be termed, encapsulated (and partially inverted) the trope of the heroic human male versus the ruthless denizen of the ocean. Sizeable sharks caught off Sydney beaches (or in the Harbour) were usually put on display, whether dead or alive. The Coogee aquarium was a favourite venue for the showing of live sharks.

On April 25, a medium-sized shark was caught on a line off Coogee. Before it could be towed in for exhibit, however, it was 'cannibalised' by a much larger shark which was then captured and deposited in the Coogee pool. Not surprisingly this extremely large shark, watched by a crowd of eager onlookers, began to exhibit signs of acute distress. Increasingly lethargic, it began to sink to the bottom of the pool, vomiting up as it did so, a human arm, distinguished, it was later discovered, by the presence of a tattoo. Subsequent police investigation showed, however, that the arm had not been bitten off the (absent) body by either shark, but had in fact been sawn off. Further delving by the police led to the Sydney underworld, a drug smuggling racket and the identity of the victim and his likely murderers.

The name by which this incident has been remembered, 'The Shark Arm Affair' is indicative of the tale's enduring fascination.[20] The Affair both reflected and temporarily destabilised the complex of symbolic associations characteristic of human/shark interactions. Although the shark had swallowed a human arm, and not just immediately before its capture, it had not begun to digest it, evidence (now backed by scientific study) that sharks, contrary to popular opinion, do not regard humans as preferred food. Secondly, while the shark, in vomiting up the arm, initially appeared in its traditional role as dismemberer, harbinger of a death redolent of inscrutable (and unjust) fate, it was instead the (however unwitting) instrument of human justice, revealing a murder that would otherwise have remained undetected. The dismemberment of the human body was in this instance performed by other human(s), not by sharks. The sobriquet 'shark arm' also conjured both the obdurate difference between shark and human anatomy, while at the same time evoking the constant association of 'shark attack' with severed human limbs. Though obviously oxymoronic, the shark's persisting associations with human dismemberment and death made the phrase instantly and popularly intelligible, its ironic destabilisation by the facts of the case serving only, in the end, to reinforce the 'vicious circularity' of the shark image.

This summary sketch can only hint at the complexities involved in the place the shark occupies in the Western and Australian psyches. It is interesting in this regard to compare and contrast attitudes of other human cultures with that of the West; it is illuminating to note the different strategies employed in negotiating the perceived similarities and differences between humans and sharks, where the often contrasting symbolic role(s) of sharks in such cultures means that respect for their power is far greater. Nevertheless the *image* of the shark remains a powerful component of the Australian beach and marine imaginary, always, in Winton's words, as that 'unacknowledged moving shadow … what the eye searched for when you weren't even looking'.

Notes

1   See *The Sydney Morning Herald Magazine* 3 February 1988: 18–25. See also M. Price, 'Something Out There', *The Australian Magazine*, 6–7 January 2001.
2   People still kill over 100 million sharks per year. See for instance Marty Synderman, *Shark, Endangered Predator of the Sea* (Toronto: Porter, 1995) 114. *Carcharias Taurus* (The Grey Nurse) was pushed to the edge of extinction before it was discovered that they had never made an unprovoked 'attack' on humans.
3   See for instance controversy generated in the Australian popular press in *The Sydney Morning Herald Magazine*, 3 February 1988: 18–23 and M. Warneminde, 'Save the Shark!', *Fisheries* 3,2, Winter (1995).
4   Frank Robson, 'A Monster of our Own Making', *The Sydney Morning Herald Magazine*, 3 February 1988: 18.
5   M. Price, 'Something Out There', *The Australian Magazine,* 6–7 January 2001: 16.

6 D. Richards, 'Sharks', *Overland* V. 128 (1992): 76.

7 See for example *The Weekend Australian*, 18–19 November 2001: 1. (Although the caption states that the shark has 'a doomed bull seal' in its jaws, the 'victim' is in fact an offal-filled plastic bag.)

8 Steve Baker, *Picturing the Beast: Animals, Identity and Representation* (Manchester: Manchester U.P., 1993) 28.

9 See for example the advertising posters for the film *Jaws*; the illustration accompanying the articles in 3 and 4 above; and the cover of *The Australian Magazine,* 6–7 January 2001.

10 Baker, *Picturing the Beast* 29.

11 Baker, *Picturing the Beast*. He also notes that 'The intelligibility of stereotypes is entirely dependent on their conformity, and that conformity is not (and never was) to some "truth" of the animal'.

12 *Jaws,* dir. Steven Spielberg, 1975.

13 Baker, *Picturing the Beast* 29.

14 Price, 'Something Out There' 16.

15 Henry David Thoreau, *Cape Cod* (Dover Value edn., 2004) 78.

16 Peter Matthiessen, *Blue Meridian: The Search for the Great White Shark* (USA: Penguin, 1997) 5.

17 Tim Winton, 'Blue Water, Dark Shadows', *The Independent Monthly*, December 1995/January 1996: 29.

18 For an extended commentary on the uses of cannibalism in 'Othering' human groups, see F.P. Barker, *Colonial World* (Cambridge: Cambridge U.P., 1998). An 'othering' is to represent such humans as 'beastly', moving them to the 'animal' side of the species boundary, even though the act which precipitates this is the alleged *human* consumption of *human* flesh.

19 Nick Fiddes, *Meat: A Natural Symbol* (London: Routledge, 1991).

20 For details of this story, salaciously recounted, see *Famous Detective Stories* 4: 7 & 8, June and July, 1950; Vince Kelly, *The Shark Arm Case* (Sydney: Angus & Robertson, 1963).

Works cited

Baker, Steve. *Picturing the Beast: Animals, Identity and Representation*. Manchester: Manchester U.P., 1993.

Barker, F.P. *Colonial World*. Cambridge: Cambridge U.P., 1998.

Fiddes, Nick. *Meat: A Natural Symbol*. London: Routledge, 1991.

Kelly, Vince. *The Shark Arm Case*. Sydney: Angus & Robertson, 1963.

Matthiessen, Peter. *Blue Meridian: The Search for the Great White Shark*. USA: Penguin, 1997.

Price, M. 'Something Out There'. *The Australian Magazine* 6–7 January 2001.

Richards, D. 'Sharks'. *Overland* 128 (1992): 76.

Robson, Frank. 'A Monster of our Own Making'. *The Sydney Morning Herald Magazine* 3 February 1988: 18.

Synderman, Marty. *Shark, Endangered Predator of the Sea*. Toronto: Porter, 1995.

Thoreau, Henry David. *Cape Cod*. Mineola: Dover Value edn, 2004.

Warneminde, M. 'Save the Shark!'. *Fisheries* 3,2, Winter (1995).

Winton, Tim. 'Blue Water, Dark Shadows'. *The Independent Monthly* December 1995/ January 1996: 29.

'Savage Printers': Beachcombing, Tattoos and Liminality in James O'Connell's Residence

ANNIE WERNER

In 1836, James F. O'Connell's memoir *A Residence of Eleven Years in New Holland and the Caroline Islands* was published in Boston. Throughout his life O'Connell was alternately known as a sailor, a traveller, a rogue, even a pirate, and later in his life, when he returned to Europe, he appeared in circuses as a man 'tattooed by savages'.

Though modern scholars have shown O'Connell's narrative to be at least partially fictionalised, it is still a valuable document, since it stands as an active engagement with a colonialist discourse that surrounds notions of liminality and transgression embodied in some of the first white men to live on the Pacific islands—the beachcombers.

Beachcombers, those men who deserted ship, escaped convict settlements or rejected the colony, crossed beaches into the Indigenous culture of the islands they inhabited, and what we know of them comes from the narratives many of them published upon their return to Europe and/or the United States, in an attempt to capitalise on their experiences. The general public's thirst for tales of the 'savages' of the new world meant that the publication of narratives in book or pamphlet form provided a quick and easy income for many sailors who had spent some time in the Pacific islands. O'Connell's *Residence* is a clear example of a text that engages not only with the conventions of the emerging and popular genre of beachcomber literature, but also with the greater dialogues involving colonialist definitions of civilization and savagery. O'Connell's editor claimed the narrative was the 'first published, circumstantial history of a community of Oceanic Indians', and O'Connell himself indicates that he intended the work as 'a compilation of facts upon portions of the world comparatively little known', and that he has 'identified [himself] with it only so far as was necessary to give it the interest of a narrative'.[1] Analysis of the text, however, shows that O'Connell's engagement with the broader discourse of colonialism and its associated genres, meant that his text became an astounding conglomeration of forms that is suggestive of what can perhaps be viewed as the prototype for the beachcomber adventure story, *Robinson Crusoe*.[2]

O'Connell introduces himself to his reader in a way reminiscent of Daniel Defoe's introduction of Crusoe. He begins his narrative by explaining his parentage. His mother was an equestrian, his father a costumer in the circus, and his early childhood was spent with an uncle. At age eleven, O'Connell went to Cobbet, London, with his uncle, whose inattention allowed him to wander about the circus, and later the ship-yards, where he became a cabin-boy who set sail for Botany Bay on a ship with a cargo of female convicts. Following a series of mishaps and adventures, O'Connell found himself on the island of Ponape, in the Caroline Islands, where the greater part of his narrative is set. By the 1830s, Ponape had developed a reputation as a haven for runaways, and something of a beachcomber community was established upon the island. Ponape was also a popular spot for whalers because of its numerous safe harbours. Ponape's 'beachcomber period' (1830–1854) is described by Martin Zelenietz and David Kravitz as a dynamic one because the beachcombers' roles on the island were constantly in flux. At the beginning of the period, the early beachcombers had little involvement with trade, but by 1839 they had assumed a more prominent position in the 'market' of the island, which peaked with the influx of beachcombers in the early 1840s. According to Zelenietz and Kravitz, the decline of Ponape's beachcomber period coincided with the establishment of permanent Christian missions in the 1850s.[3]

O'Connell is often classified as a beachcomber, and the details in his narrative certainly indicate that his position on Ponape was strongly suggestive of the archetypal beachcombers. Like many writers of what could be termed 'beachcomber narratives', however, O'Connell was perhaps wary of the opprobrium associated with the term. As Herman Melville felt compelled to do some twenty years later, O'Connell worked to distance himself from any association with those rogues of the Pacific.

O'Connell deploys various tactics in order to establish his work as a sophisticated piece of writing, self-consciously assuring his readers that he is a respectable individual. His early descriptions of his time on board the convict ship of his first voyage, and his descriptions of the female convict passengers in particular, provide a clear indication of the social position he wished to project for his readers. He is derisive toward the convicts, and clearly positions himself as morally superior, emphasising his fellow passengers' criminal status. He employs a directly phonetic, vernacular dialogue when relaying the conversations of the passengers, contrasting sharply with his own narrative language, which is rather more formal. In addition, his references to Shakespeare, poetry, and other canonical literature situate his own work as being 'literary', rather than colloquial.

O'Connell's true allegiances are often difficult to pinpoint. At various points his attitudes—towards the British, the Indigenous populations of the islands he visits, and ultimately, himself—seem confused. His representation of his first encounter with Indigenous Australians, for example, is fraught with contradiction. Initially, O'Connell mocks the 'Chief of the Sydney Cove blacks', King Bungaree, sarcastically commenting upon his second-hand officer's coat and lack of shoes. He writes:

> upon his neck was suspended the order and insignia of his nobility—a plate which might have been gold, but was brass, bearing the inscription, 'BUNGAREE, KING OF SYDNEY COVE'.[4]

While Bungaree's inferiority and paltry imitation are emphasised at first, on the following page O'Connell concedes that 'King Bungaree ... is indeed better entitled to his rank than the English to his land'.[5]

O'Connell's varying assessments of Indigenous communities he encounters are at best contradictory. They swing from the stereotypical assumed imperialist superiority, where Indigenous people are described as being 'indolent', 'vilely licentious', 'filthy', 'predatory', 'utterly degraded' and 'the connecting link between apes and men', to a more Romantic and Rousseauesque representation where he notes that 'some people claiming to be civilized might take a lesson from the humanity of these people to shipwrecked mariners'.[6]

Elsewhere, he engages with colonial discourses that construct Indigenous people as cannibals. When he is shipwrecked off Port Macquarie, with five 'Kanakas', O'Connell is solely responsible for righteously dissuading the 'savages' from their cannibalistic impulses towards each other, thereby situating himself not only as superior to the natives, but also as a kind of saviour, rescuing them from what he assumes to be debased urges.[7] He also makes sweeping generalisations about the identity of his companions, identifying them only as 'South Sea islanders' while at the same time describing them as 'countrymen'.[8] Here O'Connell assimilates what may have been a significantly diverse group of men under the general term 'Kanaka'. Like Samoa in Melville's *Mardi*, O'Connell's companions are 'identified with [their] place of origin and [their] culture, in a movement that enforces metonymy or synecdoche', and engages with the notion of a blanket primitivism that pervades much colonial literature.[9]

These contradictions in O'Connell's attitudes toward Indigenous people, not only of Australia but also of Ponape, are suggestive of O'Connell's ambivalence about his own position. It would appear that O'Connell's unease about his identity is at least partly derived from an awareness of his intended audience. Having grown up in and around the world of the circus, it is reasonably safe to assume that O'Connell had some understanding of the necessities of marketing a story. He states outright that '[t]his work is not prepared for a New South Wales market', thus making it clear that he intended his work to be read by people 'back home', not those in the colonies.[10] An awareness of this intended readership therefore allows him scope for embellishment and fabrication, since he assumes that his readers will have no first-hand knowledge of life in the colonies. In his 1997 book *Cannibals: The Discovery and Representation of the Cannibal from Columbus to Jules Verne*, Frank Lestringant points out that:

> the Island, apparently able to restrain and circumscribe fantasies, was to work rather like a fixation abcess. It inscribed and absorbed evil, and so the latter was conjured, kept at a distance.[11]

The (dis)location of the Island gave writers an opportunity to exoticise and embellish their experiences, situating and providing as the foci of their narratives the 'savagery' that the Islands allegedly contained.

Because O'Connell's 'information is so patently and flagrantly wrong' in most accounts of the island, people, and customs, Saul Reisenberg suggests that O'Connell may be a 'pathological liar'.[12] In 'The Tattooed Irishman', Reisenberg confidently claims that most descriptions of O'Connell's early life are 'pure fabrication', and it is suggested that the reason for his dubiously recounted beginnings may have been to cover up a convict past.[13] According to Reisenberg, his portrayal of nine months living with Indigenous Australians is doubtful, and a shipmate of O'Connell's claims that even the shipwreck—a pivotal event in the text that lays the foundation for the rest of the narrative on Ponape—did not in fact occur: rather, that O'Connell deserted the ship.

Significantly, many of the fabricated events in O'Connell's story reflect well-established tropes of South Sea adventure stories, explorers' accounts and, even though he attempted to distance himself from them, beachcomber narratives. Significant events in the text are easily recognisable from other texts of similar genres: the ship that is wrecked off the Caroline Islands is controlled by a 'drunken, stupid sot'; O'Connell is forcefully tattooed; he is constantly surrounded by threats of cannibalism; and he is unwittingly married to the chief's daughter.[14] In light of this, it seems likely that O'Connell's marketing savvy was behind his 'embellishment' of such events.

Upon his return to Europe, O'Connell's career hinged upon his tales of shipwreck, captivity and torture. In 1835, performing with the Lion Circus as the first tattooed man to be exhibited in the United States of America, the

Promotional poster for James O'Connell's performance.
With permission from *A Residence of Eleven Years in New Holland and the Caroline Islands by James F. O'Connell*, edited by Saul Riesenberg (ANU Press, Canberra, 1972) 40.

James O'Connell performing an Irish jig.
With permission from *A Residence of Eleven Years in New Holland and the Caroline Islands by James F. O'Connell*, edited by Saul Riesenberg (ANU Press, Canberra, 1972) 42.

ringmaster 'had a rare story about this man, of the torture inflicted by savages doing the work of tattooing'.[15] The two most prominent features of his performances at fairs and circuses around the United States were the exhibition of his tattoos—relatively novel at the time—and a rendition of the Irish jig that allegedly saved his life. These aspects of his performance, and in particular his tattooing, demonstrate the way that O'Connell's exhibitions and narrative are performances of race and national identity.

In *Residence*, O'Connell claims that his life was saved by the fortuitously timed performance of an Irish jig that apparently diverted his captors' attention for long enough to save him from being killed. Reisenberg points out that it is possible that this account was also fabricated, but regardless of its foundation in fact, the dance features prominently in his narrative and in subsequent circus appearances. O'Connell's performance of an Irish jig—a deliberately and overtly identifiable dance—simultaneously asserts O'Connell's patriotism and Europeanness, and the Empire's influence over the 'savages', who are so enamoured and perhaps 'fooled' by this jig that they spare his life. In addition to its narrative function, the dance also supplements O'Connell's circus display, substantiating his exhibition and transforming it from a mere display of his tattooed body, into a performance of his life-saving (and symbolically patriotic) dance. The motif of the jig is a reiteration of O'Connell's identity and nationality, and he writes: 'I have no doubt that in my heels was found the attraction which led the chief to select me from among my comrades'.[16] As a motif within the narrative, the jig is inserted at points within the text where O'Connell deems it necessary to reassert his Irish identity. He declares his alterity from the Ponapeans, thus resisting the possibility of acculturation, despite his tattoos and marriage.

Regardless of these efforts, however, the alterity that O'Connell asserts through his performance is contradicted by his tattooed body and the Indigenous markings it displays. Though O'Connell establishes the tattooing process as fearful and torturous—which aligns it with other captivity and beachcomber accounts of the process—it is nevertheless ultimately represented as beneficial, initiating him into a position of power within the tribe and even saving him from being eaten.

O'Connell sets a scene of suspense prior to his account of the actual process, describing an ominous journey to the place where they were to be tattooed, which 'would have been pleasing, if we had not been so utterly in the dark as to the purpose of the journey'.[17] On arrival, O'Connell and his companion busy themselves in speculation as to their 'end'. The woman who tattoos O'Connell's hand is described as his 'executioner', and the process itself is described as a 'battering' and a 'punishment'.[18] He claims to have heartily resisted any further tattooing, but to no avail: the 'savage printers' continued their torture, and O'Connell 'often thought [he] should die of these apparently petty, but really acutely painful inflictions'.[19]

O'Connell's companion in captivity, George, was apparently unable to bear the pain of being tattooed, and begged not to have the operation completed. This wish was granted, but not without 'unequivocal expressions of disgust at his cowardice and effeminacy'.[20] In O'Connell's narrative, George operates as a humorous figure, whose primary function within the text is to highlight O'Connell's superiority. George is frequently the subject of jovial derision, and in the scenes depicting the tattooing process, is emasculated by not being able to endure the pain. This in turn establishes O'Connell as brave, honourable and essentially more of a 'man'. In addition, O'Connell claims that the Ponapeans exclaimed 'Jim Chief brave!' in admiration of his endurance.[21] This exclamation does much for O'Connell's standing: he is denoted as a 'chief', with all its implications of power, authority and status, and he is also established for the reader as being 'brave' even in the eyes of the 'savages'. This status is further confirmed by George's marriage to a wife of 'no rank', whereas O'Connell is wed to a member of the ruling family.

In many captivity and beachcomber narratives, tattooing is described in terms that sexualise the process, with an emphasis being placed on penetration with 'sharp sticks', and, especially in the cases where young girls are being tattooed, the loss of blood. In O'Connell's narrative, the tattooing process is similarly sexualised, though the emphasis is more erotic and titillating than predatory. O'Connell fixates upon the 'bevy of tender ladies' who are responsible for the operation, and seems almost ecstatic when he writes that 'between every blow my beauty dipped her thorns in the ink'.[22] This also establishes a possessive relationship between O'Connell and the woman tattooing him, which pre-empts the relationship to follow: he calls her 'my beauty', and later discovers that the tattooing process was actually part of a marriage ritual whereby he becomes wedded to one of his tattooers. His wife:

> was only about fourteen years of age, affectionate, neat, faithful, and, barring too frequent indulgence in the flesh of baked dogs, which gave her breath something of a canine odor, she was a very agreeable consort. During my residence upon the island she presented me with two pretty little demi-savages, a little girl, and a boy, who stands a chance, in his turn, to succeed his grandfather in the government of the island.[23]

O'Connell is careful to outline his wife's virtues in terms recognisable and appreciable by a Western audience. He is also at pains to establish his links to the Panopean royal family.

Reisenberg indicates that O'Connell's unawareness of the marriage ritual is likely to be an embellishment. In the same way that most beachcombers implied that their tattoos were an involuntary infliction, O'Connell also suggests that he was married unwittingly. As Daniel Thorp points out, beachcombers were considered by white populations to be 'more degraded than the Natives', presumably on account of their:

> fall from civilization: while the indigenous people had never been civilized, the white man gone native had held civilization in his grasp, and thrown it away in favour of the indigenous, 'savage' way of life.[24]

For many beachcombers who aimed to sell their stories as a means of making a living upon returning to European or American society, suggestions of voluntary submission to 'savage' ways needed to be denied, especially in relation to

Indigenous tattooing and marriage. As a result, beachcombers' accounts were often modified to include suggestions of enforced captivity, tattooing, marriage and integration.

O'Connell also justifies his tattoos by evoking the previously established threat of cannibalism. O'Connell claims that his tattoos prevented him from being 'eaten' by another tribe when he was travelling through the islands:

> Notwithstanding the representations of Ahoundel that we were in danger of being eaten if we ventured out of his sight, nothing but the most courteous treatment was received by us. My tattooing, speaking of my relationship to Ahoundel-a-Nutt, was better than letters of introduction.[25]

Since Christopher Columbus' voyages to South America in the late fifteenth century, when the term 'cannibal' was actually coined, the possibility of encountering 'cannibal savages' has been a tension in explorer, traveller and beachcomber narratives; most writers seem to be obsessed by the question of whether the people they encountered actually practised anthropophagy.[26] By implying that he was shipwrecked and captured, and that his participation in the 'savage' act of tattooing was forced, and in fact justified by the equal or greater threat of being ingested by the savage body, O'Connell disavows responsibility for his participation in the Ponapean's primitive way of life.

While O'Connell carefully navigates the tenuous and shifting line that he draws between his own captive, white, Irish, civilised identity, and that of the Ponapeans, his awareness of colour deepens. O'Connell is understandably conscious of his Othered position on Ponape, but his analyses and descriptions of 'colour' are unusually nuanced, and at times even complex.

He is clearly aware of his own otherness among the Ponapeans, and notes several times the way that the blue veins that show through his relatively translucent skin are constant sources of amazement and wonder. He also remarks on the 'practical joke' of surprising people who had never seen him before, by entering:

> a house suddenly, with a howl, and [striking] an attitude … Imagine the effect which would be produced on a party of American or European ladies by the sudden apparition of an albino under such circumstances, and you will have some idea of the fright of the islanders.[27]

A fear of whiteness is identified here: a fear that someone lighter than oneself might suddenly appear. While this anecdote emphasises his Otherness on Ponape, and evinces an unusual awareness of the consequences of Othering, his treatment of the caste system on Ponape essentially negates this awareness. He is deliberate in pointing out that the lower castes are darker than the higher, and that such groups do not interrelate, though he makes no mention of the impact his own colour might have had on his ability to integrate. He also engages with the nineteenth century European fear of miscegenation, indicating that 'incestuous intercourse between the white castes and the black' is unknown.[28] He notes his own difference, and the islanders' infatuation with his difference, though he does not recognise it as a symbol or marker of class. *His own* colour is taken for granted, and therefore entrenches notions of white superiority.

After living on Ponape for almost a decade, O'Connell and his 'shadow', George, were taken from the island by the *Spy* of Salem, and then deposited in prison in Manila for being pirates and trouble-makers. When finally freed from Manila, they made their way to Macao, via Canton, where they were objects of curiosity because of their tattoos, presumably providing O'Connell with the inspiration for his future employment.

O'Connell arrived in New York in 1835 via Halifax, Canada, and was employed almost immediately with the Lion Circus. He performed on and off for almost twenty years, displaying his tattoos and performing the Irish jig. O'Connell's performances embodied perfectly the liminal position of the beachcomber: his skin was inscribed with an 'alien aesthetic', a visible and permanent signifier of the boundaries he had crossed and the 'primitive' society that he infiltrated.[29] At the same time, viewers were presented with his overt patriotism through the dance that saved his life—the Irish jig. These contradictions, evident in O'Connell's narrative, clearly highlight the complexity of identity construction that many beachcombers were subject to in their movement between cultures. When this movement became integrated into a performance, as in O'Connell's case, the question of marketability added further complication to his narrative. Ultimately many events depicted therein became distorted or fictionalised in order for the narrative and performance to engage successfully with popular tropes, attitudes and understandings of what it means to be 'civilised' or 'savage'.

Notes

1   H.H.W., 'Preface' in James O'Connell, *A Residence of Eleven Years in New Holland and the Caroline Islands: Being the Adventures of James F. O'Connell* (Boston: B.B. Mussey, 1836) x.
2   O'Connell, *A Residence of Eleven Years* 251.
3   See Martin Zelenietz and David Kravitz, 'Absorbtion, Trade and Warfare: Beachcombers on Ponape, 1830–1854', *Ethnohistory* 21:3 (1974): 223–249.
4   O'Connell, *A Residence of Eleven Years* 30.

5   O'Connell, *A Residence of Eleven Years* 31.

6   O'Connell, *A Residence of Eleven Years* 82, 109.

7   O'Connell, *A Residence of Eleven Years* 77.

8   O'Connell, *A Residence of Eleven Years* 78.

9   Juniper Ellis, 'Melville's Literary Cartographies of the South Seas', *The Massachusetts Review* 38:1 (1997): 22.

10 O'Connell, *A Residence of Eleven Years* 34.

11 Frank Lestringant, *Cannibals: The Discovery and Representation of the Cannibal from Columbus to Jules Verne* (Polity Press, Cambridge, 1997) 143.

12 Saul Reisenberg is chairman of the department of anthropology at the Smithsonian Institute, editor of O'Connell's journal and a leading figure in studies of first contact in the Caroline Islands. Saul Reisenberg, 'The Tattooed Irishman', *The Smithsonian Journal of History* (1968): 5.

13 Reisenberg, 'The Tattooed Irishman' 2.

14 O'Connell, *A Residence of Eleven Years* 102.

15 Esse Forrester O'Brian, quoted in Saul Reisenberg, 'The Tattooed Irishman', 12.

16 O'Connell, *A Residence of Eleven Years* 110.

17 O'Connell, *A Residence of Eleven Years* 113.

18 O'Connell, *A Residence of Eleven Years* 114–16.

19 O'Connell, *A Residence of Eleven Years* 116.

20 O'Connell, *A Residence of Eleven Years* 115.

21 O'Connell, *A Residence of Eleven Years* 115.

22 O'Connell, *A Residence of Eleven Years* 116.

23 O'Connell, *A Residence of Eleven Years* 122. The Ponapeans' social stratification was matrilineal, so male beachcombers generally had little impact on the distribution of social power and status.

24 Daniel Thorp, 'Going Native in New Zealand and America: Comparing Pakeha Maori and White Indians', *The Journal of Imperial and Commonwealth History* 31: 3 (2003): 1–17.

25 O'Connell, *A Residence of Eleven Years* 182.

26 For more information on the literary culture of cannibalism, see Frank Lestringant, *Cannibals: The Discovery and Representation of the Cannibal from Columbus to Jules Verne* (Polity Press, Cambridge, 1997).

27 O'Connell, *A Residence of Eleven Years* 123.

28 O'Connell, *A Residence of Eleven Years* 148.

29 Vanessa Smith, *Literary Culture and the Pacific: Nineteenth Century Textual Encounters* (Cambridge University Press, Cambridge and New York, 1998) 47.

Works cited

Ellis, Juniper. 'Melville's Literary Cartographies of the South Seas', *The Massachusetts Review* 38:1 (1997): 9–29.

H. H. W. 1836. 'Preface' in O'Connell, James. *A Residence of Eleven Years in New Holland and the Caroline Islands: Being the Adventures of James F. O'Connell*. B.B. Mussey, Boston, 1836.

Lestringant, Frank. *Cannibals: The Discovery and Representation of the Cannibal from Columbus to Jules Verne*. Polity Press, Cambridge, 1997.

O'Brian, Esse Forrester, quoted in Reisenberg, Saul. 'The Tattooed Irishman', *The Smithsonian Journal of History* (1968): 1-17.

O'Connell, James. *A Residence of Eleven Years in New Holland and the Caroline Islands: Being the Adventures of James F. O'Connell*. B.B. Mussey, Boston, 1836.

Reisenberg, Saul. 'The Tattooed Irishman', *The Smithsonian Journal of History* (1968): 1-17.

Smith, Vanessa. *Literary Culture and the Pacific: Nineteenth Century Textual Encounters*. Cambridge University Press, Cambridge and New York, 1998.

Thorp, Daniel. 'Going Native in New Zealand and America: Comparing Pakeha Maori and White Indians'. *The Journal of Imperial and Commonwealth History* 31: 3 (2003): 1–17.

Zelenietz, Martin and Kravitz, David. 'Absorbtion, Trade and Warfare: Beachcombers on Ponape, 1830-1854', *Ethnohistory* 21:3 (1974): 223-249

Errol Flynn's Lifelong Relationship ... with the Sea

MICHAEL X. SAVVAS

Dedicated to Errol's grandson, Luke Flynn

Errol Flynn once wrote about feeling the 'keen ecstasy of ... a hard driving vessel'.[1] Surprisingly, he was referring to his beloved yacht, the *Sirocco*, described in his first book, *Beam Ends*. Apart from *Beam Ends*, Flynn wrote a novel called *Showdown;* an autobiography, *My Wicked, Wicked Ways*; a film script, *Cuban Rebel Girls*; and seven articles for *The Bulletin* newspaper. Flynn's acting career and extra-curricular activities obscure the fact that Flynn was a highly talented and imaginative writer. Furthermore, Flynn's writing employs an exciting interplay between fact and fiction, which still has power and relevance today. A significant amount of Flynn's writing was about his one true love—a love he could never conquer—the sea.

In *My Wicked, Wicked Ways*, Flynn writes, 'My only real happiness is when I am near the sea'.[2] A number of significant events in Flynn's life took place on the seas. He met his first wife, the glamorous French movie star Lili Damita, on an ocean liner called the *Paris* en route to New York. Flynn was travelling to Hollywood to begin a six-month contract with Warner Brothers. Flynn had also met previously on his voyage to London 'the bell-ringing Ting Ling O'Connor'[3] on 'the *Fusham*, a small packet that plied between Hong Kong and Macao'.[4] Ting Ling turned out to be a 'high class' prostitute who swindled Flynn out of thousands of dollars and actually broke his heart: 'It was one of the worst heart drops that ever happened to me. I actually thought she cared for me'.[5]

In Hobart over ten years ago, I met and befriended an elderly gentleman called Don Norman. Norman was a childhood friend of Flynn and wrote the now rare book, *Errol Flynn. The Tasmanian Story.*[6] Norman became my guide and drove me around Hobart. At one point he showed me a dance hall he and Flynn used to go to. Norman then pointed out the beach where Flynn would escort the ladies from the dance hall to engage in a different type of dancing. Even before he became famous, Flynn associated the sea and the beach with sex.[7]

98

Flynn writes in *My Wicked, Wicked Ways* about his early life in Tasmania and his connection with the sea:

> My primary interest became the sea. I listened to anyone who would talk of it, and I relished the occasional trips we took across the Bass Strait to Sydney. And so the two main streams of thinking in the family were very much of this earth: the primordial creatures of the nearly impenetrable Tasmanian wilderness and the eternal oceans.
>
> Around the water's edge, and only there, I was happy. I used to frolic in the water with such abandon that my father once remarked that human knowledge originally came out of the sea, as well [sic] the human himself, 'But you look as if you are going from the land back to the sea'.[8]

Flynn's father, Professor Theodore Thomson Flynn, also had an affinity with the sea. According to his biographical entry in *Bright Sparcs*:

> Although his early interest was marsupials, he later developed an interest in marine biology. This led him to work towards the development of Australian fisheries, spending fifteen years harnessing the resources of state and commonwealth governments and imperial trade policies and even forming a private company to harvest pelagic fish stocks. He was involved in the establishment of CSIRO and a proposal to build a national marine research station.[9]

Apart from Errol and his father's connection with the sea, Norman goes as far as to write in his biography of Flynn, *Errol Flynn. The Tasmanian Story,* of 'the salt that is already in the blood of all men born in the old whaling port of Hobart with the sea lapping the very steps of the city'.[10]

As a child, Flynn was very aware of his maritime heritage. His maternal grandfather, Captain George Young, was a master mariner. According to Flynn in *My Wicked, Wicked Ways*, Flynn was also descended from Midshipman [Edward] Young[11], chief aide to Fletcher Christian on the *Bounty*.[12] As a young boy in his home in Tasmania, Flynn would play with a sword that Young had captured from Captain Bligh.[13] This sword and all that it represents helped shape Flynn's identity as a rebel and as a sailor, drawing on two essential conflicting stereotypes about British sailors: the first, that they were loyal participants in the English caste system; the second, that they were pirates or mutineers who rejected the hierarchies of English society. The latter group was such a threat to the status quo that mutiny was a capital offence. Flynn's character was definitely more shaped by the second. This was further compounded by the fact that he was an Australian (with an Irish background), and had been rejected by the English caste system in his days as a public school student. He writes in *My Wicked, Wicked Ways* about his formative experiences at South-West London College:

I was regarded as a 'colonial', a term uttered with contempt. I resented this very much and it might have given me for a time a complex and a feeling I had something to overcome. 'Say, my good fellow, is it true that all Australians are cannibals?' I would be asked. Or, 'My goodness, Flynn, is it true that in Australia the women eat their young?' It was a bullying spirit.[14]

What has not been mentioned before is Flynn's possible West Indian connection: for the *Bounty's* midshipman '"Ned" Young was likely born at St. Kitts in the West Indies of an English father and a West Indian mother'.[15] According to Norman, Flynn may have also been part Polynesian; this mixed heritage may well have been a consequence of the *Bounty* connection, as many of the *Bounty* sailors had children with the Tahitian women on Pitcairn Island. This is of interest in helping to explain Flynn's sense of difference and individuality growing up in a predominantly Anglo-Celtic Australia. Having mixed heritage may have influenced Flynn's identity as an outsider and rebel.

Flynn accepted that sailing enhanced his willingness to think about his self-identification as a descendant of the *Bounty's* Midshipman Young. In Flynn's first book *Beam Ends*, he writes that on the *Sirocco's* way to Cooktown in Queensland, the crew stopped at Restoration Island:

> ... out of pure curiosity. I wanted to see the island which had once been the salvation of Bligh and his men of the *Bounty* a month after they had been turned adrift in their twenty-three foot boat near Tahiti.
>
> ... The island has a high hill with forest to the water's edge and one beautiful sheltered sandy beach, without doubt the one on which Bligh and his starving men landed.
>
> We swam in the lagoon and then lay on the beach trying to recapture in imagination what had been the feeling of those men as they saw the aborigines in all their war paint, shouting and waving their spears only a short distance away, and the dread misgivings in each heart as they launched their tiny boat once more and sailed off to what must have seemed certain death.[16]

It is no coincidence that Flynn's first film, made by Australian film-maker Charles Chauvel, is *In the Wake of the Bounty*. It may also be the case that when Flynn lived in Jamaica in the latter part of his life he was still exploring this Bounty connection, remembering Midshipman Young's West Indian heritage.

Flynn's sense of identification as a rebel sailor/buccaneer was also significant. On Hinchinbrook Island he met a man called Forsythe: 'His exploits and his name were almost legendary in New Guinea and this in a land where every man [including Flynn] is something of a buccaneer himself'.[17]

Flynn further writes that 'Forsythe befitted the conception of your modern buccaneer. He was tall, lithely built and ... [had] an exceedingly handsome face ... [and] his manner was cultured and pleasant'.[18] Flynn could have been describing himself ... and probably was. It was this romanticised notion of pirate that Flynn would project throughout his life and acting career; the movie role that made him a star was as the suave doctor turned pirate, *Captain Blood*, based on Rafael Sabatini's novel. In this novel, *The Chronicles of Captain Blood*, the pirate hero of the title is unexpectedly dapper, elegant and sophisticated:

> Easterling was almost disconcerted, so different was the man's appearance from anything that he could have imagined. And now this singular escaped convict was bowing with the grace of a courtier ...
>
> Mr Blood began to speak. He had a pleasant voice whose metallic quality was softened by a drawling Irish accent.[19]

Although Flynn was not Irish, his name and background on his father's side were. This automatically sets Blood and Flynn apart from the English mariners. When Flynn wrote *Beam Ends*, he had created for himself an imaginary childhood in Ireland. Why would Flynn deliberately alter the facts about his childhood in Australia/England in an ostensibly factual book? Clearly, Flynn was either seeking some kind of literary effect, aiming to promote a certain image of himself, or both. When Flynn revised his own history, was he thinking of Captain Blood's Irish background? All that can be known is that Flynn's decision to create an imaginary Irish childhhod was a conscious one, and done for a reason.

Flynn also writes in *My Wicked, Wicked Ways* of his childhood that 'Robinson Crusoe was a figure in our folk lives, and we read *Two Years Before the Mast*'.[20] Flynn's mention of Daniel Defoe's novel is significant. Like *The Bounty*, Defoe's book *The Life and Adventures of Robinson Crusoe*[21] also involves the sea, beachcombing and mutineering. Crusoe's opportunity for escape from his island comes in the form of a band of sailors and mutineers. The mutineers take an English ship to Crusoe's island. Ultimately, some of them choose to stay on the island, rather than returning to England to hang as mutineers. It is not difficult to conceive of Flynn making connections in his imagination between Defoe's story and the story of *The Bounty*.

Both Crusoe and Flynn became beachcombers. Crusoe was, of necessity, a self-disciplined and resourceful beachcomber, whereas Flynn was a self-destructive one. Yet even towards the end of his life, when Flynn appeared to be at his lowest point, perhaps he was sustained by romantic notions of the Robinson Crusoe archetype. In *My Wicked, Wicked Ways*, Flynn portrays himself as an urban beachcomber, who lived from 1953–1956 on his schooner, the *Zaca*, at

Palma de Majorca, Spain. He drank 'steadily, daily—about a fifth of vodka a day, maybe more'[22] and 'went around with a stubble beard and didn't give a damn'.[23] Flynn also displays his use of metaphor by suggesting that he himself has been cast up on the beach, just like Crusoe. Examples of this are 'I lived the life of a guy who is washed up',[24] 'I believe I was washed up, finished',[25] 'Now I was just living, drifting',[26] 'I drifted',[27] and 'He's washed up, they said'.[28]

In his early twenties in New Guinea, Flynn was a correspondent for Sydney's *The Bulletin* between 1931 and 1932. During this time, Flynn wrote seven sporadic articles for *The Bulletin,* with the first appearing on December 2, 1931 and the last appearing on October 5, 1932. He wrote under the *nom de plume* of Laloki, just as other contributors to the Aboriginalities section of *The Bulletin* used *noms de plume*. This 'Aboriginalities' appeared to be a forum for supposedly humorous articles and illustrations, stereotyping people such as Irish Catholics and Indigenous Australians.[29] Flynn's articles in Aboriginalities do not always portray the New Guinea natives in a positive light, particularly Flynn's description of the Goiaribari: 'The Goiaribari people are by far the lowest tribe I have ever come across'.[30] Yet, given the context of the rest of Aboriginalities, Flynn's articles seem almost objectively neutral in comparison. Furthermore, in *Beam Ends*, Flynn compares the Goiaribari with another tribe, the Vialalla River men, whom he describes as 'people of the highest moral standards and fine and brave in their spirit'.[31] By the standards of the time, Flynn's perspective could even be seen as progressive.

Perhaps through laziness on Flynn's part, or perhaps through prudent creative decision-making, two of these *Bulletin* articles were eventually incorporated into *Beam Ends*, Flynn's first book. Author John Hammond Moore writes that 'It is quite apparent that, when putting his first book together a few years later, he dusted off those old clippings and adapted them to his immediate needs'.[32] *Beam Ends* was published in 1937 by Cassell in Australia and Great Britain and by Longmans, Green in America. It recounts Flynn's travels as a young man, from Sydney Harbour to New Guinea, along the east coast of Australia on the *Sirocco*. Moore also writes that *Beam Ends* was reviewed favourably in important newspapers:

> The Melbourne *Argus* (11 September, 1937) found it 'an entertaining narrative', while the *New York Times* (28 March, 1937) called the tale 'a wild one'. The *Times* noted that although much of the voyage was spent 'in merry exploits at ports of call along the Australian coast, almost every hour at sea was hair raising'.[33]

Intriguingly, the first scene from Flynn's first book begins in Port Adelaide, with the arresting opening sentence, 'Throw it down on top of the bastard!'[34]

Although this could have been his obituary, Flynn was referring to the third mate (on top of the ship the *Baltimore*) heaping coal dust on him from a great height. This was after he and his mate The Dook had 'played the roles of fire-men on shore leave only too well'[35] by returning to the ship drunk. The Dook, by the way, was the nickname for Trelawny Adams. In a historical allusion that seems more the result of Flynn's imagination than real coincidence, Flynn's ancestor Edward Young was a close friend (on Pitcairn Island) and fellow crewmember on *The Bounty* of another person with the surname of Adams, John Adams.[36] Yet this was, in fact, a real coincidence. It is just one of the many instances in which the boundaries between fact and fiction in Flynn's writing overlap.

Of Flynn's three books, *Beam Ends* is the one that most reveals Flynn's passion for and specialist knowledge of boats and sailing. A book based on an actual voyage Flynn took with three mates and which, like many sailing books, uses boating terms, could seem self-indulgent and elitist. Yet the book is engrossing, and Flynn's decision to include improbable and entertaining anecdotes from both land and sea is a shrewd one, and prevents the book from being one just for those in the know.

Whether the yarns from *Beam Ends* are true or not becomes irrelevant. At times, readers may know or sense that Flynn is romancing. For example, he makes several references to his former life in Ireland, but Flynn was not Irish: he was Tasmanian. Flynn's Hollywood publicists indicated that he was Tasmanian, yet no-one believed him. Flynn writes in *My Wicked, Wicked Ways*:

> Nor did they believe that I came from Tasmania, Australia and New Guinea. No one believed anything else I ever said about my life and adventures in that part of the world.[37]

This was more about people's ironic reluctance to believe a truth stranger than fiction than about a perception that Flynn was a liar. For at this stage, the public had no particular reason to accuse Flynn of being a liar.

Some of Flynn's anecdotes in *Beam Ends* also seem so wild as to beggar belief. When waxing lyrical about the splendours of the Great Barrier Reef, Flynn provides an amazing account of riding turtles and even racing them:

> But we had many a race. You get on the female's back and hold her at front and rear. She puts down her head and starts for the waters of the lagoon. On the beach the going is easy, but once your mount enters the water, it is a different matter. At first you find you have to let go and rise to the surface as soon as she dives, but after a while you learn the knack of holding your steed's head up in a certain way so that she is unable to dive, and then comes the real fun of turtle riding. The excited

animals swim about the surface of the lagoon clumsily trying to unseat you and you can steer in any direction you wish.[38]

This passage is interesting to focus on, for it has man, arguably most evolved of all species, going from land back into the sea astride a prehistoric animal. The implication of mastering a *lower* species is there, perhaps deliberately, as Flynn was the son of a biologist and a Darwinian. This may have held appeal to an alpha male like Errol Flynn.

The turtle riding anecdote also brings to mind the film *Pirates of the Caribbean,* in which pirate Captain Jack Sparrow reports escaping from a desert island by roping together a couple of sea turtles and making a raft out of them. Sparrow claims that he used human hair from his own back as rope.[39] This suggests that Sparrow is a highly imaginative lateral thinker, who is happy to exaggerate the truth to promote his own legend. These traits are also ones Flynn portrayed in his life, films and writing. We know when we see the pirate Errol Flynn travel down the length of a ship's sail by holding onto a sword that slowly tears the canvas that it is improbable, yet this is the kind of lie many viewers/readers enjoy as a form of escapism. In many of the James Bond films, the same occurs, where we as viewers actively participate in enjoying ridiculous and improbable action scenes unfold. Perhaps the appeal of these characters is that when everyone else is saying that it is all over and there is nothing more to do, these people find a way to negate the truth. We know we are being lied to, but it does not matter. Ironically, Flynn's turtle riding probably did happen, for turtle riding does indeed take place off the Queensland coast.

Flynn's unreliable memoirs create a sense in the mind of the reader of not knowing what to believe, but such romance invests the words with much of their power. For example, in *Beam Ends*, Flynn describes in detail a dinner party he and his *Sirocco* crewmates went to at Tavai, a New Guinea trading station. As he does elsewhere in *Beam Ends*, Flynn refers to the Ireland of his childhood, relating his host Goodyear's home to it: 'It quite took me back to Ireland for a moment'.[40] However, Flynn was not Irish and never lived in Ireland; this fabricated detail provides a context for the dinner party anecdote: we wonder how much of the anecdote is true. According to Flynn, at the dinner table, Goodyear drops his false teeth into a glass of water, shoots a native in the buttocks with a revolver and has his dinner guests served a wallaby in a pot, 'complete with fur, eyes and teeth'.[41] Whether this story is true or not remains a mystery, although Goodyear had his doubts, trying unsuccessfully to sue Flynn after the publication of *Beam Ends*. John Hammond Moore writes that according to 'Allen Innes, the Salamua hotel and store keeper, Goodyear was ... furious'[42] about Flynn's depiction of him in *Beam Ends*, but gave up on trying to sue Flynn 'because of international complications'.[43]

The boundaries between fiction and non-fiction are still often debated in Australia, which is just one of the reasons why Flynn's writing merits closer scrutiny. As the recent controversy surrounding Kate Grenville's book *The Secret River* has shown, the boundaries between fact and fiction in writing become political and engender passionate responses. Grenville was accused of presenting her fiction as history, a claim she vehemently denied. She also denied the claims (from such people as Inga Clendinnen) that she inferred historical fiction is superior to factual historical writing.[44] To even draw clear distinctions between these two categories is problematic. Donna Lee Brian writes in TEXT that 'very little fiction is not based on some wider reality and it has long been accepted that non-fiction can never be "pure" fact'.[45] With Flynn's best writing, we are very aware that we are reading an amalgam of fact and fiction, but often do not quite know which is which. This creates a sense of unpredictability, which can work to great effect in writing. It is comparable to discovering round characters in any kind of story, for knowing both the characters' good traits and bad traits, we can not always anticipate which trait will emerge and the characters are therefore unpredictable.

In *Beam Ends*, Flynn's autobiographical persona is not as round as it is in *My Wicked, Wicked Ways*, written twenty years later. In *Beam Ends*, Flynn refers to the conduct and personalities of his three shipmates, but he largely portrays himself as a neutral observer. He projects different aspects of himself onto the other crew members, particularly The Dook and Rex. This sophisticated technique is complicated by the fact that these other crew members were actual people who undertook the journey on the *Sirocco* with Flynn. The Dook is a Cambridge graduate, who is scholarly, dignified and cerebral (just as Flynn could be). The Dook is presumably a deliberate mispronunciation of The Duke; Flynn's nickname in real life was The Baron. Rex, however, is a name given to dogs, and Rex seems to embody all the animal urges. Significantly, Rex is frequently mentioned in connection with animal terms. Flynn says to Rex after he tried to seduce a female rower, 'Just tried a bit of gorilla stuff on Bow, eh?'[46] Other comments directed to Rex include, 'Don't go, you swines!'[47] and 'No, luckily I don't happen to be a promiscuous animal like you'.

Some of Flynn's 'I just work here' neutrality seems quite ludicrous with the benefit of hindsight, knowing what we do now about Flynn's predilections. For example, Flynn describes his voyage through Queensland's Whitsundays and arrival at 'a large low-lying island'[48] near Dent Island. Flynn and crew come to dine with a Mrs Wilson at her home on the island and are watched by her children (the only other inhabitants on the island). According to Flynn, Mrs. Wilson and all of the children were 'wild and scared'[49] and had never left the island. Lucy, the eldest daughter at seventeen, is being ogled not by Flynn, but inevitably, by Rex:

> Rex was looking at her in a trance, with eyes popping, so I gave him a kick under the table that lifted him out of his chair.
> 'Lay off, Casanova!' I hissed.[50]

Ultimately, Flynn and Lucy become mutually smitten:

> Then one day we went to where a shimmering mountain stream emptied in a cool, clear rock pool and we swam in it. Unashamed and laughing she flung her clothes from her and plunged in. For her there was no question of modesty—she just knew nothing of such things. I stood on the bank, tortured, knowing that it was no use; knowing how childlike innocence disarms and that for me there could be no plucking of the lotus.[51]

This is a dubiously coy response from the man who allegedly inspired the simile, 'In like Flynn'.

In a similar vein, Flynn and Rex take The Dook to a Turkish bath in Brisbane. In Flynn's account, Flynn smokes a cigarette while Rose and four other prostitutes try to have their way with the horrified Dook. Flynn observes but does not partake. By the time Flynn wrote *My Wicked, Wicked Ways* he had become so much the participant that he spoke freely of his adventures in bordellos, and that the way to discover the essence of a country was to visit its brothels. Again, this startling honesty nestles alongside Flynn's trademark imaginative escapades and makes this book a compelling read. By the end of his life, Flynn was confident enough to portray himself as a blackguard, and say in completely unapologetic terms, *This is me!*[52] Max Harris described this book as 'an autobiographical classic. It should be unashamedly part of our essential national literature. Which it isn't'.[53]

When Flynn thought his career and his life were all but over, between 1953 and 1956, he lived on his schooner, the *Zaca*, at Palma de Majorca, Spain. Here he sailed, skin-dived, and even changed nappies for his 'lovely little daughter Arnella'.[54] Born in 1952, Arnella was Flynn's fourth daughter. Her mother was Patrice Wymore, Flynn's third wife. Flynn describes his love of diving during this period as such:

> Next to this sport all others are childish: the thrills of baseball, tennis, football, golf, they are nothing compared with being a hundred feet below, with a great stone

sea wall about you, the sunlight shining down through the green illuminating an underwater seascape, and the fish moving by.

The lure of the sea, in all its forms, is probably the strongest urge in me. It is a silent world. I am always fascinated, as one is with a favourite poem. It is the indescribable beauty down there that makes you want to go to it and hold it. It is an exercise in quick reflexes. Your mind sharpens, it snaps, it works like an automatic pistol.[55]

Why else did Flynn love the sea so much? Part of the appeal seems to be Flynn's love of natural scenery. In *Beam Ends* he writes about the Passage of Hinchinbrook Island:

Inside it was as beautiful as the journey through the Whitsundays. ... Sitting out on the bowsprit and looking down into the sheltered waters ahead, the clear reflections of the ship and the many emerald-like islets, thick with tropical fruit trees and palms, nestling about larger islands, made the passage a veritable paradise.[56]

This extract, along with others from *Beam Ends,* reveals that Flynn had an aesthetic sensitivity to the beauty of nature, a beauty that could sometimes only be viewed from the perspective of beyond the coastline. It conjures stereotypes of the natural beauty of the Pacific islands, promoted by a writer such as Herman Melville in *Typee,* in which the narrator also appreciates the natural beauty around him:

Although I could not avoid yielding in a great measure to the general languor, still at times I contrived to shake off the spell, and to appreciate the beauty of the scene around me. The sky presented a clear expanse of the most delicate blue, except along the skirts of the horizon, where you might see a thin drapery of pale clouds which never varied their form or colour.[57]

Flynn's depiction of the beauty of nature is also reminiscent of the writing of R.M. Ballantyne in *The Coral Island,* in which he promulgates the stereotype of the islands being the stuff of paradise:

The island on which we stood was hilly, and covered almost everywhere with the most beautiful and richly coloured trees, bushes, and shrubs, none of which I knew the names of at that time—except, indeed, the cocoa-nut palms, which I recognised at once from the many pictures that I had seen of them before I left home. A sandy beach of dazzling whiteness lined this bright-green shore, and upon it there fell a gentle ripple of the sea.[58]

Yet Flynn makes other references to the sea which have nothing to do with its serenity or beauty and show that Flynn can also see its ugly side. For example, when the *Sirocco* passes through Sydney Heads, Flynn describes the maelstrom:

I was soaked to the skin as the ship suddenly dived into the first large head swell. Another came on top of it, and we went under that one, too.

All attempts to make some hot coffee were hopeless. No sooner was the kerosene stove lit than a sea would come over and buckets of water pour through the leaking hatch to put it out. Besides you had to hold the pot on the stove. If you left it for a second it would be on the floor. Holding the pot on the stove meant staying in the galley and staying in the galley meant being horribly seasick, but the galley seemed to hold a soul-destroying variety of its own.[59]

Surprisingly perhaps, for someone with such a romantic imagination, Flynn sabotages notions of the sea that are too idyllic. In *Beam Ends* he writes:

Man against the sea! An old story, but who has been faced with its perils and not known his weakness? Or felt that utter hopelessness and despair against its fury?[60]

In response to a poem by Masefield, 'Sea Fever', which repeats the clause 'I must go down to the sea again'—and confirms Flynn's familiarity with literature about the sea—Flynn writes:

I am no 'born sailor' type who, as bodily discomfort increases, becomes proportionately louder in expressions of delight for the sea. When I am soaked to the skin and bone by 'wind like a whetted knife', my only thought is to get dry again as quickly as possible. When 'the grey dawn breaks on the sea's face' my first instinct is to get a cup of coffee into me, while should any 'laughing fellow rover' try to tell me a merry yarn before the grey dawn, he had better watch out—I will let out a loud cry and more than likely throw him over the side.[61]

Masefield also suffered from seasickness. So, although Flynn was undeniably drawn to the sea, he also had conflicting emotions about it. This is in keeping with paradoxical feelings about any kind of relationship, where one can simultaneously love someone and hate that person or aspects of that person. Also, the sea is ultimately mysterious, so why should our human response to it not be the same?

Beam Ends uses the literary device of a circular ending. As I mentioned, *Beam Ends* begins with Flynn and The Dook getting drunk in Port Adelaide. At the very end of the book, Flynn refers to the sad death in a cyclone of The Dook:

Kindly, lovable old Dook. His death was a tragedy that left me stunned and dazed for a long time. We all felt it deeply. He had been something more than a friend ...

The *Sirocco*'s bones and his are scattered over a coral reef in the South Seas, as are the bones of many a fine ship, but never of a finer man.[62]

The only problem with this poignant ending is that in reality, The Dook had not died at all, and went on to be a partner in Flynn's tobacco venture.

Flynn's second Book *Showdown*, is a novel set in New Guinea, and also features a captain of a boat, Captain Fabian. Although Stephen Knight writes of *Showdown* that 'the fluent technique might cause some surprise'[63] and a blurb in *New Guinea Images in Australian Literature* proclaims that 'Flynn's Father Kirshner was drawn with intelligence and human warmth',[64] as a novel it is not able to engage the dynamics between truth and fantasy that give so much of Flynn's writing its originality and power. For as readers, we expect a novel to be largely a fictional construction, even if it is based on elements of reality. Yet in Flynn's 'non-fiction' writing, we have little idea about what will be factual and what will be fictional, and this can create an exciting sense of anticipation and wonder.

There is either a coincidence or an interesting literary allusion in *Showdown* which (to my knowledge) has never been mentioned before. In real life, Flynn took a boat to explore the heart of the New Guinea darkness in the Sepik River, along with a tall Austrian man called Dr Erben. Erben's name became Swartz and then Koets in *My Wicked, Wicked Ways*. A prolific reader, Flynn would have been familiar with fellow sailor, writer and visitor to Australia,[65] Joseph Conrad, and his novella *Heart of Darkness*, featuring the tall German man named Kurtz, the object of the narrator Marlow's obsessive search for meaning.[66]

Sadly, Flynn's final film script *Cuban Rebel Girls* was appallingly written. Perhaps Flynn forgot what we can all forget at times: that we are better than our worst efforts. Although Flynn is generally overlooked as a writer, at his best he wrote clearly, simply and entertainingly. He was capable of sophisticated literary devices and word play and employed literary allusions. His writing is good and interesting enough to be re-examined today, both as a contribution to the body of maritime literature and in its own right. As the debate continues in Australia and elsewhere about what constitutes fiction and non-fiction, Flynn's work may provide some partial answers. His writing elicits complicated responses from readers, whose reception of the writing is altered by our perception of Flynn as a fabricator. Flynn has traditionally been judged and denounced as a liar. Hopefully, post-modernism has taught the world that the truth is complex and multi-faceted, and what is untrue for one person is true for another. Perhaps now is the time to look at Flynn's work without the yoke of self-righteousness and judgementalism. Moral issues aside, Flynn's licence with the truth helps to create an exciting sense of anticipation and curiosity.

Flynn had many transitory relationships with women in his life, but the one relationship he maintained throughout his lifetime was with the sea. He died within days of selling his last yacht, the *Zaca*. Perhaps a life without the sea was not worth living.

Notes

1 Errol Flynn, *Beam Ends* (New York: Buccaneer Books, 1975) 27.
2 Errol Flynn, *My Wicked, Wicked Ways* (Great Britain: William Heinemann Ltd, 1960) 21.
3 Flynn, *My Wicked, Wicked Ways* 132.
4 Flynn, *My Wicked, Wicked Ways* 126.
5 Flynn, *My Wicked, Wicked Ways* 138.
6 Don Norman, *Errol Flynn. The Tasmanian Story* (Hobart: W.N. Hurst and E.L. Metcalf, 1981)
7 Personal conversation with Don Norman, n.d.
8 Flynn, *My Wicked, Wicked Ways* 21-22.
9 Biographical entry from *Bright Sparcs*, accessed 6 December 2006 from <http://www.asap.unimelb.edu.au/bsparcs/biogs/P001056b.htm>.
10 Norman, *Errol Flynn* 57.
11 In the Mel Gibson/Anthony Hopkins film *The Bounty* (dir. Roger Donaldson, 1984), Bligh says to the mutineering Young before leaving the *Bounty*, 'You've not seen the last of me, Ned Young. Take my word for it'.
12 Flynn, *My Wicked, Wicked Ways* 21.
13 Flynn, *My Wicked, Wicked Ways* 21. Interestingly, although Flynn referred to his ancestor as Richmond Young, there was no such person on *The Bounty*. Flynn is actually referring to Midshipman Edward Young.
14 Errol Flynn, *My Wicked, Wicked Ways* 26.
15 *Mutiny on the HMAS Bounty*, accessed 11 July 2006 from <www.lareau.org/young.html>.
16 Flynn, *Beam Ends* 193-194.
17 Flynn, *Beam Ends* 155.
18 Flynn, *Beam Ends* 158.
19 Rafael Sabatini, *The Chronicles of Captain Blood* (London: Pan Books Ltd., 1963) 14.
20 Flynn, *My Wicked, Wicked Ways* 21.
21 Daniel Defoe, *The Life and Adventures of Robinson Crusoe* (London: Penguin Books, 1985).
22 Flynn, *My Wicked, Wicked Ways* 9.
23 Flynn, *My Wicked, Wicked Ways* 9-10.
24 Flynn, *My Wicked, Wicked Ways* 9.
25 Flynn, *My Wicked, Wicked Ways* 9.
26 Flynn, *My Wicked, Wicked Ways* 9.
27 Flynn, *My Wicked, Wicked Ways* 10.
28 Flynn, *My Wicked, Wicked Ways* 10.
29 For example, in one edition of Aboriginalities, an illustration portrays an Indigenous Australian woman slumped under a tree, holding a bottle in one hand and looking completely inebriated. The caption under this illustration reads, 'LU'BRA-CATED'. *The Bulletin*, December 2, 1931, 20.
30 *The Bulletin*, June 15, 1932, 20.
31 Flynn, *Beam Ends* 229.

32 John Hammond Moore, *The Young Errol – Flynn before Hollywood* (Sydney: Angus and Robertson Publishers, 1975) 73.

33 Moore, *The Young Errol* 61.

34 Flynn, *Beam Ends* 3.

35 Flynn, *Beam Ends* 7.

36 *Mutiny on the HMAS Bounty*, accessed 11 July 2006 from <www.lareau.org/adams.html>.

37 Flynn, *My Wicked, Wicked Ways* 87.

38 Flynn, *Beam Ends* 133-134.

39 *Hot Movie Quotes*, accessed 19 December 2006 from <http://www.hotmoviequotes.com/quotes/movies/pirates-of-the-caribbean/page_4.html>.

40 Flynn, *Beam Ends* 220.

41 Moore, *The Young Errol* 72.

42 Moore, *The Young Errol* 72.

43 Moore, *The Young Errol* 72.

44 Kate Grenville, 'History and Fiction' accessed 15 April 2008 from www.users.bigponmd.com/kgrenville/TSR/history and fiction.html.

45 Donna Lee Brian, 'The place where the real and the imagined coincides: an introduction to Australian creative non fiction', accessed 19 December 2006 from http://www.griffith.edu.au/school/art/text/speciss/issue1/intro.htm.

46 Flynn, *Beam Ends* 62.

47 Flynn, *Beam Ends* 60.

48 Flynn, *Beam Ends* 136.

49 Flynn, *Beam Ends* 137.

50 Flynn, *Beam Ends* 137.

51 Flynn, *Beam Ends* 138-139.

52 Although ironically, the book wasn't entirely 'This is me!' for Flynn had help in writing the book from Earl Conrad.

53 Max Harris, 'Errol Flynn – Last of the Great Charmers' in *The Larrikin Streak – Australian Writers Look at the Legend,* edited by Clem Gorman (Sydney: Pan Macmillan Publishers, 1990) 206. Max Harris was a colourful figure in his own right. He was one of Australia's most important literary figures. He was a key member of the Angry Penguins; he started the remaindered book concept in South Australia; he attracted world-wide publicity with his involvement in the Ern Malley hoax; he was a founder columnist for *The Australian* newspaper and 'was acknowledged as one of the greatest lyric poets Australia had produced'. He also was a self-described feminist. So, Ern Malley aside, endorsement of one's writing by such a luminary as Max Harris is impressive to say the least. *Ern Malley – The Official Website*, accessed 19 December 2006 from <http://www.ernmalley.com/max_harris.html>.

54 Flynn, *My Wicked, Wicked Ways* 8-9.

55 Flynn, *My Wicked, Wicked Ways* 353-354.

56 Flynn, *Beam Ends* 155.

57 Herman Melville, *Typee*, accessed 20 December 2006 from <http://www.bibliomania.com/0/0/36/1007/frameset.html>.

58 R.M. Ballantyne, *The Coral Island*, accessed 20 December 2006 from <http://www.athelstane.co.uk/ballanty/coralisl/coral04.htm>.

59 Flynn, *Beam Ends* 21-22.

60 Flynn, *Beam Ends* 211.

61 Flynn, *Beam Ends* 126.

62 Flynn, *Beam Ends* 240-241.

63 Stephen Knight, *Continent of Mystery – A Thematic History of Australian Crime Fiction* (Victoria: Melbourne University Press, 1997) 164.

64 Nigel Krauth, *New Guinea Images in Australian Literature* (St Lucia, Queensland : University of Queensland Press, 1982)172.

65 Joseph Conrad visited Australia in the early 1890s.

66 The publication of *Showdown* in 1946 predates Australian author Charlotte Jay's excursion into the jungles of Papua, which also alludes to Conrad's *Heart of Darkness*. Jay's book was first published in 1952.

Works cited

Ballantyne, R.M. *The Coral Island*, accessed 20 December 2006 from <http://www.athelstane.co.uk/ballanty/coralisl/coral04.htm>.

Brian, D. L. 'The place where the real and the imagined coincides: an introduction to Australian creative non-fiction', accessed 19 December 2006 from <http://www.griffith.edu.au/school/art/text/speciss/issue1/intro.htm>.

Bright Sparks, accessed 6 December 2006 from <http://www.asap.unimelb.edu.au/bsparcs/biogs/P001056b.htm>.

Defoe, D. *The Life and Adventures of Robinson Crusoe.* London: Penguin Books, 1985.

Ern Malley – The Official Website, accessed 19 December 2006 from <http://www.ernmalley.com/max_harris.html>.

Flynn, E. *Beam Ends.* New York: Buccaneer Books, 1975.

Flynn, E. *My Wicked, Wicked Ways.* Great Britain: William Heinemann Ltd, 1960.

Flynn, E. *Showdown.* Sydney: Invincible Press, 1946.

Gorman, C. (ed.) *The Larrikin Streak – Australian Writers Look at the Legend.* Sydney: Pan Macmillan Publishers, 1990.

Hot Movie Quotes, accessed 19 December 2006 from <http://www.hotmovie quotes.com/quotes/movies/pirates-of-the-caribbean/page_4.html>.

Knight, S. *Continent of Mystery – A Thematic History of Australian Crime Fiction.* Victoria: Melbourne University Press, 1997.

Norman, D. *Errol Flynn. The Tasmanian Story.* Hobart: W.N. Hurst and E.L. Metcalf, 1981.

Krauth, N. (ed.) *New Guinea Images in Australian Literature*. St Lucia, Queensland: University of Queensland Press, 1982.

Melville, H. *Typee*, accessed 20 December 2006 from <http://www.bibliomania.com/0/0/36/1007/frameset.html>.

Moore, J. *The Young Errol – Flynn before Hollywood*. Sydney: Angus and Robertson Publishers, 1975.

Mutiny on the HMAS Bounty, accessed 11 July 2006 from <www.lareau.org/young.html> and <www.lareau.org/adams.html>.

Sabatini, R. *The Chronicles of Captain Blood*. London: Pan Books Ltd., 1963.

The Bounty, dir. Roger Donaldson, Orion Pictures Corporation, 1984.

Some Versions of Coastal:
Thea Astley, Captain Simpson and
the North Queensland Coast

SUSAN SHERIDAN

In writing about Australia, the coast has incited far fewer and less influential imaginative flights than the interior. The 'enigma of the centre', especially the conviction that a great inland sea—or at least a river system—would be discovered in the continent's unknown interior, inspired the best-known journeys of exploration by white immigrants. This imagined centre becomes the repository of all hopes, the screen on which is projected all Utopian dreams. Even coastal exploration, says Paul Carter, was designed to solve this 'enigma of the centre'.[1] And yet we are an intensively urban population, and our cities are all on the coast of the continent. Most of us live in its 'five cities, like five teeming sores' where, in A.D. Hope's lines from the satirical poem, 'Australia', 'second-hand Europeans pullulate/Timidly on the edge of alien shores'.

Even though non-Indigenous Australians are now second-hand Asians, Africans and Arabs, as well as Europeans, we still have a 'propensity to cling to the edge'. And how timid this still sounds, when from the inland desert, that 'waste'—again in Hope's words—springs 'such savage and scarlet as no green hills dare'. Here, 'that waste' echoes T.S. Eliot's 'waste land' as the place of spiritual journeying and discovery, the dry space of truth, the 'Arabian desert of the human mind' from which prophets might come. The ancient continent, dry like 'a woman beyond her change of life' has, by this final twist of Hope's poem, become the repository of truth.[2]

A 'propensity to cling to the edge' implies fear or inability to confront such truth, and such harshness. Yet architect Philip Drew, who uses this phrase in his book, *The Coast Dwellers* (1994), reflects on the strangeness of this obsession with the inland as a mythical region in the Australian imagination:

> We are in effect saying that where we live, coastal Australia, is less important to our identity than another part of the country where few people live ... Displacement has become so ingrained that we automatically look somewhere other than where we actually are for a symbolic axis in our lives.[3]

114

Here he alludes to the way that from early days the colony depended for its material and cultural resources on an external centre; such displacement continues to the present day in the desire to seek significance in an inland that is almost as remote as England was.[4] Yet 'our historical experience developed on the periphery—on the edge', Drew argues, and in fact we have not just one but 'a number of centres, each widely distributed around this edge'. Drew likens this to 'a kind of turned–inside–out diffuse centre distributed around the rim; a linear identity based on the coast'.[5]

Drew's idea of the distributed centre, linear identity based on the coast, is only one of the most recent challenges to the dominant account of the centre-periphery, inland-edge metaphor. Christina Stead, for one, imaged Sydney as a port city, positioned as a centre of world trade routes and looking outwards onto the Pacific and the world (not just England), inhabited by immigrants who were born travellers.[6] In this image the sea, not the in-land, is the expanse to which we look out. It is—or was—what links us with the rest of the world.[7]

Edge, then, might be positive, not negative. It might even attain its own difference; after all, there can be no centre without a margin, no circle without a circumference, no axle without a wheel rim. When the centre-margin metaphor is deconstructed, the first move is to reverse the usual hierarchy of value. Only when this has been done can we begin to shift the opposition from its moorings. The periphery can be conceived as the thing itself, rather than a mere margin. The coast can come into its own as a space, rather than the edge of a larger space in which significance resides, or is sought.

Here we have the makings of 'the coastal' as trope and perhaps even as literary mode or genre. My title, 'Some Versions of Coastal' is meant to evoke William Empson's book, *Some Versions of Pastoral*, where he explored variant uses of the pastoral as a space signifying simplicity, even innocence, to be contrasted with the complexities, sometimes the immorality, of the court or the city—or a space in which to parallel and sometimes parody an heroic main plot. In white Australian mythology, the inland has served as the place of pastoral, remote from cities and towns and potentially the place of spiritual discovery and renewal. In this mythology, as we see in Hope's poem, the coast represents negative qualities, and not only because it seems a mere edge or margin beyond which we dare not venture. In Hope's poem, the coast represents urban civilisation, the inland desert being opposed to 'the lush jungle of modern thought' inhabited by 'civilised apes' chattering on. This metaphor of the lush jungle carries over into a horror of fertility, as the migrant settler population 'pullulates' on the shoreline.

With this distinctly heroic version of bush or desert pastoral dominant in

Australian art, there has been little use of pastoral as parody, as Empson characterises the pastoral scenes in Shakespeare in his chapter, 'Double Plots'—though perhaps it could be said that 'Dad and Dave' enacts that version of pastoral.[8] Thea Astley, more recently, might be seen as the great exponent of anti-heroic pastoral; a major impetus of her stories is the deflation of the heroic settler ideal, whether explorers or pioneers. Her fiction is set in suburbs and small towns, mostly on the Queensland coastal fringe, so it would be more accurate to describe her as an exemplary practitioner of the Australian *'coastal'* mode of writing. The 'coastal', then, is set, not in nature—it is not a landscape, nor even a seascape—but in all those settler-populated non-urban spaces on the continental edge.

But the way she understands this 'coastal' is crucial. It isn't just the beach, the shoreline. The topography of her fiction is specific to North Queensland. It includes sea coast, mountain range and 'claypan' or rainshadow country—which is inland, but not nearly so geographically remote as the 'dead centre'. For Astley, the geographically and spiritually close relationship between these three strata is the whole point, as her two final novels demonstrate. *The Multiple Effects of Rainshadow* begins by dramatising an incident that actually happened on Palm Island in the 1920s, when the white supervisor of the mission went berserk and murdered his own children. He was shot and accidentally killed by an Indigenous man, who was eventually cleared on a charge of murder. The second half of the book—like most of Astley's later works, a series of stories each focusing on a different character—follows the later lives of those who were present. The title invokes the rainshadow effect of a coastal mountain range—that is, the dry conditions produced as the range acts as a barrier, preventing rainclouds from crossing over from the coast to the inland side. Metaphorically, the spiritual rainshadow or drought resulting from the cataclysmic earlier event continues to blight the lives of all the characters, from Indigenous Manny Cooktown and his son Normie to former schoolteacher Vine and his son Matthew, who returns to the island in the vain hope that he can do something to ease the plight of the Aboriginal people there.

Astley's final novel, *Drylands*, traces the decline of the small town of that name. It is located in rainshadow country: 'claypan, arid plain, perhaps, a flattish hinterland where the low Divide moves ever backwards as you chase the paddock grasses, wire fences, switching from verdure to an ochreous sheep-munch'.[9] It is a town to escape to, as the narrator, Janet Deakin, did when she left her single life in the city and came there to live with her husband, who has since died. Or maybe, she thinks now, 'to run from'—and by the end of the novel she is more than ready to run. The anonymity of this country also appeals to another character, the corporate whistle blower who takes on the identity of 'Franzi Massig' to escape his pursuers. He too sees it as a place to 'go to earth', a 'funk hole', in the middle of 'no man's land ... the cultivated *terra nullius* of our founding fathers, a desolation of low hills ... '[10] Here, the rainshadow country takes on specific political significance; it is a mere residue of white pioneering days, this para-doxically 'cultivated *terra nullius* of our founding fathers,' an unlovely landscape, inhabited by unlovely folk who prey on each other. A parodic pastoral, where country life may be simpler than the city, but it is equally brutal. Violence is the theme of all the stories in *Drylands*, ranging from the verbal sneers that Janet suffers, through harassment and property destruction to domestic violence and attempted rape. One by one the victims flee the town and as Drylands dwindles to a ghost town, in the end Janet too, her shop and writing table trashed, joins the other escapees. Only Bennie, the Indigenous man whose birth country it is, stays on.

Where do they go, these escapees from the inland heartland of the settler founding fathers? There is an alternative Australia, along the lush tropical coast. The necessary condition of rainshadow country, of course, is the excessive rain-fall on the windward side of the mountain range. Geographically speaking, in North Queensland this results in luxuriant rainforests and wide rivers flowing into the sea. Metaphorically speaking, the lush, tropical coastal strip is everything the rainshadow country is not—it is the place that people fleeing from Drylands want to escape to; it bears their images of paradise. The freedom and spaciousness of escape, the beauty of the coast, act as a counterweight to imprisonment in Drylands' heat, shabby small rooms, noisy pub, failing farms. But these images occupy only fleeting moments in the book's time frame: they may be only dreams. Janet, the last to leave, resolves to hit the coast in search of an isolated house she had once seen 'on the edge of a coastal lagoon somewhere north of Brisbane', its name painted on a board, 'Bateau Ivre'.[11] Rimbaud's drunken boat is a quirky image of paradise. The novelist might evoke it, but she will not go there.

The relationship between the coast and the dry hinterland constitutes Ast-ley's most recent metaphor for what angered her, and what, therefore, drove her art. The 'multiple effects of rainshadow' constitute the emotional and spiritual drylands suffered by its human inhabitants. They are separated from the para-disal tropical coast by the ranges, the Great Divide, just as Adam and Eve were driven out of the Garden of Eden to live in its rainshadow, in the fallen world. In *Drylands*, both cruelty and abjection, both the male perpetrators of violence and their feminised victims, are manifestations of this rainshadow state of being. At the level of contemporary social critique, the metaphor suggests that the rapidly depopulating rainshadow country, that 'cultivated *terra nullius*', is a disowned by-product of the material wealth of settler Australia, the 'lucky country' on the eve of the twenty-first century.[12] And—closer to the earlier novel, *The Multiple Effects of Rainshadow*—the metaphor can also signify the destructive inheritance of that originary act of violence against the Indigenous people of the land, which condemns both settler and Indigenous Australians to live in its rainshadow.

Ross Gibson, in his *Seven Versions of an Australian Badland*, presents a contemporary Queensland haunted by its bloody past, including acts of 'dispersal' of Indigenous people. In this political context he describes the literal rainshadow effect as intrinsic to the 'badlands' that is his particular geographical subject. Travellers going south from Mackay, he writes, driving up the wooded range and over the crest, 'dropped westerly into dusty air. Gone now the iodine tang of the sea-breeze that had followed them up the gradient'. Then, with 'the coastal plain behind them, they etched a line through the flatland rain-shadow while a stingy wind drifted in from the outback mining country'.[13]

In this metaphysical topography of coast and hinterland, the one cannot exist without the other—a truly reciprocal binary opposition, of suffering and longing. Their proximity is precisely the point. As she put it at the end of the essay, 'Being a Queenslander', claypan and coast, the ugly and the beautiful are 'so essential and complementary to each other in this place that they become one and the same'.[14]

If Astley's white characters look longingly outwards from claypan to coastline and the sea, my second practitioner of the coastal mode is at home on the sea. Indeed, he regards the land with some suspicion. This is Thomas Beckford Simpson—incidentally my great great grandfather—a ship's captain from Sydney.[15] He left several accounts of his voyages, mostly trading sandalwood, but some were government commissions.[16] On one of these he was commissioned by the New South Wales government in 1849 to sail his brig, the *Freak*, along the coast of Cape York Peninsula and search for traces of the expedition led by Edmund Kennedy, which had failed disastrously earlier that year. A long extract from the private log of the *Freak* recounts this journey, on which he was accompanied by 'the native Jackey Jackey'.[17]

Kennedy's was one of the iconic failed exploratory expeditions, comparable to Leichhardt's or Burke and Wills—except in this case there were several survivors: two of the white men who stayed behind at Weymouth Bay, too ill to continue, and the Indigenous man known as Jackey Jackey, who had accompanied Kennedy until his death just short of his goal at Cape York. The expedition's purpose was to explore the country between Rockingham Bay and the tip of the Cape, retracing the steps of the lost Ludwig Leichhardt, whose journal Kennedy took with him. It was a well-equipped expedition: 13 men, 28 horses, 3 carts and a flock of 100 sheep. Yet a series of disasters took the lives of all the live-stock and all but three of the men. Jackey Jackey—an Indigenous man from the Singleton area north-west of Sydney whose name was Galmarra—was rescued and brought back to Sydney.[18] There he told the sorry tale of how Kennedy was speared by local Yadhaigana men, who had been shadowing them for days, and died in his arms. Jackey buried the body and completed the journey. This was the basis for the iconic status of 'Jackey Jackey' as the faithful Indigenous servant. The other feature of the Kennedy story that gained iconic status is the explorer killed by hostile natives; Indigenous oral histories, however, claim that Kennedy and Jackey fired their guns to scare off the local men, and killed some of them, so the spearing of Kennedy was done in retribution.[19]

Beckford Simpson's log recounting that journey along the north Queensland coast provides a counter-example to Astley's coastal writing in several respects. Firstly, as an explorer story, it reiterates the tragic end of a famous failed expedition, and features Jackey Jackey as the iconic faithful native retainer in contrast to the treacherous locals who speared Kennedy. Secondly, the log represents the voice of a mariner, a man of action sent to investigate the facts, not an ironic observer dramatising human folly and cruelty. Thirdly, for the mariner, the sea is his familiar territory; sailing close to the coast is perilous—tropical storms, unreliable charts, the danger of running aground—and shore expeditions among natives are positively dangerous.

The mariner's view of the land can be deceptive, and indeed it could be said that the first disaster to befall Kennedy's party was that they chose to depart on their overland journey to the tip of Cape York Peninsula from Rockingham Bay (just north of Palm Island). This spot had been designated by Captain James Cook in 1770 as 'well sheltered and afford[ing] good anchorage', although he had not landed there to verify this impression. The anchorage was good, but the terrain behind the sandy beach where the expedition landed proved to be almost impenetrable, and so they had to travel southwest and laboriously cross three wide coastal rivers in their search for 'a gap in the high steep wall that edged the tableland'. By the time they found such a pass and resumed their northward journey, it had taken them over ten weeks merely to reach the Tully Falls, almost directly opposite the headland near their starting point.[20] The absurdist dimension of this story hardly needs underlining.

However, our mariner Beckford Simpson is more circumspect, and carefully investigates everything before making decisions. Two weeks south of the *Freak's* first destination, Weymouth Bay—where Kennedy had left behind the bulk of his party because they were too sick to travel further—Jackey and his companions point out some men waving at them from North Percy Island ('Jackey firmly asserted they were "white fellow", he knew them by their walk'). Simpson takes the men on board the *Freak*, but his suspicions are roused by their equivocating about the presence of a third member of their party. This man is found by the crew, near death. Simpson takes down the survivors' stories and compares them for inconsistencies. He concludes pretty quickly that 'they are not what they represent themselves to be', and are probably escaped convicts; indeed, 'from the fact of there being a purple mark on the deceased's throat, I have reason to fear there has been some foul work going on'.[21]

When they reach Weymouth Bay (north of Lockhart River), Simpson proceeds with his melancholy task. Finding the remains of Wall and Niblet, the last of the men to have died there and not been buried, he takes their bones back to the ship for later burial at Port Albany.[22] His men find a variety of things left by the party, including 'a portion of Leichhardt's journey overland'—apparently Kennedy took this as guidance in his journey. Simpson notes: 'I was rather surprised to find some cabbage-palm trees (Livistania) growing in the vicinity of the camp; the tops are very nutritious, and would have been very desirable for men in a starving state, had they been aware of it'.[23] The implicit criticism is unmistakable: the heroic explorers were incompetent natural scientists.

Simpson's own narrative is marked by its careful noting of botanical and geographical features of the land, as well as his mariner's observations of weather, tides and anchorages. He and his crew undertake a painstaking search for remains of the expedition at several places along the coast, and he forensically weighs up the evidence that these can yield. When they explore the Escape River area where Kennedy died, Simpson meticulously records all the sites identified by Jackey and the material proofs of his story that they find—remnants of a sextant, a compass, broken spears and so on. It seems to have been an unstated purpose of the expedition to confirm the truth of Jackey's account. Yet Simpson observes Jackey equally closely, recording that:

> poor Jackey was very quiet, but felt, and felt deeply, during the day. When pointing out the spot where Mr K died, I saw tears in his eyes, and no one could be more indefatigable in searching for the remains.
>
> He reports with obvious sympathy that his 'feelings against the natives were very bitter, and had any of them made their appearance at the time, I could hardly have prevented him from shooting them'.[24]

However, Simpson depends on Jackey's guidance to such landing places and accepts his advice about what is achievable and what is not. At Shelbourne Bay the captain 'consults' him about going to the inland camp where he and Kennedy had left the last three men, but Jackey advises against it, so 'I therefore considered all that we could do would be to thoroughly examine the coast with the whale-boat, close in shore, and the brig as near as she prudently could approach'.[25] At Albany Bay, Jackey again advises against making an overland trek to find the last stash of Kennedy's papers that he had hidden in a tree. Simpson seems only too happy to take this advice and stay on the coast.[26]

There is an interestingly reciprocal relationship between the two men, but also potential for conflict. Simpson wants to encounter the local 'natives' in order to get news of the lost men, but when a group of thirty of them appear, shaking hands with the ship's officer and his men and giving them water, 'Jackey at first thought he recognised the native who escaped from the "Ariel" [who, he claimed, has speared Kennedy] among them; he got a little excited and wanted to shoot him'.[27] On several occasions Simpson reports having to restrain Jacky when he wanted to shoot the local 'blacks' (as he calls them in his own narrative).

The anomalous position that Jackey occupied, however, is not commented upon. For example, the search party at one point finds 'a note book that Jackey had been drawing sketches in'.[28] Who was this man, who sketched in a note-book like the other 'explorers', and like them rode a horse and carried a gun? He would have had no clan loyalty to the locals—as Simpson reports him, he would have preferred to take his revenge against those who had speared him as well as Kennedy. His expressions of affection and grief were approvingly and sympathetically noted by his supervisor. On the occasion of the burial of Wall and Niblet 'poor Jackey was much affected, and could not refrain from tears'.[29] Simpson concludes his account with the following character reference:

> I cannot close my extracts without mentioning the exemplary conduct of Jackey Jackey. Since he came on board I have always found him quiet, obliging, and very respectful; when on shore he was very attentive, nothing could abstract him from his object; the sagacity and knowledge he displayed in travelling the trackless wilderness was astonishing; when he found the places he went in search of he was never flushed with success, but invariably maintained his quiet, unobtrusive behaviour; he was much concerned at not being able to find the remains of his late unfortunate master, to whom he was sincerely attached ...[30]

Simpson and Jackey shared several qualities: a similar wariness about the hinterland and its 'trackless wilderness' (not trackless for Jackey but not his own country, either), as well as a comparably 'attentive' pursuit of his objectives and to the detail of places and things. The mariner knows the sea as the 'native' knows the land. Together they travelled in the wake of the mythic failed hero, Kennedy, picking up the pieces. Yet in doing so, they also contributed to the secondary myth of the faithful native servant.[31]

These two 'versions of coastal' take different perspectives on the edge, the one looking longingly out from land to sea, the other looking apprehensively in from sea to land. What they share is an acute sense of this far North coast as the extremity of 'civilisation'. The last note in Simpson's journal records his satisfaction that they were able to capture the horse that the *Ariel* had left at Albany Island, to take it back south on board the *Freak*. For Jackey, too, it is the end point: 'I knew it was Cape York because the sand did not go on further'. When the 'blacks' reappear he feels really trapped, and wildly cooees to the boat, 'murry murry glad when the boat came for me'.[32] For Astley, Cape York is the 'vanishing point' for those of her characters who want to lose themselves, like Franzi from *Drylands*.[33] At the end of *It's Raining in Mango: Pictures from the Family Album*, Astley has Reever Laffey set off travelling north as far as he can go.[34]

However, Astley is, as always, caustic about the Great Explorer tradition. When Reever remarks that he'd like to take his Indigenous friend, Billy Mumbler, with him, his mate Molloy laughs:

> 'Doing an early explorer, eh? A Kennedy complete with Jacky-Jacky ...', and adds discouragingly, 'You've got a hope. He's into Stevie Wonder plaits and sharp cool-dude clothes these days'.[35]

Billy is not, in other words, a candidate for the iconic role of the faithful Indigenous servant—although perhaps his pleasure in 1980s popular culture brings him somewhat closer to Jackey Jackey's use of the whitefella accoutrements of horse, gun, pocketknife and sketchbook.[36]

For neither the white men nor their Indigenous friends is the far north their country. This return to the contradictions of 'civilisation' and the inescapable ties of belonging to place marks the classic Astley 'version of coastal'. Set in the towns and suburbs of the continental edge, her coastal writing incorporates Indigenous-settler relations as central, and always troubled. It entertains dreams of escape but savagely undercuts their illusions. Astley's Queensland coast is not exceptional but metaphorically represents post-colonial Australia. Her fiction, above all, could be said to establish the 'coastal' as a literary mode to contest the dominance of the pastoral in Australian writing.

Notes

1   Paul Carter, *Living in a New Country: History, Travelling, Language* (London: Faber & Faber, 1992) 9.

2   A. D. Hope, 'Australia' , *Collected Poems* (Sydney: Angus & Robertson, 1966) 13.

3   Philip Drew, *The coast dwellers: Australians living on the edge* (Ringwood, Victoria: Penguin, 1994) 32–3.

4   Drew, *The coast dwellers* 34. Drew makes the interesting—but surely anachronistic—observation that '[o]nly in the 1950s, after the artistic discovery of Central Australia, was [Australia's place as an outpost of Empire] questioned and the centralised schema adapted to Australia by resiting it within the country' (35). But the enigma of the centre had been there almost from the beginning—certainly from Leichhardt's time.

5   Drew, *The coast dwellers* 35.

6   Christina Stead, *For Love Alone* (Sydney: Angus & Robertson, 1991 [1944]), Prologue.

7   Note that Hope's final turn towards the 'desert of the human mind' is explicitly a misanthropic turning away from people and their social and economic relations.

8   Ivor Indyk suggests that the comic aspects of Les Murray's pastoral vision serve something of this purpose: His 'Some Versions of Australian Pastoral', *Southerly* 48, 2 (1988): 115–27.

9   Thea Astley, *Drylands* (Ringwood, Victoria: Viking Penguin, 1999) 6. See my extended discussion of this novel, 'Violence, Irony and Reading Relations: Thea Astley's *Drylands*' in *Thea Astley's Fictional Worlds*, eds Susan Sheridan and Paul Genoni (Newcastle, UK: Cambridge Scholars Press, 2006) 164-75.

10 Astley, *Drylands* 24. These phrases echo the description of the landscape of *An Item from the Late News*.

11 Astley, *Drylands* 294.

12 In his discussion of *An Item from the Late News* Genoni invokes the idea of white settlement 'unravelling' as evidenced by the abandoned mining towns of the hinterland: Paul Genoni, *Explorers and Exploration in Australian Fiction* (Altona, Victoria: Common Ground Publishing, 2004) 129.

13 Ross Gibson, *Seven Versions of an Australian Badland* (St Lucia: University of Queensland Press, 2002) 26–7.

14 Thea Astley, 'On being a Queenslander' in *Eight Voices of the Eighties*, ed. Gillian Whitlock (St Lucia: UQP, 1989) 178.

15 He made enough money in the sandalwood trade to have his own 245-ton brig, the 'Freak', built in 1847 (Dorothy Shineberg, *They Came for Sandalwood: A Study of the Sandalwood Trade in the South-West Pacific 1830–1865* (Melbourne: Melbourne University Press, 1967: 137)—though Norma Townsend, ('Memoir of a Minor Mariner: Thomas Beckford Simpson and New South Wales, 1839–1853', *The Great Circle* 5: 2 October 1983: 107) disputes his reputation as an entrepreneur in the sandalwood trade. Two years after the Kennedy voyage he made a similar, but unsuccessful, voyage to Port Essington in an attempt to find traces of Leichhardt's party. It was on this journey that he contracted the 'tropical complaint' that took

his life at the age of 45 in 1853 (C. Bede Maxwell, *Wooden Hookers: Epics of the Sea History of Australia* (Sydney: Angus & Robertson, 1940) 208–9).

16 'The Strathisla's Voyage' about trading for sandalwood in New Caledonia, the Loyalty Islands and the New Hebrides was published serially in the *Sydney Morning Herald* and reprinted in the *Shipping Gazette* (1845). He also left the 'Private Log Book of the *Giraffe*, 1843' (Mitchell Library MSA2621).

17 This last text, as well as Jacky Jacky's narrative, are included as appendices to William Carron (one of the survivors of the expedition).

18 According to Craig Cormick, *Unwritten Histories* (Canberra : Aboriginal Studies Press, 1998).

19 Narrative of Ted Wymarra, reported in Nonie Sharp, *Footprints Along the Cape York Beaches* (Canberra: Aboriginal Studies Press, 1992) 97.

20 Constance Mackness, *Clump Point and District: An Historical Record* (Cairns: G.K. Bolton, 1983) 5–6.

21 W. Carron, *Narrative of an expedition, undertaken under the direction of the late Mr. Assistant Surveyor E. B. Kennedy, for the exploration of the country lying between Rockingham Bay and Cape York* (Adelaide : Libraries Board of South Australia, 1965). Facsimile edition of 1849 publication, 100, 106.

22 Carron and his companion, too weak to bury them, nevertheless survived, to be rescued by the *Ariel*.

23 Carron, *Narrative of an expedition* 111.

24 Carron, *Narrative of an expedition* 119–20.

25 Carron, *Narrative of an expedition* 112.

26 He later manages to retrieve this stash by sending to the whaleboat ashore (Carron, *Narrative of an expedition* 123).

27 Carron, *Narrative of an expedition* 114.

28 Carron, *Narrative of an expedition* 123.

29 Carron, *Narrative of an expedition* 124. But he is not the only 'native' who behaves in ways that meet Simpson's approval. When his men 'fully explained' what they were doing to some 'natives' who were present, they 'conducted themselves with propriety when the funeral service was being read' (Carron, *Narrative of an expedition* 124).

30 Carron, *Narrative of an expedition* 125.

31 This continuous process of mythmaking around the Kennedy expedition is brilliantly satirised in Craig Cormick's story, 'Do you remember when you heard that Kennedy had been killed?'

32 Carron, *Narrative of an expedition* 87.

33 Or Mac Hope, in *Vanishing Points* (1992), who runs tours of the Cape York Peninsula with his 'Genteel Poverty Bus Company'. As Elizabeth Perkins, 'Hacking through tropical undergrowth', *Outrider* 10 (1993): 377 points out, Mac follows parodically in the footsteps of Edmund Kennedy, just as Kennedy himself was retracing the journey of another lost explorer, Ludwig Leichhardt.

34 This is the Australian equivalent of Huck Finn 'lighting out for the territory', a journey from which he does not intend to return.

35 Thea Astley, *It's Raining in Mango* (Ringwood, Victoria: Viking Penguin, 1987)
   239.
36 Note different spellings of Jacky Jacky in various texts. No authoritative one.

Works cited

Astley, Thea. *Drylands*. Ringwood, Victoria: Viking Penguin, 1999.

Astley, Thea. *The Multiple Effects of Rainshadow*. Ringwood, Victoria: Viking
   Penguin, 1996.

Astley, Thea. 'On being a Queenslander' in *Eight Voices of the Eighties*, ed. Gillian
   Whitlock. St Lucia: UQP, 1989.

Astley, Thea. *It's Raining in Mango*. Ringwood, Victoria: Viking Penguin, 1987.

Carron, W. *Narrative of an expedition, undertaken under the direction of the late Mr.
   Assistant Surveyor E.B. Kennedy, for the exploration of the country lying between
   Rockingham Bay and Cape York*. Adelaide : Libraries Board of South Australia,
   1965. Facsimile edition of 1849 publication.

Carter, Paul. *Living in a New Country: History, Travelling, Language*. London: Faber
   & Faber, 1992.

Cormick, Craig. *Unwritten Histories*. Canberra : Aboriginal Studies Press, 1998.

Drew, Philip. *The coast dwellers: Australians living on the edge*. Ringwood, Victoria:
   Penguin, 1994.

Empson, William. *Some Versions of Pastoral*. London: Chatto, 1950.

Genoni, Paul. *Explorers and Exploration in Australian Fiction*. Altona, Victoria:
   Common Ground Publishing, 2004.

Gibson, Ross. *Seven Versions of an Australian Badland*. St Lucia: UQP, 2002.

Hope, A.D. *Collected Poems 1930–1966*. Sydney: Angus and Robertson, 1966.

Indyk, Ivor. 'Some Versions of Australian Pastoral'. *Southerly* 48: 2 (1988): 115–27.

Jackey Jackey. 'The statement of the aboriginal native, Jackey Jackey, who
   accompanied Mr. Kennedy', Appendix 1 in *Carron, Narrative of an Expedition*.

Mackness, Constance. *Clump Point and District: An Historical Record*. Cairns:
   G.K.Bolton, 1983.

Maxwell, C. Bede. *Wooden Hookers: Epics of the Sea History of Australia*. Sydney :
   Angus & Robertson, 1940.

Perkins, Elizabeth. 'Hacking through tropical undergrowth'. *Outrider* 10 (1993):
   377–86.

Sharp, Nonie. *Footprints Along the Cape York Beaches*. Canberra: Aboriginal Studies
   Press, 1992.

Sheridan, Susan. 'Violence, Irony and Reading Relations: Thea Astley's
   Drylands' in *Thea Astley's Fictional Worlds*, eds Susan Sheridan and Paul Genoni.
   (Newcastle, UK: Cambridge Scholars Press, 2006) 164–75.

Shineberg, Dorothy. *They Came for Sandalwood: A Study of the Sandalwood Trade in the South-West Pacific 1830–1865.* Melbourne: Melbourne University Press, 1967.

Simpson, Thomas Beckford. 'The statement of Captain Simpson of the "Freak", who proceeded in search of Mr. Kennedy's papers, &c' Appendix 3 in Carron, *Narrative of an Expedition.*

Stead, Christina. *For Love Alone.* Sydney: Angus & Robertson, 1991 [1944].

Townsend, Norma. 'Memoir of a Minor Mariner: Thomas Beckford Simpson and New South Wales, 1839–1853'. *The Great Circle* 5: 2 October 1983: 105–115.

Coastal Scenes in Bessie Head's The Cardinals[1]

DOROTHY DRIVER

Despite its vigorous Indigenous art tradition, Australia is—like Canada—readily characterised as a coastal rather than a continental culture. In the United States, on the other hand, there exists a relation of tension and opposition between the culture of the interior and the two coastal cultures of colonial settlement. The South African case is different from all these. Even in its literature of settlement, where one might expect a greater focus on the coast, the interior bears the preponderant symbolic weight. Whereas Australian settler writing shows the interior as a place of desolation, failure and loss, it was the coast that South African colonial explorers found forbidding, and the settlers turned to the interior for its promise of freedom and plenty. Moreover, land conjugates considerably more readily than the coastline does with the present-day interest in national or ethnic identity and belonging. Accordingly, in South African literature, the sea, coast and beach are used as settings far less often than the interior is.

Thomas Mofolo's *Chaka*—usually thought of as the first novel in a Southern African language—makes a significant, if brief, reference to the coastal. First published in seSotho in 1925 and translated into English in 1931, *Chaka* is set in the late eighteenth and early nineteenth centuries. Its opening reference may seem rather bland: 'South Africa is a large headland situated between two oceans, one to the east and one to the west'.[2] But by the end of the book these oceans are seen as having become portals of destruction. '*Umlungu*, the white man, is coming', says Chaka to his brothers, 'and it is he who will rule you, and you will be his servants'.[3]

Writing at roughly the same time as Mofolo, but from a colonial European perspective, Roy Campbell ends his poem, 'Rounding the Cape', with a warning voice that issues from the very point where Mofolo's two oceans meet:

The prow glides smoothly on through seas quiescent:
But where the last point sinks into the deep,
The land lies dark beneath the rising crescent,
And Night, the Negro, murmurs in his sleep.[4]

Campbell's literary source is Luís de Camões' poem, *The Lusiads* (1572), which details Vasco da Gama's pioneering imperial voyage from Portugal to India in 1497–99. Canto V, which describes Da Gama's rounding of the Cape, inaugurates many of the characteristic themes of South African writing,[5] themes that spring from the social divisions instituted by European invasion. Of these social divisions Bessie Head—South Africa's first black female novelist writing in English—would later write:

> Twenty-seven years of my life was lived in South Africa but I have been unable to record this experience in any direct way, as a writer. It is as though, with all those divisions and signs, you end up with no people at all. The environment completely defeated me, as a writer. I just want people to be people, so I had no way of welding all the people together into a cohesive whole.[6]

In fact, Head did produce one South African novel before leaving South Africa on an exit permit in 1964. After settling in Botswana, she published several works of fiction and non-fiction before her death in 1986. Botswana and its inhabitants became her enabling environment. But in her first novel, *The Cardinals*, written in the early 1960s and published posthumously, she turned to the littoral in order to imagine a world beyond 'divisions and signs'. She makes no explicit reference in this novel to Camões, or to any of the early travel or settler literature that sets up the 'divisions and signs' later entrenched under Apartheid. However, tracking through some of these key moments in the making of South African literature and its critical reception will outline the discursive context against which Head was in part reacting. It will also help establish the logic through which the coastal scenes in *The Cardinals* can be most productively read.

✶ ✶ ✶ ✶ ✶ ✶ ✶

After describing in *The Lusiads* Da Gama's voyage down the west coast of Africa on his way to the Cape and then India, Camões comes to the crew's first beach encounter with the Khoisan at St Helena Bay on the Northern Cape coast. Here Camões imagines Da Gama saying:

Suddenly I saw a black-skinned man, surrounded by my crew, coming towards me. He had been captured in the mountains while gathering honeycombs. More savage-looking than Polyphemus, he was also very frightened because we were unable to communicate with each other.[7]

As the fictionalised Da Gama tells it, the encounter ends without incident: 'We let him head back to his village that was not far off.'[8] Despite the crude naming ('black-skinned', 'savage'), what takes place on the coast is a more peaceable human engagement than the capture in the mountains. But the scene is very different on the following day. After going back into the mountains to re-visit the Khoisan group, one of the crew returns to the shoreline 'in a greater hurry than when he left'.[9] And when a boat is sent to fetch him back to the ship, the crew is attacked.

In this changed atmosphere, and further south, Camões figures the Cape peninsula as a huge and malevolent landmass that forbids entry into the interior and perhaps further movement east. He draws on Greek myth to explain its etiology: the Titan Adamastor—desiring Thetis, goddess of the sea and wife of Peleus—decides to take her by force, and runs forward 'to fill myself with that goddess who was the life of this body of mine'.[10] He finds himself rendered immobile instead: 'my flesh was changed into earth, my bones into rock, these limbs that you see and this face were projected over the watery spaces. My enormous body became this desolate cape'.[11]

In the white South African imaginary, this moment symbolises a kind of creation or birth. But it is also what postcolonial criticism calls a 'self-other' division: the very forcefulness of Adamastor's behaviour eliminates fluidity and entrenches fixedness instead. Although the terms Camões specifies are those of gender, not race, Adamastor is read in white South African literary culture as 'Caliban desiring Miranda, the Beast longing for Beauty', and as a 'primal monster' groping after a 'pale' nymph whose 'privilege makes her untouchable and whose advanced society punished unwarranted affection with all the powers of a superior technology'.[12] Laurens van der Post puts the critical position more bluntly: Adamastor is black, Thetis is white. The black man was denied the white woman, 'and in the process his heart was turned to stone'.[13]

The assumption that Canto V of *The Lusiads* is about the generic black man's frustrated desire for the generic white woman is coterminous in the white South African imaginary with other readings of early coastal encounters. To use Head's formulation, all of them unerringly register 'divisions and signs'. Ethnographic writing about the wreck of the passenger ship the *Grosvenor* (1782) on the Pondoland coast pays pornographic attention to the salvation of the white women castaways—or not—from the Indigenous hordes.[14] In an earlier episode, the wreck of the *S. João* (1552), sentimental interest focuses likewise on the fate of the Portuguese noblewoman who survived the wreck with her husband and children. Camões refers to her briefly;[15] the fuller tale is told in Bernardo Gomes de Brito's compilation of *Historia Tragico-Maritima* (1735–38). Its conclusion, which describes how the Indigenous inhabitants of the Natal coast attacked and stripped some of the castaways, reads as follows:

> It is said that D. Leonor would not allow herself to be stripped, defending her body by fists and blows since it was her nature to prefer being killed by the Kaffirs than to find herself naked in front of everyone. [...] Once naked, D. Leonor threw herself on the ground immediately and covered herself with her very long hair. She made a hole in the sand and buried herself in it up to the waist; she never again would rise from the sand. [...]
>
> I can truly say that I know of no one who could hear of this without great pity and sadness. To see a noble woman, daughter and wife of two honourable *fidalgos* so mistreated, and with such lack of respect! When the men in the company beheld Manuel de Sousa and his wife naked, they retreated a bit, ashamed in finding their captain and Leonor thus.[16]

Josiah Blackmore develops a rich argument about the redolence of loss, defeat and perdition in Portuguese shipwreck literature. He claims, for instance, that shipwreck is represented in such a way as to be metonymic of the undoing of empire. Analysing shipwreck literature as an early form of what would later be called colonial discourse, he focuses on those divisions of race, class and gender that had to be re-entrenched or negotiated whenever a ship contacted the African coast. In brief, Blackmore first reads Leonor de Sá as a feminine and maternal body. On the arduous march after the shipwreck she then becomes a masculine body; and now—in the passage just quoted—she 'appropriat[es] a masculine code of honor' in her self-defence as a woman.[17] At this point, Blackmore claims, 'she can no longer survive the re-gendered body shipwreck has forced her to occupy.'[18]

In the face of this inexorable reproduction of a colonial discourse so firmly in the grip of a patriarchal symbolic, I am driven to ask a question on behalf of Head and her disavowal of 'divisions and signs': How else might we read Leonor de Sá if we wish to avoid naming her as no more than a masquerading male, a naked noblewoman before the ship's company, and a naked white woman before 'Kaffirs'? How else, that is to say, might Head herself have read such a moment if she wished not to re-entrench 'divisions and signs'?

Leonor de Sá's attempted and actual obscurings of the upper and lower parts of her body may be read as a desperate attempt to ward off her registration in the pejorative: as a white woman stripped naked and shamed. In effect, she refuses to become a sign in a discourse obsessively concerned with dominion, control and penetration as metaphors for meaning-making; and with the kind of identity-formation that depends on the categories of gender, race and class. Of course, Leonor de Sá cannot but figure in such discourse as a white noblewoman naked and shamed. But in a performance that strives to unspeak itself at the very moment at which it starts making meaning, she resists that repressive nominalisation by functioning also as a verb—burying, covering, obscuring. In this respect, I will shortly argue, she is like Camões' Thetis, whose ductile figure resurfaces centuries later in Head.

The reception of these three early coastal stories—the wreck of the *Grosvenor*, the wreck of the *S. João*, and Diaz's rounding of the Cape—manifests misreadings generated by rigidly schematised modes of representation, and typifies the dominant critical context within which South African writing has had to operate. Yet re-reading Canto V of *The Lusiads* can tell a different story from the one that typecasts Adamastor as male and black, and Thetis as female and white. This different story foregrounds the littoral as the site of a discursive escape.

Forewarned of Adamastor's intent, and knowing that her abduction would bring about a war between the Titans and Neptune's fleet, Thetis casually says: 'Well, I doubt if a nymph can satisfy the love of a giant. But if it's a choice between my honour and interminable war, I will save the oceans so much destruction'.[19] Refusing to have her 'honour' the occasion for war, Thetis promises to give herself to Adamastor instead. Yet at the moment of their union he is metamorphosed into earth and rock, thus giving shape to the promontory of the Cape, and she too becomes stone, 'a cold mountain', 'her gorgeous face [...] no more than a rocky cliff'.[20] Perhaps this is how Adamastor—creating his own reality—experiences her in their embrace. In any event, Thetis at the same time remains the sea. 'To increase my suffering', Camões imagines Adamastor saying, 'the gods encircled me with these waters of Thetis herself'.[21]

This Cape-coastal encounter is a superlatively generative moment not just for a reading of Head but for postcolonial feminist criticism in general. Thetis is not simply a woman defined by rape (and stonily immobile in her rapist's embrace) but also the signifier—variously conceptualised by Friedrich Nietzsche and Jacques Derrida, Hélène Cixous and Luce Irigaray—of that which eludes conventional representation by escaping definition and therefore control. In naming this figure the 'feminine' they do not necessarily exclude men. The term 'feminine' denotes an ontological and epistemological position whose signifier registers the incapacity of discursive language to release itself from a patriarchal symbolic in order to define what creative writing can perform. To essentialise Thetis as 'elusive'—if only partially—would risk yet another stagnation into 'meaning'. Yet engaging with the 'femininity' Thetis puts into play productively addresses the problem of representation raised in writing and reading: the necessity to marshall standard meanings, on the one hand, and to reject or exceed these meanings, on the other hand.

Head does not explicitly refer to Thetis and the Adamastor myth in *The Cardinals*, yet the figure of Thetis silently presides over this first novel. Specifically, Thetis's mode of refusing rape is central to the novel. Conventionally a defining moment for women and men, rape positions them in a binary structure that distinguishes victim from assailant. Yet Thetis's adoption of a doubled—or duplicitous—and partially elusive position not only allows a cunning escape but also creates an Adamastor endlessly lacking and perhaps yearning for the fluidity he has lost. Head's focus on the coastal in her first and only novel with a South African setting invites the kind of reading that is responsive to Thetis's refusal. It also invites the kind of reading that responds to Leonor de Sá's ordeal as the ordeal of those around her as well: human figures read only in terms of 'divisions and signs' and denied the full scope of their potential selves; human beings reduced to the spectacle of their bodily form.

In this regard Head's *The Cardinals* prefigures or sets in motion a subtradition in South African writing in which figurations of the littoral unsettle the discourses of national or ethnic identity and belonging generally associated with the land. Lewis Nkosi's *Mating Birds* (1987), for instance, uses the beach—a place of warmth and naked bodies—as the site on which to strive to undo the regulatory control of race and gender that characterized South African life under Apartheid; and in *David's Story* (2000) Zoë Wicomb uses the sea and sea pools—although the coast is not a consistent focus of her novel—to address just that dynamic of meaning and unmeaning that *The Cardinals* proposes.

* * * * * * *

Given the circumstances of Apartheid and the mystery of her origin Bessie Head must have suspected that others would think her own conception the outcome of rape. Gillian Stead Eilersen, a biographer writing years after Head's death, said that Head's mother, Bessie Emery, had been admitted to what was known as the Pretoria Mental Hospital, before her daughter was born, because of uncontrollable grief at the loss of her young son. She would sometimes spend time out in her family home in Johannesburg, and on one occasion visited her sisters in the coastal city of Durban. On the basis of interviews with Head's white relatives and other research, Eilersen concludes that Head was the child of 'a love affair or a rape', although '[t]here is no record of how it happened or where'.[22] But Head rejected rape as her origin. As a self-fashioning woman, she kept returning in her writing to the story of her parents' interracial sexual union in order, literally, to re-conceive herself and the world: to re-write this sexual union as a kind of re-birth, not simply of her parents and herself but also of the world she wanted for the characters in her fiction, and for those in the world outside.

Head had no direct contact with her mother, and never knew her father's identity. In an autobiographical essay published in 1982, Head romanticised their incompletely known story by fabricating a tale of racehorses and a groom, and explaining her mother's institutionalisation as an Apartheid plot, although months were to elapse before the baby was declared not 'white':

> I was born on July 6, 1937, in the Pietermaritzburg mental hospital. The reason for my peculiar birthplace was that my mother was white and my father black.
>
> No details were ever available about my father beyond the fact that he worked in the family stables and took care of their racehorses.[23]

The truth is that the family did not own racehorses, and Head's father could not therefore have been the family groom. But Durban is a city associated with horseracing, and a large national race-meeting—'the Durban July'—takes place there each year in the month of Head's birth.

By the time she wrote this, Head had already moved to Botswana. She had also by this time published three novels. In the third—*A Question of Power* (1974)—she recycled the story of racehorses and groom. In *The Cardinals*, however, the love affair between fictional mother and father is set not in the family stables but on the beach.

Written before she left South Africa, but then apparently lost, *The Cardinals* was not published until 1993, seven years after her death. The novel engages to some extent autobiographically with Head's experience as the only black female reporter in the Cape Town office of *Drum* publications,[24] where black as well as white men either patronise the central character or treat her with contempt. But—for the purposes of this essay—the more important autobiographical engagement is the novel's oblique re-telling of Head's own conception, the first of Head's revisionist narratives about the creation of both self and worlds. From this new construction of herself would stream 'pattern[s …] invented in her own head'[25]—stories that one of the narrators in her story collection entitled *The Collector of Treasures* (1977) calls 'gold amidst the ash'.[26] In this 'work of a beautiful design'[27] her characters could be 'people' rather than 'divisions and signs'.

At the start of *The Cardinals* we see an unnamed woman getting out of her car and picking her way through a slum in order to hand over her newborn child to a woman called Sarah. The date is 1937. South Africa is at this time governed by the pro-British United Party. In 1936 the Natives Representative Act had withdrawn the Cape African franchise, which meant that now in all four provinces only those deemed white had the right to vote. And 1934 had seen the formation of the National Party, the party of Afrikaner nationalism that would in 1948 win the 'national' whites-only elections and formalize racial segregation. In this context the unnamed woman who opens the novel is understood to be white, and Sarah is understood to be either of mixed race or black. The child will grow up to be classified 'coloured' under Apartheid legislation, and her father is thus presumed not to have been white. At no point, however, does the narrator name race.

The slum is flanked on one side by a graveyard; on the other side are a rubbish dump and a highway the text calls the National Road. Beyond them lies the sea. In the rubbish dump the child Miriam finds a storybook that portrays a resilient and light-hearted bear on a seaside holiday, and from this book a kind old man teaches her to read. The first word the child learns to read is *sea*.[28]

Acts of reading and, especially, writing are crucial in this novel, and are closely linked to escape. When the child Miriam runs away after being sexually abused by her foster-father, the implication is that her determination has been fuelled by the same spirit that drove her to learn to write and read. And when as a young woman she finds a job on a newspaper called *African Beat*, a fellow journalist called Johnny takes it upon himself to teach her how to write. That his intent is also to teach her how to love introduces into the novel an erotics of writing that will again be related to both the coastal and the motif of escape. However, it is in the structural relation between acts of writing within the novel that the littoral makes its most subtle and interesting appearance.

The journalists on *African Beat* name this quiet and timid young woman Mouse. As an exercise, Mouse re-writes for her self-proclaimed tutor and would-be lover an episode from his boyhood that he has sketched out for her. Her story seems to him so accurate that it spurs him to remember something else, and the novel at this point includes a brief subordinate plot detailing this additional episode in Johnny's life. As it turns out, it is from this brief subordinate plot that much of the novel's mystery and energy spring. In the subordinate plot, Johnny is a fisherman living on the beach, his only social link with a small group of fishermen living a carefree coastal existence. He meets on the beach a young woman with whom he has a passionate love affair, and it is this young woman who, we come to understand, is the unnamed woman who walks into the slum with a newborn baby at the start of the novel. Thus it is this woman—Ruby—who gives birth to Mouse, and Johnny is now Mouse's biological father as well as her would-be lover.

The ontological status of this subordinate plot is a pressing issue throughout the novel, as is the question of whose consciousness it emanates from or dramatizes. When the main narrative resumes, neither Johnny nor Mouse are given any inkling of their biological relation, and their flirtation proceeds, as do their discussions about writing. The truth value of the subordinate plot is uncertain; it may be an authorial flashback; it may emanate from either Johnny's or Mouse's consciousness; it may be a new memory for Johnny, instilled in him by Mouse. Its status may, in other words, have more to do with desire than with fact (a possibility stressed through its use of a stylistic register associated with the love romance and altogether uncharacteristic of the main plot). Nonetheless, for the rest of the narrative, focussing as it does on the developing love affair between Johnny and Mouse, impending incest is the theme. How we read this theme, and how it relates to Head's interest in writing, depends fundamentally on the structural ambiguity of the relation between plots; that is, between the main narrative and the insertion that may be flashback, memory or desire. This ambiguity takes up—I argue—the figure of the littoral. On occasion, too, the developing love affair between 'father' and 'daughter' deploys sea imagery reminiscent of that earlier 'remembered' beach encounter, so that the peculiar doubling that thus occurs is fundamentally underwritten by figurations of the littoral. All in all, the coastal scenes in *The Cardinals* work with its complex composition to produce intricate and tantalizing possibilities about the relation between writing and the Incest Taboo that in effect develop Head's narrative about evading 'divisions and signs'.

The inclusion in *The Cardinals* of the beach encounter between Johnny and Ruby in what I call the subordinate plot produces a strange combination of narrative possibilities. On the one hand, as Johnny and Mouse fall in love, father–daughter incest appears inevitable, but on the other hand incest is *not* represented as part of the action, and any notion of its inevitability may be based on an imaginative insertion rather than the truth of the story. Therefore, on the one hand, the novel may be read as staging the impossibility of evading what Jacques Lacan called the Law of the Father, according to which subjectivity, language and writing itself emerge with the prohibition of incest. However, on the other hand the novel may be read as registering the fictive nature of this Law, which inserts into an innocent sexual coupling and act of creation (subjectivity, language, writing) the No of prohibition. Nonetheless, given the co-presence of the narrative plots (the main narrative and the mysterious insertion of the subordinate plot), and the productive ambiguity of their connection, neither one nor the other of these possibilities can stand alone. This means that the novel in effect simultaneously names and unnames its two central characters: *father* and *daughter* here represent their naming, *man* and *woman* their provisional unnaming. These two characters—who double into four across the two plots—stand both inside and outside the Law of the Father, on what this essay is calling the cusp of the littoral. The cusp of the littoral marks what is simultaneously inside and outside the Law, and what is simultaneously a part of and yet free from 'divisions and signs', standing on the threshold or liminal line between land and sea.

Head further complicates her novel and takes us deeper into the nexus of language and subjectivity, writing and taboo, by juxtaposing the allegedly universal Incest Taboo with South Africa's culturally specific Immorality Act. (In 1927 sexual union outside marriage was prohibited between whites and Africans; Apartheid legislation later extended the prohibition to include sexual relations between whites and all those classified as non-white.) Writing becomes, then, a necessary scene of transgression not just in the allegedly universal sense, but also in the culturally specific sense. The novel includes another story stemming from Mouse's writing, this time from her journalistic endeavours. In court she covers the case of a Norwegian sailor who is bewildered at being arrested and brought to trial for having sex with a woman whose Apartheid label—'non-white'—is beyond his ken.

Although the Immorality Act and the Incest Taboo are historically incommensurable, one being apparently universal and the other culturally specific, each functions or has functioned as a form of social organisation: the Incest Taboo defines familial relations in terms of gender, and the Immorality Act—which criminalised interracial heterosexual desire—defined social relations in terms of race as it intersected with gender. As an outsider the Norwegian sailor marks a position structurally and symbolically similar to that of *man* and *woman*—Johnny and Ruby—in the subordinate plot, before that plot enters, as it were, the main plot and takes on the assumed 'divisions and signs' of the main plot. The sailor is also as ignorant of Apartheid legislation as the father and daughter are of their 'real' relation to each other— 'real', that is, within the familial relations structured by the Incest Taboo. If, this novel asks us to ask, geography enables the Norwegian sailor to escape South Africa's Immorality Act, is there a comparable world in which subjectivity may develop outside the legal and symbolic systems established by the Law of the Father? Can the act of writing itself create a world independent not only of Apartheid South Africa's 'divisions and signs' but also of the supposedly universal 'divisions and signs'? Or are subjectivity and desire, and language and writing, altogether dependent upon already established laws? These questions are posed, as it were, on the cusp of the littoral.

As already suggested, Head's novel dramatises the littoral in part structurally—through deft narrative footwork that allows a subordinate plot to stand both inside the main plot (as flashback) and outside it (as a fiction)—and in part tropologically. Fish and fishermen, pools and waves, beach and sea, mark the lovers as wild and autonomous, as if they are primal parents who know nothing of the conventions of gender and, until Ruby's street betrayal of Johnny, the conventions of class and race as well. On the other hand, the main plot struggles to evade 'divisions and signs', whether in Miriam's life in the slum, where the line of the national highway intervenes between slum and beach, or in her life as a journalist, where the political world constantly intervenes. The act of writing, too, is contaminated by the social. When Johnny teaches Mouse how to love and to write, he teaches her how to love and write *him*: both verbs acquire a specific transitivity under the direction of Mouse's unknown father. If the plot juxtaposition creates between Johnny and Mouse a potential sexual transgression, and colours their creative union, too, as transgressive, Mouse's apprenticeship cannot shake free of subordination.

Yet the text insists on ambiguity in the incest theme, and thus in the regulation of gender. Johnny tells Mouse about his early acts of near-sexual love with his sister, a prostitute from the age of ten, from whom he never withheld 'the kind of love she wanted from [him]' when at night she would lie down crying next to him.[29] If we interpret his desire for Mouse as comparably curative, we will see him as substituting love for the foster-father's sexual abuse. On the other hand, because the text frequently characterises him as overbearing, we may think him merely self-justificatory and unable to distinguish care from abuse. His masculine position is both protective and abusive, both loving and self-serving.

This ambiguity of the relation between the two characters takes us to the heart of a problematic that has preoccupied many women writers besides Head, and re-writes those terms *man* and *woman* that were earlier posited as provisionally neutral. Although Johnny proclaims freedom from regulation in everything—'I live without a code or a law'[30]—the form of love he offers Mouse (whether as father to daughter, or as man to woman) places her in a dangerous and contradictory position. 'Because I love you', Johnny says at one point, 'I can wait until you are able to love me'.[31] In the moral framing provided by the subordinate plot, that time may of course never come. But by now the text has made up its mind about this matter: 'I can't come and live with you', Mouse says to him at a slightly earlier moment. 'You're a man', she adds; and later, 'I cannot love'.[32] Even though it is not known here that Johnny is the father, the text not only encourages us to regard the lover as the (sometimes) kind but nevertheless dominating father-figure, but also requires us to understand that male-female relations are structured inevitably by inequalities of power. The act of loving necessarily consigns Mouse to the object-position in the grammatically transitive syntax of heterosexuality: to love (for her) is to be a woman loving a man. Yet Head's thinking takes her in a direction other than that of women writers whose concern rests on gender inequality, for her deeper interest is in the difficulties and dangers of representation, in writing and taboo.

* * * * * * *

We return, now, to Thetis. How does her impossibly doubled movement enter the text? And what does Head's sea-imagery in the main plot bring to the problematic of representation opened up in her writing?

Just after Johnny has told her at great length how to love, Mouse throws herself into the sea's 'swirling, tumultuous waves',[33] as if to enter the 'elemental ecstasy' her mother Ruby had felt in 'the savage, battering beat of [the] high sea' that symbolised Johnny's love-making at that time.[34] If Mouse tries to be her mother, and thus to turn back the clock against her own social becoming, the 'swirling monster that had engulfed her rose again and flung her out some twenty feet ahead of him'.[35] The monster recalls Johnny—elsewhere described in such terms[36]—as well as the Adamastor figure from Camões and subsequent white South African poetry. Gone now is whatever possibility of escape that might have been signified either in Mouse's jump into the sea or even in her finding herself 'twenty feet ahead': Johnny saves her, slaps her, and calls her a stupid woman. After parroting that circular definition of woman-as-lunatic which lies deep in the patriarchal imaginary, he jokes about throwing her back into the ocean, as if like a discarded fish. Incapable of making a return to the sea, or of being like Thetis in Camões' poem, Mouse appears to have no option but to submit. We are reminded of the sea as described in the storybook found at the rubbish dump: both promising a seaside holiday and unpropitious, for the storybook bear swims in a wave that the child Miriam suddenly feels rising to 'swamp her'.[37] This (at the level of the plot) is why Mouse resists Johnny's advances even as she responds.

In its use of the Immorality Act, as in its use of the Incest Taboo, *The Cardinals* gestures towards alternative worlds outside the normative, while at the same time registering the manner in which these alternatives come to be tied back into the normative, and even demanding that readers acknowledge their complicity in this regard, for no one but the reader calls Johnny and Mouse 'father' and 'daughter'. If we connect up its main and subordinate plots, *The Cardinals* appears to be saying that there is no way out of the symbolic system that names gender, even though there is a world and a language beyond the reach of the Immorality Act. That reading would confirm both Lacan's observation about the Oedipus story (we cannot stand outside language) and Derrida's point that there is no meaning outside the text. So much for Thetis, one might say. Yet the disjuncture in the narrative creates an imaginative space outside the symbolic system underpinning the social world of 'divisions and signs', a space from which one may reflect on the binary terms of that symbolic system's various cultural constructions: 'father' and 'daughter', 'man' and 'woman', 'black' and 'white'. The coastal imagery grounds that imaginative space in a particular place, and helps us make connections across the novel's spatial, temporal and ontological disjunctions. But the disjuncture remains a disjuncture, recalling the simultaneity of freedom and entrapment signified in Thetis's story. It is as if the sea itself both remained the sea and yet also became as the land itself has become: owned, controlled, and divided up. In the figurations I began with in this essay, sea and coast sometimes exemplify fluidities of meaning that are not readily replicated socially on dry land. However, the picture has now become more complex.

One of Head's concerns in *The Cardinals* is language, the symbolic system that names things—gender, for example—in oppositional and hierarchical terms. Another is family structure, the kinship system that positions father and daughter, brother and sister, in relations of power and taboo. And a third is Apartheid, the oppositional and hierarchical system that legislates the social and political positions of black and white. In a deft deployment of doubled plots, as I have argued, the novel juxtaposes the Immorality Act with the Incest Taboo in order to connect language, family and Apartheid. Yet the metonymies of the coastal (ocean, wave, beach, seaside holiday, sailor, fisherman, fish) that materialise these connections enable the novel to investigate three possibilities: being either inside or outside the 'divisions and signs' of society, or both inside and outside at once.

The novel thus explores how its four main characters (read across the two plots) are both inserted into and evade a Family Law constructed in terms of the Incest Taboo. The contiguity of the two plots posits that relations between males and females are haunted by those between fathers and daughters. As we have seen, both plots are crucial to the problematics of representation, which the structural doubling of mother and daughter allows us to evade by reading each as a revision of the other. The novel also positions these characters in relation to the Immorality Act. It refuses to name them racially, but race is implied through the class distinctions that creep into the plot, as well as by the narrative proximity of the Norwegian sailor and the plot about the Immorality Act. Again, the contiguity of all these plots (or, to put it more simply, the juxtaposition of the Incest Taboo and the Immorality Act) produces an effect of doubling. Being outside signifies escape, while being inside signifies entrapment. The four characters are, as suggested earlier, sometimes inside or outside, and sometimes both inside and outside at once.

These doubled plots instantiate the acts of writing and re-writing which then become part of the novel's themes, and not merely a structuring device. By juxtaposing Apartheid's Immorality Act with the Incest Taboo, Head raises the question of the relation between these two radically different but equally fundamental laws of subject-formation, inducting us into a process Michel Pêcheux has called 'identification' and 'disidentification'.[38] If—Head's novel asks us to ask—one can remain as easily outside a discourse of race as of class by refusing to identify and be identified in such terms, can one similarly 'disidentify' from the Incest Taboo? How can one construct a world and a language that do not use the Incest Taboo to legislate family relations in the way that the Immorality Act polices race? By revealing the contingency of both these repressive apparatuses, Head appears to be positing a different kind of social configuration which would provide an antidote not simply to Apartheid but also to those confining structures we call representation and the 'world'. Such a claim is borne out by both the title of the novel and its explanatory epigraph: '*The Cardinals*, in the astrological sense, are those who serve as the base or foundation for change.' Assuming that Head is equating the four cardinal points of a new cosmology with the four characters in two of her doubled plots (Johnny-as-lover and Ruby, Johnny-as-father and Miriam/Mouse), what is she saying about the procedures or possibilities for change?

Head's opening reference to the cardinals crucially signposts her novel's interest in reading and writing as transformative acts that depend fundamentally on acts of interpretation. What we glimpse momentarily and fleetingly in *The Cardinals* is an attempt to imagine a new kind of human subject which is *not* (in that now famous Derridean phrase) 'always already' a social creature, born into a language and culture structured invariably by divisions and oppositions. *The Cardinals* performs loving, writing, and being human—whether as a man or a woman—in metaphorical synchronicity. Each is at some point and in some way associated with the coastal; each is on the cusp between freedom from and entrapment in social 'divisions and signs'; each is engaged in a process of risk and even of danger, crossing the lines of taboo. The novel thus interrogates the symbolic order which underpins the social one in a poetic register created largely through the littoral imagery of beach and sea. But the poetic register is itself a site of doubling. It produces a disidentification even while it necessarily remembers—takes meaning from—the identification and counter-identification it refuses. And if it is not endlessly buffeted from one to the other position and back again, it moves restlessly between, above or beyond them. Even when the creation of non-meaning or the non-subjective position exists only by virtue of the prior existence of meaning, it may remain poised—as I have suggested—on the cusp between an established meaning and a meaning-to-come.

Head's novel is radical in its treatment of such impossible feats as collapsing the distinction between inside and outside or treating stasis as a point of becoming. The ambiguities generated by writing on the cusp of the littoral elevate the literariness of *The Cardinals* above its referentiality at a political moment in South African cultural life that would soon give over to protest writing and the sovereignty of the 'real'. Although there are many ways in which the novel does not fully work as a novel, these ambiguities are the source of its narrative attraction. The latter might be called its 'godliness', deriving as it does from the 'impossible' task of being obliged to make meanings within the terms of a law that the writing is also trying to stand outside of. In this formulation, the writer—which is to say, the act of writing—is something like René Girard's archaic priest-figure, whose potency lies in his transgression.[39] It is in this sense that I see Thetis presiding over the potentially immense power, the generative magic, of the text's refusal to follow the route that is at the same time marked out as the route to be taken. Like the four characters who make up 'the cardinals', Thetis stands both inside and outside the symbolic order, on the cusp of the littoral—as indeed does the author, which is to say, the 'author-effect' produced through the text.

Later in her writing career Head would develop a new imagery, this time from a land-locked Botswana. Here she would deploy the elemental figurations of moon, earth, sky and planets, some hints of which we see in *The Cardinals*. Like a figure in J.M. Coetzee's *Dusklands* (1974) who imagines 'eyes [so] free, they reach out to the horizon all around',[40] or Homi Bhabha's fantasied critical subject who dwells in the 'revisionary time' of the 'in-between' and 'beyond',[41] she develops characters and creative moments between characters that escape the discourse bequeathed by Apartheid.

In 1984 Head travelled to Adelaide at the invitation of the Adelaide Festival of the Arts, where she gave a talk entitled 'Living on an Horizon' to what she felt was 'the most responsive audience in the world', although she commented, too, on how 'closed and narrow' she found the 'white-dominated' life of Australia generally.[42] She also corresponded with Sreten Božić, writing under the name

B. Wongar, whose *Walg* she admired for its capacity to depict spiritual links between human beings and the world around them lost to the civilised world. He invited her to spend writing time on his property in Gippsland. One can only assume that Head would have been sympathetic to Wongar's desire to identify with Indigenous Australians (and shocked by the steps the Commonwealth took to suppress his exposé of the impact of uranium mining and nuclear testing in the Northern Territory), for she was not one to support identity politics, whatever their source. But she did not take up his invitation, and died soon afterwards, in 1986.

Over twenty years after *The Cardinals* was written, the black South African writer Zakes Mda made the connections between South Africa and Australia that Head herself did not live to make. In *The Whale Caller* (2005), Mda uses a story drawn from Aboriginal Dreaming about a time before humans and animals were divided, and by means of the coastal he connected the two countries' first peoples. Calling up an epistemology foreign to Enlightenment Reason, the Whale Caller, he writes, knows 'many Dreamings, told to [him] by travellers from those big islands during the days when [he] used to walk the coast'.[43] One might think, here, of the coast as no longer the portal of destruction named in Mofolo's *Chaka*, now that the black South African gaze has turned east, across 'the vast Indian Ocean'.[44] But Mda's novel is not sanguine: the ocean is red with the blood of whales killed under the aegis of a global capitalism that renders impotent the freedom achieved with the ending of Apartheid and the ardently longed-for demise of its 'divisions and signs'.

Notes

1   My thanks to Ken Ruthven and Shannon Burns for useful comment on an earlier version, and to the Centre for African Studies, University of Cape Town, for office space for part of the time this essay was being prepared. I engage here with difficult questions about Head's first novel that have been usefully addressed by several critics: M.J. Daymond, Introduction, *The Cardinals with Meditations and Stories*, by Bessie Head (Cape Town: David Philip, 1993) vii-xviii; Annie Gagiano, *Achebe, Head, Marechera: On Power and Change in Africa* (Boulder, Co. and London: Lynne Rienner, 2000) and Desirée Lewis, *Living on a Horizon: Bessie Head and the Politics of Imagining* (Trenton, N.J. and Asmara, Eritrea: Africa World Press, 2007). My focus on the coastal has taken my reading in a direction other than theirs, and expands on my two reviews of Head's novel: Dorothy Driver, 'Gestures of Expatriation and Belonging', *Southern African Review of Books* 5. 5 (Sept./Oct. 1993): 16-18; and Dorothy Driver, Review of *The Cardinals, with Meditations and Short Stories*, by Bessie Head, *New Contrast* 21. 4 (1993): 83-86.

2   Thomas Mofolo, *Chaka*, 1925, Trans. Daniel P. Kunene (London: Heinemann, 1981) 1.

3 Mofolo, *Chaka* 168.

4 Roy Campbell, *Selected Poetry* (London: Bodley Head, 1968) 17.

5 Stephen Gray, *Southern African Literature: An Introduction* (Cape Town: David Philip; London: Rex Collings, 1979) 17.

6 Bessie Head, 'Some Notes on Novel Writing', *New Classic* 5 (1978) 30.

7 Luís de Camões, 'Rounding the Cape', *Writers' Territory*, Ed. Stephen Gray (Cape Town: Longman Southern Africa, 1973) 2.

8 Camões, 'Rounding the Cape' 2.

9 Camões, 'Rounding the Cape' 3.

10 Camões, 'Rounding the Cape' 5.

11 Camões, 'Rounding the Cape' 5.

12 Gray, *Southern African Literature* 25.

13 Laurens van der Post, 'The Turbott Wolfe Affair', *Turbott Wolfe*, by William Plomer (Johannesburg: Ad Donker, 1980) 145.

14 Ian E. Glenn, 'The Wreck of the Grosvenor and the Making of South African Literature', *English in Africa* 22.2 (1995) 5.

15 Camões writes of the survivors of the *S. João*: 'They shall see the rough, grasping Cafres strip the gorgeous lady of her garments after a long and painful trek along the burning sands, leaving her limbs exposed to the rigours of the elements' (4).

16 Josiah Blackmore, Trans. 'Account of the Very Remarkable Loss of the Great Galleon *S. João* […]'. *The Tragic History of the Sea*. Ed. C.R. Boxer (Minneapolis: University of Minnesota Press, 2001) 23.

17 Josiah Blackmore, *Manifest Perdition: Shipwreck Narrative and the Disruption of Empire* (Minneapolis and London: University of Minnesota Press, 2002) 75.

18 Blackmore, *Manifest Perdition* 75.

19 Camões, 'Rounding the Cape' 5.

20 Camões, 'Rounding the Cape' 5.

21 Camões, 'Rounding the Cape' 5.

22 Gillian Stead Eilersen, *Bessie Head: Thunder Behind Her Ears: Her Life and Writing* (Portsmouth, N.H.: Heinemann; London: James Currey; Cape Town and Johannesburg: David Philip, 1995) 7.

23 Bessie Head, *A Woman Alone:Autobiographical Writings* (Oxford: Heinemann Educational, 1990) 3.

24 *Drum* publications put out two magazines owned and formally edited by white men, and researched and written by journalists classified under Apartheid as non-white, almost all of whom were male.

25 Bessie Head, *The Collector of Treasures* (London: Heinemann, 1977) 90.

26 Head, *Collector of Treasures* 91.

27 Head, *Collector of Treasures* 90.

28 Bessie Head, *The Cardinals, with Meditations and Stories* (Cape Town: David Philip, 1993) 48.

29 Head, *Cardinals* 49.

30 Head, *Cardinals* 7.

29 Head, *Cardinals* 78. See also: 'I used to kiss her the way a man kisses a woman' (78).

30 Head, *Cardinals* 85.
31 Head, *Cardinals* 91.
32 Head, *Cardinals* 72, 88.
33 Head, *Cardinals* 89.
34 Head, *Cardinals* 52.
35 Head, *Cardinals* 89.
36 'Why don't you come down and lie next to me? I'm not really a monster' (Head, *Cardinals* 100).
37 Head, *Cardinals* 8.
38 Michel Pêcheux, *Language, Semantics and Ideology* (London: Macmillan, 1982). 159. Pêcheux refers to three processes of subject-formation and the construction of meaning: identification, counter-identification, and disidentification. Identification accepts the image of self/meaning projected by the dominant discourse; counter-identification rejects that image/meaning, yet even in its opposition it accepts the terms through which the image/meaning is proposed; and disidentification takes up a non-subjective position in such a way that threatens to 'rearrange' or even 'overthrow' the discursive terms (whether dominant or oppositional) through which the image/meaning is proposed. Disidentication thus displaces dominant practices of ideological subjection.
39 René Girard, *Violence and the Sacred*, trans. Patrick Gregory (Baltimore and London: Johns Hopkins University Press, 1972) 105. For Girard, this figure is 'the catalyst who converts sterile, infectious violence into positive cultural values' (107).
40 J.M. Coetzee, *Dusklands* (Johannesburg: Ravan Press, 1974) 79.
41 Homi K. Bhabha, *The Location of Culture* (London: Routledge, 1994) 7.
42 Bessie Head, Letter to Paddy Kitchen, 18 June 1985; cited Eilersen, *Thunder* 271.
43 Zakes Mda, *The Whale Caller* (Johannesburg: Penguin, 2005) 140.
44 Mda, *Whale Caller* 138.

Works cited

Bhabha, Homi K. *The Location of Culture*. London: Routledge, 1994.

Blackmore, Josiah. Trans. 'Account of the Very Remarkable Loss of the Great Galleon S. João [...]'. *The Tragic History of the Sea*. Ed. C.R. Boxer. Minneapolis: University of Minnesota Press, 2001. 3-26.

Blackmore, Josiah. *Manifest Perdition: Shipwreck Narrative and the Disruption of Empire*. Minneapolis and London: University of Minnesota Press, 2002.

Camões, Luís de. 'Rounding the Cape.' *Writers' Territory*. Ed. Stephen Gray. Cape Town: Longman Southern Africa, 1973.

Campbell, Roy. *Selected Poetry*. London: Bodley Head, 1968.

Coetzee, J. M. *Dusklands*. Johannesburg: Ravan Press, 1974.

Daymond, M.J. Introduction. *The Cardinals, with Meditations and Stories*. By Bessie Head. Cape Town: David Philip, 1993. vii-xviii.

Driver, Dorothy. 'Gestures of Expatriation and Belonging'. Review of *The Cardinals, with Meditations and Short Stories*, by Bessie Head; and *A Gesture of Belonging: Letters from Bessie Head, 1965-1979,* ed. Randolph Vigne. *Southern African Review of Books* 5. 5 (Sept./Oct. 1993): 16-18.

Driver, Dorothy. Review of *The Cardinals, with Meditations and Short Stories*, by Bessie

Head, ed. and intro. M.J. Daymond. *New Contrast* 21. 4 (1993): 83-86.

Eilersen, Gillian Stead. *Bessie Head: Thunder Behind Her Ears: Her Life and Writing.* Portsmouth, N.H.: Heinemann; London: James Currey; Cape Town and Johannesburg: David Philip, 1995.

Gagiano, Annie. *Achebe, Head, Marechera: On Power and Change in Africa.* Boulder, Co. and London: Lynne Rienner, 2000.

Girard, René. *Violence and the Sacred.* Trans. Patrick Gregory. Baltimore and London: Johns Hopkins University Press, 1972.

Glenn, Ian E. 'The Wreck of the Grosvenor and the Making of South African Literature'. *English in Africa* 22. 2 (1995) 1–18.

Gray, Stephen. *Southern African Literature: An Introduction.* Cape Town: David Philip; London: Rex Collings, 1979.

Head, Bessie. *A Woman Alone: Autobiographical Writings.* Oxford: Heinemann Educational, 1990.

Head, Bessie. 'Some Notes on Novel Writing'. *New Classic* 5 (1978) 30.

Head, Bessie. *The Cardinals, with Meditations and Stories.* Ed. and intro. M.J. Daymond. Cape Town: David Philip, 1993.

Head, Bessie. *The Collector of Treasures.* London: Heinemann Educational, 1977.

Lewis, Desirée. *Living on a Horizon: Bessie Head and the Politics of Imagining.* Trenton, N.J. and Asmara, Eritrea: Africa World Press, 2007.

Mda, Zakes. *The Whale Caller.* Johannesburg: Penguin, 2005.

Mofolo, Thomas. *Chaka.* 1931. Trans. Daniel P. Kunene. London: Heinemann, 1981.

Nkosi, Lewis. *Mating Birds.* Johannesburg: Ravan Press, 1987.

Pêcheux, Michel. *Language, Semantics and Ideology.* London: Macmillan, 1982.

Van der Post, Laurens. 'The Turbott Wolfe Affair'. *Turbott Wolfe.* By William Plomer. Johannesburg: Ad Donker, 1980.

Wicomb, Zoë. *David's Story.* Cape Town: Kwela Books, 2000.

Wongar. B. *Walg: A Novel of Australia.* 1983. London and Melbourne: Macmillan, 1986.

Indian Ocean Poetry

STEPHEN MUECKE

I have been encouraged to write poetry by two of my colleagues in Sydney. One, the poet Keri Glastonbury, has written a piece whose title perfectly expresses the popular Australian sport of poet-bashing. It's called, 'Shut-up, no-one wants to listen to your poetry', and it has appeared in the *Cultural Studies Review*.[1] The other colleague who encouraged me was Martin Harrison, who offered the gentle reassurance that the texts you are about to hear are not poetry at all, but rather 'talk pieces'.

Now, I'm happy to go along with that, since that phrase is something like the *Sprechstücke* of Peter Handke fame.[2] But in this contemporary Australian context, or rather oceanic context, I want to identify some features of the poetic underlying these texts which depart from the dominant lyrical mode. They are all about the external. They do not emerge from some personal interior, or metaphoric depth; nor are they inspired from anything above. They are about geographies: horizons, lines that connect places on a map. These are pieces I have written to express some continuities in Indian Ocean culture.

Now, it isn't just me inventing these continuities, for the more I look, the more I find they are there already: they exist in religion, trade practices, cuisine; they are carried by natural patterns like monsoon winds. In addition, continuities like this can only be perceived if one is looking for them. Broome, for instance, is a town in North-West West Australia, or is it an Indian Ocean port? Is it national or transnational? New ways of seeing are created with our interpretative tools, and of course the notion of *creolisation* is one of them. Françoise Lionnet, talking about Creole vernacular theatre in Mauritius says:

> Finding useful ways of articulating Creole texts (oral, written or visual), not just with their European generic 'models' but also with postcolonial creative texts and performances, is an important step in the process of conceptualizing the links among the varied cultures of the so-called 'peripheries'. More lateral comparisons among 'minor' texts and genres or marginalized artistic productions and languages will eventually allow us to bypass altogether the mediation by a center, and the usual comparison of the margin with its hierarchical other that becomes inevitable in studies of intertextuality, literary influence and cross-pollinations.[3]

So *performing* these texts, linking them laterally with other texts, and making explicit those connections, is a way, for me, of not thinking in terms of centres and margins. There are connections in a network which can be coaxed to grow new 'shoots', as it were. So the approach is not by way of postcolonial *critique*, but by way of performing *potentiality*. To talk of this Indian Ocean context, between Australia and Mauritius, as creolised, is not to assume that either language or tradition, here or there, is dominant. The principle is to not take the major or the powerful as an assumed point of reference. It is to attend to the swell of a rising tide which might carry us forward.

My first *Sprechstücke* owes it existence to Françoise Lionnet's work 'Reframing Baudelaire: Literary History, Biography, Postcolonial Theory, and Vernacular Languages'. To her I owe the idea of locating Baudelaire in the Indian Ocean; that certain of his poems were born of his experience there, and are thus part of the Indian Ocean heritage since they are a creolisation, as it were, of his French with local Creole:

> Perhaps the time has come [she says] to reconsider Baudelaire's poetry as one of the first places of emergence of the native Creole woman's voice, a ventriloquized voice to be sure, but the only one we have from the first half of the nineteenth century.[4]

Baudelaire was doing a powerful thing in his time, speaking to Europe with a slightly exotic voice, but without this necessarily being *exoticism*. This is why I have used the concept of post-orientalism as the title for the poem. The argument it carries—these talk pieces are fictocritical in that they tell stories while making arguments—is that the orientalist critique of artists as appropriators or misrepresenters misses something important: their necessary right, and desire, to be influenced, to activate, as Lionnet says, a 'baroque aesthetics by using creative "mélanges" and parodying the original as well as contemporary cultural scenarios.'[5] We should not criticise Western artists for appropriating, while we celebrate Indigenous artists for their creative *mélanges*. The mistake here is not so much with artists' practice, because we are all appropriators and mixers, it is with the critical assumption that the Western forms are generically stable.

Post-orientalism
Baudelaire never made it to India,
sent there in '41 by his mother and step-father
to cure his dissolute ways, his *flânerie*,
his ratbaggery and incurable genius.

Couldn't they see that a trip *là-bas* could only feed the fever?
So of course he agreed, embarking on a steamer at Le Havre,
with enough opium and books to keep him company;
the ship's chambermaid, also, mesmerised no doubt
by his melancholy and his outlandish style.

The captain spoke of his percentage in the Compagnie des Indes,
and the propagation of vanilla in Réunion and Madagascar
while prising the wine carafe gently from young Charles' grip.

At Saint-Denis he descended, under instructions,
the sea so rough that landing from the launch required climbing a rope ladder
hanging at the end of a jetty, two cannon balls attached to the bottom end.
'Grab the rungs at the crest of the wave, no sooner', they yelled.
But Baudelaire, the formalist, the agent of urbanity, insisted on climbing the
ladder with books under his arm,
and slowly, pursued by the next rising wave,
reaching and engulfing him and tearing him from the ladder.
Then fished out (with some difficulty) but, amazingly, the books
       unrelinquished.
So finally he consented (*Voyons, Monsieur! Enfin!*)
to leave them in the boat.
And on his way up again, rinsed gently by another wave.
Kept hold, arrived on top and set off for the town, calm and cool,
his hat turning and drifting in the Indian Ocean depths.

The immersion transforms the oeuvre, or is it
Emmelina de Bragard, a creole woman *aux charmes ignorés*
whom he knew

in a perfumed country caressed by the sun
under a canopy of trees ablaze with purple.

Baudelaire, our urban dandy, is suddenly provincialised.
Standing wet and dripping on a jetty in the Indian Ocean,
the aesthetic hemispheres turn: now he will invent
from là-bas
a modernism metropolises never knew.
Oceanic feeling now flows, unstoppable, from the exploited places

(whose spices and perfumes literally funded the literatures of the modern,
giving the bourgeoisie time, money, dissolution).

The war of economic domination is won as soon as declared.
But now the postcolonial subjects set up shop
in the tourist-infested tropics, with an inexhaustible resource:
the forever incomplete desires for *luxe, calme* and *volupté*.
And sure, they spin a subtle, but substantial, economic revenge.

Like a strange and beautiful Trojan horse, our Indian Ocean poet
released an army of weird desires into the metropolis;
such an infection is never, ever misrepresentation.
You cannot argue with a virus or a verse, it takes hold, or not.[6]

This next poem, sorry, talk piece, is about alternative modernities:

JÉROME'S HAPPY HOUR

Time is suspended so sweetly,
Jérome might think, but he's not,
not like that.

On a Friday afternoon at Black River,
he has come back from the reef,
pulled up his blue catamaran on the beach,
and is hailing his friends, as Ayeesha looks after the catch.

They gather under the palms
with a bucket of sweet rum coco.
Before time starts again.

They spot the green Landrover
coming from Flic-en-flac
with the white-shirted driver.
And have time for one 'Missié James' joke,
before he stops and walks over (*Bonzour, bonzour!*).

Mr James Merryweather, an agent of the modern,
sent from the UK:
to inject new life and vitality into the fishing industry

'Come on Jérome. This is a glorious day for fishing.
Why aren't you working?'

'I don't have to, Missié James. I came back yesterday with 75 pounds of capi-
taine and vacoas. I've got enough money to last the weekend!'

'Look, Jérome …'
He is ignoring the others who are smirking or sleeping.
'If you get more fish,
you can buy a big boat with an outboard.
And then take tourists out,
and make more money!'

Jérome's eyes open a little wider
in mock-negro surprise:
'A big white house, more children
a gold necklace … for Ayeesha'.
(kissing the illusory jewel away,
with a theatrical gesture, for the drinkers).
Takes a puff of one of Merryweather's du Mauriers.

'And when I am rich, Missié James, what then?'

'You'd be an old man by that time, Jérome.
You could then stop working
and lie on the beach and enjoy the sun!'

'So what am I doing now? Enough fish, no work, plenty of sun!'
and he cackles until he coughs and spits.
And takes a good slug of rum coco.

And the Englishman goes off to his own clubby happy hour
at Flic-en-Flac,
watching the sun set in the ocean as
five women in red saris make *pujas* to Lakshmi on the beach.

And he complains to the teacher Ramesh Ramdoyal
who writes it all up in
Tales from Mauritius: A Supplementary English Reader.

There are questions at the end for the pupils,
who were also becoming modern, in 1979,
as the reef fishing is running out and
ocean trawlers are coming in.

'In the story "Live Now, Pay Later" who do you think is more sensible—
Jérome or Mr Merryweather? Give reasons for your choice.'

As soon as you have choice,
you are a modern subject.
You can hone a moral technology,
becoming professional,
going about giving people advice.

But they might think.
Did Jérome really have a sensible choice?
Or Mr Merryweather?
The only thing that can really compete
with a fleet of trawlers,
is the happiness of rum coco
in the filaments of a long hour.[7]

Paul and Virginia

When I was doing fieldwork in Port Louis, Mauritius in 1998, I was rummaging in an old photography studio-cum-museum, and came across a couple of reel-to-reel audio tapes. I asked the proprietor what was on them and he didn't know. I said I had a machine at home that could play them. Who knows? I said, they might be something interesting. So he let me take them away on the promise of keeping him informed.

And I did, coming back excitedly the next day with the machine and we sat down and listened to an old creole man tell the story of Paul and Virginia, in his own vernacular style; that is, in Mauritian Creole. *Paul and Virginia*, as you know, is the classic novel of Mauritius, a bestselling romance from Bernardin de St Pierre, published in France in 1788. As far as Jean Baladin (the proprietor of the photo shop) and I were concerned, this more contemporary version was a literary gold-mine. Someone—we didn't know who: in the nineteen fifties, judging from the age of the tapes—had had the foresight to record on old man who must have been renowned for his abilities in recounting epic oral narratives. My grasp of Mauritian French creole was far from perfect, but it was one of the languages Jean had grown up with. So in the end, between us, we were able to prepare two versions: a creole transcription and my English translation.

For the method of transcription I borrowed the techniques I had used for the narratives of Paddy Roe, from Broome, not that far away on another Indian Ocean shore.[8] There I had found that oral narratives are formed more naturally in phrases rather than the proper sentences of written languages, and that the narrator's pace is physically governed by the body, by lung capacity. So a line is often a phrase, punctuated by a pause at the end where the narrator takes a breath. In my translation I found myself falling in to the patterns of Paddy Roe's style. I hope he would have been able to accept it as a compliment that the beauty of his technique could only be imitated, somewhat poorly here, by his old editor and pupil, for this first version of a vernacular Paul and Virginia, transcribed and translated here without any embellishments.

[tape begins as two men are talking, one in standard French (he is probably a planter or a visitor to the island), and the other voice is that of an old man talking creole]

… yes, of course. When you are ready.
[coughing]
—You are ready now? This thing is on is it?
—Yes
—Oh! [laughs] Oh, OK, then…

Well, these two mothers gave birth the same day,
at a place called Pamplemousse
just up here in the hills, you know.

And the old ladies helping them came up there.
Oh, they weren't old, but they were young,
Malagasy women, from over there,
friends of the two young mothers,
and they were French, but poor,
oh, very poor those French mothers were.

But they knew what to do, the midwives, you know.
They didn't have too many doctors in those days.
Only one, for the planters really.

You could hear them crying out
at the same time, these two mothers,
from their huts on both sides of that clearing,
up there in the hills,
around Pamplemousse.

And then, around four in the afternoon,
everyone heard the two babies crying,
first one side then the other: *waaa ... waaa.*
Two babies born, then.
'Oh good!' everyone said.
All the people was happy.

So, the two midwives brought the babies out,
all wrapped up, a boy and a girl, they said,
a beautiful boy and beautiful girl.
Put them to sleep side by side in the same crib,
while their mothers had a sleep too.

Ah well, after that those two kids started to grow,
growing up together in that place.
The mothers had two helpers, like slaves,
but not really, more like friends.
Domingo, I think the man's name was,
and his wife was Mary, she was one of those mid-wives.
He married her after Paul and Virginia were born.

Oh the old people used to talk about that wedding too
old Tjamba was playing music, plenty of rum.
And dancing all night, right through the night,
down on the beach at Black River.

So all together they made a farm,
up at Pamplemousse.

Domingo was a good farmer, while Mary looked after the poultry.
She took the produce down to the market in Port Louis.

On the fertile ground Domingo sowed wheat,
and on the poor ground maize.
Rice too, in the marshy areas.
Pumpkins and cucumbers grew well at the foot of rocks,
sugar-cane in the clayey soil;
cotton-tree and coffee in the high spots.

Oh he knew what he was doing, that old fella.
And Paul used to follow him around when he was little.
After he grew up he helped the old man.
Oh, Domingo and Mary they loved those two kids,
they was always playin' around with them.

So one day come, Paul and Virginia were getting big now
Virginia was a woman really now, so pretty, you know
and embarrassed, she hid away in the house,
hiding away because she was shy, lil' bit.

Poor Paul didn't know what to do, he'd lost his playmate.
So Domingo took him hunting, out in the bush
they might find birds, or an old Dodo egg.
Things like that you could sell in town.
oh good price you get too, for those Dodo eggs
no matter if it is broken, you can patch it up, no worries.

So one day come, Domingo is working in the garden
and he's looking, rubs his eye and looks again
oh! something there, in the pumpkin patch, he keeps looking.
Like a pumpkin, only moving, up and down
you know … [laughter]

Mus' be … oh can't be! Someone's bottom!
That Domingo took off! back to his hut,
running, and he's panting and asks Mary, where Paul?

I dunno, where Virginia? ... Oh, you'd better come, he said.
So they both crept back, have a look,
from around the side of a tree, you know, two heads
and they were laughing little bit, giggling.

Anyway, no more pumpkin there,
but there's Paul and Virginia walking on the other side
holding hands you know, those two lovely kids.

Domingo and Mary had a good laugh then.
After that Mary always called her old man *coco-fesses*[9]
But they didn't tell the mothers,
'cos they went to church and everything.

So what happened then?
Nature must take its course you know.
Mary talked to Virginia of course
about all that women's stuff
but mighta been too late, I think.

Soon as she knew ... soon as she knew
(must have been that pumpkin I think!)
Well Mary said, 'we gotta tell your mother'.
The old lady has to know what to do.

She had that same thing too, when she was carrying Virginia
her man just took off, somewhere in France
and she had to go up to Pamplemousse with Paul's mother
and her husband had died or something.

Oh, they was really cross those old ladies
when they found out
About Virginia and Paul
what they done, ooh, very cross.

And so they had to send the girl away
that's what those French people do, you know
they think it a big shame.

'Cos that mother had a auntie in France.
And a boat was leaving in a couple of weeks.
'We'll send you there', she said.
'You can help your old Auntie, she's been asking for you.
And carry a letter with you.'

That's how it went, you know
Virginia didn't want to go,
she was crying all the time.
And Paul wanted her to stay
he was just hanging around.
'Cos those two grew up together,
together they wanted to stay,
on the island, where they grew up.

Now I dunno what happened in France
Paris it might of been, or maybe Rouen
but Virginia stayed there about a year,
with a young girl who went with her,
to keep her company on the ship.
Creole girl, from that family, ah, whatname now?
Can't remember that family name, doesn't matter.

After that nobody heard any story, no letter, nothing.
'What happen to Virginia?' everyone been askin'.
And Paul hanging about, down by the sea,
just sitting carving a bit of wood, or might be bone.
He was making picture of his girl, you know, how they do.
Like the *barhai* do, we call 'em *barhai*, wood carvers.[10]
scrimshaw English call it, eh? *scrimshaw*.
Old Pierre in Flic-en-Flac got some of that stuff, you seen it?

So one day come, they got word,
mighta been the governor I think,
said those girls coming back, on the next boat.
Virginia and her girlfriend,
or her helper, or whatever.

Governor himself went up to Pamplemousse
to talk to those mothers.
That old Auntie dead too, in France, he said.

And she gonna leave some money to you lot.
Looks like no more worries.
Everyone got happy then.
'Cos they really missed their girl
and Paul, like he woke up again after a long sleep.

Started to get everything ready then.
Boat was coming in about a month.
That was the old days then
sailing boats, very slow, you know all the way from France,
around past Cape Town, then across to Mauritius, and on to India.

So when they gonna come, one night I think
people was saying, 'oh! cyclone comin' up'.
In the morning everyone was down at a place called *Poussière d'or,*
waiting waiting waiting, watching the sea,
see if they could see that boat,
and they could see the storm coming from the other side.

Soon as that boat got near the shore, crash! the cyclone hit it.
They couldn't control the boat,
and it was close up on the reef.
You could see the people on the deck,
and then it hit the reef.

And some people got little boats out to help,
get out there to rescue them, you know
Paul was there, yelling out to Virginia
and telling her to jump in.
But she was too frightened.
She didn't want to jump into the sea.
Boat started to break up then,
with the storm and lightning all around.

It was a big bloody mess they say,
dead body washing up on the beach, you know
and poor Paul, running from one to another,
after the storm, running around
and looking for his beloved, and he didn't find her.
Someone else found her, half buried in the sand.
After the storm.

And they took him away and the poor boy lost his mind.
After that he couldn't talk, and just got thinner and thinner.
I think it mighta been a few months after that, he was dead.

So that was the story of Paul and Virginia.
Some bloke made a book out of that, eh?
long long time ago.

[noise of chairs moving around] ——

But that's not the finish yet, of the story,
'cos they found that other girl, the creole girl you know.
Someone musta pulled her out of the water,
and she came in on one of those little catamarans.

And she had a baby in her arms, little baby
but that wasn't her baby, no.
this was a little white baby, blond hair, everything.

Nobody knew, where this baby been come from, you know.
But we knew, you know, us creole mob.
That girl musta told her mother after a while,
who that baby belong to, you know.

Virginia musta kept that baby.
Somehow she talked to that old auntie, talk her around
and she let her keep the baby,
Virginia wanted to bring it home for her and Paul, you know.

That creole girl kept the baby, with her people in Black River, I think
nobody worried too much, those days,
plenty o' lil' brown kids running around.
So he grew up there, in Black River,
but they knew where he come from, really.
'cos of Domingo and Mary.

So that's how that little boy got his nickname,
'Pumpkin', they called him, and the old people knew why,
but they kept it to themselfs, my old creole mob.
That little Pumpkin was a happy kid, strong.
but he never knew who his real mummy and daddy were.

that's the finish now, of that story.

Notes

1 Keri Glastonbury, 'Shut Up, Nobody Wants to Hear Your Poems!: Painter versus Poet', *Cultural Studies Review*, Vol. 12, No. 2.

2 Thanks to Edward Scheer for the information that Peter Handke's first play, *Publikumsbeschimpfung* ('Offending the Audience', 1966) was published in the German under that title with the sub title 'und andere Sprechstucke' (trans. London Methuen, 1971). John Kinsella has said: 'I think that's a good description of [your pieces], but I'd go for "dialogics" as there's more theory at work than the other indicates. They are also less addressing than they seem, almost being vocal distractions 'pretending' to be interactive conversations. I think there's more artifice than 'talk' allows as well. But still, it's a fair enough label.' (Email, 19 January 2006)

3 Françoise Lionnet, 'Creole Vernacular Theatre: Transcolonial Translation in Mauritius', *Modern Language Notes*, 118:4 (Oct. 2003) 913.

4 Francoise Lionnet, 'Reframing Baudelaire: Literary History, Biography, Postcolonial Theory, and Vernacular Languages', *Diacritics* 28.3 (1998) 84.

5 See my paper outlining this idea: 'The Fall: Fictocritical Writing', *parallax*, 25, October–December 2002 108–12; Lionnet, 'Creole Vernacular Theatre' 919.

6 First published in *Meanjin* 64.4, 2005 78–9.

7 First published in *Westerly* 50, November, 2005 208–10.

8 Paddy Roe, *Gularabulu: Stories from the West Kimberley*, ed. and introduction by Stephen Muecke, Fremantle, Fremantle Arts Centre Press, 1983.

9 A rare double coconut from the Seychelles which looks like a bottom.

10 See Lee Haring, *Indian Ocean Folk Tales* (Chennai, National Folklore Support Centre, 2002) 63.

Works cited

Handke, Peter. *Publikumsbeschimpfung* ('Offending the Audience', 1966). Trans. London: Methuen, 1971.

Haring, Lee. *Indian Ocean Folk Tales*. Chennai: National Folklore Support Centre, 2002.

Lionnet, Françoise. 'Creole Vernacular Theatre: Transcolonial Translation in Mauritius'. *Modern Language Notes,* 118:4 (Oct. 2003) 913.

Lionnet, Francoise. 'Reframing Baudelaire: Literary History, Biography, Postcolonial Theory, and Vernacular Languages'. *Diacritics* 28.3 (1998) 84.

Muecke, Stephen. 'The Fall: Fictocritical Writing'. *parallax* 25, October–December 2002 108–12.

Roe, Paddy. *Gularabulu: Stories from the West Kimberley*. ed. and introduction by Stephen Muecke. Fremantle, Fremantle Arts Centre Press, 1983.

Kingdoms of Neptune: seas, bays, estuaries and the dangers of reading skua poetry (it may embed in your skull)

JOHN McLAREN

> The skua flew into our heads in 1968—
> a new kind of poetry, a scavenging predator
> frequently attacking humans …
> One was found
> in Tasmania, its beak embedded in the skull
> of a spotted quoll …
> … if you read skua poetry, beware:
> one could fly out from the page
> and change the expression of your face.[1]

Since Neolithic times, civilisations have been built on the abundance of water. It came to irrigation societies from the Nile, the Ganges, the Indus and the Euphrates. It came to the societies of northern Europe and the islands of the North Atlantic from precipitation, and the rivers carried away their excess. As the division of labour separated the genders, women, as Kate Llewellyn puts it, were water and men were fire, but together they built wetlands cultures.[2] Women were givers of life, but also creatures driven by tempestuous passion who reflected men's lust back on them and turned them to stone. Men wielded power, brought destruction. They also channelled the waters, turned them to their own purposes. Then they came to Australia, where the land was dried out, a barren, threatening mother they could not control. They would not or could not learn from the hunter gatherers whose way of life had conserved the waters. They tried instead to impose their waterlands culture on a drylands continent. When it resisted, they turned on it in fury and hatred.

The tyranny of distance that has dominated Australian history was driven by water, both as presence and absence. The rivers and waterholes that were sacred sites for the first dwellers determined the patterns of their habitations and journeyings, and through the millennia the expanses of the oceans surrounding their continent kept them apart from foreign intrusions as they adapted a dry land to their economic needs and developed a culture responsive to its demands. Some 12,000 years ago the rising of these oceans set the Tasmanians still further apart from the mainland. However, 600 years ago along the north coast Indigenous people were making regular contact with traders and fishers from Asia and its islands. The ocean that had been a barrier for some became a roadway for others, eventually bringing sailors and then settlers from the wetlands of Europe.

For centuries, Europeans had seen the world as a mass of land with the Mediterranean Sea at its centre and the ocean marking its boundaries. The Mediterranean and the Euxine, and the rivers flowing into them, were their highways. As they spread across the world, the oceans became their highways to wealth. When they stumbled on to Australia the north and west shores proved inhospitable, but the vision of wealth the oceans had discovered for them in the east never quite dropped away. Luis Vaz de Camões wrote of gold and luxury abounding in Irian South, and, after Ferdinand Magellan opened the Pacific to European eyes, his successors sought through its islands for the Great Southland of the Holy Spirit.[3] The pragmatic James Cook and the scientific rationalist Sir Joseph Banks replaced these rumours with a utilitarian vision of a curious country fit for reformatory and pastoral settlement.

Kenneth Slessor later gave high drama to Cook's choice of 'a passage into the dark', west rather than north from New Zealand.

'Choose now!'
The winds roared, blowing home, blowing home,
Over the Coral Sea. 'Choose now!' The trades
Cried once to Tasman, throwing him for choice
Their teeth or shoulders, and the Dutchman chose
The wind's way, turning north, 'Choose Bougainville!'
The wind cried once, and Bougainville had heard
The voice of God, calling him prudently
Out of the dead lee shore, and chose the north,
The wind's way. So, too, Cook made choice,
Over the brink, into the devil's mouth,
With four month's food, and sailors wild with dreams
Of English beer, and smoking barns of home.
So Cook made choice, so Cook sailed westabout,
So men write poems in Australia.[4]

Writing in the 1930s, Slessor did not consider the reality that men and women had for millennia been composing, and remembering, poems in Australia. The pragmatic Cook had sailed west because his discoveries had already 'reduced the only possible site of a continent in the southern hemisphere ... to so small a space that it would be a pity to leave that unexamined'.[5] His greater interest was in the Pacific islands themselves. But he too saw them only from a European perspective.

The New Zealander Allen Curnow, writing of Tasman's discoveries, sees them first as a seaman for whom 'Exhilaration went off like a gun'. But he then shows the discovery through the eyes of the islanders, to whom

> danger
> Is what comes over the sea;
> Over the yellow sands and the clear
> Shallows, the dull filament
> Flickers, the blood of strangers:
> Death discovered the Sailor
> O in a flash, in a flat calm,
> A clash of boats in the bay
> And the day marred with murder

The poem ends with another reminder that New Zealand is an island, involved by bloodshed in the life of other lands.[6]

This sea and its winds continue to blow through James Baxter's 'Pig Island Letters', a sequence about the New Zealand of his own time, where his listeners are 'aware of the albatross', and that:

> In the Otago storms
> Carrying spray to salt the landward farms
> The wind is a drunkard. Whoever can listen
> Long enough will write again.[7]

The poet is not the beneficiary of the discoverers, but a creature of the land they have left him, and which he must make his own through his own as he takes his words from the same winds that continue to shape it. By contrast, when Slessor writes his seafaring poem in Australia he ends it in Scotland, where the voyaging has become only a romantic memory. The voyagers remain remote from the land they have discovered.[8]

As the newcomers traversed and named the Australian inland, they found no fertile river valleys to sustain the dream of a new civilisation that they carried with them. They built trading ports on the coast, and they exploited the Pacific to their purpose, but these places gained no purchase on their imagination. In contrast to New Zealanders, they looked to Neptune's inland realm, searching for a sea that did not exist, exploring, draining and polluting rivercourses, or paddling by the shores of the threatening ocean. They carried with them new plants and beasts, new tools and new dreams. These dreams rested on a free and prosperous rural citizenry, but this depended on a plenitude of water. Instead of an inland sea that would generate a bounteous climate, the explorers found a dry inland, a dead heart, and the settlers on the intermediate plains encountered a frequency of drought.

As well as being geographic facts, oceans, seas and rivers are cultural constructs that determine the way we perceive and use or live with our material and human environment. It did not take long for the language the settlers brought to Australia to change in order to accommodate their new reality. Rivers retained their currency, even when they were reduced to strings of muddy puddles or dry watercourses. Thomas Mitchell inscribed grandiose names on the dry inland plains, conjuring up visions of lofty mountains and well-watered valleys, thus reinforcing the myth of inland fertility. Squatters named their stations after glens in Scotland, but gullies, waterholes, and creeks replaced the vales and fountains, pools, rivulets, streams and brooks of England. The creeks were often designated with such terms as Homestead, Dry or Deadman's, or the matter-of-fact Seven Mile. Even when they flowed with water after sudden rains, they offered an impediment rather than a path to progress, as the immortal sunburned stockman found when he 'apostrophised his bloody cuddy'.

> 'This bloody steed must bloody swim,
> the same for me as bloody him!'
> The creek was deep and bloody floody;
> So ere they reached the bloody bank
> The bloody steed beneath him sank—
> The stockman's face a bloody study,
> Ejaculating bloody! bloody! bloody![9]

When Australian writers turn to their shores, they avoid direct encounter, bloody or otherwise, with the sea. Vance Palmer set a novel among fishermen in *The Passage*, but the estuary where his characters work is only a background to the lives they lead on shore. Thea Astley ventured into the Pacific in her *Beachmasters,* but in the book she kept to her island, and when she returned to Australia she had a deluge sweep her bolder characters out into the oceans, where they were heard of no more. The novelists Tim Winton and Robert Drewe are among the first writers to draw attention to the importance of the littoral in Australian culture. Winton took on Herman Melville's whale and whalers, but his characters are outsiders and his action was confined to the shore, as it is in *Dirt Music,* another novel of a fisherman. In *The Bodysurfers* (1983), Drewe uses the beach as a site of personal affairs rather than as a place where his characters may live out their lives.

Popular television series have taken a similar perspective, using the beach as an exotic background for personal affairs. At first glance, the ABC's *SeaChange* appears more firmly grounded in daily life and work, but its framework is a pastoral idyll where refugees from the city seek to protect rural innocence from developers who relish the pace and greed of the city.[10] In Anne Reeves's film *The Oyster Farmer* (2005), a more complex relationship is set up, as the newcomer has to overcome the hostility of locals whose lives are shaped by the harsh realities of economic survival and past violence.[11] The river offers the possibility of freedom, but only to those who are prepared to pay the economic and emotional price of learning to live with it and its people.

The credits to this film acknowledge the assistance of the poet Robert Adamson and the photography of his partner, Juno Gemes. The Hawkesbury and its littoral are fully present in Adamson's own poems, which are comple-mented by Gemes's photographs.[12] Throughout his work, Adamson has been, as T.S. Eliot says of Shakespeare, 'occupied with the struggle—which alone constitutes life for a poet—to transmute his personal and private agonies into something rich and strange, something universal and impersonal'.[13] The violence of humans and nature persist along Adamson's Hawkesbury, but his people learn to balance it in their lives. There is a stillness about Gemes' photography, gen-erated by the immobility of artefacts waiting use, or of people captured in the midst of action, and by the sheen off the water, but it is a stillness that implies labour. It gives us glimpses of a way of life along the river, but at the same time it withholds its full meaning, which is accessible only to those who work there. Adamson has lived and worked there as fisherman and as poet, and his words capture the river in its time and place, and in the struggles, violence and passion that constitute its life.

In his autobiography, Adamson shows how as a youth he had found an island of sanity with the paternal grandfather who had introduced him to the world of the Hawkesbury and the work and craft of fishing. When he escaped from domestic violence to life as a tearaway, he suffered the awful consequences of the New South Wales gaol systems.[14] Eventually he found salvation in words when other prisoners and their visitors introduced him to prose fiction, to Niccolò Machiavelli, and to the songs of Bob Dylan and the poetry of Les Murray, Geoffrey Lehmann, Sappho and Gerard Manly Hopkins. He learned to write, filling an exercise book with his first collection of poems. But before he could escape to the company of other poets and back to boats and fishing on the Hawkesbury, he suffered a traumatic loss. As he prepared to leave the Maitland prison with his poems clutched under his arm, a brutal warder intervened.

> 'Your poetry … is written on government property. If you take this through the gates, it's stealing.'
> … I stood there feeling sick … I was standing near the open gate. I had only to move forward. It was like stepping into space.[15]

He returned to his river, where he again started his writing from the beginning, transforming his life by working on its waters as he transformed his experience into words.

The sea and its creatures represented for Adamson a nature that is neither indifferent, as in Marcus Clark, hostile, as in Henry Lawson, or redemptive, as in Judith Wright. The river and the ocean comprised a force that shapes those who work with it. Or perhaps better it is a presence, from which, as in the poem of the same name, he moved '[t]owards abstraction/possibly a gull's wing'.[16] From his grandfathers he had learned respect for craftsmanship, and he himself became a crafty worker with boats and tackles, and with words. Like others on the river, he constructed his freedom through his craft.

The symbolism of water as life, flight as freedom, and the fisherman as the participant observer who brings them into unity, remains central to his later poetry. Once Adamson takes to the water his words become anchored in an objective world that is a metaphor of inner reality. So, as he trails his nets in 'The River' (1977), they seem to gather the universe reflected in the waters, but they also trawl up his love to

> *go forth to the world's end*
> *to set our lives at the centre*
>
> though the tide turns the river back on itself
> and at its mouth, Ocean.[17]

The lovers remain at the centre of their world despite the river and the Ocean, yet Ocean, standing ungrammatically alone at the close of the poem, also absorbs them. The poem moves from perception to perception so as both to annihilate and discover the individuals.

The various sources of Adamson's poetry come together in a later poem, 'The Language of Oysters' (1997).[18] The poem moves from the logic of symbolism to the mundane logic of the oyster-farmers of Mooney Creek. It shows their nights in tin shacks, their dawns opening on to 'our great brown river', their battered punts and Yamaha engines and the dream where 'clinkers crack, where mud sucks them under'. It then swerves to the past, as the poet sees his grandfather's hands, 'fumbling accurately, lessening the knots', and the hessian sacks waiting back on the wharf to be filled with oysters. The words suggest the precise actions of the boatman's craft, but the exact references cannot be supplied by the uninitiated reader. The generic connotation is of a skill learned with patience and giving mastery. The poem then turns from the concerns of the fisherman to the indifferent world of nature:

> On the bank spur-winged plovers stroll in pairs,
> their beak-wattle chipped by frost,
> each day they ping at the crack of the sun.

The observation continues to be precise, but it is now directed not to human concerns, but to the enveloping and indifferent world of which the human is a part. The final lines take the reader back to human concern and Australian history, but now with its dreams made absurd by the labours of the fisherman and the indifference of nature that have preceded them:

> Stalking for corruption? Signs.
> Blue algae drifts through your brother's dream
> of Gold Coasts, golf courses. The first settlement.

Again the sequence is directed by the images, not by formal logic. The corruption nurtures the oysters, but also refers to the consequences of white settlement of this continent. The brother's dream of meretricious development is also the driving force of settler history.

The waterlands in Adamson's work function both metonymously and ironically. They are part of a whole order of nature and humanity, but they are also separate, an order that cannot be reduced to human purposes. Human agents can sail them, fish them, use them to cultivate their oyster farms, but they can do so only by learning the laws of the waters themselves. Water is not a resource to be exploited, but a resource to be used. Adamson is a mythologer, an Orpheus who endows his river-world with meaning, but it is never able finally to hold it or his Eurydice. Paradoxically, this sense of the separateness of water enables him to be at home with nature in a way that the dreamers of waterlands and the settlers of drylands never could be. Their alienation from the land meant that their home was always elsewhere in time and space: as a dream of the future or a nostalgic recall of their source country. Adamson knows the waterlands through the work of fishing and writing that makes his home in the present.

Adamson is too much of the postmodern to look at water, or nature, as a source of human meaning, but equally he is too much the realist to reduce it to a construct of words. He is aware that his own life has been shaped by chance and necessity that words cannot change, but can turn to meaning. As a poet he uses words in the same way that, as a fisherman, he uses rods and nets, as powerful tools to sustain his life in his environment. From the first, as he ignored regulations and drifted through closed waters at two in the morning, wondering 'do we exist?' or whether 'Augustine still loved his wife', or watched as an amateur fisherman 'flicks a lure / at the racks of oysters …/ then gives up and swigs a bottle of whisky. / Ah the way that first drink braces' he has known only that 'Stars fracture the sky with light' and 'Jesus / didn't walk the water in this river valley'.[19]

The estuary waters of the Hawkesbury bring Adamson to an awareness of both his separateness and his integrity. They themselves are neither simply resources to be exploited, mere backdrop for human action, nor gendered metaphors. There is no romantic identification with nature, nor any attempt to appropriate the Indigenous concept of people belonging to the land. His is a western consciousness that observes, classifies and uses. This consciousness perceives human life as part of a wider order that includes the animate and the inanimate, brought together around the estuary that supports them all. The poems may show us how to live without illusion with our immediate environment. Yet this environment remains landlocked. Its very specificity keeps it local. Unlike Curnow or Baxter, who knew that the ocean brought danger to their island, Adamson's world is imaginatively disconnected from the traffic of the ocean and the unsettling forces of a globalisation he might seem culturally to endorse.

Like Adamson, Kate Grenville uses the Hawkesbury river in her novel *The Secret River* as a participant in the action, rather than simply as a setting.[20] It carries the characters—the ex-convict William Thornhill, former Thames waterman, his wife Sal, and their children—into its hinterland, and is a part of the place where they work. But while William sees it as a route to the future, Sal sees it as the link back to the Thames, the escape route to London, where she really belongs and which is the destination of her hopes. For a while the river opens to them the alternative possibility of sharing the land with the Indigenous people, but they are too closely tied to an imported culture that represents the Indigenous people as a threatening other. The land remains alien, even after William tries to make it his own by participating in a massacre of the blacks to make it safe for his family. William and Sal prosper, building a high wall where they make a simulacrum of England, but, separated from both the country and the river, they are never at home.

At the end of the novel, William reflects that 'Looking down at his estate, it was possible to imagine it a version of England … This bench, where he could overlook all his wealth and take his ease, should have been the reward. He could not understand why it did not feel like triumph'.[21] His only peace comes from gazing at the cliffs, hoping to see one of the people still dwelling among them as they had come before he came. He has missed the chance, taken in part by his son, to make himself part of the land and its people. The light on the river now separates from the land he is joined to, as the ocean remains as an uncrossable barrier to his past. His land, rather than being the foundation of a future, is a just base from which future settlers will carry their English wetland visions into a dryland interior. Only a later generation that Adamson represents will overcome personal alienation as it comes to respect the river and its environs on its own terms. Yet even Adamson's poetry remains haunted by a violence that, like the skua, comes from the unknown beyond the estuary.

Notes

1 Robert Adamson, 'The southern skua', *Mulberry Leaves: new and selected poems 1970–2001* (Sydney: Paper Bark Press, 2001) 279.

2 Kate Llewellyn, 'Water', *The Floral Mother and other essays* (Sydney: HarperCollins, 1995) 53–4.

3 Quiros's vision has been celebrate in poetry by Marie EJ Pitt, 'The Promised Land', *Poems* (Melbourne: EdwardA Vidler); Vincent Buckley, 'Land of No Fathers', *The World's Flesh* (Melbourne: Cheshire, 1954) 37–54; James McAuley, 'Captain Quiros', *Collected Poems* (Sydney: Angus & Robertson, 1994) 137–21 [1964].

4 Kenneth Slessor, 'Five Visions of Captain Cook', *Collected Poems*, edited by Dennis Haskell and Geoffrey Dutton (Sydney: Angus & Robertson, 1994) 88.

5 *Captain Cook's Voyages 1768–1779*, selected by Glyndyr Williams (London: Folio Society) 91.

6 Alan Curnow, 'Landfall in Unknown Seas', *Selected Poems* (Auckland: Penguin, 1982) 74–5.

7 James K. Baxter, 'Pig Island Letters', *Selected Poems*, selected and edited by J.E. Weir (Auckland: Oxford University Press, 1982) 60–9.

8 Slessor, 'Five Visions', 94, lines 210–13.

9 Adapted from 'The Great Australian Adjective: the Australian Poem', in Bill Wannan (ed.), *The Australian* (Melbourne: Australasian Book Society, 1954) 114–15.

10 *SeaChange*, three series, 1998-2000, produced by Artist Services for the Australian Broadcasting Corporation, Executive Producer, Sue Masters, Producer, Sally Ayre-Smith, sundry Directors.

11 *The Oyster Farmer*, 2005, Director/Writer Anne Reeves; producers Anthony Buckley and Piers Tempest.

12 For Gemes's photographs, see Robert Adamson and Juno Gemes, 'The Language of Oysters', *Overland 141*, Summer 1995, 11; also Gemes's photographs in Adamson, *Mulberrry Leaves*.

13 TS Eliot, *Selected Essays* (London:Faber, 1949) 137.

14 Robert Adamson, *Inside Out: an autobiography* (Melbourne: Text, 2004).

15 Adamson, *Inside Out* 239.

16 Adamson, *Mulberry Leaves* 62.

17 Adamson, *Mulberry Leaves* 126–7.

18 Adamson, *Mulberry Leaves* 260–1.

19 Adamson, *Mulberry Leaves* 32–3.

20 Susan Sheridan, during discussion of this paper, drew my attention to the importance of the Hawkesbury River in this novel: Kate Grenville, *The Secret River* (Melbourne: Text, 2005).
21 Grenville, *The Secret River* 330, 334.

Works cited

Adamson, Robert and Juno Gemes. 'The Language of Oysters'. *Overland* 141, Summer 1995.

Adamson, Robert. *Inside Out: an autobiography.* Melbourne: Text, 2005.

Adamson, Robert. *Mulberry Leaves: new and selected poems 1970-2001.* Sydney: Paper Bark Press, Australian Humanities Research Foundation, 2001.

Baxter, James K. 'Pig Island Letters', *Selected Poems*, Ed. J.E. Weir. Auckland: Penguin, 1982.

Buckley, Vincent. 'Land of No Fathers', *The World's Flesh.* Melbourne: Cheshire, 1954.

Curnow, Alan. 'Landfall in Unknown Seas', *Selected Poems.* Auckland: Penguin, 1982.

Eliot, TS. *Selected Essays.* London: Faber, 1949.

Grenville, Kate. *The Secret River.* Melbourne: Text, 2005.

Llewellyn, Kate. *The Florid Mother and other essays.* Sydney: HarperCollins, 1995.

McAuley, James. 'Captain Quiros', *Collected poems*, Ed. Dennis Haskell and Geoffrey Dutton. Sydney; Angus and Robertson, 1994.

Pitt, Marie EJ. 'The Promised Land', *Poems.* Melbourne: Edward A. Vidler, n.d.

Wannan, Bill (ed). *The Australian.* Melbourne: Australasian Book Society, 1954.

Film

The Oyster Farmer, 2005, Director/Writer Anne Reeves; producers Anthony Buckley and Piers Tempest.

Television series

SeaChange, three series, 1998-2000, produced by Artist Services for the Australian Broadcasting Corporation, Executive Producer, Sue Masters, Producer, Sally Ayre-Smith, sundry Directors.

What Was and Is and Shall Not Be

HEATHER TAYLOR JOHNSON

There were other days

when like some flourescent kite
pink from sun and yellowed hair
I swayed with rushes
and lost my stomach
and laughed and ran,
threw sand with my toes
and swam until I seeped out salt.

And there was a man,

who built with me dreams of densely watered dirt
and sat beside me, sharing stories from shells
and we held the world between the hairs of our skin
that smelled of sweet coconut sweat.

This place was a watercoloured picture book.
This place was fish and chips.

But I was younger,

knew what to do with what I had,
I knew the taste of a sunscreened man,
knew how to take off my clothes,
run till I fell
and splash and dive
and swim.

Ten years later

this place is darker
and I could mean the clouds
or the overall feel
because there's something about metal cranes
and concrete stacks in the distance of my ocean
or the beach that's not sand but boulders
the size of my weakened back
when it's slouched in gloomy defeat.

This place is starving seagulls.

I could just be brooding
because my spectrum of sky is grey to dark grey,
because I'm older and I get this way,
alone and extinguished,
cold and alone.

This place is for sinking stones

as small as these tied to each finger and toe
or those that dangle from both my ears
or as large as the one that hangs from my neck
or the one that cuts my wrists.

Poems

GRAHAM ROWLANDS

The Seacave
The morning sun rips
through scarves of salmon cloud &
drills into the seacave
opening to the day
like stomach walls of
a gutted animal.

DANGER is red on signs
about waves above waves
plugging you (or whoever)
headfirst into the
most inward tunnelling deadend
away from the Southern ocean's ice.

Alone
you follow small arrows
in & out of the pitted boulders
& around the rusty escarpments
& the green pools full of big marbles—
pools like new stainless steel hotplates
when you glare at them
against the sun.

You follow the painted
red arrows as if following the footprints of
some sea-going bird until
they follow you &
can no longer
follow
you

under the rotting green fungus of
copper-stained molars two metres through—
the upper lip of the cave's mouth
receded & too old for
a lower jaw.

Sea & salt & rain
& only the dawning sun's heat
have squeezed the soft gizzards of
limestone from granite ribs
opening up & leaching more
sepia & ochre & olive mineral skeins
draping down inner walls of
tripe for the sea air's
rank eroding.

Rimmed by a seaward ridge of granite,
in the centre of the seacave—
water, deep, pooled, marooned
& not to be tasted.

Out of brine, suddenly
two frogmen in flippers. I
feel the Antarctic ice melt, chilling
me in a breaker of blue air
curling down & curdling around
& up my back
& over me

& I see the ceiling grinding down on me
like a slab of prehistoric mutton
weighing a precipice

& I run.

Days
Small crabs scuttle on the beach, scatter
like marbles spilled from a bag
as we slip down sand hills.
They always run away.

Sometimes, we, the two of us,
chafe against each other, hand in hand,
as we slide down a damp crease
in the wind-folded dunes.

I feel I cannot resist,
I resent this sand.

Sting-Ray, Whyalla
Under iron circles still turning
search-lights on the invisible enemy—
under concrete bunkers blocked into the hill
like Moroccan postcards of Mediterranean sun
framing the sea into long horizontals from shadow
where paint leaves blood on the concrete
& blood leaves a message from
no one to no one
but
a helicopter pilot over
an ingenious DROP DEAD
on the roof—

the cry goes out.

Along the jetty, through rails,
the boys are gloating over
a sting-ray, hooked. A sting-ray gaffed
with cross-gaffs (one in one breathing-hole).
They're working it around the pylons.
They're clearing the decks. They're
wearing their gloves, their knives.
  It's making their day—

this sea-swelling black on blue sea-kite
no longer flying black through blue
but floating, now, on ripple ribs,
tail limp, then thrashing
as a gloved arm disarms it—
the spike. The boy lifts up the ray by
the hand-holds of breathing-holes
as if holding the handles of a bicycle
to cut the hook out of the white underside of black &
then turns it over again
like flipping a flounder on a plate
with a kind of etiquette
before letting it slip back
like a black umbrella opening & closing
then flapping, slowly flapping
back into blue—

two metres of wing
slowly flapping.

Sea Mullet

You kept your eyes open
for the fishermen's eyes open
for deep-sea mullet running
close to the sky, the coast.
You'd see the Jeeps tread sand
& the rowing boat unfold the net
& the professionals leaning
against the undertow, wet
in their cut-sleeve flannels.
Everyone helped. Everyone hindered.
Waves spawned patches of net
above the burying sand.
The pros didn't have to sell.
Still they sold for a song,
for silver—schooners.
Later, there seemed to be roe
fat as your thumb &
long as your longest finger
in every fish. You ate
the rich egg-grains of
millions of mullet.

Shipwrecks, Castaways and the Coorong Aborigines

KAY MERRY

In the early years of white intrusion, the beaches and coastline of Australia were sites of first encounter between Europeans and Indigenous people; they were places of tragedy for the victims and survivors of shipwrecks and also places of collision between disparate cultures. Writing on the significance of the beach as a first contact site, Greg Dening noted that '[h]istory always begins there … [t]hat is its first theatre'.[1] This chapter examines the differing experiences, interactions and outcomes of the European castaways and local Indigenous people following the shipwrecks of the *Fanny*, the *Maria*, and the *Mariner* along the Coorong within the first decade of South Australian settlement.[2]

Following European settlement of Port Phillip, Adelaide and the Swan River, the maritime industry was the life-blood of the fledgling southern colonies, which were totally dependent on the regular arrival of ships from the older colonies of Sydney and Van Diemen's Land as well as from overseas destinations. In the 1830s and 1840s, literally hundreds of ships plied the waters of the Southern Ocean with cargoes of immigrants, mail, food, and other essential supplies. The arrival and departure of ships was announced on the front page of newspapers, often with detailed passenger lists and advertisements describing eagerly awaited imported wares. But there was also a perilous aspect to the shipping industry in the early nineteenth century, before the establishment of lighthouses and other navigation aids, and soon many shipwrecks littered the southern Australian beaches, coasts and reefs.[3]

In 1840, more than 150 ships arrived at Port Adelaide: approximately thirty per cent came from Van Diemen's Land, thirty per cent from Great Britain, ten per cent from Sydney and another thirty per cent from other destinations, including New Zealand, India, Java, and Singapore.[4] The presence of rocky reefs to the west of Cape Jaffa at the southern end of the Coorong, the strong coastal currents and prevailing westerly winds combined, especially during times of extreme weather patterns, to reveal the treachery of the south-east coast as a site of many shipwrecks.

In June 1838, the *Fanny*, a brand-new twenty-three ton schooner, was travelling from Hobart to Western Australia carrying the Swan River mail and three passengers: Wesleyan missionary, Reverend William Longbottom, his wife and young son.[5] Strong westerly winds off Kangaroo Island blew the ship off course and after a fierce six-day battle with the elements it was finally driven aground on a Coorong beach, in the early hours of the morning, about thirty miles to the east of Encounter Bay.[6] With great difficulty, everyone managed to get ashore safely. At daybreak the crew salvaged as much clothing and provisions as possible; unfortunately everything else was lost, including Reverend Longbottom's library.[7] Next morning, nine Indigenous people visited the freezing castaways, bringing firesticks. They showed them their water holes and fed them for almost seven weeks, until they were able to secure assistance from the Encounter Bay whale fisheries and proceed on to Adelaide. Three months after the shipwreck, Captain James Gill, master of the *Fanny,* stated in the press that the 'natives … were every way well-disposed; and during our stay among them … they at all times evinced the greatest friendship. They are decidedly the most inoffensive race I ever met'.[8] As Graham Jenkins points out, the castaways owed their lives to the compassion and practical assistance of the Milmenrura or 'Big Murray tribe' of the Coorong and Murray Lakes area.[9] The *Register* noted in August, 1838, that two men named Roach and Delve had gone to the wreck of the *Fanny* about three weeks previously and had not been heard of since. Following a thorough search, only their clothes were found; everything else on shore from the wreck was ransacked, and it was supposed that both men had been killed by the 'natives'. [10]

Two years later Adelaide's newspapers announced intelligence of a vessel being wrecked 'on the coast to the eastward' of Encounter Bay, and of the murders of several of her crew and passengers by local Indigenous people.[11] The ship was identified as the *Maria*, an inter-colonial brigantine of 136 tons. She had departed for Hobart from Port Adelaide in ballast on 26 June 1840 with sixteen passengers and a crew of ten.[12] A preliminary investigation by Captain William Pullen and a group mustered from the Encounter Bay fisheries, including three Indigenous people, confirmed the veracity of the early reports as they encountered the 'truly horrible' spectacle of naked, mutilated and, in some cases, dismembered bodies of eight Europeans, partially covered with sand or thrust into wombat holes in the sand-hills behind the beach. After identifying and describing their findings, the party buried the remains and for more than a week continued searching unsuccessfully for survivors.[13]

When Governor George Gawler received Pullen's report he commanded Police Commissioner Thomas O'Halloran to lead a punitive expedition consisting of a large party of mounted police troopers and volunteer militia to the Coorong to 'apprehend, and bring to summary justice' no more than three of the

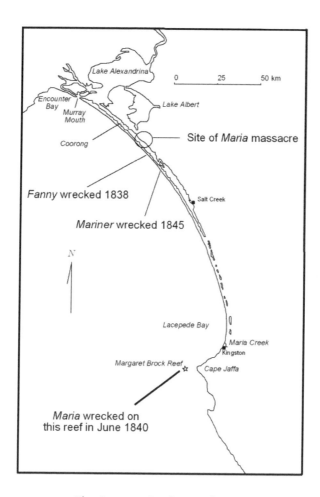

The Coorong, South Australia

ringleaders in the massacre.[14] After arriving at the Coorong, the mounted police scoured the peninsula, and then shot and wounded two men who were fleeing across the Coorong. They went on to capture more than sixty Ngarrindjeri, most of them women and children. O'Halloran noted that

> upon the persons of almost every man and woman, and in almost every wurley we examined (and they were numerous), we found various articles of European cloth-ing belonging to males and females, as well as children … many of them stained with blood.[15]

Many valuables belonging to the *Maria* castaways were also found, providing evidence that clearly proved that 'those in custody were participators in, if not actual perpetrators of, the late horrible murders'.[16]

A member of the punitive party, Inspector Alexander Tolmer, noted in his journal that, with the assistance of a Ramindjeri man from Encounter Bay, the captives pointed out one of their number as the murderer of sailors Roach and Delve who had visited the *Fanny* wreck two years earlier. The captives also indicated where one of the murderers of the *Maria* crew might be located.[17] Some volunteers fetched the accused who, O'Halloran observed, 'was quite unconscious till secured, of our being aware that he was one of the murderers'.[18] Tolmer described the men as being tall and powerfully made 'with countenances the most ferocious and demon-like I ever beheld'.[19] That night, around a blazing fire, all the captives were made to sit with their arms pinioned with tether-ropes while O'Halloran conducted a drumhead court-martial 'regulated on strict principles of martial justice' on the two culprits voluntarily given up by their group.[20] After taking evidence from various members of the group through the interpreters and consulting some members of his party and the accompanying Encounter Bay (Ramindjeri) Aborigines, O'Halloran pronounced sentence of death upon the prisoners.

The next day the bound and captive Milmenrura (the clan of the Ngarrind-jeri) and the condemned men were escorted to the place of execution where gallows were erected; the hanging of the prisoners took place over the graves of the eight *Maria* victims.[21] O'Halloran stated later in his report that the men 'died almost instantly and both evinced extreme nerve and courage to the last'.[22] However, conversely, Tolmer's account portrays the hanging as a horrifying, botched and grisly affair.[23]

The assembled Ngarrindjeri were then released and warned by O'Halloran to leave the bodies to 'hang till they fall in pieces' as a reminder of 'the white's punishment for murder'.[24] Several days were spent searching for the remaining castaways and the wreck of the *Maria*, examining the contents of the native huts and setting fire to them after confiscating all European clothing and objects from the natives.[25] O'Halloran's report also noted that several more bodies from the *Maria* were discovered and buried, accounting for seventeen murders committed by the 'hostile' Milmenrura: fifteen belonging to the *Maria* as well as the two whalers, Roach and Delve. Then the expedition returned to Encounter Bay and Adelaide; O'Halloran noted in his report that they had spent almost three weeks in the field, 'actively employed at this very inclement season ... in a portion of the province so difficult and so little known'.[26]

The long-boat and some wreckage of the *Maria* were discovered a few days later, strewn along the shores of Lacepede Bay, near Kingston, about 100 miles south-east of the Murray Mouth, by two men from Kangaroo Island. They supposed that the ship had come to grief on 'Bundin's [Baudin] Reef' (now known as Margaret Brock Reef), off Cape Jaffa.[27] A vigorous and divisive public debate ensued regarding the 'Milmenrura murders' and the legality of Governor Gawler's conduct that persisted for a year and 'created the strongest sensation in England', attracting the attention of the Aborigines Protection Society in London.[28]

Five years later, in November 1845, on a voyage from Port Phillip to Adelaide, the schooner *Mariner* was struck by a heavy gale near Kangaroo Island. It lost both masts and then drifted at the mercy of the wind and waves for several days before being wrecked on a Coorong beach, about forty miles south of the Murray Mouth.[29] As with the *Fanny* and the *Maria*, all seven passengers and crew survived the wreck and struggled ashore, one by one, in the intervals between the waves. They lit a fire and at daybreak began to salvage the cargo, which was mostly damaged. Two days later they were visited by some Ngarrindjeri, 'principally women', as the men had remained concealed until the women reported back to them. When the Ngarrindjeri men approached the castaways, they tried to persuade them to shoot ducks 'doubtless to see if they had guns to fire'. They had two guns but no percussion caps.[30] The plundering then began in earnest; the terrified castaways gave them everything they demanded, and when threatened with the police, the natives defiantly replied 'gammon'.[31] One of the crew had gone for assistance and when news of their plight reached Adelaide, three mounted police left immediately for the wreck site and were joined by volunteers from Encounter Bay and Goolwa.[32] As they approached the wreck, they found the beach and sandhills strewn with cargo, but no people—black nor white—just footprints which they followed over the dunes until they arrived at an encampment

formed of spread sails, around which a great number of natives were seen, who on perceiving the quick approach of the three horsemen, and recognising them as police, immediately scattered, some of them dropping plunder from the wreck. On their disappearance the wrecked people showed themselves.[33]

The next day a large 'mob of wild natives' from Salt Creek arrived at the scene but they quickly retreated upon seeing the police. Before long there appeared some Encounter Bay whalers who had carried their boat overland to Goolwa and then sailed down the Coorong to the camp. The castaways and salvageable cargo were speedily transferred to Goolwa to await the arrival of a dray to convey them all to Adelaide.[34] A report in the *Southern Australian* speculated that, had the rescue been delayed a single day longer, 'the passengers and crew would, in all probability, have experienced the fate of the unfortunates in the *Maria*'.[35] John Bull maintained that, from then on:

the blacks did not … show themselves in any number as they had not forgotten the punishment which had been inflicted on them by Major O'Halloran for the murders which had been committed a few years before.[36]

The Milmenrura of the Ngarrindjeri people, who had contact with the white castaways of the *Fanny*, the *Maria* and the *Mariner*, owned this bountiful country and lived in densely populated, semi-permanent villages around the Murray Lakes and northern end of the Coorong, which provided them with abundant food and materials for all of the necessities of life.[37] Long before the official settlement of South Australia by the British in 1836, the Milmenrura had experienced contact with Europeans which must have conditioned their attitudes and, indeed, responses to white people.[38]

First of all, groups of sealers had based themselves on Kangaroo Island from at least 1804.[39] These rough outcasts, many of whom were runaway sailors and ex-convicts, were superb mariners and crossed to the mainland with ease to hunt and also to abduct Indigenous women whom they treated as slaves. For example, in the mid-1820s, sealer George 'Fireball' Bates combed the beaches from Encounter Bay around to the mouth of the Murray River for the bones of stranded whales to be sold in Sydney.[40] He and his mates and their 'native' women hunted on the Adelaide Plains in 1826 and 1827 where they found the kangaroo plentiful, taking 7,000 skins in one trip.[41] Around 1830, he and two others walked from Cape Jervis to Lake Alexandrina where they waited until the native men were hunting and '[a]t a signal, all rushed forward and snatched their prizes. With their hands tied behind their backs, the girls were then marched back to the boat and hurried across the Passage' to Kangaroo Island.[42]

In the mid–1840s, when Mrs Christina Smith went to live among the Booandik people near Rivoli Bay, south of the Coorong, she found that the Booandik were all too familiar with the effects of guns, for which they had a name: 'bung-bung'.[43] She was also told of an incident more than twenty years earlier when they sighted the 'first ship in Rivoli Bay' and of the subsequent abduction of one of the native women by two white men (most probably sealers), who surprised her with several other women and children as they were collecting shellfish on the beach. She managed to escape and return to her people a few months later when the boat 'put into Guichen Bay', a little further south and later she gave a very unfavourable account of the treatment she received from the crew. Smith noted that 'as late as 1846 the black women, in speaking of this event, made all sorts of grimaces signifying disgust'.[44]

As explorer Charles Sturt made his epic voyage down the River Murray in

1829–30, he found that as his party approached Lake Alexandrina, the Indigenous groups became increasingly hostile. When intimidated by a group of them during a brief stay on the lake's shores, he took up his gun and they immediately retreated. Sturt concluded that they were obviously familiar with guns and 'attributed this awareness and their hostility to the behaviour of the sealers on Kangaroo Island'.[45]

In later years, the Reverend George Taplin, missionary to Point McLeay Aboriginal Reserve, spoke to several Indigenous men who remembered Sturt's arrival and told of 'the terror which was felt as they beheld his boat crossing the Lake Alexandrina'. They also recounted to Taplin their first encounter with horned cattle in the area, which similarly evoked 'great terror' (as they were widely believed to be 'demons'), soon after British settlement in the colony.[46]

The former officer in charge of the Swan River Colony, Captain Collet Barker, was given the task of examining the eastern shore of St Vincent Gulf and of locating and surveying the mouth of the River Murray in 1832. He and some others walked overland from Yankalilla Bay to the Murray Mouth, where he was fatally speared after swimming two hundred yards to the southern side in order to take bearings from the hillock from which Sturt had stood only a few months earlier.[47] Later, John Bull was told by the Indigenous group concerned that Barker would not have been killed but he ran away and would not stop when they gave him friendly signs, so he was ambushed and speared.[48] Others claimed that he was killed 'just to prove that a blackfellow had power to harm a white man'.[49] Anthropologist Philip Clarke concluded that Barker was probably attacked because he was mistaken for a sealer from Kangaroo Island and killed in reprisal for earlier overland raids and abductions of women.[50]

Overland parties bringing cattle and sheep from Sydney and Port Phillip were responsible for the deaths of hundreds of Indigenous people. Even before the *Maria* murders in mid-1840, almost twenty groups had made the long journey along the River Murray to South Australia and, while the early parties experienced few problems with the Indigenous people, hostilities became increasingly common. In November 1839, Alexander Buchanan, in company with eight other young men driving 5,000 sheep to Adelaide, recorded shooting at least six 'spear-waving natives' before destroying their canoes and burning all their nets.[51] In October 1840, a letter was published in the *Register* by 'A Colonist of 1836' addressing this. It was a response to a comment by the advocate-general regarding the seeming 'conversion of the once friendly' Coorong natives into a 'tribe of ruthless murderers'. Defending the Milmenrura, the colonist pointed out that:

[t]here has seldom been an arrival by land from Port Phillip or Sydney, which on its first reaching Adelaide did not bring some tale of boasting and butchering the natives on the way. There are few in Adelaide who ... have not heard them vaunt of their exploits in shooting or 'peppering' the natives in their route. And there are well authenticated instances where both the stockkeepers and their masters have related tales of their shooting or hunting down the natives, which they have promptly recanted when it was ascertained that they were affording grounds for a dangerous enquiry into their own conduct.[52]

The author of the published letter was in no doubt that firearms had been 'unhesitatingly and unscrupulously' used by the overland parties and concluded that white aggression was responsible for changing the Milmenrura 'from friendly to hostile'.

Less than a year after the *Maria* murders, in April, 1841, an 'affray' between the local Indigenous people and an overland party of twenty-six men, 6,000 sheep and 500 cattle, occurred on the Rufus River, near the 'elbow' of the Murray and was reported in the press.[53] Once again, Major O'Halloran and 'a strong body of mounted police', volunteers and the Protector of Aborigines, Dr Matthew Moorhouse, were sent to render assistance to the party, and to demonstrate to the belligerent natives that 'the whites are not to be trifled with'.[54] Tragically, during this engagement, 'from thirty to forty were killed, and as many wounded' and four others were taken hostage.[55]

Thus, in a very short period of time, a vicious cycle of increasing hostility and resistance towards the frequent intrusions of overlanding parties, (with their bullock teams and thousands of cattle and sheep) and their subsequent response of violence and retaliation, soon took its toll. News of the inhumanity and barbarity of the white man would have travelled swiftly up and down the River Murray. Sturt noted a decade earlier the custom of sending ambassadors forward from one community to another in order to prepare for their approach.[56] The abuse of Indigenous women and outrage over the white men's failure to keep promises of food and other goods as compensation for the privilege of passing through and permanently damaging their territories and eco-systems, caused relations between the traditional owners and the intruders to deteriorate into open warfare within the first few years of white invasion. This happened in spite of the original intentions of the colony's Founding Fathers that guaranteed both land rights and protection by law for the 'Aboriginal Natives'.[57]

Between the time of the *Maria* shipwreck in 1840 and that of the *Mariner* in 1845, rapid pastoral expansion occurred to the south of the Coorong. The subsequent atrocious treatment of the Booandik of the Rivoli Bay district, near present-day Robe, was mentioned in a report to the governor by the police commissioner, stating that:

> damper poisoned with corrosion sublimate was given them. Another method of ill-treatment which can be vouched for is that of driving the Natives from the only watering places in the neighbourhood. The Native women appear likewise to have been sought after by the shepherds, whilst the men were driven from the stations with threats.[58]

In this period, Henry Melville, a stock-keeper near Lake Albert, was often engaged in conflict with the Milmenrura, whom he detested. In his journal he referred to the aftermath of the *Maria* incident and of the gold coins that the natives had acquired from their victims. He wrote that:

> [s]ome of the Coy's shepherds got several sovereigns from the natives ... I knew that a party of whalers from Encounter Bay went up the Coorong in 1843 and got well paid for their enterprise in gold obtained from the darkies and at the same time avenged the murder of their countrymen. Major O'Halloran's executions ... gave these savages a severe lesson but the raid of the whalers was worse by far ... [59]

According to archaeologist John Mulvaney, it is necessary to establish the protocols of the living Indigenous culture before any encounter may be set into historic context because 'only in this way is it possible to understand Aboriginal responses to contact situations'.[60] All of the first encounters between white and black occurred upon Indigenous land, although this was rarely acknowledged by the Europeans. Nor were they aware, in the early years of settlement, of the structures, customs, rituals and complexities of Indigenous societies, including the importance of reciprocal obligations. Some of the sealers, however, were well versed in some of the 'native protocols'. William Cawthorne, author of *The Kangaroo Islanders*, described one such occasion. A sealer, 'Georgy', swam from a boat in Rapid Bay to the beach and was greeted by about fifty 'native warriors':

> Georgy rose from the water, and imitating native etiquette, sat down on the sand in silence. Thereupon, the natives squatted, too. Thus both parties continued for at least ten minutes, then Georgy spoke, and explained their visit. They were friends, fishing and hunting up the Gulf. They had plenty to eat—they wanted to come ashore. The whites would leave their guns, and the blacks were to leave their spears. They were to have a grand dinner, to bring down their wives and daughters, and have a great corrobboree [sic].[61]

Missionary George Taplin wrote that custom was rigidly observed by the Ngarrindjeri nation (to which the Milmenrura group belonged) and contributed to the social stability of the community.[62] In reference to the native concept of *territoriality*, George French Angus, artist and son of one of the founders of South Australia, observed that:

> The possession of the soil is claimed by them, each tribe having its own hunting-ground or fishing locality, and the infringement upon these rights frequently leads to war amongst them.[63]

In a similar vein, Simpson Newland, son of one of the earliest settlers in the Encounter Bay area, observed that 'the lines of demarcation between the tribes of the lakes, the Coorong, and the lower Murray and Encounter Bay appear to have been very clear, and hostilities were very frequent'.[64] A few months after the *Maria* events, the Milmenrura people explained the reason for the massacre of the white castaways to Dr Richard Penny, surgeon to the Encounter Bay fisheries. He was quoted in the *Register*, saying that he had

> gathered from them (the natives), that they had brought the whole people up a long way, *showed them water, fished, and carried their children for them a long time*. That when they came to this point, they could not take them any farther, as their country ends there, and the picannini Murray begins. They then claimed some clothes and blankets for their trouble, *but the white people refused to give them*, yet said, if they would take them to Adelaide, they should have plenty. This they could not do, so they began to help themselves, and *this being resisted*, ended in the murder of the whole.[65]

The *Register* concluded that 'the unfortunate passengers of the *Maria* were not murdered in cold blood but in an affray evidently provoked by the resistance and ungrateful conduct of the white party'.[66] But it appears that inter-clan rivalry may have been yet another factor in the *Maria* tragedy; in April, 1841, the Milmenrura people explained to Dr Penny that they were also jealous of the next group, into whose territory they would there have passed, 'and who, being in the habit of visiting Adelaide, could have taken them [the castaways] up and obtained the reward promised to them'.[67]

Reciprocity and trade are fundamental principles common to Indigenous societies and the Milmenrura people clearly expected to be rewarded for the hospitality, labour and generosity of their people. The *Fanny* and *Maria* shipwrecks occurred on the Coorong in mid-winter—and clothing was coveted by the Milmenrura. The overlander Alexander Bucchanan wrote in his diary that the natives along the River Murray expected to receive goods such as tomahawks, fishing hooks, clothing, and food (they were particularly partial to 'jumbucks' or sheep) in exchange for fish and permission for the parties to pass through their territories.[68] But although Bucchanan would not hesitate to shoot

Indigenous people if they became 'troublesome', he gave them unwanted or drowned sheep when it suited him. Speaking of an encounter along the Murray with 'a noted chief', on 26 November 1839, he wrote: 'Bluebeard started with us and we gave him a lame sheep that was not able to travel and he went away quite contented.'[69]

But the cross-cultural sexual liaisons should not be underestimated and probably played a large role in fuelling the tragic outcome. There are numerous oral and written accounts of the abduction and abuse of Indigenous women by a succession of white sealers, whalers, overlanders, shepherds, stockkeepers and settlers in the first half of the nineteenth century, a few of which have already been alluded to above. In 1934, one of the last initiated Coorong men told anthropologist Norman Tindale that the molestation of Indigenous women by sailors of the *Maria* and the ensuing scuffle had led to the deaths of the survivors.[70] In relation to the 1838 murders of the sailors Roach and Delve, Reverend Longbottom had often publicly stated that while awaiting rescue following the *Fanny* wreck:

> he never entertained any apprehensions from these natives, and that the chief difficulty he had to contend with in his friendly intercourse with them was to restrain the loose conduct of the sailors with the native women. It is a singular fact that the man Roach … was one of the crew of the *Fanny*.[71]

The Milmenrura would have justly believed that, along with all the natural resources *within* their territorial boundaries and surrounding waters, they were also perfectly entitled to the spoils of shipwrecks that washed upon their shores, including the cargo and wreckage from the *Fanny* and the *Mariner*. They would have resented Roach and Delve returning to salvage valuables from the *Fanny*. They probably saw an opportunity to exact revenge, especially if Roach *had* exhibited 'loose conduct' with the Indigenous women a few weeks earlier, as Reverend Longbottom asserted.[72] No one bothered to enquire about a *motive* for their murder, two years later, when one of the men responsible was offered up to O'Halloran when he was seeking 'two, but not more than three' scapegoats to punish for the *Maria* murders.[73] The first person, in fact, to suggest that there may have been a motive for the massacre, was the 'Colonist of 1836' who wrote in the *South Australian Register* in October 1840:

> You maintain the tribe to be wholesale butchers—ruthless murderers of defenceless beings; but your opinion would be qualified were it to be supposed that the passengers [or crew?] of the *Maria* were the aggressors; or even that … some sudden jealousy or dispute, or improper interference, on one side or the other, among parties who but a moment before were on friendly terms, may have led to a melé, [sic] in which the weaker party was exterminated.[74]

The relationship between the Coorong Ngarrindjeri and the castaways of the shipwrecks of the *Fanny* in 1838, the *Maria* in 1840 and the *Mariner* in 1845, reflects the broader experience of black and white contact in those first years of South Australian colonisation. Perhaps it was an amalgam of factors: the history of abduction and abuse by Europeans of their women; a lack of gratitude for their services leading to an increasing distrust and animosity towards all white people, prompted initially by the behaviour of the sealers and overlanders that led to the massacre of the *Maria* castaways. Three years later in 1843, when the South Australian Company began taking over large tracts of their land for cattle,[75] it was little wonder that when the *Mariner* was wrecked in 1845—less than eight years after the arrival of the British in South Australia—the Milmenrura reacted in such an intimidating and provocative manner towards the white survivors. By then, it was becoming all too obvious that their traditional way of life was coming to an end and they were being dispossessed of their country, their resources and their very identity.

Notes

1 Greg Dening, *Beach Crossings* (Carlton: Mieganyah Press, 2004) 348.
2 The Coorong is an elongated tidal lagoon that runs parallel to the Southern Ocean for about 100 kilometres. It is never more than a few kilometres wide and in 1840 the waters of the Coorong are likely to have been brackish. A system of sand-dunes, the Younghusband Peninsula, separates the lagoon from the sea. These dunes are largely vegetated and reach about thirty metres at their highest point.
3 Paul Clark, *Shipwreck sites in the South-East of South Australia 1838–1915* (Australian Institute for Maritime Archaeology, Special Publication No 5, 1990) 8.
4 E.A.D. Opie, *South Australian Records Prior to 1841* (Adelaide: Hussey and Gillingham, 1917) 91–102.
5 *South Australian Register and Colonial Gazette*, September 8, 1838: 5b.
6 *Southern Australian*, September 22, 1838: 4c; Clark, *Shipwreck sites* 14.
7 *Register*, August 25, 1838: 3d; *Southern Australian*, August 11, 1838: 1c.
8 *Register*, September 8, 1838: 5ab. From statement of Captain Gill, master of the *Fanny*.
9 *Register*, October 3, 1840: 2cd; Jenkins, *Conquest of the Ngarrindjeri* (Adelaide: Rigby, 1979) 21, 56. According to Rev. Taplin, who ran the Point McLeay Mission on the Raukan Peninsula from 1859–1879, in the early days of the colony, the Coorong clans of the Narrinyeri who inhabited the northwest portion of the Coorong, the Murray Mouth and around Lakes Alexandrina and Albert, were generally known as the 'Milmenrura Tribe'. In recent years, historian Graham Jenkins was informed that a Coorong clan, called 'Milmenroora' dwelling near McGrath's Flat had long undergone a name change and were now called 'Milmenyeriam'. Due to the ubiquity of the 'Milmenrura' name in the early

days of the colony, however, I will continue to use this name. Taplin explains that the Narrinyeri (Taplin's spelling) were a sort of confederacy of eighteen tribes and, although 'they often fought and quarrelled among themselves, they always presented a united front to the neighbouring natives'.

10 *Register,* August 25, 1838: 3d.

11 *Register,* August 1, 1840: 6b.

12 *Register,* June 7, 1840: 4a; *Adelaide Chronicle,* July 29, 1840: 3bcd.

13 *Register,* August 15, 1840, 6a; *Adelaide Chronicle,* August 19, 1840: 3def; also A. Tolmer, *Reminiscences of an Adventurous and Chequered Career at Home and in the Antipodes,* Vol. 1 (London: Sampson, Low, Marston, Searle and Rivington, 1882) 175. `

14 *Register,* September 19, 1840, 3d; Tolmer, *Reminiscences* 181–2.

15 *Register,* September 12, 1840: 2b. O'Halloran's report to Governor Gawler.

16 *Register,* September 12, 1840: 2b.

17 Tolmer, *Reminiscences* 187.

18 *Register,* September 12, 1840: 2c.

19 Tolmer, *Reminiscences* 188. Tolmer explains that in the early days of the colony it was a recognised law among the Indigenous people that although a number may have combined to commit a murder, the person known to have thrown the actual fatal weapon was considered to be the murderer and the remainder of the tribe considered innocent of the crime, 'hence their willingness to give up these two men especially'.

20 Tolmer, *Reminiscences* 188.

21 Tolmer, *Reminiscences* 188–9; *Register,* September 12: 1840: 2c.

22 *Register,* September 12: 1840: 2c.

23 Tolmer, *Reminiscences,* 189–90.

24 *Register,* September 12, 1840; 2c. Tolmer, *Reminiscences* 189–90.

25 *Register,* September 12, 1840: 2c; Tolmer, *Reminiscences* 190; John Wrathall Bull, *Early Experiences of Life in South Australia and an Extended Colonial History* (Adelaide: E.S. Wigg & Son, 1884) 124.

26 O'Halloran in *Register,* September 12, 1840: 2d.

27 Bull, *Early Experiences* 125–6. The men, referred to as Thompson and Walker, who found the wreckage of the *Maria* were travelling (most probably by boat) up the Coorong and signed a statement, taken down by Captain Nixon, on their observations.

28 *Adelaide Chronicle,* June 30, 1841: 2g–3a; July 28, 1841: 2c, 2e; August 4, 1841: 2g. The *Maria* affair was also widely reported in the other Australian colonies; see the *Supplement to the Sydney Herald,* 25 September, 1840: 1e and *Colonial Times* (Hobart), 1 September, 1840: 7d.

29 Clark, *Shipwreck* 21; Jack Loney, *Wrecks on the South Australian Coast* (Yarram: Lonestone Press, 1993) 44; *Observer,* 15 November 1845: 5a; *Southern Australian* 26 November, 1845: 1c.

30 *Southern Australian,* 21 November, 1845: 2e, 3a.

31 *Southern Australian,* 21 November, 1845: 2e. 'Gammon' roughly translates as 'humbug'.

32 *Observer*, 15 November, 1845: 5a.

33 Bull, *Early Experiences* 45–6.

34 *Southern Australian*, 21 November, 1845: 2e, 3a.

35 *Southern Australian,* 21 November, 1845: 2e, 3a.

36 Bull, *Early Experiences* 46. However, according to the memoirs of Henry Melville, a stock-keeper for the SA Company, who lived and worked on a cattle run located between the Coorong and Lake Albert from 1843–1845, tensions and a form of covert guerrilla warfare had continued between the local Indigenous people and the white settlers, shepherds and stock-keepers, at least until the *Mariner* shipwreck in November, 1845.

37 Jenkins, *Conquest* 13.

38 Jenkins, *Conquest* 25.

39 Jean M. Nunn, *This Southern Land: A Social History of Kangaroo Island 1800–1890* (Hawthorndene, SA: Investigator Press, 1989) 21.

40 H.P. Moore, 'Notes on the Early Settlers in South Australia Prior to 1836', *Royal Geographical Society of Australasia – SA Branch Proceedings,* Vol. XXV, 1923–4: 110.

41 Nunn, *This Southern Land* 38.

42 *Advertiser*, 27 December, 1886, quoted in Nunn, *This Southern Land* 38–9.

43 Mrs James Smith, *The Booandik Tribe of South Australian Aborigines* (Adelaide: E. Spiller, Govt. Printer, 1860) 43.

44 Smith, *The Booandik Tribe* 25.

45 Nunn, *This Southern Land* 41; J.S. Cumpston, *Kangaroo Island 1800–1836* (Roebuck Society, Canberra, 1970) 113. Sturt must have had contact with sealers in Sydney before his voyage down the River Murray because they gave him a description of the land around Port Lincoln, Spencer and St Vincent Gulfs and the southern coast of South Australia.

46 George Taplin, 'The Narrinyeri', in *Native Tribes of South Australia* (Adelaide: E.S. Wigg & Son, 1879) 3.

47 John Mulvaney and Neville Green, *Commandant of Solitude: The Journals of Captain Collet Barker 1828-1831* (Melbourne: Melbourne University Press, 1992) 22–26.

48 Bull, *Early Experiences* 75. Bull's interpreter was a woman who had been recently stolen from the Adelaide tribe and could speak some English.

49 Charles White, *Early-Day Tragedies on the Coorong.* (Manuscript, Mortlock Library, written in 1937 by Charles White, who lived most of his life on the Coorong. He died 'a very old man' in 1945).

50 Philip Clarke, 'Early European interaction with Aboriginal hunters and gatherers on Kangaroo Island, South Australia', *Aboriginal History*, 1996, 20: 67, 70.

51 Alexander Buchanan, 'Diary of a journey overland from Sydney to Adelaide with sheep', July–December, 1839, *Royal Geographical Society of Australia – SA Branch,* Vol. XXIV, Session 1922–3, 72.

52 *Register*, October 3, 1840, 2d.

53 *Register*, April 24, 1841, May 1, 1841, September 11, 1841.

54 *Register*, September 11, 1841, 2e: Report of Aboriginal Protector, Matthew Moorhouse.

55 *Register,* September 11, 1841, 2e: Report of 'Mr Robinson', one of the overlanding party.
56 Jenkins, *Conquest* 28.
57 See Letters Patent and the Proclamation by Governor Hindmarsh in B. Dickey and P. Howell (eds), *South Australia's Foundation: Select Documents* (Adelaide: Wakefield Press, 1986) 74–7.
58 South Australian Archives, GRG 24/1 1845/116. Quoted in Jenkins, *Conquest* 63.
59 Henry Melville, *Reminiscences of Henry D. Melville* (Manuscript, State Library of South Australia, D 6976 (L), 1887) Vol. 1.
60 D.J. Mulvaney, *Encounters in Place: Outsiders and Aboriginal Australians 1606-1985* (St Lucia: University of Queensland Press, 1989) 1.
61 W.A. Cawthorne, *The Kangaroo Islanders* (Adelaide: Rigby, 1926) 111.
62 G. Taplin, *Native Tribes* 8.
63 George French Angas, *Savage Life and Scenes in Australia and New Zealand* (London: Smith, Elder and Co., 1847) 88.
64 Quoted in Rod J. Hamon, *Victor Harbor and Encounter Bay: Mysteries and Tragedies* (South Australia: Seaview Press, 1999) 115.
65 *Register*, April 24, 1841: 3c. (Italics as in original.)
66 *Register,* April 24, 1841: 3c.
67 *Register,* April 24, 1841: 3c.
68 Bucchanan, 'Diary of a journey' 68, 70-72,
69 Bucchanan, 'Diary of a journey' 74.
70 Norman B. Tindale, 'Vanished Tribal Life of Coorong Blacks: Tragedy of a Supplanted Race', *Advertiser*, April 7, 1934: 11d.
71 *Register*, October 3, 1840: 2cd. Letter to the editor from 'A Colonist of 1836'.
72 See *Register,* October 3, 1840: 2cd.
73 Instructions to the Commissioner of Police, Major O'Halloran, from Governor Gawler, on August 14, 1840. *Register*, September 19, 1840: 3d.
74 *Register*, October 3, 1840: 3d.
75 Melville, *Reminiscences* Vol. 1.

Works cited

Angas, George French. *Savage Life and Scenes in Australia and New Zealand.* London: Smith, Elder, & Co., 1847.

Buchanan, Alexander. 'Diary of a journey overland from Sydney to Adelaide with sheep, July-December, 1839, *Royal Geographical Society of Australasia – SA Branch*, Vol.XX1V, Session 1922–3. 51–76.

Bull, John Wrathall. *Early Experiences of Life in South Australia and an Extended Colonial History.* Adelaide: E.S. Wigg & Son, 1884.

Cawthorne, W. A. *The Kangaroo Islanders.* Adelaide: Rigby, 1926.

Clark, Paul. *Shipwreck Sites in the South-East of South Australia 1838–1915.* Australian Institute of Maritime Archaeology, Special Publication No. 5, 1990.

Clarke, Philip. 'Early European interaction with Aboriginal hunters and gatherers on Kangaroo Island, South Australia'. *Aboriginal History*, Vol. 20, 1996.

Cumpston, J.S. *Kangaroo Island 1800–1836.* Canberra: Roebuck Society, 1970.

Dening, Greg. *Beach Crossings.* Carlton: Mieganyah Press, 2004.

Hamon, Rod J. *Victor Harbor and Encounter Bay: Mysteries and Tragedies.* South Australia: Seaview Press, 1999.

Dickey, Brian and Howell, Peter (eds). *South Australia's Foundation: Select Documents.* Adelaide: Wakefield Press, 1986.

Jenkins, Graham. *Conquest of the Ngarrindjeri.* Adelaide: Rigby, 1979.

Loney, Jack. *Wrecks on the South Australian Coast.* Yarram: Lonestone Press, 1993.

Melville, Henry. *Reminiscences of Henry D. Melville.* Manuscript, State Library of South Australia, D 6976(L), 1887.

Moore, H.P. 'Notes on the early settlers in South Australia prior to 1836'. *Royal Geographical Society of Australasia – SA Branch Proceedings*, Vol XXV, 1923–4.

Mulvaney, John and Green, Neville. *Commandant of Solitude: The Journals of Captain Collet Barker 1828–1831.* Melbourne: Melbourne University Press, 1992.

Mulvaney, D.J. *Encounters in Place: Outsiders and Aboriginal Australians 1606–1985.* St Lucia: University of Queensland Press, 1989.

Nunn, Jean M. *This Southern Land: Kangaroo Island 1800–1890.* Hawthorndene: Investigator Press, 1989.

Opie, E.A.D. *South Australian Records Prior to 1841.* Adelaide: Hussey and Gillingham, 1917.

Smith, Mrs James. *The Booandik Tribe of South Australian Aborigines.* Adelaide: E. Spiller, Government Printer, 1860.

Taplin, G. *Native Tribes of South Australia.* Adelaide: E.S.Wigg & Son, 1879.

Tolmer, Alexander. *Reminiscences of an Adventurous and Chequered Career at Home and at the Antipodes*, Vol. 1. London: Sampson, Low, Marston, Searle and Rivington, 1882.

White, Charles. *Early-Day Tragedies on the Coorong.* Manuscript, 1937, SLSA.

Newspapers

Adelaide Chronicle

Observer

Southern Australian

South Australian Register

Colonial Gazette

Sydney Herald

Otim Singh in White Australia

MARGARET ALLEN

By the sea-front at Kingscote, Kangaroo Island, the Indian, Otim Singh, ran a store and was a valued member of the local community during the first three decades of the twentieth century. During his life, Otim Singh made a number of journeys and crossed a number of seas and many shores. His migration from India to Australia in 1890 bought about a number of sea changes. He prospered in Australia, crossing many boundaries and barriers. Coming to Australia before the passing of the Immigration Restriction Act of 1901, he was able to remain a resident, after which date his fellow country-men were classified as 'prohibited immigrants'. Living in this white community, he prospered with his successful business in Kingscote and married a woman from a prosperous white family. However, there were some boundaries which he did not breach and his final journey across the sea marked a return to his religious and cultural roots.

It has been estimated that there were up to 7,637 Indians in Australia during the first decade of the twentieth century.[1] This number dwindled as Indians were excluded from entering Australia after 1901 and as those who had been resident for some years and went back to visit India were then unable to reenter. Just as these men were excluded from Australia, they have also been marginalised in written Australian history.[2]

The Indian diaspora to Australia, which developed strongly from c1880, saw some thousands of men coming to Australia to work as cameleers, hawkers, shop-keepers, cameleers, farmers and agricultural labourers. Some stayed only a few years, while others spent many years in Australia, often interrupted by long periods back in India, before returning to Australia to carry on their work. If they could establish that they were resident in Australia, they could return.[3] While some men had wives and children in India, others married in Australia and established families here; a number lived out their lives alone, and by the 1920s were a dwindling number of elderly men, living out their days without the support of family.

There are relatively few historical sources on these men. Certainly for those seeking to leave Australia temporarily after 1901 for a trip back to India, a Domicile Certificate or Certificate Exempting the Dictation Test (CEDT) was produced by the Commonwealth Government Customs and Excise Service, which was charged to administer elements of the Immigration Restriction Act.[4] Such a certificate made it possible for that person to re-enter Australia without having to take the dictation test that was administered to exclude Indians and other prohibited immigrants. These certificates typically included brief personal descriptions of the applicant, together with two photographs and hand or thumb-prints. Surviving applications include further details of the applicant's activities in Australia along with references attesting to good character. Such documents provide some basic information about a number of British Indians who lived in Australia in the period in question.

In the case of Otim Singh, sufficient resources make it possible to explore his biography in a more extensive manner and to gain some understanding of his life. Some of these documents were created by him and provide richer information than the brief remarks on an official form, and give us a greater insight into the ways in which he negotiated living as the representative of what was seen as an inferior race in a determinedly white Australian community.

He was born a Sikh in the Punjab in 1862. According to a personal entry which he prepared for the *Cyclopedia of South Australia* in c. 1909, he left home at the age of nineteen before going to Sumatra, where he worked as a 'super-visor in a large tobacco-plantation on behalf of an English firm for about five years' and where he had '200 coolies under his control …whilst in Sumatra [he] served four years in the British Mounted Police.'[5] In other versions of his story, it is claimed that 'crossing to Java, [he] took service for several years under the Dutch, in the police force'.[6] He was able to benefit from the opportunities that the British Empire offered. As Tony Ballantyne has noted, the Sikhs were seen as 'reliable, "fairly incorruptible", [and] hard-working', and believed to be suited to police work and supervisory roles.[7]

The migratory worker often set out on his travels to recoup the family honour, its *izzat* and its fortunes at home. When such a worker had amassed sufficient funds, he might return to India to purchase land. Thus Otim Singh returned home and purchased some land, but only stayed for nine months.[8] It seems that the family farm was still not large enough 'to provide for all members of the family at an adequate standard of living'[9] and he left home again, to visit his brother who was working in Java. His brother may well have been one of the Sikhs brought over by the British firms Ocean Liner or General Motors to act as watch-men at Tanjung Priok, the port near Batavia.[10] It is likely that he heard from other Sikhs in the Punjab or in South East Asia, that Australia or '"Telia" was open'.[11] After a couple of months Otim Singh went on to Australia, arriving in Melbourne in 1890. W.H. McLeod has noted that the Punjabi Sikhs often left India for the first time when posted as soldiers or police to Hong Kong or Malaya, then later moved into civilian employment there and subsequently ventured further in the 1880s when they heard, via their Sikh information networks, of opportunities in 'Telia' (Australia) and 'Miktan' (America).[12] Otim Singh's experience was slightly different; he worked either for an English firm in Sumatra from c. 1882 or in the Dutch police force in the Netherlands East Indies, before finally moving on to Australia.

Otim Singh records receiving his English education in Melbourne; he must have been quite familiar with English, for in three months he had 'a sufficient mastery of the language … to enable him to continue his travels inland'.[13] He went to Ballarat and Colac and learned from one of his compatriots how to be a hawker. He pursued this occupation in southern centres, both in Western Victoria and into South Australia, for the township of Wolseley in South Australia became his headquarters. Presumably he ordered goods from Melbourne and Adelaide, collected them from the railway station at Wolseley and then distributed them to customers across the South-East of South Australia and the Western Districts. Perhaps the hostility to what was termed the 'Indian hawker nuisance' in Victoria, or perhaps the opportunity to find greener pastures, led to his proceeding to Adelaide in 1897 and shortly thereafter going to Kangaroo Island. He later recalled that, 'in those days no commercial travellers visited the island', so he had a 'free field before him'.[14] He did well and set up a store in Kingscote in c. 1902 that he ran until his death in 1927. He made only one return trip to India, in 1927, just before his death.

Otim Singh made numerous sea voyages during his life-time. On his first trip to Sumatra, he was probably going to a job for which he had been contracted in Delhi. Nevertheless it appears that he was among the earliest wave of Sikhs to venture outside of India in pursuit of work.[15] As he crossed the seas from India to Sumatra, to Java and then on to Melbourne he probably travelled on the deck or in third class. Such Indians usually travelled cheaply, usually in third class.[16] As he became more prosperous on his regular short business trips between Kingscote and Adelaide and on his final return trip to India, presumably he would have moved to travelling in better style.

As he made these voyages he was helped by others, chiefly by a network of Sikhs who shared their knowledge about potential greener pastures. Information from other Sikhs probably led to his going to Sumatra, and when he visited his brother at Batavia in Java he would have found information about Australia. In Victoria, one of his countrymen instructed him 'in the trade of a hawker'. In Adelaide, a friend advised him to 'settle on Kangaroo Island, where it was averred he would find excellent scope for his business'.[17] This network helped him to launch himself across the unknown.

While in his earlier voyages Otim Singh was relatively free from surveillance from governmental authorities, to make his trip back to India in 1927, he had to apply to the Australian Customs service for a CEDT. Given that he was a respected businessman by that time, possibly he was spared the indignity of having to give his hand-prints.[18] CEDT holders had their presence on a ship noted by the customs boarding officer, as it reached and departed from each Australian port, as if the officer were recording the passage of dangerous cargo. Indeed, in June 1927 the Collector of Customs in Western Australia advised his counterpart in Adelaide that Otim Singh, the holder of SA CEDT 325/57, had been on the *Moldavia* when it left Fremantle for Colombo.[19]

During the years he spent working in Australia, Otim Singh moved up the hierarchy of hawkers, from one who carried his goods on his back to having a horse and a cart to travel between farms, stations and townships in the bush. Later, on Kangaroo Island, he crossed over from the marginal position of itinerant hawker, one largely occupied by Indians and Syrians, to become a business owner with a house, an individual with real property, and with a real stake in the community.

The lowest level of hawker went around on foot with his pack on his back, and presumably Otim Singh began hawking on foot. Certainly when he first travelled around Kangaroo Island he went by foot; he later records that 'he trudged along with his bundles on his back'.[20] Here he would have had to 'study the needs and wishes of the little farmers … and visit the little farming hamlets in the countryside, with the things they would need, things like pins and needles and buttons and sewing cotton'.[21] Presumably he graduated to a horse and cart, but like their colleagues the pedestrian hawkers, those who went about in their carts in itinerant fashion were also positioned outside of the norm of Australian society. Jewan Singh, another South Australian hawker, on one occasion gave his address as c/- Post Office, at Tanunda. But the local police reported: 'Jewan Singh is not a resident of Tanunda, but occasionally camps on the reserve and collects his mail at the local PO'.[22] When he was in Adelaide he camped where he stabled his horse and cart. The proprietors of the Central Horse and Carriage Bazaar in Bentham Street Adelaide noted, 'Jewan Singh for several years stabled his Hawker Van turnout in our stable and latterly camped here when he came to town to buy new stock'. They attested to his good character: 'we always found him strictly honest in all his dealings and a very decent steady man on whose word you could place every reliance'.[23] But his manner of life and his 'race' put him outside mainstream society.

During the 1890s there was a certain amount of concern in both Victoria and South Australia about itinerant hawkers.[24] Racial prejudice was crucial to this social anxiety. Indian hawkers, although they were British subjects, were marginal in emerging white Australia, because of their 'race'. While the controversy in Victoria seemed to focus upon Indians, in 1893 in South Australia the authorities refused to renew hawking licences of Afghans, Assyrians and Chinese.[25] Popular understandings tended to include all those seen as not-white into an inferior category. As a *Register* columnist candidly admitted:

> With true British arrogance we virtually regard all such, whether Chinese, Afghans, Syrians, Hindus, or Persians, as the scum and offscouring of the earth. They have committed the unpardonable sin of being coloured, and although they were not consulted in the choice of their complexion they must perforce be Ishmaelites.[26]

Concerns about Indian hawkers surfaced from time to time, and there seemed to be an on-going discussion of their worth. In 1905 a 'Country Schoolmistress' wrote to the *Register,* in defence of Indian hawkers, suggesting there should be some reciprocity within the British Empire:

> I … have always found them civil, honest, and obliging. I for one would be genuinely sorry if their licences were stopped … [Considering many of our countrymen have made their fortunes in India, and that Calcutta owes its name, 'City of Palaces,' to the splendour of the British merchants' residences, is it fair to deny our Indian subjects the right to earn a decent living in our colonies?][27]

Individuals became known and liked in the white community. A Punjabi Muslim who worked as a hawker in Victoria from c. 1899, commented that he got to know the farmers he served 'very intimately'. He reported having friendly relations with his customers would 'ask [him] to put up [his] horses in the stable and come and have tea with them'.[28] However, another hawker noted the dominance of white people: 'We are nobody, we are of no consideration in this country: the white man is everything.'[29] Similarly, Indians in Adelaide reported in 1922 'that there was a general attitude of contempt on the part of people, as though it were shameful and humiliating to be an Indian … the ordinary people have a very poor conception of Indians'.[30]

Otim Singh moved beyond being a hawker to establishing a store and buying a house. While the histories of Indians living in Australia have scarcely been researched, it seems that some at least were able to establish successful businesses. The transnational Sindhi company, Wassiamull Assomull and Company, had offices and representatives in Sydney, Melbourne, Brisbane and briefly in Adelaide, while Marm Deen was in partnership with the Syrian man Jaboor in Melbourne for a number of years until c 1913.[31] In Adelaide in 1930, 'Professor' Ali Haider, Qualified Optician and Herbalist, had an office in Union Chambers

Mr Otim Singh

in Wakefield Street. He owned real estate in Queenstown valued at £1,000.[32]

The self-made man who rose in the ranks of society, securing for himself and his family a good living, was a key element of the narrative of settler society. In the second volume of H.T. Burgess, *Cyclopedia of South Australia* published in 1909, there are scores of such accounts: of men and families who made good in the colony, each penned by the subjects of a short biographical statement and then converted to the third person by the editors. Many included photographs not only of the men but also of their farmhouses and business premises. Otim Singh's entry appears to be the only one about a non-white subject. It includes a photograph of him as well as one of his shop in Kingscote. This entry is highly anomalous in a collection of white settler men. No Indigenous people are similarly represented as individuals making their way in the society.

In the *Cyclopedia* we read the story of Otim Singh's business life framed within a narrative of success. We discover that while trudging about with his pack on his back, he liked the island and decided

Mr O. Singh's premises, Kingscote

to give the place a fair trial with the ultimate result that success so crowned his
efforts that he was able to establish himself in a store. His first premises, which were
built of tin, were in time replaced by a stone building 20 feet long, which afterwards
was enlarged, and finally, in 1907, the present fine premises were erected. The
People's Stores, which has a frontage of 60 by 48 feet, is one of the best shops in
Kingscote, and Mr Singh's connection extends throughout the length and breadth
of the island.[33]

Otim Singh's pride in his achievement is almost palpable. The photograph
of the substantial corner shop with attached residence, with his name and the
store's name in large letters, underlines this.

He seems to have been a very enterprising business man catering to the Kangaroo Island community of farmers, fishermen and townspeople. The relatively
isolated nature of the island, with small communities scattered across it, meant
that the residents could be quite dependent upon local stores for a wide variety of
goods. Many of the people would not have been able to afford to go to Adelaide
by boat to buy clothing and many other requisites. In addition, Kingscote was
a very popular holiday destination for many from Adelaide, on the mainland,
who would come and stay in the local hotels and boarding houses for a week or
two in the spring and summer.

From 1908 Otim Singh ran a large advertisement for his store on the front
page of the *Kangaroo Island Courier*, noting that he sold a wide range of groceries,
goods and gifts such as watches and clocks. He also sold drapery items, footwear,
clothing and offered tailoring services, and for the tourist trade he offered post
cards with a 'Fine Assortment of KI views' and 'Best Quality Chinaware with
views of Kingscote'.[34] He was agent for a number of companies and seemed to
have always been open to new business opportunities. In 1907 he was 'Agent

for Aachen and Munich Fire Insurance Company' and in 1908 for 'Edison Pho-
nographs and Records' and 'Universal Cycle and Motorworks'. In 1909 he had
opened a branch store at the small community of MacGillivray at the farm of
Reed and Coy, although it is not clear how long this lasted. In 1917 he could
advertise that he had a 'Six Cylinder Buick Motor Car On Hire 'and would
arrange trips to suit visitors'.[35] In 1924 he was an agent for Harrington's Photographic Supplies and in the following year he became an agent for Buick and
Chevrolet Cars and Trucks. In that year he owned two Buicks, a four cylinder
and a larger six cylinder one, 'with all the latest improvements' advertising 'trips
arranged to any part of KI'.[36] By 1926 he was also the sole agent for Golden
Fleece Benzine'.[37]

He was now a prosperous man. In 1927 he was described as owning

> freehold property at Kingscote, consisting of a large shop and dwelling valued
> at £4000, and also two houses valued at £800. He carries stock in his General
> Store valued at about £1800. His turnover averages between £5000 and £6000
> per annum and he estimates his income as varying between £200 and £500 per
> annum.[38]

At his death, his estate was valued at £10,240.[39] Otim Singh was very much
the self-made prosperous man. Such material success on the part of an Indian
could well have aroused resentment and jealousy among some in the white community, but there is no evidence of that occurring.

As he made this transition from itinerant hawker to becoming a man of sub-
stance within the community his appearance changed. In a photograph taken in
Mount Gambier in 1895 he is shown as Otter Singh.[40] Photographed with two
other Indian hawkers, Gunga Singh and another un-named man, he wears a
turban and sports facial hair, a full beard and moustache. He wears a suit with a
watch chain across his mid-riff. He and the other hawkers wear white dust-coats
over their suits, which may have been a sign of their occupation.

By the time he is photographed for the *Cyclopedia of South Australia* in 1909 he
has cut his hair short and discarded his turban; now he is clean-shaven apart from
a moustache, and wears a three-piece suit with a watch chain on his vest. He had
modified his appearance to leave behind the features which marked him as a Sikh
man. There is a suggestion in the Burgess entry that he had cut his connections
to other Indians in South Australia: 'Since coming to this state he has no dealings
with his countrymen, preferring to make his purchases direct from the business
houses in Adelaide.'[41] While it is said that he separated himself from business
dealings with other Indian hawkers, it is possible to read this to mean that he
cut himself off more generally. Certainly he maintained contact with his family

Indian hawkers at Mount Gambier 1895: (left to right) Gunga Singh; Otter Singh; unidentified. Credit State Library of South Australia

in the Punjab. He would have done this by post and most probably was sending them money via money orders or by other means.

A number of the Indian men living in Australia at the time married white women; others married Indigenous women, while some remained single. Yet others had wives and children in India, whom they visited from time to time. When he visited Australia in 1922, V.S. Sastri, the Indian envoy, was somewhat surprised to find that '[a] good many Indians have married Australian wives from whom they have children and live in harmony and friendship with their neighbours.'[42] Australia never had generic laws about miscegenation such as those introduced in the United States.

In 1906 Otim Singh married Susannah Buick, a white woman, the daughter of David Buick, a long-established farmer of Hog Bay, Kangaroo Island. She was aged thirty-four, although she gave her age as twenty-nine years on the marriage certificate. Otim was forty-four, although his age was recorded as thirty. Otim married into a prosperous and significant family on the island. By 1909, Susanna's brother, Alexander, had added 2,000 acres to his late father's holding. However, we cannot assume that such a marriage was totally un-problematic.

Rebe Taylor has recently explored the fate of the descendants of the Indigenous Tasmanian women who lived in the Dudley area of Kangaroo Island. She notes that marriage patterns among the larger landowners excluded marriages with Indigenous-descended families, even though these families also had significant land-holdings in the district. When interviewing people on the island in the 1990s she met comments such as 'I would always say, stay white, keep away from the colour' and 'no white person, parents wouldn't have wanted their daughters to marry them'.[43] Taylor notes that the racial prejudice was greatest against those with Aboriginal forebears, but she also quotes a woman descended from 'a French national from Mauritius' that '[t]here was a very strong racist attitude' and '[h]aving black grandchildren ... that's at the back of the minds of these Kangaroos Islanders'.[44]

It seems likely that the marriage between Otim Singh and Susanna Buick was seen as controversial. Susannah was thirty-four when she married and the marriage may have been seen as more acceptable to some as she might have been seen as being past the first flush of youth and perhaps her child-bearing years. It is not clear how long Otim and Susannah knew each other, but it is possible that they could have met when he first went to the island in 1897, when she was only twenty-five years old. One can speculate that their marriage was delayed for a number of years, due to her family's opposition. For a woman to marry at such an age was certainly well above the average age of marriage at the time, but, in fact, it was not beyond the age of child-bearing. It is significant that Otim and Susannah did not have any children. Taylor notes that at least one couple, Mary Seymour, of Indigenous descent, and her husband, Frank Abell, decided not to have children as '[s]he didn't want to have children who had stigma attached to them'.[45] The Kangaroo Island community was a small one and as Taylor notes: 'Almost everyone knew everyone on Kangaroo Island.'[46] Thus it is also equally possible that Otim and Susannah made a similar decision. Perhaps being childless was the cost they had to pay for their marriage.

Certainly after 1901 Indians were not thought of as possible settlers; that is, as people who had a future in this land for their children and grandchildren. Rather, they were anomalies, relics left over from an earlier era, from before the passing of the Immigration Restriction Act. Under later changes introduced in 1919, Indians resident in Australia were able to bring in their wives and minor children to live in Australia if they could show that they could support and house them properly. However only a few people availed themselves of this opportunity, which allowed some communities, such as Woolgoolga, New South Wales, to have a significant number of Sikh families.[47] But, generally, Indians were not seen as settlers and when they did settle in Australia, they were often viewed with suspicion. In 1911, the NSW Minister of Lands, Niel Nielsen noted the following about Indians gaining land in northern New South Wales:

The Hindoo applicants are undesirable settlers in many ways and in any community of white settlers are regarded with much disfavour amounting almost to complete aversion. The majority of the Hindoos in this state have started as small hawkers or pedlars and saved a fair amount of money; they are naturally acquisitive.[48]

Nielsen alleged that these Indian men posed a sexual threat to white women and their children:

On the northern rivers, where many of these undesirables have obtained farms the white settlers cannot leave their wives and families on the adjacent properties without protection, nor will the women-folk stay on the farms if their men folk are away.[49]

In the white society, there could be a certain level of anxiety about the sexual propensities of these 'coloured' men. Otim Singh would have had to work against such prejudices. Perhaps his marriage into a respected and white land-owning family would have shored up his position.

Otim Singh's manliness could always be suspect. This becomes evident in the correspondence relating to a request he made to the customs officials in 1926. He applied for permission for his nephew Sunda Singh to come to Australia to work in his business while he had a trip back to India. Otim Singh already employed an assistant but was concerned that an employee might leave his position during his absence and thus cause difficulties for his wife. A family member would be more reliable. In all he asked that his nephew be able to stay for three years.

As was normal with regard to such applications, the Investigation Branch was asked to assess Otim Singh's worth and his standing in the community and also whether 'his white wife would be able to manage the business during her husband's absence.' The officers were required to make inquiries 'of principal business houses in Adelaide and at Kingscote'.[50] The local police at Kingscote made inquiries and the report reads: 'Otim Singh had an old established business as a General Storekeeper at Kinsgcote, Kangaroo Island and is well spoken of by residents of good standing there.' Further, they questioned Otim Singh and their report reads:

Mrs Otim Singh who is a white woman will he states hold his power of attorney during the time he intends to be away, and although she is capable of looking after the business, doing the necessary buying etc Mr Otim Singh desires that his nephew Sunda Singh should be permitted to enter Australia.[51]

They also checked whether Susannah Singh would be supported in Otim's absence. The implication here was that an Indian man might just leave and abandon his wife, that he may not know how to behave in an appropriately masculine manner. When Indians applied to bring their wives and minor children in, as allowed under the 1919 regulations, inquiries were made about their incomes and their residences. Some were refused permission to admit their family as their residence was not seen as suitable. The suggestion was that an Indian man might not know how to look after his wife and family in a manner appropriate to a 'civilised' community. Something of Susannah Singh's feelings about such inquiries can be heard in the officers' report of her reply: 'Mrs Singh intimated that if her husband left Australia he would do so with her full knowledge and consent and that she had no reason to doubt that she would be fully provided for.'[52]

It is not clear whether Sunda Singh came to Australia, but within six months of this request, Otim Singh went to India in May 1927. He travelled on the *Moldavia* and he may have arranged to travel with some other Punjabis for Gainda Ram, Mahdo Ram and Keshan Singh were also on the same ship.[53]

It seems that Otim Singh, now aged sixty-five, was not well and he made the trip to India in the hope of recovering his health. Presumably he also wanted to visit his family and his homeland. However, his illness recurred and he returned to Adelaide where he was for 'several weeks' in a private hospital under the care of Dr De Crespigny and Dr Pulleine.[54] In December 1927, he returned to his home in Kingscote, where despite his doctors' efforts, he died shortly afterwards.

The day after his death, a long obituary appeared in a prominent position in the local newspaper, which began: 'The residents of Kangaroo Island will hear with regret the death of Mr. Otim Singh'.[55] He had been in an unusual position, an individual and prosperous Indian man in a white community. While it cannot be claimed that every white Australian absolutely and energetically supported the 'White Australia policy' without allowing for any individual exceptions, he clearly occupied a liminal position. Some strategies that he employed to strengthen his position can be discerned in this obituary. His public-spiritedness was emphasised, and we read that he 'interested himself in local affairs, always being willing to assist in any movement for the good of the town and district'.[56] The *Kangaroo Island Courier* for 1916–17 reveals that he was often a generous donor to fund-raising activities. Late in 1915 he contributed prizes to the Kingscote school prize-giving. During the years 1915–17 he made contributions for the Wounded Soldiers Club and the South Australian Soldiers Fund. On New Year's Day 1916, he presented an 'ambulance car', presumably a toy for an Art Union raffle which raised £1.16.0. When some South African Soldiers had a rifle shooting match against the Kingscote Club, Otim Singh presented £1.1.0 to the highest scorer in the match.[57] At the Australia Day celebrations at Kingscote in August 1917, he was one of the 'staid and dignified townsmen' who dressed up in the Ugly Man Competition to raise money for soldiers.[58] A member of the local Vigilance Committee, which seems to have been a group of businessmen seeking to advance the interests of Kingscote, he spoke at valedictory dinners for departing bank managers and other prominent citizens.[59]

Otim Singh's fine store, which was enlarged once more in 1916, was seen as a community asset. A report of some festivities held there, quoted here at length, gives some idea of this as well as the local regard for Otim and Susannah:

A Pleasant Evening

A very enjoyable evening was spent by a number of the townspeople on Thursday evening at the 'warming' of the additions to the People Stores. The ample floor space of the new room made it ideal for dancing and the large numbers of young folk of Kingscote, who are always so ready to 'step the light fantastic', spent a merry time until the 'wee sma' hoors' of Friday, to music supplied by Mr. L. Wright on the good old accordeon. At a suitable hour a dainty supper supplied by Mrs Otim was served and was done justice to by all present. The additions are a great improvement to Kingscote and reflect credit both on Otim Singh and the contractors.[60]

In all the accounts of Otim Singh, there is a continual emphasis upon his family's loyalty to Britain and Empire. In his entry to the *Cyclopedia of South Australia* we read: 'In earlier life he had a great ambition to join the British Army in India, and whilst in Sumatra [he] served four years in the British Mounted Police'. His obituary reads: 'His father and uncles were soldiers and fought with the British forces during the Indian Mutiny of 1857/8.'[61] From the late nineteenth century, Sikhs had been constructed as particularly martial and also very loyal, and it seems that he was able to present himself in this light for his obituarist noted, he 'belonged to that fine type of Hindoo known as Sikhs'.[62]

Some weeks after his death, his widow published an extensive and effusive return thanks, which can be read as a statement of his worth. With her detailing of others' care and kind wishes, she seems to be reminding the readers that he was a loved man of some standing:

Mrs Otim, widow of Otim Singh, wishes sincerely to thank all relatives and friends for all telegrams, letters and personal expressions of sympathy extended to her during her recent sad bereavement. Thanks is extended to the officers and members of the Kingscote Lodge of the RAOB, to Mrs Lermitte and all friends who rendered personal help during her husband's last illness. Especially desiring to thank Drs Des [*sic*] Crespigny and Pulleine and nurses for their care and attention to her husband during his illness in Adelaide, and also to Dr Lermitte for his unceasing attention and medical skill during her husband's last illness.[63]

Otim Singh had crossed many boundaries and many shores in his life-time. He had travelled far from his birth-place and had lived in Australia for almost forty years. But in death, there were further crossings which linked him back to his home. There was no funeral at Kingscote, rather his body was shipped back to Adelaide for cremation. In a codicil to his will added in 1923, he specified that he wanted his ashes delivered to the Secretary of the Import-Export business, G. and R. Wills, Adelaide, presumably for their ultimate return to India.[64] He left his widow all of his estate, for her use during her life time. However, upon her death it was to revert to his three nephews, Sundar, Eishar and Kham Singh, of Bhgalawalla Village, Ferospur District, P.O. Druli, in the Punjab. Mrs Otim ran the business for some years after his death. It seems that finally his estate was returned to his family in the Punjab, where they could contribute to one of the quests which sent Otim on his many journeys, namely, the strengthening of the family's *izzat*.

Notes

1   A. Palfreeman, *The Administration of the White Australia Policy* Melbourne, Melbourne University Press, 1967, p.146.

2   But see Marie de Lepervanche, *Indians in White Australia* Sydney (Allen and Unwin, 1984), Rashnere Bhatti and Verne A. Dusenbery (eds), *A Punjabi Sikh Community in Australia: from Indian sojourners to Australian citizens* (Woolgoolga N.S.W.: Woolgoolga Neighbourhood Centre Inc, 2001); Margaret Allen, '"Innocents Abroad" and "Prohibited Immigrants": Australians in India and Indians in Australia 1890-1910' in Ann Curthoys and Marilyn Lake (eds) *Connected Worlds* (Canberra, ANU E-Press, 2005) 111–24.

3   For a brief discussion of this see Margaret Allen, 'Innocents Abroad' 120–2.

4   The State Collectors of Customs reported to the Secretary of the Department of External Affairs and after 1916 to the Department of Home and Territories.

5   H.T. Burgess, *Cyclopedia of South Australia* (Adelaide: Cyclopedia Company, 1909 volume 2) 1019-1020.

6   See his obituary in *Kangaroo Island Courier* 10 December 1927: 2. Also see *Register* 18 May 1927: 10 and *Register* 14 December 1927: 13.

7   Tony Ballantyne, 'Entangled pasts: colonialism, mobility and the systematisation of Sikhism' un-published conference paper presented at CISH, University of NSW July 2005, 7.

8   Burgess, *Cyclopedia* 1019.

9 Tom. G. Kessinger,. *Vilyatpur 1848-1968 Social and Economic Change in a North Indian Village* (Berkeley, University of California Press, 1974). p. 138.

10 A. Mani, 'Indians in Jakarta' in K. S. Sandhu and A. Mani (eds), *Indian Communities in South East Asia* (Singapore: Times Academic Press, 1993) 103.

11 Quoted in Ballantyne, 'Entangled pasts 8.

12 W.H. McLeod, 'The First Forty Years of Sikh Migration', in W.H. McLeod, *Exploring Sikhism Aspects of Sikh Identity, Culture and Thought* (New Delhi, Oxford University Press, 2000) 250.

13 Burgess, *Cyclopedia* 1019.

14 Burgess, *Cyclopedia* 1019.

15 W.H. McLeod, 'The First Forty Years of Sikh Migration', in W.H. McLeod, *Exploring Sikhism Aspects of Sikh Identity, Culture and Thought* (New Delhi, Oxford University Press, 2000) passim.

16 In the files of the National Archives there are a number of such third class tickets sent from India by Indians seeking to show that they had been in Australia.

17 Burgess, *Cyclopedia* 1019.

18 In 1912, Rochimull Pamamull, a Melbourne businessman was thus excused from having to give his handprints. National Archives of Australia (NAA) Collector of Customs, Melbourne, General Correspondence B13 1912/5677 Roehumull Pamamull Certificate of exemption from Dictation Test.

19 NAA Australian Customs Service, South Australia Correspondence Files SB D1976 Immigration Act Gainda Ram application for CEDT and passport. Otim Singh's CEDT has not currently been located.

20 Burgess, *Cyclopedia* 1020.

21 Quoted in S K. Datta, 'India and Racial relationships', *Young Men of India* v. 35 (8) August 1924, 500.

22 NAA Australian Customs Service, South Australia Correspondence Files D596 1921/3865.

23 NAA D596 1921/3865.

24 See Athol Brewster, 'The Indian Hawker Nuisance in the Colony of Victoria 1890–1900', Honours history thesis, University of Melbourne 1978. My thanks to Dr Andrew Brown-May, University of Melbourne and Athol Brewster for access to this thesis.

25 See reports in *Register* 22 April, 1 May, 5 July and 7 July 1893.

26 *Register* 5 July 1893, 4.

27 Letter to *Register* 1 Dec 1905. See another supportive letter from Dumosa in *Register* 7 December 1905. Brackets in original.

28 Quoted in S.K. Datta, 'India and Racial relationships' 500.

29 Quoted in S.K. Datta, 'India and Racial relationships' 500.

30 *Argus* 12 June 1922.

31 See Claude Markovits, *The Global World of Indian Merchants, 1750-1947* (Cambridge, Cambridge University Press, 2000) Passim; NAA B13 1909/9567 Fatah Singh.

32 NAA Investigation Branch, Investigation Case Files S. A. D1915/2634 Admission of Hadi Haissan.

33 Burgess, *Cyclopedia* 1020.
34 See advertisements in *Kangaroo Island Courier* on 2 November 1907, 13 January 1926 and also on 6 June 1925.
35 *Kangaroo Island Courier* 22 December 1917: 5.
36 *Kangaroo Island Courier* 28 February 1925.
37 *Kangaroo Island Courier* 13 January 1926.
38 NAA D191/1589 Singh Otim
39 Last will of Otim Singh Probate Registry Office, Supreme Court Adelaide Number 48675/1927.
40 Indian hawkers at Mt Gambier Photograph B16740 State Library of South Australia.
41 Burgess, *Cyclopedia* 1020.
42 *Report by the Honourable V.S.Srinvasa Sastri P.C. Regarding his Deputation to the Dominions of Australia, New Zealand and Canada* (Simla: Government Central Press, 1923) 3.
43 Rebe Taylor, *Unearthed: The Aboriginal Tasmanians of Kangaroo Island* (Adelaide, Wakefield Press, 2002) 225.
44 Taylor, *Unearthed* 226.
45 Taylor, *Unearthed* 236.
46 Taylor, *Unearthed* 233.
47 See Bhatti and Dusenbery (eds), *A Punjabi Sikh Community*
48 Public Record Office (London) Colonial Office (CO) 886/4/21 Further correspondence relating to treatment of Asiatics in the Dominions.Enclosure in no 37 NSW Minister of Lands, Niel Nielsen wrote this minute in 1911.
49 Public Record Office (London) CO 886/4/21 Enclosure in no 37.
50 NAA D1915/1589. Singh Otim.
51 NAA D1915/1589. Singh Otim.
52 NAA D1915/1589 Singh Otim.
53 See NAA D1976 Immigration Act Gainda Ram application. See also *Register* 18 May 1927, 10.
54 *Kangaroo Island Courier* 10 December 1927.
55 *Kangaroo Island Courier* 10 December 1927.
56 *Kangaroo Island Courier* 10 December 1927.
57 *Kangaroo Island Courier* 29 April 1916, 5.
58 *Kangaroo Island Courier* 1 September 1917, 3.
59 *Kangaroo Island Courier* 9 May 1916, 4 and also see *Kangaroo Island Courier* 13 June 1908, 7.
60 *Kangaroo Island Courier* 4 October 1916, 2.
61 Burgess, *Cyclopedia* 1020 and *Kangaroo Island Courier* 10 December 1927.
62 Mrinalini Sinha, *Colonial Masculinity The 'manly Englishman' and the 'effeminate Bengali' in the late nineteenth century* (Manchester and New York: Manchester University Press, 1995).
63 *Kangaroo Island Courier* 17 January 1928.
64 Last will of Otim Singh

Works cited

Allen, Margaret. '"Innocents abroad" and "prohibited immigrants"; Australians in India and Indians in Australia 1890-1910' in Ann Curthoys and Marilyn Lake (eds) *Connected Worlds History in Transnational Perspective*. Canberra, ANU E Press, 2005.

Argus

Ballantyne, Tony. 'Entangled pasts: colonialism, mobility and the systematisation of Sikhism' un-published conference paper presented at CISH, University of NSW July 2005.

Bhatti, Rashmere and Dusenbery, Verne A. (eds). *A Punjabi Sikh Community in Australia: from Indian sojourners to Australian citizens*. Woolgoolga N.S.W.: Woolgoolga Neighbourhood Centre Inc, 2001.

Brewster, Athol. 'The Indian Hawker Nuisance in the Colony of Victoria 1890-1900'. Honours history thesis, University of Melbourne, c. 1978.

Burgess, H.T. *Cyclopedia of South Australia*. Adelaide, Cyclopedia Company, 1909, volume 2.

Curthoys, Ann and Lake, Marilyn. 'Introduction' in Ann Curthoys and Marilyn Lake (eds) *Connected Worlds*. Canberra: ANU E-Press, 2005.

Datta, S.K. 'India and Racial relationships'. *Young Men of India* v. 35 (8) August 1924.

de Lepervanche, Marie. *Indians in White Australia*. Sydney: Allen and Unwin, 1984.

Kangaroo Island Courier

Kessinger, Tom G. *Vilyatpur 1848-1968 Social and Economic Change in a North Indian Village* Berkeley, University of California Press, 1974.

McLeod, W.H. 'The First Forty Years of Sikh Migration' in W.H. McLeod, *Exploring Sikhism Aspects of Sikh Identity, Culture and Thought*. New Delhi: Oxford University Press, 2000.

Mani, A. 'Indians in Jakarta' in K. S. Sandhu and A. Mani (eds) *Indian Communities in South East Asia*. Singapore: Times Academic Press (1993).

Markovits, Claude. *The Global World of Indian Merchants, 1750–1947*. Cambridge: Cambridge University Press, 2000.

Palfreeman, A. *The Administration of the White Australia Policy*. Melbourne, Melbourne University Press, 1967.

Probate Registry Office, Supreme Court Adelaide Last Will of Otim Singh, No. 48675/1927.

Public Record Office (London) Colonial Office (CO) 886/4/21 Further correspondence relating to treatment of Asiatics in the Dominions.

Report by the Honourable V.S.Srinvasa Sastri P.C. Regarding his Deputation to the Dominions of Australia, New Zealand and Canada (Simla, Government Central Press, 1923.

Register

Sinha, Mrinalini. *Colonial Masculinity The 'manly Englishman' and the 'effeminate Bengali' in the late nineteenth century.* Manchester and New York: Manchester University Press, 1995.

Taylor, Rebe. *Unearthed: The Aboriginal Tasmanians of Kangaroo Island.* Adelaide: Wakefield Press, 2002.

A 'Quixotic Escapade' at Recherche Bay

LUCY FROST

Recherche Bay, in the far south of Tasmania, is a remote and secretive place at the end of a gravel road, the most southerly drive you can make in Australia. Until recently when the Bay has become a cause celebre among environmentalists, it had seemed a place erased from history. Almost no one remembered that French explorers had anchored in its sheltered waters more than two hundred years ago to undertake some of Australia's first major scientific experiments, or that among the crew on the expedition's ships was the first European woman to step onto a Tasmanian beach. Louis the ship's steward was actually Marie Louise Victoire Girardin in male disguise. It is said that 'Louis', riled by taunts about her manhood, threatened another crew member with a kitchen knife and was in her turn challenged to a duel fought in this idyllic wilderness setting with its dramatic mountain ranges louring in the background.[2] There are various ways to tell the story of this cross-dressed adventurer from Versailles. The diminutive but fiery-tempered swashbuckler with a kitchen knife could invite a comic rendering, as could the improbably named Fortestsodo Santo,[3] an Iberian sailor who tried to escape the British convict system by building a boat on the shores of Recherche Bay in 1814. Santo might have vanished from history if he had not almost escaped to Chile little more than twenty years after the French had been there and only a decade after the British had founded their colony. The sequence of events which brought Santo to the shores of Recherche Bay can be pieced together from the record of his trial at the Old Bailey, newspaper reports, registers of courts martial, convict records, and the unpublished autobiography of a man who believed fervently in his own importance. In re-constructing this story I want to suggest that while bringing 'lost' places like Recherche Bay into national consciousness is bound to be a serious endeavour, it need not be grim. A place may be valued in part for the comic tales it has engendered, tales like the 'Quixotic escapade' which adds an Iberian connection to the ennobling story of the French scientists.

Santo arrived in Hobart Town on 19 February 1812.[4] He was aged about thirty-five and was sentenced at the Old Bailey to seven years' transportation for stealing a watch. 'Me no got the watch', the shop assistant remembered Santo saying in his fractured English after his companion, Francisco Perera,

had rushed out the door.[5] Santo arrived in the penal colony before Lieutenant Governor George Arthur developed his elaborate system of recording-keeping.[6] The sailor is remembered because he is represented in the narrative of a man who became sufficiently prominent to believe his reminiscences worth recording half a century later, John Pascoe Fawkner. Fawkner is described by his biographer C.P. Billot as a 'truculent, fiery little man whose influence dominated the early days of Melbourne's history', continues to be remembered for his insistent claim that he—and not John Batman—should be recognised as that city's founding father.[7] But during the period when his life became entangled with Santo's, Fawkner was only twenty-one, and according to Billot, it 'seems likely that by this time he had realized that he would always be short, and that all his actions from now onwards would need to be larger than life if he was to make any impression on life at all'.[8]

Reminiscing fifty years later as a man past seventy concerned for his place in history, Fawkner would remember himself as an idealistic youth embarking upon a 'Quixotic Escapade':

I had taken from my father a shop and house in Hobart Town, and set up a bakery, to enable me to sell the wheat produced on my father's farm: unfortunately, the baker I employed was not only a prisoner but also a foreigner, born in Piedmont, had been a soldier under Bonaparte in Spain, taken prisoner by the English, and as he stated induced to enter the British army to prevent being sent to prison; he took the first opportunity to desert, was caught, and sentenced to transportation for desertion: He collected around him other foreigners, who stated they were transported for the same offence, trying to get home to their friends and relations. These men instilled into me the notion that they were unjustly suffering.[9]

Fawkner's baker from Piedmont, like Samuel Taylor Coleridge's traveller from Porlock, resists authentication. Even young Johnnie seems a figment of reminiscing imagination. The verifiable John Pascoe Fawkner was born in London where he lived until 1803 when his father, sentenced to transportation for receiving stolen goods, was ordered onto the *Calcutta,* and his wife and children went too.[10] After an abortive attempt to establish a colony on the shores of Port Phillip Bay (near the present-day town of Sorrento), the *Calcutta* sailed across Bass Strait in 1804 and founded Hobart Town instead.

The reminiscing Fawkner, however, portrays himself not as a savvy chap who was a foundation member of a penal colony, but as a naïf formed within a literary, pastoral tradition:

> I had been brought up chiefly away from companions, a great portion of my time passed in the wild woods reading Plutarch's Lives and tales of heroism, and fancifully agreed to help these men escape from the slavery of convictism.[11]

'Fancifully agreed' seems an understatement for buying into a scheme by which, in Fawkner's own words, 'every requisite of canvass, iron work, rope and other things to enable a small vessel to be built in the woods, should be provided by me also provisions for them to last for a voyage to South America'.[12] Fawkner was going to arrange the escape of seven convicts, four of whom bore names sounding foreign to an Englishman: there was Fortestsodo Santo, of course, and then Antonio Martini, a soldier court-martialled in Spain; Vivenza Buchheri, another soldier, court-martialled in Malta; and Antonio Janni, sentenced to death for cutting and maiming a man, had been commuted to transportation for life.[13] A fifth convict, Patrick McCabe, court-martialled like Martini after deserting in Spain, qualifies as 'foreign' in the sense of being Irish, but the other two bear English-sounding names: William Green, court-martialled in Quebec, and Montrose Johnson, transported for stealing a sheep.[14]

Because secrecy was of paramount importance for an escape in which the logistical complications required considerable time and planning, the convict conspirators must have known each other well enough to make judgments about trustworthiness. Although they were assigned around the Hobart area to various masters and gangs, they had arrived in the colony aboard just two ships: Martini, Buchheri, and Janni were with Santo on the *Guildford* to Sydney and then on the

Ruby to Hobart; Green, Johnson, and McCabe shared a passage on the first ship bringing convicts directly from England to Van Diemen's Land, the *Indefatigable,* which arrived on 19 October 1812, exactly eight months after the *Ruby.*[15] The connection between these two ship-based networks may have been Martini and McCabe, both court martialled in southern Spain for deserting, Martini on 14 January 1811 and McCabe three months later.[16] They may have known each other at that time, or once they were both in Hobart they may have struck up a conversation about their experiences of deserting from the British army as it fought the troops of Napoleon—or the connection may lie somewhere else entirely. Interestingly, Pierre Reine, the other Private in the Regiment of Chasseurs Britanniques with whom Martini was convicted of 'Deserting with a view to join the enemy', was not part of the conspiracy, though he had shared the voyage to Hobart via Sydney with the others on the *Guildford* and *Ruby,* as had Buchheri's co-accused from his Malta Court Martial, Guiseppe La Rosa, who was also excluded from the plot.[17] Something about those earlier unsuccessful attempts to desert may have disqualified Reine and La Rosa from the attempt to escape, or one of them may have been a missing eighth convict, who according to Fawkner had 'promised' to join the others—'he failed on the night of evasion but kept the secret truly'.[18]

While one can construct a kind of logic to explain how these seven conspirators got together, the crucial question remains: how did they persuade young Fawkner to get involved?[19] Granted that the reminiscing Fawkner romanticises both his own naïveté and the circumstances of the convicts, he must nevertheless have been moved by their stories, because he knowingly agreed to take terrible risks. Weeks, even months, would have been required to stockpile the materials for a serious attempt at escape. Although Fawkner is adamant that everything was paid for through good honest work (mostly his own), it seems more likely that in the chaotic world of early Van Diemen's Land, where the criminality of those who came free was often breath-takingly more spectacular than the petty crimes of the convict transportees, the conspirators were well-positioned through their assigned work to make significant contributions of their own. Antonio Janni could have helped himself to some portion of the massive quantities of spirits, grain, and sugar which his master, Lieutenant Colonel Andrew Geils, would soon be accused of removing from the government store while he was acting lieutenant governor.[20] Antonio Martini was brilliantly placed to divert goods from the commissariat, which was under the temporary control of his erratic master, Patrick Gould Hogan, because the man who ordinarily held the appointment was in Sydney awaiting trial.[21] Perhaps it was because Patrick McCabe's master had little to offer the conspirators' accumulating pile of goods, that the Irishman courageously decided to rob Hobart's most conspicuous house, 'a noble town house complete with castellations and roof-top cannon'.[22] The compass stolen by McCabe might have been most useful if he had not been caught and sentenced to 500 lashes.[23] While the pain may well have fuelled McCabe's desire to escape, the episode casts some doubt on his judgment—and on young Fawkner's for risking involvement with such bunglers. And as for the Iberian sailor, Fortestsodo Santo, the experience he was gaining as a member of the Hobart boat builder's gang would prove invaluable, as would the local knowledge and the skills Fawkner himself had gained if Robert Sharman is right in saying that he 'earned his living in the years 1810 to 1812 as a builder and timber-splitter'.[24]

Presumably boat-building materials and supplies coming in from the convict conspirators were stored at Fawkner's bakery until 'the quixotic escapade' began. 'The night fell, the clouds of evening set on the night of the 15th of April 1814', and Fawkner with the help of one of the convict escapees loaded Fawkner's own whaleboat, and rowed out of the harbour 'under the very eyes of the sentry at the wharf'.[25] A little further down the Derwent they picked up the other six, and all 'took our places in the boat; five as oarsmen myself as steersman, and without noise or show, we pushed off, passed the guard boat and soon up sail and away with a fair breeze', bound 150 kilometres down river to Recherche Bay, the site chosen by Fawkner as 'a good place to build the craft'.[26]

Fawkner, who does not mention what happened to the bakery in his absence, claims he thought he could spend months helping the convicts build a seaworthy vessel, and then return to 'my own farm at Glenorchy, [and] no person would know where I had been'.[27] On 21 May, however, the *Van Diemen's Land Gazette and General Advertiser,* the official publication of the colonial government, carried on its front page a 'Public Notice':

> The following Prisoners having made their escape in a Boat.
> Antonio Martinio, Servant to P. G. Hogan Esq.
> Forteso De Santo [sic], from the Boat builder's gang.
> Patrick McCabe, Servant to Mr Lang.
> Vissanso Boucherie, Servant to the Military Hospital.
> Antonio Janio, Servant to Lieut. Colonel Gells.
> Montrose Johnson, Servant to John Rebley Settler.
> William Green, Clerk to the Naval Officer.
> John Fawkner Junr. Free man—having aided and assisted the said Persons in making their escape, and also accompanied them … Any Person or Persons harbouring, concealing, or maintaining any of the Absentees, will be prosecuted for the Offence.

An abbreviated version of this notice was also published in the *Sydney Gazette* on 16 July.

The first newspaper report appeared when the escapees were some five weeks missing. There is no evidence that anyone was sent to look for them; why should a small settlement on a large island divert precious resources in search of convicts who would probably die or return, or draw attention to themselves as marauding bushrangers? Recherche Bay was well beyond the boundaries of the penal colony's surveillance system, an appropriately secret place for the very visible and noisy activities involved in cutting down trees to build and launch a sailing vessel complete with masts and rigging. The boat, after its capture, was described in the *Sydney Gazette* as a 'lugger-rigged vessel of very singular appearance ... about 36 feet keel, & well modelled: their cordage was contrived of twisted bark'.[28] They named their ship the *Liberty*, resonating with the rhetoric of the American and French revolutions, and their own desire to be free.[29]

The halcyon days of Tasmanian autumn changed into winter during the months when they built the *Liberty*, the winds hitting Recherche Bay making their first landfall straight off the Southern Ocean and Antarctica. When the boat-builders first arrived, members of the Indigenous band Lyluequonny band may still have been on the coast, watching as these strange rough characters came up the beach, a far different mob of visitors than the polite and well-mannered French.[30] Did the Lyluequonny show the convicts the French garden? Did they dig potatoes there? Or did the escapees threateningly demand food and sex from them? Does the objectionable behaviour of these intruders explain why, little more than a year later, Captain James Kelly met real hostility on the same shore? Kelly, in a similar sized five-oared whaleboat with a crew of four, was circumnavigating Van Diemen's Land. As he reported in his logbook, on 13 December 1815 'we attempted to haul the boat up on the south side of Recherche Bay, but were prevented by a large body of natives giving us a tremendous volley of stones and spears'; this was the only time on the voyage when Aborigines refused to allow Kelly's boat to land.[31]

However, the boat-builders managed to feed themselves, whatever shelters they built, their comforts would have been few, and among this motley crew with 'foreigners' whose English was rudimentary, fractiousness and quarrelling seem inevitable. Perhaps this explains why, in their eagerness to be off after four months in the wilderness, they made a mistake. 'They had actually sailed', reported the *Sydney Gazette* on 8 October, 'but when 60 miles at sea were obliged to put back, from the fear of perishing, their water, for want of secure vessels, having all leaked out'. Their luck was up. At the mouth of the Derwent River, the government schooner *Estramina*, always on the look-out for run-aways, met the strange-looking *Liberty*, boarded her:

> found two prisoners on board, and learnt from them that she had been built by a number of bush rangers, near the South west Cape, with a design of leaving Van Diemen's Land entirely.[32]

The other crew of the *Liberty*, according to Fawkner, were off 'seeking for water casks'.[33] Certainly we know that one of them, the quintessential Irish bungler Patrick McCabe, was caught breaking and entering the house of a settler on a property south of Hobart on 24 August.[34] The day before, to his apparent surprise, Fawkner himself was arrested, charged, taken before two magistrates, and sentenced. Before the *Liberty* put out to sea, Fawkner had been landed 'near Hobart Town', and in his reminiscences he claims that his involvement would have passed unnoticed, but for the dastardly betrayal of two 'foreigners'.[35] 'The names of the traitors', he wrote, 'were Antonio Martini, Piedmontese, and Vicenso Bucharsh Russian or Bulgarian'.[36] In the imagination of the reminiscing Fawkner, a young man is seduced and betrayed by foreigners.[37]

Fawkner never tried to blame Fortestsodo Santo, with whom his name was bracketed on the list of prisoners to be transported by the *Lady Nelson* to Newcastle, the secondary punishment station north of Sydney. Santo is described as a prisoner, sentenced to three years by the Hobart magistrates, and Fawkner as a free man, sentenced to two. Fawkner had initially been sentenced to three years and 500 lashes; Santo would not have been spared the lash, and his original sentence too may have been reduced.[38] It is understandable that the Iberian ship builder should come in for the heftiest punishment among the conspirators: his skills made him a dangerous man.[39] It was Fawkner's status that made him a threat to the small community—for free men to help the unfree in their midst conjured the stuff of nightmares.

The tale of Santo and his mates makes no claim on the noble realm where the environmentalists have recently been re-staging the drama of the French scientific expeditions at Recherche Bay, but these escaped convicts and their benefactor offer a comic gloss, a wry whiff of boys' adventures that undercuts the earnestness with which most stories of early European experience in Australia is told. John Pascoe Fawkner was wrong about many things, and yet in evoking the memory of Spain's famous tilter at windmills, he hit precisely the right key: it had been indeed a 'Quixotic' escapade.

Notes

1 An earlier version of some material from this chapter was included in Lucy Frost, 'The Vanishing Iberian Connection', eds Susan Ballyn, Geoff Belligoi, *Changing Geographies* (Barcelona: Centre d'Estudis Australians, 2001) 21–41.

2 Bruce Poulson, *Recherche Bay: a short history* (Southport, Tasmania: Southport Community Centre, 2004) 8.

3 Probably because Santo was illiterate and spoke in heavily accented English, his first name was transcribed with no consistency. I have used the spelling from the Indent of the *Ruby* (CON 13/1 Archives Office of Tasmania), the ship which brought him to Van Diemen's Land.

4 Santo had been transported on the *Guildford* to Sydney, arriving on 18 January 1812. Most of the 199 men stayed in New South Wales, but about 60 were sent on the *Ruby* to Van Diemen's Land, arriving in Hobart Town on 19 February.

5 Trial of Zoortestoodo [sic] Santo and Francisco Perera, 5 December 1810, *The Proceedings of the Old Bailey*, www.oldbaileyonline.org/, accessed 2 January 2006.

6 Few public records, including convict records, survive for the period (1813–1817) when Thomas Davey was Lieutenant Governor of Van Diemen's Land. Davey told a House of Commons enquiry in 1820 that upon his return to England, he had sent 'all the Papers connected with my office' to his patron (quoted P.R. Eldershaw, *Guide to the Public Records of Tasmania* (Hobart: Tasmanian State Archives, 1957) ii.

7 C.P. Billot, *The Life and Times of John Pascoe Fawkner* (Melbourne: Hyland House, 1985) xi.

8 Billot, *The Life and Times* 60.

9 John Fawkner, 'The reminiscences of John Pascoe Fawkner' (MS 8512, State Library of Victoria) 59, 57.

10 Marjorie Tipping, *Convicts Unbound* (South Yarra, Victoria: Viking O'Neil, 1988) 272.

11 Fawkner, 'The reminiscences of John Pascoe Fawkner' 57.

12 Fawkner, 'The reminiscences of John Pascoe Fawkner' 57.

13 On 14 January 1811 Antonio Martini was convicted of desertion at a General Court Martial held at Isla de Léon, near Cádiz on the southern coast of Spain, and was sentenced to fourteen years' transportation (Registers of Courts Martial, War Office 91/5, National Archive, Kew, England); Vincenzo Buchieri and Guiseppe La Rosa, Privates in the Sicilian Regiment, were tried (charges unspecified), at a Court Martial held on 9 August 1810 at La Valette, Malta. Found guilty, they were sentenced to transportation 'for the natural term of their Lives' (Registers of Courts Martial, War Office 91/5, National Archive, Kew, England); Antonio Janni, charged with 'Cutting and maiming a Man', was tried at the Hampshire Summer Assizes on 10 July 1809, convicted, and sentenced to death (Record of Conviction, Home Office 27/5, National Archive, Kew, England).

14 On 13 April 1811, Patrick McCabe, Private in the 87th Regiment of Foot, was tried before a Court Martial at the Isla de Leon, Spain, convicted of desertion, and sentenced to transportation for life (Registers of Courts Martial, War Office 91/5, National Archive, Kew, England). Upon arrival in Van Diemen's Land,

McCabe was described as a native of King's County (Ireland), 33 years old, with a pock-pitted scar over the right eye (Alphabetical Register of Male Convicts CON 23/1 Archives Office of Tasmania, Hobart, Tasmania); Serjeant William Green of the Royal Newfoundland Feusilliers was tried before a Court Martial at Quebec on 29 January 1811, convicted of desertion, and sentenced to transportation for life (Registers of Courts Martial, War Office 91/5, National Archive, Kew, England); Montrose Johnson was sentenced to transportation for life at the Kent Assizes on 21 August 1811 (Assignment List CON 13/1; Convict Conduct Record CON 31/23, Archives Office of Tasmania, Hobart, Tasmania).

15 Charles Bateson, *The Convict Ships 1787–1868* (Glasgow: Brown, Son & Ferguson, 1969) 202, 342–343, 356–357.

16 Registers of Courts Martial, War Office 91/5, National Archive, Kew, England.

17 Registers of Courts Martial, War Office 91/5, National Archive, Kew, England; Santo's co-accused from the theft the watch in London, Francisco Perera, had been on the *Guildford,* but was disembarked at Sydney.

18 Fawkner, 'The reminiscences of John Pascoe Fawkner' 57–58. Billot, without giving a source, names 'Obadiah Wood, a carpenter' as the one who 'failed to turn up' *The Life and Times of John Pascoe Fawkner* 61.

19 Robert C. Sharman claimed that the convicts 'came upon' Fawkner 'while he was working as a sawyer in the bush, and prevailed upon him to help them make a cutter, in which they were to escape from the colony' ('John Pascoe Fawkner in Tasmania', *Tasmanian Historical Research Association Papers and Proceedings* 14:3 (1955): 58). Such an encounter seems highly unlikely: seven or eight convicts assigned to various masters or gangs in different places would scarcely have had an opportunity to go wandering around the bush together.

20 Geils was described by Lachlan Macquarie, Governor of New South Wales, as 'a Man of weak judgment, extremely venal and rapacious, and always inclined to sacrifice the interests of the Public to his own sordid and selfish views' (quoted P.R. Eldershaw, 'Andrew Geils', ed. Douglas Pike *Australian Dictionary of Biography* (Melbourne: Melbourne University Press, 1966) I, 436.

21 According to R.L. Wettenhall, Hogan's 'command of the Van Diemen's Land commissariat was short: accused of drunkenness and of irregular use of commissariat bills, he was himself superseded in 1816, tried by court martial in Sydney, convicted of neglect of duty and of fraudulent use of his powers, and dismissed from office' ('Patrick Gould Hogan', ed. Douglas Pike, *Australian Dictionary of Biography* (Melbourne: Melbourne University Press, 1966) 549). Peter Bolger comments: 'Every single commissary officer before 1820 was known to have fiddled his books' (*Hobart Town* 13).

22 Peter Bolger, *Hobart Town* (Canberra: Australian National University Press, 1973) 13.

23 According to his convict conduct record, McCabe was charged with 'Stealing a Compass in the Dwelling House of T.W. Birch', and sentenced on 23 February 1814 'To receive 500 Lashes and labour in the Gaol Gang' (CON 31/6, Archives Office of Tasmania, Hobart, Tasmania).

24 Sharman, 'John Pascoe Fawkner in Tasmania' 58.

25 Fawkner, 'The reminiscences of John Pascoe Fawkner' 58.

26 Fawkner, 'The reminiscences of John Pascoe Fawkner' 58.

27 Fawkner, 'The reminiscences of John Pascoe Fawkner' 58.

28 *Sydney Gazette* 8 October 1814.

29 Fawkner, 'The reminiscences of John Pascoe Fawkner' 60.

30 Poulson, *Recherche Bay* 1.

31 [James Kelly], *The Log of the Circumnavigation of Van Diemen's Land by Captain James Kelly 1814–1815* (Hobart: Government Printer, 1986) 7.

32 *Sydney Gazette* 8 October 1814.

33 Fawkner, 'The reminiscences of John Pascoe Fawkner' 59.

34 McCabe was sentenced to 500 lashes for breaking and entering the house of James Nairn at Sandy Bay (Convict Conduct Record CON 31/6, Archives Office of Tasmania, Hobart, Tasmania). One of the two Magistrates who heard his case, Rev. Robert Knopwood, had sentenced Faulkner the day before.

35 Fawkner, 'The reminiscences of John Pascoe Fawkner' 58.

36 Fawkner, 'The reminiscences of John Pascoe Fawkner' 60.

37 Fawkner's claim that the two convicts on the *Estramina* were running away from the comrades 'in order to deliver the lugger up and save themselves at the expense of their fellows and the betrayal of their benefactor' makes more sense if the names of the 'traitors' are William Green and Montrose Johnson, the two Englishmen whose names do not appear on Fawkner's official convict record ('The reminiscences of John Pascoe Fawkner' 59. See also note 49).

38 On 23 August 1814 John Faulkner was charged with 'aiding and assisting Fortros Desantos Antony Jenny Patrick McCabe Antonio Martini Vizcenza Bucheri convicts to escape from the colony 500 lashes & labor for Govt 3 years' (Convict Conduct Record CON 31/13 Archives Office of Tasmania, Hobart, Tasmania). According to Sharman, 'legend' has it that the lashes 'were administered before his father's door' ('John Pascoe Fawkner in Tasmania' 58); There is no convict conduct record for Santo, who (unlike Fawkner) did not return to Van Diemen's Land after Lt-Gov Arthur instituted the new system of record-keeping.

39 The only recorded punishments are for Fawkner, McCabe, and Santo; the paucity of records makes it impossible to determine what happened to the others; According to Tipping, the *Liberty* came into the possession of a man who had been transported with Fawkner's father on the *Calcutta,* and for some years was used to trade produce between Hobart and the other settlements (272). If this is true, the ship's durability is testimony to the care and skill with which it was built under extremely difficult circumstances.

Works cited

Bateson, Charles. *The Convict Ships 1787-1868*. Glasgow: Brown, Son & Ferguson, 1969.

Billot, C.P. *The Life and Times of John Pascoe Fawkner*. Melbourne: Hyland House, 1985.

Bolger, Peter. *Hobart Town*. Canberra: Australian National University Press, 1973.

Eldershaw, P.R. 'Andrew Geils'. *Australian Dictionary of Biography,* ed. Douglas Pike. Melbourne: Melbourne University Press, 1966. I, 435–436.

Eldershaw, P.R. *Guide to the Public Records of Tasmania*. Hobart: Tasmanian State Archives, 1957.

Fawkner, John. 'The reminiscences of John Pascoe Fawkner', MS 8512, State Library of Victoria.

Frost, Lucy. 'The Vanishing Iberian Connection'. *Changing Geographies,* eds. Susan Ballyn, Geoff Belligoi. Barcelona: Centre d'Estudis Australians, 2001, 21-41.

[Kelly, James]. *The Log of the Circumnavigation of Van Diemen's Land by Captain James Kelly 1814–1815*. Hobart: Government Printer, 1986.

Poulson, Bruce. *Recherche Bay: a short history*. Southport, Tasmania: Southport Community Centre, 2004.

Sharman, Robert C. 'John Pascoe Fawkner in Tasmania'. *Tasmanian Historical Research Association Papers and Proceedings* 14:3 (1955): 57–63.

Tipping, Marjorie. *Convicts Unbound*. Melbourne: Viking O'Neil, 1988.

Wettenhall, R.L. 'Michael Hogan'. *Australian Dictionary of Biography,* ed. Douglas Pike. Melbourne: Melbourne University Press, 1966. 548–549.

Christopher Koch: Crossing Sea Walls

CHAD HABEL

Since the beginning of his career, Christopher Koch has written fiction with a persistent interest in the notion of crossing boundaries and entering new places and spaces. Often his characters undertake sea voyages that are prompted by a sense of exile or a drive towards some sort of adventure, often occupying liminal spaces where almost anything is possible, especially the transformation of identities.[1]

In Koch's novels, the sea wall represents a boundary which serves to prevent a crossing. In contrast, the sea itself is a liminal space which characters pass through as a rite of passage or a path to potential personal transformation. Some novels, such as *Boys in the Island* and *Across the Sea Wall*, narrate a literal sea journey, while others, such as *The Year of Living Dangerously* and *Highways to a War* emphasise the metaphorical nature of the journey. Nonetheless, all of these novels focus on liminal spaces of one type or another. However, the transformative potential of such liminal spaces is rarely fulfilled. For many of Koch's characters, the force of habit is too strong.

The Boys in the Island (1958) establishes many of Koch's enduring concerns. The narrative employs a Wordsworthian nostalgia when telling of the coming-to-age of Francis Cullen. His escape from a prison-like Tasmania to the Mainland promises adventure and fulfilment. Cullen imagines Melbourne as a place of vibrancy, the place where he can develop into maturity freed from the restrictions of his home island. However, this is an empty dream; the novel ends with crushing disillusion as Cullen experiences a tragedy that prompts him to return to Hobart defeated. In this way Koch establishes the themes of broken dreams and illusions that pervade his fiction; his protagonist returns broken from the Otherland.

The Boys in the Island establishes the crucial themes of imprisonment and escape which recur throughout Koch's fiction. Francis Cullen is enamoured of the mainland; he dreams of going to Melbourne, where he imagines the 'real world' might be. 'He would break free from the hillbound circle of the island: now a mocking prison, its every corner and scene stabbing him with the joke.'[2] His eventual journey to the mainland is both a rite of passage and an adventure;

as he travels to a new place and crosses the line between his familiar past and unknown adulthood. This implies the travelling towards a mature adult identity, but this expectation does not come to fruition. Cullen must journey over water literally as a rite of passage. Although Bass Strait is not quite a sea, this passing through liminal space prefigures the sea crossings in his later fiction.

Cullen and his friends find it difficult to make a living, and the dream of a new, adult life disintegrates. Moving to Sydney does not help, and adventure on the Mainland is thwarted when a close friend dies through an accident during horseplay:

> Dead. Forever. That didn't happen to boys. His young, pallid, bony face with its pimples and freckles, its thin nose, his sandy crew-cut hair; all rotting forever in the ground. *That doesn't happen*, the boy protested.
> But it had. Shane had refused to grow up. His destination had not been possible.[3]

The stark disenchantment with the dream of adventure on the Mainland is the focus of the novel. Ultimately, through parties, gambling and drunkenness, the men turn to abuse and violence against a main female character; the macho drinking bouts have gone too far.[4] The novel concludes with a surreal car accident and Francis returning to Hobart to recover. This is a type of 'crossing over' which breaks its promise; the protagonist is unable to develop his identity in any positive way and the dream of adventure shatters into nightmare.

Across the Sea Wall (1965) further develops Koch's concerns with travel across boundaries and the consequences of breaking out of established modes of thought. Here, the sea wall acts as a metaphor for isolation and enclosure; the novel suggests that Australians tend to be inward-looking, but that international travel provides the opportunity to enter a world from which Australia has been shielded since settlement. Furthermore, this novel narrates a journey across the ocean, and so the metaphorical during occurs concurrently with a literal one. Here Koch uses travel as a vehicle for boundary crossings; on the boat the characters enter a liminal space where normal certainties are eroded and personalities can develop unfettered.

Across the Sea Wall ventures into unusual territory for the 1950s: 'Young Westerners simply didn't travel much in Asia; and that included young Australians. All that Australian voyagers saw of Asia was the ports, en route to their lost home in Britain.'[5] Koch's second novel begins his complex engagements with Asia through the representation of Australians in Asia, a motif which has since characterised his work. His narrator expresses a keen sense of adventuring forth as he leaves Australia on a ship:

> I was being raced out of my life, out of my past, out of everything I knew and which had made me, being sped away by this thundering machine—into what? Into darkness and sea, towards teeming unknown countries, with nothing but my few travellers' cheques, and Jimmy.[6]

In Indonesia and India the protagonist experiences different places and different cultures. In *Across the Sea Wall* Koch may well be accused of using 'local colour' in his depiction of Asia, as well as of portraying characters who are misogynistic and cruel. Nonetheless, what is valuable is his focus on the importance of crossing the geographical and psychic boundaries surrounding Australia; Koch's fictions wrestle with the difficulty of disrupting established modes of thinking.

As in many of Koch's other novels the positive potential in travel is not fulfilled. Once again, the protagonist returns defeated to his home and this time is particularly self-reproachful. The nostalgia is painful and he cannot help but brood on the past and blame himself:

> Once, remarkably long ago, I had an affair with a Latvian showgirl called Ilsa Kalnins; once, I was in India. I won't be able to work tonight; maybe the best way to get through the evening would be to go and drink in a pub: but I find I don't want to go out either.
>
> I don't want to go out into Sydney at all: I don't want to be in Sydney. It is not only herself she's woken in me, but the journey ... Well, I say, you had it all, you had it as much as Jimmy did, and you botched it, lost it, ran home, like a dog to its vomit![7]

At the end of this novel the possibilities inherent in sea travel, in crossing boundaries, are not fulfilled. Instead the narrative ends with a sense of hopeless failure and lost opportunities.

The Year of Living Dangerously (1978) is set entirely outside Australia where the focus is less on the journey than on the possibilities and potentials inherent in another place and another time. Jakarta in 1965 is another liminal space for expatriates; it is on the cusp of great changes, and Koch develops an atmosphere of intense anticipation which he develops further in later novels, particularly *Highways to a War*. The story of President Sukarno's final days and the political disintegration of Indonesia is narrated as a prelude to the coup and, after it, the great conflict in Indochina. The novel focuses on expatriates who are stationed in Jakarta as correspondents, but once again the potential for them to learn from the experiences in the liminal zone is curtailed. The novel has a tragic conclusion as the established illusions are shattered and the protagonist flees back to the safety of the West. A change in Hamilton's character is certainly suggested in his contact with Jill at the end, but it is not made explicit within the plot itself.

It is in *The Year of Living Dangerously* that Koch begins to more fully inhabit the tradition of adventure fiction. One marker of this is that the novel is set in a place which is unfamiliar to most Australian readers: Jakarta, Indonesia, 1965. Although the novel is set only thirteen years in the past, Koch indicates that its vision is self-consciously retrospective; the great conflict in Indochina intervenes between the action and the narration of the novel. This is the historical vision that has become a trademark of Koch's work. Most importantly, Koch builds a strong sense of anticipation in this novel; the narrative continually gestures towards the violent cataclysm which occurs at the end, in the coup and the military's reprisals. Jakarta is depicted as a liminal space; it teeters on the edge of a chasm:

> There is a definite point where a city, like a man, can be seen to have become insane ... For a long time, a man may be unbalanced, given to irrational hopes and irrational rages; and though these signs are disconcerting we continue to think of him as eccentric but sane. It's always difficult to believe that someone we know well has crossed into that other territory where no one from our side can reach him, and from which messages crackle back that no longer make any sense. But finally something happens to jar us into seeing this. That's how it was with Sukarno's Jakarta, in the middle of that weird August, at the end of the dry monsoon. [8]

This crossing over into new territory is crucial; the protagonist, Guy Hamilton, experiences adventure and is extended by going to this new place. During his first night in Jakarta the narrative is filtered through his Western vision and the place is depicted with a marked kind of 'local colour': 'It was hard not to see the place as gay, and the poverty as a game.'[9] However, as he spends more time in Indonesia, he comes to know the place better and the narrative establishes some familiarity with the place. This becomes particularly noticeable when Hamilton visits the markets and the countryside. Nonetheless, by the end of the novel Hamilton is still naïve and arrogant; he attempts to force his way past a military guard but suffers a detached retina after a rifle butt to his head. Immobilised during his convalescence, he comes to realize the error of his ways, and the way he has taken both Billy and Jill for granted. Through a dialogue with Kumar, his Javanese assistant, he even comes to realise his role as a privileged voyeur in the Javanese tragedy: 'He was a watcher, a watcher merely: a Peeping Tom, as Billy had said. And Peeping Tom had lost an eye.'[10] What is crucial about this revelation is that it is made possible by crossing over the boundaries which separate the known world from the unknown; it is within the liminal space of Jakarta just before the coup that Hamilton has the opportunity to reshape his identity and his sense of himself. Once again, though, Koch depicts the possibilities for change as limited.

Highways to a War (1995) returns to many of these concerns; it is also set in Asia, but as the title implies in a conflict zone and a place where the worst is still to come. The Cambodia episode constantly gestures towards the fall of Phnomh Penh and the tragic victory of the Khmer Rouge. The novel's protagonist, Michael Langford, escapes from his wounded past in Tasmania into a liminal space where he enacts rites of passage. This is where the notion of mapping identities becomes central; Koch portrays characters who journey across boundaries as a means of redefining their sense of themselves. However, again this is a failed task that ends in tragedy. Langford remains stuck in his personal and ancestral past and the novel concludes with him disappearing in an apotheosis.

As in *The Year of Living Dangerously*, Koch depicts an Asian location which is characterised by conflict, danger, and impending tragedy. As in previous novels, the protagonist escapes a constricting rural lifestyle in Tasmania, this time fleeing a cruel and heartless father who lives in denial of the family's ancestral secret. Just like Guy Hamilton, Michael Langford first experiences Asia with a clearly marked Western naïveté: 'Asia was disclosed to him for the first time, like a video show arranged for his pleasure.'[11] However, as he spends more and more time in Asia—first in Singapore, then Vietnam and Cambodia—he comes to understand the space more as place on its own terms, and feels more and more at home. He even shows signs of wanting to protect the innocents, according to his deep sense of chivalry. In Saigon he attracts a crowd of street children who think of him as saviour-figure. In Cambodia he goes so far as to begin helping the local military operation to resist the advance of the Khmer Rouge. This means that when the inevitable end comes, the reader is prepared for the devastating personal loss which Langford experiences. Since there is no actual sea crossing in this novel, the journey is more metaphorical than literal.

More than any other novel, *Highways to a War* demonstrates the potential for developing and transforming personal identity through crossing boundaries into unknown territory. Langford's career as a combat journalist in Asia enables him to establish his identity and place in the world; it gives him real fame among the community of expatriate journalists and especially among his friends. This is only possible through crossing over into new territory, and he does have a guide in Aubrey Hardwick:

> Langford began to see that he stood on the brink of everything he'd ever wanted: that he had only to walk through the door … Uncle Aubrey was the envoy of the future, smiling at the entrance to the world. He swung the door open and Langford hurried through, without a second's thought.[12]

Indeed, the stories told about Langford through his own audio diaries and interviews with his friends confirm that he had a profound effect on the people who knew him best. It is Claudine Phan who understands him most intimately; she notes that Langford has the nature of a warrior, and it is brought out most forcefully during his time in Asia. However, his fierce idealism and attachment to the Cambodian cause does not work positively for him, and leads him to virtual suicide as he returns to Cambodia after the fall of Phnomh Penh. This reinforces Koch's pattern of failed identity transformation through crossing boundaries.

Koch's *Out of Ireland* (1999) is a companion volume to *Highways to a War* and mirrors its themes. It features an extended sea travel episode where the protagonist meditates at some length on his position as an exile from the known world. When he reaches Van Diemen's Land he finds it a pre-modern, pastoralist idyll where he can start a new life as a colonial farmer. However, he refuses the temptations of this dream and rejects the opportunity to reshape his identity within the liminal space offered by the new frontier.

In *Out of Ireland* the protagonist, Robert Devereux, is at sea in both senses of the word. Having exiled from his native Ireland, he spends a long time in the agonising liminal space of a sea journey. He also becomes lost within himself: he feels his attachment to his homeland and his wife in particular weakening. This part of the novel draws heavily on literary precedents, especially 'The Rime of the Ancient Mariner': it comes complete with albatross, grotesquerie and redemption. This novel is the one where the literal sea journey most clearly complements the inner journey of the protagonist.

Like his historical counterpart John Mitchel, Devereux was convicted as a felon for inciting insurrection in the Irish countryside, and was confined in prison hulks at Bermuda before being transported to Van Diemen's Land. Koch emphasises the journey as a type of adventure, a crossing over into new spaces which has positive potential:

> As I looked at her [the steamship], I found I had the fast-beating pulse one always has when setting out on a voyage, and a paradoxical illusion of freedom! Appalling though my situation was, there was also something tremendous in the prospect of being borne three thousand miles across the Atlantic, clad in my grey summer frock coat and old, dark-blue cap, with its glazed peak.[13]

However, the adventure does not last long as Devereux is soon to discover the horrors of the convict hulks and finally agrees to make a deal with the colonial authorities in order to be given the luxury of life on land in Australia. This life among his former comrades, who were also transported, contains various adventures, including a confrontation with a traitorous informant, a romance with an Irish convict girl and a battle to the death with a bushranger. However, it also includes the lure of an idyllic pastoralist lifestyle as a colonial farmer, and although Devereux always feels the acute sense of exile of a romantic national-ist, he learns the potential for reconstructing himself in a different light. His time in Boeotia gives him an opportunity for self-reflection, and he particularly reconsiders his attitude to violence.

> Ironically enough, although I'm described by the British as a terrorist and a man of violence, I do not like the idea of violence. Nor do I wish to turn to it unless it can be avoided. If my blood were up, and I faced an enemy who had to be dealt with, then I believe I would fight, and fight giving no quarter ... How brave a warrior I would have been [during the uprising], I cannot know; no man can know, until the time comes.[14]

Despite his attraction to a life in Van Diemen's Land, Devereux cannot escape his sense of exile from the Northern Hemisphere and he escapes in glittering fashion to join his friends in America. The liminal spaces of the ship and the Tasmanian hop-glades have not fulfilled their potential. 'It seems that I lost everything in the Antipodes ... and that all I came away with was grief.'[15] Like many of Koch's protagonists, Devereux misses the potential for developing his identity and escapes back to a familiar territory with nothing but bad memories. His sea journey has reinforced his essential traits, rather than changed them. However, Koch ends the novel on a more upbeat note; through Devereux he notes that O'Neill has settled in the Southern Hemisphere.

> I know you are not confined in your spirit. Wandering with your sketchbook and notepad, you've discovered that contentment which my friend James Langford has achieved—but which seemed to me like surrender, and so could not be mine. You hear an unknown music in the Roaring Forties winds; you are lulled by a croon-ing in the bush ... I wonder if you've come to prefer being out of the world? If the door should open, would you actually leave your Antarctic forests and mountains? Or will you remain content there, among those easy colonial settlers for whom Bothwell and their flocks are the cosmos?[16]

In this passage Devereux gives voice to some of Koch's most enduring con-cerns: the difficulty of making a home in a new place, the contentment made possible through settling in a new hemisphere, and the isolation and inward-ness of colonial frames of mind. While Devereux remained at sea for the whole novel, O'Neill made a final landing. This is Koch's most complete example of the change which can occur in passing through a liminal space. Here the posi-tive potential within sea journeys and liminal spaces is fully elaborated, although admittedly only in the figure of a minor character.

Ultimately, the notion of 'crossing over' serves to help understand Koch's fiction as a unified body of work. It combines his use of adventure narrative, his portrayal of the potential for transforming identities, and his depiction of liminal space into one framework. Through his career these concerns have shifted in focus and emphasis, but together they represent the coherent vision which is embodied in his novels. Many of his characters do not make the most of the liminal space they find themselves in; they end up as mere littoral on the shore.

Notes

1 This chapter does not discuss *The Doubleman*, because it is more concerned with metaphysical boundaries than geographical ones, and it is less concerned with the development of identity through crossing boundaries.
2 Christopher Koch, *The Boys in the Island* (Sydney: Vintage, 1958) 122.
3 Koch, *The Boys* 175.
4 Koch, *The Boys* 190.
5 Christopher Koch, *Crossing the Gap* (Sydney: Random House, 1987) 3.
6 Christopher Koch, *Across the Sea Wall* (London: William Heinemann, 1965) 29.
7 Koch, *Across* 210.
8 Christopher Koch, *The Year of Living Dangerously* (London: Michael Joseph Ltd, 1978) 221.
9 Koch, *The Year* 21.
10 Koch, *The Year* 289.
11 Christopher Koch, *Highways to a War* (Port Melbourne: William Heinemann, 1995) 68.
12 Koch, *Highways* 90–3.
13 Christopher Koch, *Out of Ireland* (Milsons Pt: Random House, 1999) 25.
14 Koch, *Out of Ireland* 542.
15 Koch, *Out of Ireland* 700.
16 Koch, *Out of Ireland* 699.

Works cited

Koch, Christopher. *The Boys in the Island*. Sydney: Vintage, 1958.

Koch, Christopher. *Across the Sea Wall*. London: William Heinemann, 1965.

Koch, Christopher. *The Year of Living Dangerously*. London: Michael Joseph Ltd, 1978.

Koch, Christopher. *Crossing the Gap*. Sydney: Random House, 1987.

Koch, Christopher. *Highways to a War*. Port Melbourne: William Heinemann, 1995.

Koch, Christopher. *Out of Ireland*. Milsons Pt: Random House, 1999.

'on the white beach': beach encounters in The Kangaroo Islanders

RICK HOSKING

Catherine Helen Spence's *Clara Morison: a Tale of South Australia During the Gold Fever* is one of the first novels written and published in South Australia; her second chapter is entitled: 'Will probably be missed, for it only describes a long voyage'. What does happen on board ship—mostly to do with the class hierarchy of the vessel, social connections and food—takes place in the ship's equivalent of indoors, with only this single tiny view of the sea and eventual arrival on the beach:

> But the voyage was got through at last, and, after seeing a very unpromising-looking island, about which Miss Waterstone fell into raptures, and misquoted some sentimental poetry about you green isle, and which, they were informed, was called Kangaroo Island, they took a pilot on board, and slowly went up the creek till they got into Port Adelaide.[1]

Catherine Spence's feelings about the tedium of sea voyages in general, and the Southern Ocean in particular, have been shared by many writers since the 1850s; there have been relatively few fictions by Australians about the waters of the Southern Ocean.[2] There seems to be much more writing about those other oceans that girt the Australian nation, the Indian and the Pacific; significantly, there has been a considerable archive of both life and creative writing representing the experience of Australia's tropical coastlines, where detail and symbolism of the archetypal (Pacific) littoral can be deployed.[3]

In 1878 the Adelaide newspaper the *Register* published the recollections of Nathaniel Hailes, who had arrived in South Australia 21 March 1839, on the East Indiaman *Buckinghamshire*, the largest immigrant ship to reach South Australia to that time, on which he had been the Superintendent of Emigrants.[4] Hailes' memoirs are significant for many reasons, not least because they are among the most witty and readable of those that have come down to us. Neatly titled 'Self Transportation', his first article appeared in the *Register* 8 January 1878 and records the moment of arrival at Holdfast Bay 22 March 1839:

> One passenger, a Sussex farmer, amused me greatly. He was a Dandie Dinmont

in his way; a fine, powerful, frank, warm-hearted and simple-minded fellow. He subsequently acquired good property in the colony, but died comparatively young. His particular idiosyncrasy was dread of the natives. Immediately after we had cast anchor in Holdfast Bay Mr Elles [*sic*] came to see me in his Sunday clothes for wear ashore, to wit, a blue coat with brass buttons, yellow waistcoat with similar brass buttons, and breeches, and top boots, and enquired of me 'Mr Hailes, what be those black things on the shore yonder?' I answered, 'They are native Aborigines.' And looking through the ship's telescope, added, 'and fine athletic fellows they are.' 'Well now,' said Elles, 'if I meet any of the Bodginees when I get ashore I'll shoot 'em that I will.' (He had his loaded rifle on his arm.) 'Now do you think the Governor would do anything to me for shooting Bodginees?' 'Oh!' I replied, 'he would hang you, that's all.' 'Would he now! What a shame!' was his response. Years after I saw many natives at work on his freehold and laughed with him about his former terrors.[5]

This is a revealing moment, often found in colonial narratives, when the new arrivals gaze on the beach, the first glimpse of the new land, searching for signs that will give some intimation of a possible future. Hailes' littoral view is that seen through a ship's telescope; he is able to both frame and focus on what is there to be seen, and he chooses to focus on Indigenous people. He discovers that the beach is the contact zone; the space of encounter, exchange, negotiation and transition; things might happen on the beach. Before the beach can be crossed and the traveller or settler heads off inland, preliminary encounters must be experienced and relationships tested. For the intending settlers, the beach is the place of first encounter where they will establish the preliminary social relations that will determine the ongoing dynamics of co-presence with Indigenous people.[6]

Hailes' travelling companion, Ellis, is in dread as a result of their discovery that the beach is already inhabited; Ellis's arrival on deck flourishing his firearms reminds us that, in the minds of at least some of the immigrants, settling down the other side of the beach will only occur after any resistance from Indigenous people had been overcome, if necessary by force of arms. While the colonial administration back in London certainly expected a little give and take from the colonists, Ellis's firearms remind us that under duress, dominance must be demonstrated from the beginning, especially for people who have travelled so far. The settlers begin as they intend to continue.[7]

William Cawthorne wrote what may well be the third novel in South Australia, which was first published as *The Islanders* in serial form in 1865–66 and then reprinted in 1926 as *The Kangaroo Islanders: A Story of South Australia Before Colonization 1823.*[8] The novel represents first comers in episodes of encounter and conflict with Indigenous people on the beaches facing the Southern Ocean. It ends with a shipwreck; at least since Shakespeare's *The Tempest* and Daniel Defoe's *Robinson Crusoe*, the communal nightmare of the shipwreck has been among the most fertile of starting (or finishing) points for popular narratives, so it is not surprising that this Australian historical novel from the nineteenth century should feature a shipwreck that provides an appropriate moment of high drama.[9] Such narratives represent individuals faced with elemental forces over which they have little or no control, stressing the fickleness of fortune and man's capacity to respond *in extremis*. The perilous voyage across the trackless wastes of the seas takes the traveller into realms where it is manifestly evident that Britain does not rule the waves; the journey ends in disaster, the survivors castaway on a beach, left stranded between the sea and the land.

This passage written in 1812 by Sir John Graham Dalyell describes the significance of the shipwreck for the British; such attitudes must have been held even more strongly by colonials who had made the long sea voyage from Britain to the Antipodes, sometimes sailing as far as forty or fifty degrees south through the Roaring Forties:

> In a country such as Britain, where every individual is either immediately or remotely connected with the fortune of the sea, the casualties attendant on the mariner must be viewed with peculiar interest … Shipwreck may be ranked among the greatest evils which men can experience. It is never void of danger, frequently of fatal issue, and invariably productive of regret. It is one against which there is least resource, where patience, fortitude and ingenuity are unavailing, except to prolong a struggle with destiny, which, at length, proves irresistible. But amid the myriads unceasingly swallowed up by the deep, it is not by numbers that we are to judge of the miseries endured. Hundreds may at once meet an instantaneous fate, hardly conscious of its approach, while a few individuals may linger out existence, daily in hope of succour, and at length be compelled to the horrible alternative of preying on each other for the support of life.[10]

Crusoe must be shipwrecked before he can walk his beach and eventually encounter the Other, that solitary 'Print of a Man's naked Foot on the Shore, which was very plain to be seen in the Sand'.[11] Shipwrecks result in an (enforced) sojourn, and for some, the end of travelling altogether, and in the colonial space the possibilities and challenges of co presence with the Indigenous.

Significantly, William Cawthorne had extensive personal contacts with Indigenous people that inform his historical novel. He claimed to speak (some) language; he wrote at length about personal contact, recording an involvement in the politics of on-going relationships between settlers and Indigenous people, drawing on an archive of mostly oral sources and family reminiscence rather than mainstream published historical sources. He even gave three of his children Kaurna names.[12] Cawthorne was also a painter and a poet, writing one of the first Australian poems to represent an Indigenous Dreaming story in English: *The Legend of Kuperree, or, The Red Kangaroo*, published by his son in Adelaide in the 1860s.[13]

Cawthorne knew Dr Matthew Moorhouse, the South Australian Protector of Aborigines from 1840 to 1870; he records meeting him several times in his diary, and although at first he initially found him difficult and supercilious, he later had a number of dealings with him, travelled with him to the South East to exhume a body, and was even given access to his papers.[14]

Cawthorne wrote both ethnographic essays and filled his memoirs with his experiences with Indigenous people; his diary entries in his 'Literarium diarium' about on-going relations with people in the Native Location on the north side of the River Torrens remain one of our most detailed records of day-to-day encounters and interactions with the people of the Adelaide Plains. While Cawthorne's ethnographic essays were *written* in the 1840s, they did not appear in print in his lifetime but were published by the Royal Geographical Society of Australasia (South Australian Branch) three decades after his death; his long essay appeared in 1926, when the writer and politician Simpson Newland was president of this influential body.[15]

The Kangaroo Islanders is the first attempt in Australian fiction not only to represent the southern littoral but also to depict the lifestyles and histories of the sealers who worked on the offshore islands and reefs between 1795 and about 1830 during that curious hiatus between European discovery and settlement, as his subtitle makes very clear. The novel is based on conversations with (ageing) Islanders, men and women still living on Kangaroo Island whom he met when visiting his father, the former whaler Captain William Anderson Cawthorne, who was the first lighthouse keeper at the Sturt Light at Cape Willoughby on Kangaroo Island in the 1850s.[16]

There is a great deal in Cawthorne's novel about sealing, including details about coastal trading in seal skins and salt. There are also descriptions of ship handling and fine descriptive seascapes. This extended description is a typical set piece from early in the novel, no doubt it reflects something of Cawthorne's own experience while crossing Backstairs Passage in a small boat on a summer's morning on his way to visit his father at Cape Willoughby:

> It was early morn, and such a morn as only Australia can boast, a clear, pellucid morn with not a cloud to mar the sky, not the faintest mist, nor any visible thing

to blemish the unrivalled beauty of the early day. Looking up into the heavens the eye could perceive unfathomable depths; gazing upon the land, could realise its uttermost distances; and, scanning the sea beneath, could see as in a looking glass. There, at the very bottom, on a floor of pure white sand, the hungry shark was rising and falling or pausing as he watched the huge ship darkening his pathway. There, again, was the ill-shapen 'stingerree,' flapping its huge sides, as a bird does its wings when, hastening on some furtive expedition, it is driven like a small cloud across the expanse of heaven, or with marvellous deception covering itself with the sand until invisible to all eyes. There were the voracious schnapper in countless numbers, moving rapidly along in all the glory of purple and gold in their search for new marine pastures. The supernatural clearness of the atmosphere caused the neighbouring highlands, the distant capes, and the range of mountains in the vicinity of what is now called Cape Jervis, to appear singularly close. On the black rocks, black as ink, that lined some parts of the bay, sat a mass of wild sea fowl, contrastingly white. A little higher up, on another ledge of jutting rocks sat another group of white birds, and higher still a third. In the calm morning, though so far off, their solemn chattering, their spiteful pecking, their clamorous disputing, could be distinctly heard, tipping, tripping, and modulating with the gentle swell of the sea. Anon one of them would rise in order to visit some more favourite spot, and, clattering and spattering upon the water with outstretched wings, would leave behind, straight as the flight of an arrow, an agitated pathway, gradually melting to the finest line; or one would slyly pounce upon an unwary fish, and enjoy the whole relish without a squabble with his brethren as to the lion's share. High in the air could be seen a line of birds, with very long necks and very short bodies, but with flight even and swift. They were black swans making a beeline across the straits to the lakes and islands of the Lower Murray. Over the island could be seen several hundreds of unwieldy pelican flying in their peculiar way, and marking on the blue expanse as far as the eye could follow, the singular outline of the letter 'W.' They were winging their way to the seat of the primeval haunts of their race—the inland lagoons of the island.[17]

This is a fine set piece, where pellucid sea, dramatic coastline and the Antipodean cloudless sky are combined with rich details of undisturbed fish and bird life in a visually engaging seascape. It is a long time since we have seen snapper in such numbers.

Given that *The Kangaroo Islanders* is a novel about the lives of early nineteenth-century seamen, there are many nautical expressions in this novel. Cawthorne notes in his diary that when he arrived on the *Amelia* in South Australia in May 1841 he 'was a black skinned sailor boy full of the sayings and habits of the boatmen'.[18] A little over a decade later, when he came to write his novel, he was able to make good use of those sayings, no doubt helped along by his father's knowledge and experience. As a result, one of the small pleasures on offer in *The Kangaroo Islanders* is its display of colourful nautical slang and quotations from various chanteys. Given that so few colonial Australian novels reflect such maritime experience, this feature is memorable. One or two examples will suffice. At one point a character is described as a 'son of a gun'; this is a British naval expression for an illegitimate child, originating on the West Indies station. On some ships on blockade duty women were allowed on board; if children were born (the father unknown), then the entry 'son of a gun' would be made in the ship's log.

At another point one of the ship's company is lost in the scrub around Pelican Lagoon on Kangaroo Island and is later rescued; this is how he is addressed by one of the Islanders after he is found, in Cawthorne's approximation of working-class and regional dialectal English in the style of novelists Sir Walter Scott and of Charles Dickens:

> And here, you bale away cold water on his nob; we'll soon set yer up all a-taunt-o; but I hopes yer will be werry pertickler arter this how yer goes toddling about in this garden o' ours, which is summet like oursels, werry poorty in some places, and werry ugly in t'other.[19]

The expression 'all a-taunt-o' means a fully rigged vessel; with all sails set; RH Dana Jr has the meaning: '[s]aid of a vessel when she has all her light and tall masts and spars aloft', in other words set up right.[20] The novel has many such examples: no other Australian colonial novel pays as much attention to the language of the sea.

In *The Kangaroo Islanders* Cawthorne also tells the story of a sealer, 'Captain Meredith' (his first name not given), who is represented as a melancholy, introverted and fastidious master of an unnamed sealing and trading vessel who sails from Sydney to Kangaroo Island to buy skins and to load salt. Most of his crew desert to join the Islanders; after his ship is wrecked on Troubridge Shoals, the remaining crew still loyal to Meredith sail south for Kangaroo Island.

There are a number of beach scenes in the novel; two deserve some discussion. The first is to be found in Chapter XVII, which concludes with 'The Rape of the Black Sabines', culminating in the abduction of a number of Indigenous women from the beach at Rapid Bay. The sealers have left Creek Bay on Kangaroo Island by whaleboat, and they sail for the North West Bluff, now called Rapid Head. Cawthorne describes the place as follows:

> As they approached, the scene became exceedingly beautiful, the valley, the mouth of which formed the bay, was enclosed by high, rolling hills, and the coast presented

a broken wall of bold rock. A stream of fresh water issued and ran over the sand, and noisy cockatoos and parrots resounded on every side; the kangaroo grass stood as thick as a hay-field, and as high as a man. Altogether it was a lovely spot, and even now, though denuded of trees, and dotted over with settlers' homes, though the rotund hills are marred with lines of fences, and a jetty stands on the spot where the Islanders were in the habit of landing, still the place is beautiful, and is certainly the most picturesque on the whole coastline of Gulf St. Vincent. The locality is now called Rapid Bay, so named after the brig that brought out the first surveying party, including the Surveyor-General, Colonel Light. It was the first place at which the surveyors landed.[21]

Given the events that follow, this is an intrusive description, stressing the advantage of hindsight in the representation of the double vision that is so much a part of the appeal of historical fiction. When Cawthorne asks us to see such places as palimpsests of history, he prepares the way for the tragedy that will occur on this picturesque beach.

The Islanders 'killick' the boats just outside the surf and 'just beyond a spear's throw' of the beach, and wait to see how the Kaurna react to their arrival.[22] When one of the crew suggests they go ashore, Georgy warns that they are under surveillance, and that if they were to land on the beach they run the risk of being attacked: 'they'll take yer kidney-fat out of yer'. Then a native steps out on the white beach, and the Islanders recognise him; he is a man called Conday.[23] Old Sam then advises Georgy to take care how he 'lays the strand seamanlike', to be careful in his negotiations with the people ashore, and (shades of Mr Ellis) to remind them that they carry no guns:

> Georgy was soon ready. It would have scared the natives to have pulled [the whaleboat] in, so he slipped quietly overboard and swam ashore. As he neared the beach he spoke to old Conday, who immediately recognised him. A yell of delight brought from rock and rise, bush and brake, some fifty warriors, who with a rush soon joined their companion. Georgy rose from the water, and imitating native etiquette, sat down on the sand in silence. Thereupon, the natives squatted, too. Thus both parties continued for at least ten minutes, then Georgy spoke, and explained their visit. They were friends, fishing and hunting up the Gulf. They had plenty to eat—they wanted to come ashore. The whites would leave their guns, and the blacks were to leave their spears. They were to have a grand dinner, to bring down their wives and daughters, and have a great corroboree. This was agreed to, but not without dissent.
>
> 'Where's my sister?' asked one; 'why have yer ate her?'
>
> Georgy said it was some other white man that had her, but the last time he saw her she was well and fat.

'You lie!' replied the other, 'you ate her.'[24]

Here Cawthorne demonstrates his understanding of the hybrid identity of the Islanders, one or two of whom had taken on some of the language, customs and practices of the Indigenous people of the mainland. Georgy is shown as respecting the protocols about encounters that still exist in many Indigenous communities today, participating in the 'sit-down' ceremony, if only here to deceive, to gain their confidence and then await the opportunity to abduct as many women as possible. Even given Islander motives and their hidden firearms, this is still an uncommon attempt to represent the complex processes of give and take, of reciprocity, of interaction on the frontier where Europeans treat such protocols with (seeming) respect. Then they speak. While it is not clear what language is being spoken on the beach, there is no doubt that information and opinions are exchanged. Cawthorne also presents an ironic reversal of the nineteenth-century stereotype of Indigenous cannibalism; here it is the Kaurna who think that the *Europeans* are cannibals.

The Islanders then come ashore, and on the beach a 'grand roasting of fish, wallaby, and kangaroo' takes place. After night falls, a couple of corroborees are performed; their Kaurna hosts never suspect that the Islanders might have sinister motives for arranging the gathering on the beach. When the blacks are resting, rolling about on the sand 'laughing, quite exhausted with their efforts in the dance and song', the Islanders seize the moment, grabbing six women and then fleeing in their whaleboats, from which one of the women escapes. The Islanders spend the night just offshore in the whaleboats, the five captive women 'wailing their sorrowful song'. Here Cawthorne covertly recognises the generally taboo subject of miscegenation; so many of the edgy and complicated transracial relationships that occurred between Islanders and Indigenous women must have had their origins on beaches in something like the circumstances described in this scene.

Next morning in the early morning light, when things are still misty on the water, they discover that one of their companions, Long Bill, is dead, a spear through his 'callous heart'. They tip the body overboard. Cawthorne ends the chapter with this authorial observation:

> High up in a cavern containing a singular stalactite, and only visible from the sea, overlooking the spot where this tragedy happened, is yet to be seen the strong resemblance of the skeleton of a man. It is known to all coasters as 'Bill's Ghost.'[25]

The Kangaroo Islanders ends with a representation of the murder of 'Captain Meredith' on the beach at Yankalilla on Fleurieu Peninsula, south of present-day

Adelaide. 'Chapter the Last' opens with his shipwrecked crew coasting in another whaleboat. They anchor off Yankalilla, to the north of Rapid Bay; all along the coast there are native fires. The Indigenous man with them says 'Lauty [plenty] blackfellow', and advises they stay aboard for the night.[26] Next morning 'not a native or a smoke was visible. The stillness of death was on the land; and there was every appearance of a terrific hot day'.[27] While Meredith's companions sit on the gunwales with their feet in water; their Indigenous companions swim 'like two porpoises' around the boat. Meredith decides to go ashore to find some shade and read his Bible. He climbs the coastal dunes to a bare knoll with some low bushes. There, while deep in Psalms, he is murdered.

This episode is of considerable historical interest, referring to a series of events that, in spite of Cawthorne's subtitle of 1823, actually occurred in South Australian waters in the mid-1830s, and possibly as late as February or March 1836, just a month or two before the first of the South Australian Company ships arrived.[28] Meredith is murdered by two Kaurna men whom he has never met. They strike him down with a *kutta*, a digging stick, having mistaken him for one of the Islanders who had broken protocols and the rules of hospitality and abducted the five women a few days previously.

Cawthorne makes it very clear that Captain Meredith is killed because he is suspected of being one of the 'white thieves', an Islander. The two 'warriors' who see Meredith come ashore assume he had been a member of the raiding party that had taken the five women. As one warrior says to the other, 'They have two of my sisters. They have stolen your wife'. Meredith's killing is thus an uncommon mid-century representation of justified resistance and retaliation by Indigenous people, contesting the widely-held South Australian view from later in the nineteenth century and beyond into our own times that settlement was peaceful and without violence.

In this chapter Cawthorne uses the controversial detail of the taking of Meredith's kidney fat by his killers. There is no evidence that his body was so mutilated; Captain George Martin of the South Australian Company immigrant ship *John Pirie* found Meredith's body, and his account mentions only hair on the tomahawk, suggesting a head wound.[29] Cawthorne, however, insists that his kidney fat was removed. Many other colonial writers record the practice; the detail is often found in memoirs and reminiscences written by 'old hands' and is usually presented to demonstrate the hideously Manichean and irredeemable otherness of Indigenous people.[30] Cawthorne uses the detail here not to represent accurately the grotesque circumstances of a real-life murder—after all, he only knew something of this event and where it happened because the old sealer Nathaniel Walles ('Nat') Thomas had shown him the place—but instead the detail is used to suggest Cawthorne's *insider* knowledge.[31] The accretions of such details no doubt contributed to Captain Meredith's murder being remembered through the nineteenth century as an event that contributed to the perception of an unbridgeable difference between Indigenous and non-Indigenous people. However, the Islanders were to blame, says Cawthorne. Ironically, he seems not to have known that the real-life Meredith was directly implicated in two brutal episodes, one in Port Phillip in late 1833, the second at Port Lincoln in November 1834, in which Indigenous women were abducted from the beach and men and children shot. Here, however, in Cawthorne's novel, Meredith is remembered as an innocent and mutilated victim; there is thus a considerable if unintended irony that he dies on a white sandy beach; the biter is bitten.

The reaction of the sealers to the news of Meredith's death is revealing. While Old Sam (based on Nat Thomas) swears revenge, one of his companions responds with a recognition that they are on edge: 'that's the way in this country, we lives pertickler easy, but it's a wery oneasy life to such as yer are … kill the ——wretches'. But Georgy responds: 'Softly, softly … we kills too much, that's how they kills us; it's all our fault', an anxious and unsettling recognition of the power of reciprocity. On the beach, in this contact zone, this liminal space, Cawthorne would have us believe that at least some of the sealers realised they had to stop the killing and instead negotiate with the Ngarrindjeri and the Kaurna. Such edgy moments are rare in colonial fiction.

The confusion of identity that leads to Captain Meredith's murder by Kaurna warriors keen to avenge crimes against their women is on one level a simple plot device, but on another level the detail suggests a complicated spatial hierarchy of beaches as liminal spaces in this pre-colonial interregnum. The Islanders live offshore from the main *before colonization*, on islands, living on the edge and in the spaces between the sea and the land; Cawthorne describes them as living 'beyond the pale'.[32] The Kaurna think Meredith is an Islander because he sails in a whaleboat; they assume it is the same whaleboat that has been raiding down the coast a day or two before. Meredith is damned by association.

Cawthorne deploys a string of devices earlier in the novel to introduce the idea of this liminal period of spatial history, of a time between discovery and colonization when confusions and uncertainties abounded and where the littoral was the contact zone. In Chapter Three he describes the occasional bizarre atmospherics in these island spaces, especially when the north wind blows, when the Australian inland exhales on the southern strand, stressing the strange, in-between quality of this place:

… cat's-paws of wind were visible here and there, scarring the smooth face of the sea; but little other sign of a breeze was abroad. The sun shot down his fervid rays, and the mirage already danced its mystic mazes out and away in the straits—now called Backstairs Passage—commingling with the heave of the waters, and causing the most deceptive and singular phenomena that can well be seen; now sinking the distant capes till barely visible, then elevating and distorting their outline, till it became a difficult matter to retain one's belief that the land was the same as that seen a couple of hours before ...

The vessel soon glided through the glassy, yet singularly perturbed waters. Far and wide—right away to the middle of the passage—the waters heaved and blinked and swirled, sank and rose, and here and there danced in gigantic riplets; now bearing the appearance of a mirrored repose, anon assuming the smooth, swollen, glistening of mighty blisters, scalded, as it were, by some fiery blast. Headland and cape and distant mountains, all partook of the mystic forms of some supernatural change. Behind the distant panorama to the northward, a bright glow of red-hot air defined the sharp outline of the break between earth and heaven. All nature seemed troubled, as if it were a living sentient being, instinctively cowering before the dread outpouring of the northern gale—the withering blasts of the terrible hot wind. Higher and higher grew the reddening arch; puffs of contrary and circular currents flew hither and thither; fish leapt from the surface of the water; the vessel moved in an unsteady manner; the sea-birds darted tip and down, seaward and landward, and remained not a minute in one place; the distant patches of tall scrub on the island, ever and anon, shook their heads violently, and then lapsed into immobility. The mirage gambolled abroad in its wild career, revelling in its mad pranks with rock and wave—with a dash sinking the boldest promontory, then lifting up from obscurity the tiniest stone, commingling sky, earth, and sea in a fluid phantasmagoria, and shaping, altering, renewing dissolving, and distorting everything within the range of vision. Now great belts of ripples, miles in extent, barred the ocean in alternate stripes, in mirror-like bands, like a sea of quicksilver relieved by deep scarifications of indigo blue. A distant, though faint roar, came booming seaward; another and a quicker reverberation ran along the cliffs; quicker still and louder came a third thundering over the main. Very thin, but peculiarly distinct, could now be seen on the extreme verge of the horizon a line of the deepest hue, advancing with rapid strides down the gulf, while a continued hum and a deep moaning preceded it.[33]

Cawthorne also uses a number of traditional tropes to reinforce this sense of strangeness and peculiar difference of the island beaches and the sea around Kangaroo Island, on the edge of the continent.[34] There are eight references to Defoe's *Robinson Crusoe* in the novel, delivered not just to draw the literal comparison with the archetypal solitary man on the desert island but rather to stress that the Islanders live beyond the pale, live like savages. Dressed in the skins of animals, they smell like foxes.[35] There are also a number of related descriptions of the wildness of the Islanders, who live close to nature in a land of extremes. As their language always reveals, these are working class Englishmen, and thus more susceptible to the lure of the wild. The real-life Meredith, on the other hand, was the son of one of the richest and most powerful free settlers in Van Diemen's Land.[36]

Cawthorne also deploys a number of other ideas that are usually delivered as exclamations of wonder by various members of Captain Meredith's crew, describing amazed reactions to this 'enchanted' island'; the island is 'full of smart tricks'; a 'queer land', a 'land o' wonders' and 'an outlandish island, a dreary and weird waste'.[37] This idea of the weirdness and edginess of the island is best captured in the representation of 'A Kangaroo Island Dinner' in Chapter Eleven, in which Meredith and his men sit down to dine on island curiosities: baked dog, ant eggs, wallaby, the heart of the grass tree *(Xanthorrhoea semiplana ssp. Tateana)*, wakeries (witchetty grubs) and 'porkies', or echidna.

The final detail in Cawthorne's novel is also enlightening. Right at the end Cawthorne uses a conventional colonial trope of the sun setting on this history, but here it is given a twist. While it is usually Aboriginal culture and traditions that are normally described in colonial texts as being in their twilight, here night closes over 'native warriors' and non-Indigenous sealers alike. While the magic of dawn may only be revealed when the officially endorsed settlement begins, it is a curious irony that that dawn will also signal the end of the sealers and their edgy interregnum.[38] They fade from sight as they are 'swallowed by darkness', and are now as invisible as any traces of Meredith's grave through the picture windows (with beach views) of the expensive beach houses that now line the coast at Normanville and Carrickalinga where he died.

The Kangaroo Islanders presents us with ambivalent histories, and hints at edgy complexities. To an extent not often seen in Australian colonial fiction, it offers a narrative that is even occasionally double-visioned, here and there representing the perspectives of both Indigenous people and the Islanders on beach encounters, the symbolic zone where sea meets land and strangers meet indigenes. Cawthorne represents the beach as an ambivalent place, a zone of intercourse and exchange one moment, of conflict and death the next.

To return to Mr Ellis and his fear of the 'Bodginees'. William Cawthorne's *The Kangaroo Islanders* offers some justification for Indigenous resistance and retaliation. The unfinished business that ends his novel reveals a degree of ambivalence about the extent to which settling down in this country has been possible, even if the views from the holiday house windows of the expensive houses that now cover the beaches he wrote about appear so innocent and beguiling. In the time before colonization and before history, southern Australian beaches were anxious sites of confrontation, confusion, violence, misunderstanding and death. Greg Dening notes that voices

> from the beach are hard to hear. They can be snatched from the lips by the wind or drowned in the white noise of the waves. There are also beaches on which voices are hard to hear because they are in a silence ... It is the silence of vast spaces. It is also the cold silence of death. [39]

A coda. Eventually Europeans like Mr Ellis came to cross the beach, head off inland and settle down. In 1987 Murray Bail published his novel *Holden's Performance* in the South Australian section of which is a remarkable scene set where the River Murray meets the sea. Holden Shadbolt, Les Flies and Gordon Wheelwright visit the beach in the course of Gordon's flotsam research; Wheelwright wanting to test his theory that

> the wandering streets of the ocean must carry all kinds of information. Not simply information of one city, but the entire world and its contents, the contemporary history of man ... A study of the charts ... suggested that many of these currents would deposit their messages in the Southern Hemisphere. In fact, along our coast. [40]

They walk to the beach, leaving the Wolseley with its doors open; Holden wonders if 'any other man had ever trudged here before'.

> Around the circumference so many layers of flotsam had been deposited by recent world history ... If he'd discovered the secret whereabouts of all this ... Gas masks lay tangled among tins of regulation jam and bully. Empty life rafts sloshed with puke and inflated toad-fish. There were bales of rubbers, shattered deck chairs. Names of ships stencilled on logs and cork. Musical boxes contained angled levels of sand imprinted with anemones. In the shallows the goggles of bomb-aimers transformed into masks of channel swimmers. Wheelright picked up buckles and belts, and bits of the *Bismarck;* he kept counting and scribbled notes. Turbans unfurled and floated and strangled perforated helmets. The remains of river towns, wreckage from mountain-tops had found their way here: Dresden soup plates, Tudor gables embedded with sewing machines, carcases of glockenspiels. There'd be gold fillings on the bottom. Friends were mixed up with enemies. Between naming names—chopsticks, Mae West, anemometers ...
>
> But Holden soon became lax. These objects were the same as the daily contents of the *Advertiser.* They'd leapt from the pages, disintegrated, and now lay dumped at his feet in 3-D. He stubbed his toe on them; cut his fingers on Venetian glass and a Polish coffee percolator: a pawn-broker's collection of everyday objects.
>
> Among the cargo of torpedoed kettledrums and lightning conductors it became

necessary to isolate matador capes from the cardboard suitcase Holden had originally seen clutched by a boy much smaller than him and frightened (would never forget his ghetto cap and black socks, nor the cardboard suitcase) and isolate them from the South Australian muscat bottles and the imported fountain pens, displayed in local advertisements. Drosometers and boxes of alphonins were identified by Vern. Lapilla-encrusted hookah and dancing pumps, sardine tins from Norwegian waters.

There was so much material here Wheelright would have to come back.
'We've only seen the tip of the iceberg,' he cried in a hoarse voice.[41]

By the mid-twentieth century, Bail says, Australia was no longer in the remote Antipodes; in our age there are no more edges to the world. International history had arrived, and even the beaches facing the Southern Ocean are littered with the detritus of the Second World War and its aftermath, the flotsam of contemporary history. As we step carefully around the carcases of glockenspiels and torpedoed kettledrums that now line this littoral, if we look closely enough we might still find traces of sea-washed footprints and hear voices in the sou'west wind.

Notes

1 Catherine Helen Spence, *Clara Morison: a Tale of South Australia during the Gold Fever* ed. Susan Magarey (1854; Adelaide: Wakefield Press, 1994) 20.

2 There are several recent novels representing the Southern Ocean: Patrick O'Brian, *Desolation Island* (London: HarperCollins, 1978); William Golding, *To the Ends of the Earth: A Sea Trilogy* (London: Faber and Faber, 1991); Matthew Kneale, *English Passengers* (London: Penguin Books, 2000); Annamarie Jagose, *Slow Water* (Sydney: Random House, 2003) and Sarah Hay, *Skins* (Sydney: Allen and Unwin, 2002).

3 Some favourite texts that represent the Australian tropics include Louis Becke, *By Reef and Palm* (London: T. Fisher Unwin, 1894); Jack McLaren's *My Crowded Solitude* (London: T. Fisher Unwin, 1926) and E.J. Banfield, *Confessions of a Beachcomber: Scenes and Incidents in the Career of an Unprofessional Beachcomber in Tropical Queensland* (Sydney: Angas & Robertson, 1933).

4 http://members.tripod.com/~GEKKOS/ships/buckinghamshire.htm, accessed 20 December 2005.

5 Allan L. Peters, ed. *Recollections: Nathaniel Hailes' adventurous life in colonial South Australia* (Adelaide: Wakefield Press, 1998) 6. Dandie Dinmont is a character in Sir Walter Scott's novel *Guy Mannering*, who kept a pack of terriers; there is now a breed of terriers named after him. The list of passengers on the *Buckinghamshire* does not include anyone called Elles, but several people named Ellis are recorded. See http://members.tripod.com/~GEKKOS/ships/buckinghamshire.htm, accessed 20 December 2005.

6   Greg Dening, *Beach crossings: voyaging across times, cultures and self* (Carlton, Vic.: Melbourne University Press, 2004).

7   This paragraph owes a great deal to Pratt's ideas about the 'contact zone', in Mary Louise Pratt, *Imperial Eyes: Travel Writing and Transculturation* (London: Routledge, 1992) 6–7.

8   W[illiam] A[nderson] Cawthorne, *The Kangaroo Islanders: A Story of South Australia before Colonization 1823* (Adelaide: Rigby, 1926). There is something of a puzzle about the history of *The [Kangaroo] Islanders*, given that a number of sources assert it was first *published* in 1854. In a Publisher's Note to the 1926 Rigby Edition, it is claimed that the manuscript was '*written* about the year 1854' [my emphasis]. Cawthorne's daughter, Miss F.W. Cawthorne, of Manly NSW, gave the manuscript to Rigbys in the 1920s, so it is likely that this date (1854) reflects a Cawthorne family history about the *writing* of the manuscript. There is reasonable circumstantial evidence that Cawthorne might first have heard stories about Islanders like Nathaniel Walles Thomas and their lifestyles around that time, in that he travelled to Kangaroo Island with Nat Thomas for the 1852–3 Christmas holidays. Thus it is quite likely that Cawthorne wrote a first draft of the novel between 1853 and 1854, entitling his manuscript 'The Islanders'. There are one or two topical references in the text that circumstantially support this assertion; for example, Cawthorne mentions the 'Vaterland' expatriation, referring to the large numbers of Germans who left Germany—most to the United States, some to South Australia—after the collapse of the Märzrevolution (the March Revolution) of 1848. Numbers peaked in 1854 when a quarter of a million Germans migrated. 'The Islanders' was eventually published in serial form in 1865–6 when it appeared in *The Illustrated Melbourne Post* under that title. The first issue appeared on page 14 of number 70, dated 25 January 1865; the serial ran for a little over a year and ended in number 83, 23 February 1866. Each issue was introduced with the note: "The Islanders': a South Australian tale of the year 1823.' Written expressly for 'The Post.' Founded on fact, and illustrative of the wild life and barbarous exploits of the first white settlers on Kangaroo Island. By William Anderson Cawthorne.'

9   William Shakespeare, *The Tempest*, ed. Virginia Mason Vaughan and Alden T. Vaughan, (1611; Walton-on-Thames: Thomas Nelson, 1999); Daniel Defoe, *Robinson Crusoe* ed. Michael Shinagel, 2nd ed. (1719; New York, London: Norton & Company, 1975).

10 Sir John Graham Dalyell, *Shipwrecks and Disasters at Sea,* quoted by T.S.R. Boase, 'Shipwrecks in English Romantic Painting', *Journal of the Warburg and Courtauld Institutes* 22:3/4 (July 1959) 332.

11 Defoe *Crusoe* 112.

12 Cawthorne's 'Diary 1849–1859', entry 14 September 1854 records the naming of his son Charles Witto-Witto Cawthorne, Mitchell Library, State Library of New South Wales.

13 William Cawthorne, *The Legend of Kuperree, or, The Red Kangaroo: an Aboriginal tradition of the Port Lincoln tribe; a metrical version: by the author of The Islanders* (Adelaide: Alfred N. Cawthorne, 186?).

14 William Cawthorne, 'Literarium Diarium', entries for 4–16 March and 1 November 1844, Mitchell Library, State Library of New South Wales.

15 William Cawthorne, 'Rough Notes on the Manners and Customs of the Natives', *Proceedings of the Royal Geographical Society of Australasia (South Australian Branch).* Session 1925–26. Vol. XXVII (1927): 47–77.

16 Cawthorne's novel has been acknowledged as a source by Rebe Taylor in her recent book about the Islanders, *Unearthed: the Aboriginal Tasmanians of Kangaroo Island* (Adelaide: Wakefield Press, 2004). *Unearthed* won the 2004 Adelaide Festival Award for Non-Fiction, and the 2004 Victorian Premier's Award for a First Book of History. There are also several fictions about the Islanders: Vernon Williams, *The Straitsmen: a Romance* (London: Cassell, 1929); Robert Drewe, *The Savage Crows* (Sydney: William Collins, 1976) ; Brian Castro, *Drift* (Port Melbourne: Heinemann, 1994); Ann Clancy, *Rebel Girl* (Sydney: Pan Macmillan, 1999); and Sarah Hay, *Skins* (Sydney: Allen and Unwin, 2002).

17 Cawthorne, *The Kangaroo Islanders* 12–13.

18 William Cawthorne kept a log during the voyage: 'Log of the brig *Amelia*, kept by W.A.C. on journey from Table Bay to Adelaide, March–May 1841'. Mitchell Library Acc. No. A434.

19 Cawthorne, *The Kangaroo Islanders* 60.

20 RH Dana, Jr. *The Seaman's Friend: Containing a Treatise on Practical Seamanship, with Plates; A Dictionary of Sea Terms; Customs and Usages of the Merchant Service; Laws Relating to the Practical Duties of Master and Mariners* (Boston: Thomas Groom & Co., 1851), http://www.winthrop.dk/danalex.html, accessed 26 August 2006. Charles Dickens uses the term in *Bleak House* (1852–3), in Chapter XIII, Esther's Narrative: 'The dear old Crippler!' said Mrs. Badger, shaking her head. 'She was a noble vessel. Trim, ship-shape, all a taunto, as Captain Swosser used to say. You must excuse me if I occasionally introduce a nautical expression; I was quite a sailor once.'

21 Cawthorne, *The Kangaroo Islanders* 109. The Kaurna called Rapid Bay *Tankulrawun*.

22 To kellick a boat is to anchor with a stone tied to a rope. I have also made the assumption that the country around what is now called Rapid Bay was owned by the Kaurna people of the Adelaide Plains.

23 An historical character, aka Condoy or King Con; his name may have some connection with the word for whale, *Kondili*. At Kleinigs Hill Lookout at Victor Harbor is a community based art project representing Kondoli the mosaic whale, a dreaming story of the Ramindjeri/Ngarrindjeri people. See http://www.victor. sa.gov.au/site/page.cfm?u=352, accessed 2 September 2006. Condoy's name first appears in the report written by Dr Robert Davis in 1831 describing the circumstances of Captain Collet Barker's disappearance at the Murray Mouth. When looking for Barker, Davis met an Indigenous woman called Sally whom he took to Kangaroo Island to find the Islander George 'Fireball' Bates to assist with the search. They returned to the mainland and met Condoy, Sally's father, who then interrogated Ngarrindjeri people to determine Barker's fate. Conday is also named by 'Fireball' Bates as a man from the mainland who with his son 'Friday'

accompanied Bates to Hog Bay on Kangaroo Island. When the son died, Bates returned to the mainland with Conday where both men lived with Conday's people for some time. Eventually Bates was found ill in a cave by other Islanders and taken back across Backstairs Passage; Conday, Friday and Sal were taken with them as punishment for Bates's treatment. Condoy is also mentioned several times in John Woodforde's Journal, see for example the entry 31 August 1836, PRG 502/1/2, Mortlock Library of South Australiana. It is possible Cawthorne learned of Conday through talking with George Bates at Hog Bay. See *Advertiser* 27 December 1886, 6c; Rob Amery, 'Sally and Harry: insights into early Kaurna contact history,' *History in Portraits: Biographies of nineteenth century South Australian Aboriginal people* Eds. Jane Simpson & Louise Hercus (Aboriginal History Monograph 6. Sydney: Aboriginal History, 1998) 49–87.

24 Cawthorne, *The Kangaroo Islanders* 111. 'Georgie' seems to be based on George 'Fireball' Bates, who Cawthorne probably met at Hog Bay on one of his trips to the Island. Bates seems to have been on rather better terms with the Kaurna and the Ngarrindjeri than some of his fellow-Islanders. An article in *Advertiser* 27 December 1886, 6c–f is based on an interview with him, then in his eighty-sixth year and records his participation in ceremonies and even what is described as his initiation by 'the blacks of Cape Jervis', the Ramindjeri clan of the Ngarrindjeri from Encounter Bay. In comparison, Nat Thomas (Old Sam in the novel) seems to have been nervous and unsure of himself in the company of the 'Onkaparinga and Encounter Bay blacks'. There is a revealing episode when Thomas led a group of settlers into country around the Onkaparinga River in early 1837 searching for lost horses; he was forced to hide himself when the party came into contact with a group of Onkaparinga people, afraid they might recognise him as an Islander who had abducted women from their community. See John Wrathal Bull, *Early experiences of life in South Australia and an extended colonial history* 2nd ed. (Adelaide, London: E.S. Wigg & Son; Sampson Low, Marston, Searle & Rivington, 1884) 33.

25 Cawthorne, *The Kangaroo Islanders* 113. In his travel piece 'Journal of a Trip to Kangaroo Island', *Observer*, 15 January 1853, 3d, Cawthorne records this description: 'At 5 p.m. reached Rapid Bay, hauled up the boat; in passing the cliffs a very large niche is observable, about 400 or 500 feet high, and in it a huge white stalactite, and of such a form as to resemble a human skeleton: it is a most singular curiosity'. BHP's dolomite mining operations at Rapid Bay in the twentieth-century seem to have led to the destruction of this feature.

26 Cawthorne, *The Kangaroo Islanders* 118.

27 Cawthorne, *The Kangaroo Islanders* 118.

28 For an account of the story of George Meredith Junior, see Rick Hosking, 'The Kangaroo Islanders: The Historical Basis', *Sharing Spaces: Indigenous and non-Indigenous Responses to Story, Country and Rights* eds. Gus Worby and Lester-Irabinna Rigney (Perth: Bentley API Network, 2006) 197–216.

29 John Woodforde's diary records Captain George Martin of the *John Pirie* at Rapid Bay 8 September 1836, sailing in a whaleboat on a tour of Saint Vincent's Gulf. Sexton records him leaving Nepean Bay 7 September 1836 on William Walker's

whaleboat. Walker undoubtedly showed Martin the site at Yankalilla (the nearest landing to the north of Rapid Bay) where Meredith was murdered: Walker was paid £2 for his services. John Woodforde, 'Abstract of a voyage to South Australia in the surveying brig 'Rapid'—Capt. Light—written by John Woodforde, M.R.S. & L.A.H., surgeon of the surveying party, August 19th 1836', PRG 502/1/2, Mortlock Library of South Australiana.

30 See, for example, Ernest Giles, *Australian Twice Traversed, The Romance of Exploration*, http://etext.library.adelaide.edu.au/g/giles/ernest/g47a/part8. html#book1, accessed 26 August 2006. While the significance of this mutilation of bodies remains controversial, here Giles represents it as bush gossip, designed to frighten young people, here ironically his young *Aboriginal* companion Richard Giles Kew.

31 [William Anderson Cawthorne] 'Journal of a trip to Kangaroo Island.' *Observer* 15 January 1853: 3d.

32 The term 'beyond the pale' means outside the limits, the other side of the fence; the phrase 'fence paling' still preserves a little of this meaning. In Ireland 'the pale' refers to those territories over which the British had jurisdiction after 1547. Cawthorne is not alone in deploying the term. See Stephen Murray-Smith's study of the Straitsmen of Bass Strait, 'Beyond the Pale: The Islander Community of Bass Strait in the 19th Century', *Tasmanian Historical Research Association*, Vol. 20, No. 4 (December 1973): 167–200.

33 Cawthorne, *The Kangaroo Islanders* 12–13. Matthew Flinders sensed something of this spatial complexity when he named the passage between Cape Jervis and Kangaroo Island, suggesting it offered a 'private entrance as it were, to the two gulphs; I named it Back-Stairs Passage. The small bay where we had anchored is called the Ante-chamber', Matthew Flinders, *Voyage to Terra Australis* 2 vols. (London: G. and W. Nicol, 1814), entry for 7 April 1802. It was named 'the dirty gutter' in later colonial accounts: see *Register* 14 September 1895: 5e.

34 Cawthorne uses the word 'peculiar' seventeen times in *The Kangaroo Islanders*, in a novella of 122 pages in the Rigby edition.

35 Cawthorne, *The Kangaroo Islanders* 22, 26. Cawthorne cites the source for this famous remark about the Islanders, *Evidence respecting the Soil, Climate and production of the South Coast of Australia*, a document prepared for the committee formed in London for the purpose of establishing a colony in South Australia. Captain George Sutherland, of the brig *Governor Macquarie*, had visited Kangaroo Island on a salt and seal-skin buying voyage in 1819. In 1831 he reported to the committee about Kangaroo Island: 'There are no natives on the Island; several Europeans assembled there; some who have run from ships that traded for salt; others from Sydney and Van Diemen's Land, who were prisoners of the Crown. These gangs joined after a lapse of time, and became the terror of ships going to the Island for salt, etc., being little better than pirates. They are complete savages, living in bark huts like the natives, not cultivating anything, but living entirely on kangaroos, emus, and small porcupines, and getting spirits and tobacco in barter for the skins which they lay up during the sealing season. They dress in kangaroo skins without linen, and wear sandals made of sealskins. *They smell like foxes.* They

have carried their daring acts to extreme, venturing on the mainland in their boats, and seizing on the natives, particularly the women, and keeping them in a state of slavery, cruelly beating them on every trifling occasion; and when at last some of the marauders were taken off the island by an expedition from New South Wales, these women were landed on the main with their children and dogs to procure a subsistence, not knowing how their own people might treat them after a long absence. There are a few even still on the island, whom it would be desirable to have removed, if a permanent settlement were established in the neighbourhood'. Sutherland's report is given in *South Australia: Outline of the plan of a proposed colony to be founded on the south coast of Australia, with an account of the soil, climate, rivers &c. with maps 1834* (Hampstead Gardens, SA: Austaprint, 1978) 50–51). My emphasis.

36 See Hosking 2006 for a discussion of the historical basis for *The Kangaroo Islanders*.
37 Cawthorne, *The Kangaroo Islanders* 44, 46, 52, 53, 58.
38 The allusion here is to Mrs Henry Doudy, *The Magic of Dawn: A Story of Sturt's Explorations* (London: Hutchinson and Co, [1924]), a historical novel set in the South Australian colony in 1839.
39 Dening, *Beach Crossings* 55.
40 Murray Bail, *Holden's Performance* (Ringwood, Vic.: Viking Books, 1987) 99.
41 Bail, *Holden's Performance* 100–101

Works cited

Amery, Rob. 'Sally and Harry: insights into early Kaurna contact history,' *History in Portraits: Biographies of nineteenth century South Australian Aboriginal people*. Eds. Jane Simpson & Louise Hercus. Aboriginal History Monograph 6. Sydney: Aboriginal History, 1998: 49–87.

Bail, Murray. *Holden's Performance*. Ringwood, Vic.: Viking Books, 1987.

Banfield, E.J. *Confessions of a Beachcomber: Scenes and Incidents in the Career of an Unprofessional Beachcomber in Tropical Queensland*. Sydney: Angas & Robertson, 1933.

Becke, Louis. *By Reef and Palm*. London: T. Fisher Unwin, 1894.

Boase, T.S.R. 'Shipwrecks in English Romantic Painting'. *Journal of the Warburg and Courtauld Institutes* 22:3/4 (July 1959): 332–346.

Bull, John Wrathal. *Early experiences of life in South Australia and an extended colonial history*. 2nd ed. Adelaide, London: E.S. Wigg & Son; Sampson Low, Marston, Searle & Rivington, 1884.

Castro, Brian *Drift*. Port Melbourne: Heinemann, 1994.

Cawthorne, W.[illiam] A.[nderson]. *The Kangaroo Islanders: A Story of South Australia before Colonization 1823*. Adelaide: Rigby, 1926.

[Cawthorne, William]. 'Journal of a Trip to Kangaroo Island', *Observer*, 15 January 1853, 3d.

Cawthorne, William. 'Log of the brig *Amelia*, kept by W.A.C. on journey from Table Bay to Adelaide, March–May 1841'. Mitchell Library Acc. No. A434.

Cawthorne, William. 'Rough Notes on the Manners and Customs of the Natives', *Proceedings of the Royal Geographical Society of Australasia South Australian Branch* Session 1925–26. Vol. XXVII (1927): 47–77.

Cawthorne, William. *The Legend of Kuperree, or, The Red Kangaroo: an Aboriginal tradition of the Port Lincoln tribe; a metrical version: by the author of The Islanders* Adelaide: Alfred N. Cawthorne, 186?.

Clancy, Ann. *Rebel Girl*. Sydney: Pan Macmillan, 1999.

Dana, RH Jr. *The Seaman's Friend: Containing a Treatise on Practical Seamanship, with Plates; A Dictionary of Sea Terms; Customs and Usages of the Merchant Service; Laws Relating to the Practical Duties of Master and Mariners*. Boston: Thomas Groom & Co., 1851, http://www.winthrop.dk/danalex.html

Defoe, Daniel. *Robinson Crusoe*. Ed. Michael Shinagel. 2nd ed. 1719; New York, London: Norton & Company, 1975.

Dening, Greg. *Beach crossings: voyaging across times, cultures and self*. Carlton, Vic.: Melbourne University Press, 2004.

Doudy, Mrs Henry. *The Magic of Dawn: A Story of Sturt's Explorations*. London: Hutchinson and Co, [1924].

Drewe, Robert. *The Savage Crows*. Sydney: William Collins, 1976.

Flinders, Matthew. *Voyage to Terra Australis*. 2 vols. London: G. and W. Nicol, 1814.

Giles, Ernest. *Australian Twice Traversed, The Romance of Exploration*, http://etext. library.adelaide.edu.au/g/giles/ernest/g47a/part8.html#book1.

Golding, William. *To the Ends of the Earth: A Sea Trilogy*. London: Faber and Faber, 1991.

Hay, Sarah. *Skins*. Sydney: Allen and Unwin, 2002.

Hosking, Rick. '*The Kangaroo Islanders*: The Historical Basis', *Sharing Spaces: Indigenous and non-Indigenous Responses to Story, Country and Rights*. Eds. Gus Worby and Lester-Irabinna Rigney, Perth: Bentley API Network, 2006 197–216.

http://members.tripod.com/~GEKKOS/ships/buckinghamshire.htm

http://www.victor.sa.gov.au/site/page.cfm?u=352

Jagose, Annamarie. *Slow Water*. Sydney: Random House, 2003.

Kneale, Matthew. *English Passengers*. London: Penguin Books, 2000.

McLaren, Jack. *My Crowded Solitude*. London: T. Fisher Unwin, 1926.

Murray-Smith, Stephen. 'Beyond the Pale: The Islander Community of Bass Strait in the 19th Century', *Tasmanian Historical Research Association*, 20: 4 (December 1973): 167–200.

O'Brian, Patrick. *Desolation Island*. London: HarperCollins, 1978.

Peters, Allan L. ed. *Recollections: Nathaniel Hailes' adventurous life in colonial South Australia*. Adelaide: Wakefield Press, 1998.

Pratt, Mary Louise. *Imperial Eyes: Travel Writing and Transculturation*. London: Routledge, 1992.

Register, 14 September 1895: 5e.

Shakespeare, William. *The Tempest*. Eds. Virginia Mason Vaughan and Alden T. Vaughan, 1611; Walton-on-Thames: Thomas Nelson, 1999.

South Australia: Outline of the plan of a proposed colony to be founded on the south coast of Australia, with an account of the soil, climate, rivers &c. with maps 1834. Hampstead Gardens, SA: Austaprint, 1978.

Spence, Catherine Helen. *Clara Morison: a Tale of South Australia during the Gold Fever*. Ed. Susan Magarey. 1854; Adelaide: Wakefield Press, 1994.

Taylor, Rebe. *Unearthed: the Aboriginal Tasmanians of Kangaroo Island*. Adelaide: Wakefield Press, 2004.

Williams, Vernon. *The Straitsmen: a Romance*. London: Cassell, 1929.

Woodforde, John. 'Abstract of a voyage to South Australia in the surveying brig 'Rapid'—Capt. Light—written by John Woodforde, M.R.S. & L.A.H., surgeon of the surveying party, August 19th 1836', PRG 502/1/2, Mortlock Library of South Australiana.

From Landing Place to Meeting Place: The Heritage of Cross-cultural Encounters on the Beach[1]

MARIA NUGENT

There were other encounters between the voyagers and locals at Botany Bay in 1770 aside from the famous one on the beach when the Captain made his landing and the two local men—one young, one old—brandished their spears at him. There were other attempts at communication apart from shouts in mutually unintelligible languages across a stretch of calm water as the longboat with James Cook and his men aboard approached the shore. There were other exchanges in addition to musket balls and spears flying in opposite directions through the air as the sailors stepped ashore. All seem to have been little understood by Captain Cook and Joseph Banks at the time, and subsequently rarely interrogated by those who have later told the history of the *Endeavour* in the bay.

It is easy to forget what else happened at Botany Bay in 1770 other than the first landing because the entire encounter, which lasted eight days in all, has become so truncated, so condensed, so stripped of its complexity, through the myriad processes that transform real time action into story, or history, or myth, or a mixture of all three. This is a scene that has been visually represented in images that have circulated widely; it has been repeatedly performed on historical anniversaries, including in 1970 on the occasion of its bicentenary when the re-enactment staged at Botany Bay in front of Queen Elizabeth II was televised and beamed into the lounge rooms of thousands of Australians.[2] In these recurring renditions of the encounter, the moment of the first landing has been so accentuated that it has come to assume the space of the whole story. This moment had been singled out early by Australian storytellers for what it symbolised—for what they believed it had enacted and enabled.[3] To their minds, although not necessarily to Cook's, the act of landing at Botany Bay enacted possession and enabled settlement. This was *the* historic event that was a necessary precursor to colonisation. And as an event that was previous to the messy history of settlement, it was at times useful to those who told the story of Australia because it could be used to shift attention away from the troubling histories of convictism and the violent dispossession of Indigenous people.

It was neither possession nor potential settlement that Cook and his men had on their minds in their impatience to get ashore at Botany Bay in late April 1770. For them, this was a stopover on a much longer and still unfinished journey. The attractions of getting ashore were what they needed to acquire in order to move on. Voyagers came 'to refurbish their ships or they came to trade or they came because they needed a stopping place on their way to somewhere else', observes Greg Dening.[4] On this occasion Cook and his men had landed not to claim possession of territory, but to find water and to scout for timber. It was within the everyday business of their voyaging enterprise, which saw them cutting down trees for timber, collecting water in casks, surveying the land and its shoreline, that other less well-known, but no less intriguing, encounters with the locals took place at Botany Bay. These other encounters ought to become part of the popularly known and repeatedly rehearsed story of Captain Cook at Botany Bay in 1770, not only because each is loaded with its own meaning but because they all, either separately or collectively, can help to illuminate in new ways that all-too-familiar landing scene.

Yet, pulling the curtains back on other scenes that make up the entire encounter while the *Endeavour* was anchored in the bay, such as when some of the locals and voyagers accidentally crossed each other's paths, or when one group gingerly approached the other, does not seriously alter the fact that relations between voyagers and locals can best be described as distant. The art historian, Bernard Smith, explained that the paucity of drawings made by the expedition's artists during the Botany Bay sojourn was because 'Cook and his company had difficulty in making contact with Aborigines of a kind stable and amicable enough to permit detailed drawings from being produced'.[5] The anthropologist Nicholas Thomas has recently described the ultimate outcome of this difficulty in making contact as 'a failure of communication'.[6] About Cook's choice of the name Botany Bay, Thomas writes: 'it is not surprising that the science it commemorated dealt with plants rather than people. What name could express the failure of communication that took place here?'[7]

What happened over the course of the encounter, and not just the fifteen minutes in which the first landing was made, does not necessarily provide us with evidence that relations between the voyagers and the locals were closer than has hitherto been represented. Some recent retellings attempt to revise and recast the encounter as friendly not hostile, close not distant. One example of this type of revision is the reappearance of some obscure wordlists, allegedly compiled at Botany Bay in 1770 by two crew members on board Cook's expedition.[8] The journalist and historian, Keith Smith, has been using these wordlists of dubious provenance to suggest that 'their existence contradicts the accepted historical account that there were no friendly meetings between the Aboriginal people and Cook's voyagers'.[9] Smith's claims have been published in various journals, and reported in the *Sydney Morning Herald*.[10] They are appealing primarily because it would suit our reconciliation times if the encounter, which has been long cast as foundational to the national story, should turn out to be more harmonious and mutually satisfying than the extant records produced by Captain Cook, Joseph Banks and others suggest.

This example is only one among a series of interventions aimed at revising the orthodox interpretation of the encounter at Botany Bay, and especially in ways that highlight a hoped-for exchange of words between the voyagers and the locals. In a more creative mode, in 2001 when Cook's landing at Botany Bay was re-enacted it began with a dialogue between the two sides that did not actually take place.[11] When a replica *Endeavour* sailed into Botany Bay two hundred and thirty one years after the original event, the man playing Captain Cook asked permission to come ashore from the local Dharawal people who today live around the Botany Bay area. A local Dharawal woman, who claims direct descent from those who were on the beach in 1770, asked whether the contemporary Cook had come in peace, and when he said he had, she welcomed him onto the land. This re-enactment, with its sensitive new script, symbolically transforms what had long come to be understood as an 'invasion' into an 'invitation'.

Playing the role of welcomer serves to acknowledge the way in which it was once the prerogative of the local Indigenous people to issue an invitation to strangers who wished to enter their territory. In this way, the contemporary performance of Captain Cook landing at Botany Bay can be interpreted as addressing something of an enduring concern among Indigenous people, both locally and more generally, about how the British, as embodied by the figure of Captain Cook, had immorally assumed possession of their territory by not recognising the rights of those who occupied it.

The recent re-enactment of the landing at Botany Bay allowed the Captain to do the right thing: to ask permission to land and to be invited onto the shore on terms set by the locals. This creative act provided a little space to imagine momentarily how the course of history might have been different. Yet, the imaginative (utopian?) re-enactment on the beach at the actual original landing site goes little way to addressing the enduring problem of the effects of the imposition of 'Captain Cook's law', which continues to be felt by contemporary Indigenous communities. Indeed, one might argue that creative performances of this kind, which re-interpret past events in ways that the current generation wish had happened, simply help to elide that the failure of the British to recognise Indigenous people's sovereignty over territory remains unfinished business today.

Another example of contemporary efforts to re-interpret the Botany Bay encounter in ways more attuned to the post colonial politics of late twentieth and early twenty-first century Australia is a recommendation to rename the spot where Cook first landed. A recently prepared master plan for the management of the national park which contains the 'landing place', endorsed by the then Premier of New South Wales, Bob Carr, recommended that the name 'Captain Cook's Landing Place' be changed to the 'Meeting Place'. The spot had been popularly known as Captain Cook's landing place for much of the nineteenth century, and this had been made official in 1899 when the land in question was turned into a public reserve in order to preserve it as a historic site. The latter had been an initiative of one of Carr's predecessors, Sir Joseph Carruthers, also one-time Premier of New South Wales.

From Carruthers to Carr, the place where Captain Cook first set foot on the east coast has been deemed historically significant and worthy of preservation by the New South Wales government and for 'the people', but the context within which the two politicians argued for its importance, and justified the commitment of their respective government's resources to it, was somewhat different. Carruthers made his case in the lead up to the federation of a 'white Australia'; Carr's case was made in the context of commitments to reconciliation between black and white.[12] The two men, a century apart, fashioned their respective cases for the preservation of this historic spot in ways that suited their times.

Carr has had the greater challenge. He has had to find ways to represent the historical importance of Captain Cook, his voyage, his achievements and his landing for Australians in ways that do not offend and marginalise Indigenous communities, both local to Botany Bay and further afield. How he negotiates this tricky task is evident in his preface to the master plan referred to above. The document is introduced by spelling out the histories attached, however tenuously, to the site in question:

> The Meeting Place area where Indigenous Australians first met with Captain Cook in 1770 is a place of unique and varied national significance. It is part of the traditional lands of the Dharawal people of Botany Bay. It is a place to recognise the astonishing achievements of Cook's expedition to the east coast of Australia. It is the location of some of the earliest, and certainly the most influential, meetings to take place between Indigenous Australians and European explorers, and later settlers. It is a place that serves as a symbol for both the beginnings of a nation and the dispossession of a people.[13]

This is national history told locally. Sentence by sentence, the preface moves from pre-colonial times to Captain Cook and discovery, to exploration, colonisation and settlement, to nation building and the celebration of it, to the ultimate dispossession of Aboriginal people, culminating in what must be one of the most abbreviated versions of the history of Australia ever written, all through reference to this one specific site. It acknowledges both British possession and Aboriginal dispossession. And it implicitly recognises that what Cook stands for in an Aboriginal historical imagination is contrary to what he stands for in an Australian national historical imagination: an ending for one, a beginning for the other.[14] The challenge, the preface notes, for those responsible for the future development of the site is 'to unite these differing views'. (It is worth noting the use of the term views, not pasts or even histories, which suggests that this is understood simply as a matter of perspective.) In this context, the shift in the name from landing place to meeting place signals a somewhat paradoxical desire to tell the story of Australia from the two (opposing?) sides of the beach, yet in a cohesive, indeed unifying, way.

In this way, the new vision for the future interpretation of the landing-cum-meeting place has much in common with some recently proposed treatments of the story of Captain Cook in other prominent public sites charged with telling the story of Australia. For instance, it has some similarities to the scenario that the review panel of the National Museum of Australia headed by sociologist John Carroll suggested for a retelling of the Captain Cook story at the Museum, which it outlined in its final report. The panel proposed replacing the current multimedia presentation in *Circa*, which introduces visitors to the themes of the Museum, with a three-scene treatment of Captain Cook's arrival at Botany Bay in 1770. In the first scene, the audience would experience the event as sailors in the longboats approaching the shore for the first time; in the second they would be cast as the local Indigenous people in which 'an attempt to make sense of the approaching longboat and its weird-looking occupants through *Dreaming* stories might be incorporated'. The film, *The Last Wave*, was suggested as a model.[15] The final scene would be the present, in which the 'audience is moved into a contemporary setting juxtaposed with what has preceded, to convey a sense of vast change in two centuries'.[16] This final scene is, presumably, a vision shared by the imagined descendants of the sailors in the boat and the Indigenous people on the shore. This rendition of the landing and its consequences distances the past of Botany Bay in 1770 from the present of contemporary Australia. The emphasis is on how far from that opening scene contemporary Australian society has travelled.

In response to the review panel's suggestions about how Captain Cook might be represented in the National Museum of Australia, historian Bain Attwood has made a counter proposal. In his vision of how the Museum might tell the story of Captain Cook, which draws largely from the work of cultural theorist Chris Healy, Attwood agrees in principle that Cook could be used for telling Australian history from two perspectives, but argues that the emphasis in the retelling should be on his meaning as a 'mythical' or 'symbolic' rather than an 'historical' figure. In making this proposal, Attwood foregrounds the contemporary stories, or myths, or sagas, which Indigenous people across Australia, such as Hobbles Danayari, have told about Captain Cook.

Attwood argues that 'Captain Cook is a suitable subject for an exhibit in a national museum in Australia, not so much because of what happened in the past in terms of action but because of what has happened in terms of the telling of stories or histories'.[17] His two-sided representation of the story of Captain Cook would involve an exhibition that showed how a mythologised figure of Cook had been used by settler Australians to mask the immorality of colonisation, and by Indigenous people to expose it. Taking this approach, which focuses on a history of history-making rather than the history of the event itself, visitors to the Museum would learn about what Cook stands for, and, indeed, stands *in* for, in the Australian and in the Australian Aboriginal historical imaginations respectively.

Yet, surely there is scope to provide a treatment of Cook that is simultaneously concerned with what actually happened and with what the historical characters involved have subsequently come to symbolise. It should be possible to convey something of the process and purpose of mythologising Cook without ignoring his history, just as it ought to be possible to tell the history of Cook without losing sight of what he has come to symbolise subsequently and the ways in which what happened at Botany Bay in 1770 has continued to resonate up until the present. This is the challenge of telling the story of Captain Cook anew in a range of cultural institutions, but it is a particularly charged challenge at the very place where he first stepped ashore on the east coast of the continent and came into contact with local Indigenous people. This is *the place* where the past action was actually performed so it is imperative that the history of that past action be told there as accurately as possible. But, at the same time, the commitment to the continued preservation of the spot where *the event* happened as a site of historical significance takes place within the contemporary political context, and must be sensitive to these changed and changing times. In particular, the new interpretation of the spot where the past action occurred must negotiate the shifting terrain in respect to relations between blacks and whites, most notably in the period since Captain Cook's bicentennial anniversary in 1970, in which he has loomed large as a contested figure and his historical meaning has been unsettled.

What would the encounter at Botany Bay in 1770 look like if one were to draw on some of the insights provided by contemporary Indigenous accounts of Captain Cook told in places where he did *not* go and a couple of centuries *after* he had sailed along and landed on the east coast? Could those two moments–the moment of the action and the moment of later Aboriginal storytelling about it–be brought productively together?

The story that Hobbles Danayari tells about Captain Cook, which has been interpreted and circulated to a broad audience by anthropologist Deborah Bird Rose, is perhaps best-suited to this task because it draws attention to something that was especially germane to the actual encounter.[18] In his narrative, Danayari suggests that the original 'sin' of Captain Cook was that he failed to say 'hullo' when he stepped from his ship onto shore. In place of that 'hullo', the Captain fired four, possibly five, shots.[19] Danayari's concern with the failure of Cook to address properly the local Indigenous people at the moment of contact is interpreted by Rose as representing, or signalling, a general failure on the part of colonisers to give Aboriginal people 'a fair go', and to behave in accordance with their moral law. This unresolved situation in which the immoral law of Captain Cook still reigns explains the enduring trouble between black and white.

The 'failure' of Captain Cook to say 'hullo' can be read in general terms as characterising the whole colonial experience; but it also has many localised inflections. Plenty of historical examples can be given of particular white men who did not ask for permission to enter and who took territory belonging to Aboriginal people. Captain Cook stands in for them all. Yet, at the same time, it is worth underlining that Danayari's symbolic story about Captain Cook is powerful precisely because it references something that actually happened involving the real Captain Cook.

Knowing that Captain Cook failed to say 'hullo' properly to those whose land he was seeking to enter at Botany Bay in 1770, and that some contemporary Aboriginal storytelling about Cook identifies this as the origin point for the subsequent and enduring trouble between black and white, one question that now comes to the surface is whether or not what happened can accurately be called a meeting? Is it appropriate to call the spot where this 'failure' occurred, the meeting place? Does this new proposed nomenclature help with telling a true story about the past action? Or is its old, but now somewhat dated, designation as the landing place a more historically accurate, albeit lop-sided, description for it?

Although there was not a proper meeting between the voyagers and the locals, as evidenced by the absence of a 'hullo', it nevertheless seems a legitimate conclusion to draw from the available, albeit fragmentary, evidence that there was a straining towards one, at least on the part of the local Indigenous people. On the basis of her analysis of descriptions of encounters between strangers on the west coast of the continent, both before the time of Captain Cook and afterwards, archaeologist Sylvia Hallam claims that 'a meeting [between local and stranger] is an event, a staged event' and 'the entire proceedings are formalised, ritualised, ceremonious—a staged drama'.[20] In this drama, 'avoiding, ignoring, repulsing are the Aboriginal reactions which form a repeating pattern, and sometimes a sequence' and a 'final movement was retreat'.[21] Hallam argues that the staged event which brings local and stranger together is concerned with 'reaffirming rights to land, defusing or actualising potential conflict and hostility, and establishing links of reciprocal obligations and amity'.[22]

All of the actions and reactions which Hallam catalogues can be found in various sequences in the encounter at Botany Bay in 1770. For example, when the *Endeavour* sailed through the heads, small groups of men congregated on the north and south points to shout at it, appearing to *repulse* the ship and its occupants. And both Banks and Cook commented in their journals on the way that at different times the locals seemed content to *ignore* them. If these actions are thought about as a part of an orchestrated effort to stage a meeting with the uninvited strangers, then the stylised retaliation of the two men on the beach when the landing was made can also be interpreted as part of this repertoire. But, if considered in isolation from what else occurred before and after the landing scene, then the action of the two men looks more like straightforward 'resistance', which was the interpretation made by the voyagers at the time and one that has remained popular ever since.

But resistance does not adequately account for their actions. It cannot explain, for instance, why the couple of spears thrown by the two local men from a relatively short distance into a huddle of sailors perched on the landing rock failed to strike. Joseph Banks recorded that they 'fell among the thickest of us but hurt nobody'.[23] Following Inga Clendinnen's re-reading of the infamous spearing of Captain Phillip at Manly in 1790, which she insists should be interpreted as ceremonial not combative,[24] we need to ask: was the skill of the spear-thrower in hitting or missing his target? Was this stylised retaliation ultimately aimed to bring about a proper meeting and right relations?

If it were, and if some of the other actions and reactions of the locals over the course of the entire encounter were likewise directed toward the staging of a 'proper meeting', then disappointingly they were, by and large, ultimately fruitless. At Botany Bay in 1770, something happened that meant 'real meeting' could not and did not occur. That something was probably more than the *Endeavour* sailing away. The locals perhaps abandoned their quest prior to this, although it is not absolutely clear from the records precisely when they realised, or indeed decided, that it would be the case that this potential *meeting place* would become *a no-meeting place*.

By reconsidering the actions and reactions of the local Indigenous people during the encounter at Botany Bay in 1770 in terms of an effort to bring the strangers into their social world on proper terms, and thus as expressing some-thing of their sovereignty, new possibilities for telling the other side of this two-sided story are opened up. But just as importantly, by concentrating on questions about how through their actions they sought to stage a meeting on proper terms, and how and why this did not eventuate, some space also becomes available for reflecting on the unfinished business between black and white, which continues in the present and which has been explained by some contemporary Aboriginal people as having its (symbolic?) origins in the failure of Captain Cook to say 'hullo'. It is the act of Cook coming ashore without properly acknowledging the people whose land he entered that is today understood by Aboriginal people as having made it difficult, if not impossible, for a proper meeting to take place between black and white, both then and there at Botany Bay *and* many times and in many places since.

Notes

1   Some of the research on which sections of this paper is based was carried out in the preparation by the author of a contextual history of Botany Bay National Park (Kurnell Section) for the Department of Environment and Conservation (NSW). The author also acknowledges the generous assistance of the National Museum of Australia through its National Museum Research Fellowship Program.

2   The best known image of the landing is E. Phillips Fox's 'Landing of Captain Cook at Botany Bay, 1770', 1902. Others include: John Alexander Gilfillan, 'Captain Cook Proclaiming New South Wales a British Possession', 1889, and one called 'Captain Cook's Landing at Botany Bay, A.D. 1770', which appeared in the *Country and Town Journal*, 1872.

3   For more detailed discussion of this point, see: Maria Nugent, 'A contextual history of Botany Bay National Park (Kurnell Section)', unpublished report prepared for the Department of Environment and Conservation (NSW), 2005, especially chapter 3; Maria Nugent, *Botany Bay: Where Histories Meet* (Sydney: Allen & Unwin, 2005) 22–4.

4   Greg Dening, *Islands and Beaches: Discourse on a Silent Land, Marquesas, 1774-1880* (Melbourne: Melbourne University Press, 1980) 23.

5   Bernard Smith, 'The first European depictions'. Eds Ian Donaldson and Tamsin Donaldson. *Seeing the First Australians* (Sydney: Allen & Unwin, 1985), 21.

6   Nicholas Thomas, *Discoveries: The Voyages of Captain Cook* (London: Allen Lane, 2003) 114.

7   Thomas, *Discoveries*, 114.

8   The word lists are from: Peter A. Lanyon-Orgill, *Captain Cook's South Sea Island Vocabularies* (London: Published by author, 1979).

9   Keith Smith cited in Debra Jopson, 'Endeavour crews language lists throw new light on first contact', *Sydney Morning Herald*, 5 April 2003, 13.

10 See for example, Keith Vincent Smith, 'Words are clues'. *National Library News*, 14:5 (February 2004) 7–8; 17–18; Debra Jopson, 'Endeavour crews language lists throw new light on first contact', *Sydney Morning Herald*, 5 April 2003, 13.

11 For a more detailed discussion of this, see Nugent, *Botany Bay* 196–7.

12 For a discussion of Carruthers' vision, see Nugent, *Botany Bay* 67–9; Nugent, 'A contextual history' chapter 3.

13 'Meeting Place Precinct Master Plan, Botany Bay National Park, Kurnell' (Sydney: New South Wales National Parks and Wildlife Service, April 2003), n.p.

14 For a discussion of the different ways that the figure of Captain Cook has featured in the social memory of white and black Australians, see Chris Healy, *From the Ruins of Colonialism: History as Social Memory* (Melbourne: Cambridge University Press, 1997) chapters 1 and 2.

15 *Review of the National Museum of Australia: Its Exhibitions and Public Programs: A report to the Council of the National Museum of Australia* (Canberra: NMA, July 2003) 19. This treatment of Captain Cook's encounter at Botany Bay in 1770 was only a suggestion made by the Review Panel. The National Museum of Australia is currently developing a new script for *Circa*, but it is not envisaged that the encounter will be depicted in the way proposed by the Panel.

16 *Review of the National Museum of Australia*, 19.

17 Bain Attwood, 'Too many Captain Cooks, How many Captain Cooks?: Nation, history and perspective in Settler Australia', paper presented to the Museums Australia National Conference, May 2005, 6.

18 Versions of the narrative can be found in: Deborah Bird Rose, *Hidden Histories: Black Stories from Victoria River Downs, Humbert River and Wave Hill Stations* (Canberra: Aboriginal Studies Press, 1991); Deborah Bird Rose, 'Remembrance', *Aboriginal History*, 13:2 (1989) 135–48; Deborah Bird Rose, 'The saga of Captain Cook: Morality in Aboriginal and European law', *Australian Aboriginal Studies*, 2 (1984) 24–39; Deborah Bird Rose, 'The saga of Captain Cook: Remembrance and morality', in Bain Attwood and Fiona Magowan (eds), *Telling Stories: Indigenous History and Memory in Australia and New Zealand* (Sydney: Allen & Unwin, 2001) 61–79.

19 For a description of the landing, see James Cook, *The Journals of Captain James Cook on his Voyages of Discovery, Volume 1, The Voyage of the Endeavour, 1768–1771*, ed. J.C. Beaglehole (Cambridge: Hakluyt Society at the Cambridge University Press, 1955) 305; Joseph Banks, *The Endeavour Journal of Joseph Banks: 1768–1771*, ed. J.C. Beaglehole (Sydney: The Trustees of the Public Library of New South Wales in association with Angus and Robertson, 1962) 54–5.

20 Sylvia Hallam, 'A view from the other side of the western frontier: Or "I met a man who wasn't there…"', *Aboriginal History* 7:2 (1983) 136.

21 Hallam, 'A view from the other side', 150.

22 Hallam, 'A view from the other side', 136-7.

23 Banks, *The Endeavour Journal of Joseph Banks: 1768–1771*, 55.

24 Inga Clendinnen, *Dancing with Strangers.* (Melbourne: Text Publishing), 2003, 110-132, esp. 124–6.

Works cited

Attwood, Bain. 'Too many Captain Cooks, How many Captain Cooks?: Nation, history and perspective in Settler Australia', paper presented to the Museums Australia National Conference, May 2005.

Banks, Joseph. *The Endeavour Journal of Joseph Banks: 1768–1771*, ed. J.C. Beaglehole. Sydney: The Trustees of the Public Library of New South Wales in association with Angus and Robertson, 1962.

Clendinnen, Inga. *Dancing with Strangers.* Melbourne: Text Publishing, 2003.

Dening, Greg. *Islands and Beaches: Discourse on a Silent Land, Marquesas, 1774–1880.* Melbourne: Melbourne University Press, 1980.

Hallam, Sylvia. 'A view from the other side of the western frontier: Or "I met a man who wasn't there…",' *Aboriginal History* 7:2, 1983.

Healy, Chris. *From the Ruins of Colonialism: History as Social Memory.* Melbourne: Cambridge University Press, 1997.

Jopson, Debra. 'Endeavour crews language lists throw new light on first contact', *Sydney Morning Herald*, 5 April 2003.

'Meeting Place Precinct Master Plan, Botany Bay National Park, Kurnell'. Sydney: New South Wales National Parks and Wildlife Service, April 2003.

Nugent, Maria. *Botany Bay: Where Histories Meet.* Sydney: Allen & Unwin, 2005.

Nugent, Maria. 'A contextual history of Botany Bay National Park (Kurnell Section)', unpublished report prepared for the Department of Environment and Conservation (NSW), 2005.

Review of the National Museum of Australia: Its Exhibitions and Public Programs: A report to the Council of the National Museum of Australia. Canberra: NMA, July 2003.

Rose, Deborah Bird. 'The saga of Captain Cook: Remembrance and morality', in Bain Attwood and Fiona Magowan (eds), *Telling Stories: Indigenous History and Memory in Australia and New Zealand.* Sydney: Allen & Unwin, 2001.

Smith, Bernard. 'The first European depictions'. Eds Ian Donaldson and Tamsin Donaldson. *Seeing the First Australians.* Sydney: Allen & Unwin, Sydney, 1985.

Thomas, Nicholas. *Discoveries: The Voyages of Captain Cook.* London: Allen Lane, 2003.

Encountering the Common Knobby Club Rush: Reconciliation, Public Art and Whiteness

STEVE HEMMING AND DARYLE RIGNEY

As early as I can remember,
I was made aware of the differences,
And slowly my pains educated me:
Either fight or lose.
'One sided', I hear you say.
Then come erase the scars from my brain,
and show me the other side of your face:
the one with the smile painted on with the
colours of our sacred land you abuse.
[Extract from Robert Joseph Walker's poem
Okay: Let's Be Honest, 1981: 11]

At Victor Harbor the public artwork designed by Margaret Worth, 'on/occupied Land', standing on the foreshore between the sea and the Soldier's Memorial Square, commemorates the encounter in 1802 between Matthew Flinders and Nicholas Baudin in the Ngarrindjeri/Ramindjeri waters of Ramong (Encounter Bay).[1] For the Ngarrindjeri this encounter is less a celebration than a painful remembrance of the loss of land and water and the impact of colonisation on their nation. The artwork consists of three large metal pole-like structures emerging from a concrete base featuring the large words 'on/occupied territory'. The French nation is represented by a pole, the colours of the Tricolor, topped with an anemometer. The British nation is represented by a red, white and blue pole, topped with an octant.

The third green and yellow pole represents the common knobby club rush and the local 'Aboriginal people'.[2] The artist provides the following symbolic explanation of the meaning of the third pole and the use of cables in the memorial:

Bending but not breaking under the force of the prevailing wind, it celebrates the endurance of the land and the Aboriginal people. At certain times the wind may produce an Aeolian sound in the cables. It is a reference to Ngarrindjeri singing of the land.[3]

The public artwork was erected as a positive step towards reconciliation. What does reconciliation really mean though as we encounter the common knobby club rush? An 'ethical remembrance' would recognise the 'celebration' as an encounter between two imperial powers in the Southern Ocean before South Australia had become a British colony.[4] As Ngarrindjeri leader George Trevorrow noted at the official opening, it would also recognise that 'our [Ngarrindjeri] nation had not been party to the discussion held on that day in 1802'.[5] Attentiveness to this important point positions 'On Occupied Territory' as a site of cultural politics involving introduction to, engagement with and legitimation of particular ways of seeing, knowing and behaving within this space. David Gruenewald calls this a critical pedagogy of place where critical pedagogy 'offers an agenda of cultural decolonization' and place-based education 'leads the way toward ecological "reinhabitation"'.[6]

On Occupied Territory now occupies an important space in the Victor Harbor littoral, and if the purpose of the artwork is to engage citizens in commemorating the encounter as an act of remembrance—as an act of educative social practice—what are its implications for thinking about ideas of community, embodiment, resources, reputations, relationships, reconciliation, responsibility, rights, recognition?[7]

One clear implication for Ngarrindjeri is the need to continue to resist and challenge hegemonic ideologies and relations of power which marginalise Ngarrindjeri voices and ways of knowing because 'spaces and places are expressive of ideologies and relationships of power'.[8] And so it was again with the 'Encounter 2002 Poles', when last minute interventions from the Ngarrindjeri Heritage Committee confronted the pre-determined representation and mode of recognition of Ramindjeri Ngarrindjeri in the original plans for the commemorative artwork. As a result, important changes were called for. The Ngarrindjeri place name for the location—Pultung—was added; the original ambiguous title of the artwork, 'un/occupied Territory' was modified to now read *On Occupied Land* and a small plaque included with the text of a 'Sorrow and Apology statement' to the Ngarrindjeri nation signed by the Mayor Robert Crompton on 28 March 2003. These changes, as important as they are, do not represent a transformation because Ngarrindjeri understandings of place, history and politics are still marginalised and sanitised in its ultimate form. There is no substantial unsettling of the taken-for-granted histories and cognitive maps carried by visitors to this space on the Victor Harbour foreshore. Something as seemingly unimportant as the positioning of the three poles—with the so called Ngarrindjeri pole on the right hand side—still implies a hierarchy, given the Western convention of reading from left to right.

Robert Crompton was not returned at the elections held soon afterwards. The new Mayor Scott Schubert had the following to say in the *2002/2003 Annual Report of the City of Victor Harbor*:

> The long awaited Encounter 2002 Artwork, 'On Occupied Territory', was launched on 28th March 2003. The artwork is representative of our connections with the past when the British and French came face to face in the waters of our bay in 1802. Matthew Flinders and Nicolas Baudin met on friendly terms at a time when their nations were at war in the homeland. The artwork also reflects the indigenous inhabitants of this land, the Ngarrindjeri people. We were fortunate to have the aboriginal community participate in the artwork launch and the occasion provided the opportunity to reflect and acknowledge the injustices they have faced in the past. The Council and the Ngarrindjeri community jointly signed a 'Sorrow and Apology Statement' as a first step in a reconciliation process.[9]

Ngarrindjeri leadership hoped that the City of Victor Harbor would sign a full *Kungun Ngarrindjeri Yunnan* (KNY) agreement (Listen to what Ngarrindjeri

Figure 1: Sorrow and apology statement to the Ngarrindjeri people, Victor Harbor, 28 March 2003

people are saying) as a firm foundation for a new relationship between the local council and the Ngarrindjeri nation.[10] The apology statement is usually an essential first step in developing a KNY agreement (see Figure 1). Unlike the neighbouring Alexandrina Council, the City of Victor Harbor is yet to sign a KNY agreement.

> To the Ngarrindjeri people, the traditional owners of the land and waters within the region, the City of Victor Harbor expresses sorrow and sincere regret for the suffering and injustice that you have experienced since colonisation and we share with you our feelings of shame and sorrow at the mistreatment your people have suffered.
>
> We respect your autonomy and uniqueness of your culture. We offer our support and commitment to your determination to empower your communities in the struggle for justice, freedom and protection of your Heritage, Culture and interests within the Council area and acknowledge your right to determine your future.
>
> We commit to work with you. We acknowledge your wisdom and we commit to ensuring our actions and expressions best assist your work. We accept your frustrations at our past ways of misunderstanding you.
>
> We are shamed to acknowledge that here is still racism within our communities. We accept that our words must march our actions and we pledge to you that we will work to remove racism and ignorance.
>
> We recognise your leadership, we honour your visions, and we hope for a future of working together with respect for each other.
>
> We look forward to achieving reconciliation with justice.
>
> We ask to walk beside you, and to stand with you to remedy the legacy of 166 years of European occupation of your land and waters and control of your lives.
>
> The work of the City of Victor Harbor will be guided by your vision of a future where reconciliation through agreement making may be possible and we may walk together.
>
> The City of Victor Harbor acknowledges the Ngarrindjeri People's ongoing connection to the land and waters within its area and further acknowledges the Ngarrindjeri People's continuing culture and interests therein.

For Ngarrindjeri people much has changed in the 200 years since Flinders and Baudin met, and the non-Indigenous invasion of *Ngarrindjeri Ruwe* (country) has not been something to celebrate. In recent years the Ngarrindjeri Nation has made it a priority to use the words of Elders who managed to get their perspectives of colonisation on the record. The recently published *Ngarrindjeri Nation Yarluwar-Ruwe Plan* (Caring for Ngarrindjeri Sea Country) is a public statement of Ngarrindjeri views of invasion and a plan for living in a shared space into the future.[11] It draws on elders such as Reuben Walker, a Ramindjeri Elder from the Victor Harbor area who in 1935 wrote an account of his life story for the South Australian Museum ethnologist Norman Tindale. Towards the end of his account, which includes his experiences of living at Raukkan (Point McLeay mission) in the 1860s, and witnessing his grandparents' land being 'occupied' by 'Europeans', Walker made the following heartfelt statement that borders on a curse:

> I always thought of my kind [o]ld Grandfather and grand mother that took care of me never a child was cared so much as I was and being a half caste shame on the white race I would sooner be a full Blooded aborigine my blood boil at time I scorn the white man because I know I know He is the low wicked blaggard that took the country from my Grandmother ... my father or Grandfather [,] on the white man side the European did He have any [th]ing that he got lawfully ... That day will come when the white man will have to account for what they have done God is Good the venge[a]nce of the almighty shall they reap.[12].

It is unlikely that a selection of Rueben Walker's words might ever have been considered appropriate as part of the Victor Harbor public artwork. Walker's is a strong statement which may remind those who read his story of the dreadful impact of the invasion of South Australia on Indigenous people and the illegitimate nature of British 'settlement'.[13] This story did not change after 1934. Reuben Walker lost his son in the First World War and his great grandson Robert Joseph Walker died in 1984 in custody, 'after a struggle with warders'.[14] His collection of poetry *Up Not Down Mate! Thoughts from a Prison Cell* was first published in 1981 and contributed to the public pressure that led to the Royal Commission into Aboriginal Deaths in Custody. Perhaps his words could also have appeared on the memorial at Victor Harbor.

Some writers describe Australia as a postcolonial space—a problematic concept from an Ngarrindjeri perspective.[15] For Ngarrindjeri, Ruwe (country) is still colonised by non-Indigenous interests—the Victor Harbor Council has continued to dispossess and control Ngarrindjeri lands and waters since its establishment in the nineteenth century. In the early twentieth century the council, with the support of the police and the 'Protector of Aborigines' forcibly removed Ramindjeri/Ngarrindjeri people from their camp at Pultung, very near the present-day monument.[16] The *ngowanthis* (camps) were burnt and the people were transported to mission stations or other reserves. The Ngarrindjeri *ngownathis* had become a problem for the council's growing tourist industry. Around the same time the Protector W.G. South had developed a policy of stealing children from their parents as part of an ongoing threat to those Ngarrindjeri people living in camps.[17] These policies are examples of what historians Ray Evans and Bill

Thorpe have called Indigenocide and they worked in tandem with racist anthropological and archaeological accounts of southern South Australian Indigenous people as unauthentic and effectively extinct.[18]

In 1923 the Ngarrindjeri presented a petition to the South Australian parliament in an attempt to stop legislation designed to remove Indigenous children from their families.[19] The following is an extract from the petition published in *The Register* (1923):

'GIVE US OUR CHILDREN'

The Aborigines' Plea

Opposition to New Act

The *Register*, Adelaide, Friday December 21st, 1923

Mark well, the two forces, arrayed against each other. There stands the advocates, and supporters of the Bill that has passed, strongly fortified, their guns of 'intellect' trained and ready for action, they represent 'Right.' There, on the opposite and facing them is the rank of the enemy, strongly opposing the Bill, a very strange army, possessing no weapons of war, no intellectual powers, no parliamentary eloquence, not a grain of science in the whole body, that makes the army of motherhood. The only piece of artillery which possesses is the weapon called love. And thus equipped, the army of motherhood has taken up their position in opposition to the Bill.[20]

Tragically, but not surprisingly for the time, the petition was lost before being formally accepted. Its eloquence, its questioning of the power of western empiricism and its desperation remind the reader of contemporary challenges to practical reconciliation and more broadly economic rationalism. In 2003 the Ngarrindjeri re-presented the petition to the Governor along with a Declaration of Dominion over Ngarrindjeri Ruwe. This declaration was presented by Matt Rigney, Ngarrindjeri leader and chair of the Ngarrindjeri Native Title Management Committee. As a senior Ngarrindjeri man and Ramindjeri descendant we wonder if he would have included an extract from the Ngarrindjeri Declaration of Dominion in a major piece of public artwork commemorating the 1802 encounter between British and French in Ngarrindjeri waters. The following words are important ones when reflecting upon the context and consequences of voyages of exploration such as those being undertaken by Flinders and Baudin.

7. WHEREAS by Letters Patent of 1836 issued to Governor Hindmarsh in London the Crown of the United Kingdom of Great Britain purported to allow the said Colonizing Commissioner to begin embarking British subjects upon certain commercial terms on ships and sail for South Australia on condition:

'*that nothing in these Letters Patent contained shall effect or be construed to effect the* **rights** *of any aboriginal Natives of the said province to the actual* **occupation** *or enjoyment in their persons or in the persons of their* **descendants** *of any lands now actually occupied or enjoyed by such Natives*' *[C.O. 13/3]*

8. WHEREAS clause 34 of the Instruction to the Resident Colonizing Commissioner guaranteed that –

'*no lands which the natives may possess in occupation or enjoyment be offered for sale until previously* **ceded** *by the natives*' *[The Select Committee on the Aborigines, Report, 19 September 1860, Legislative Council of the Parliament of South Australia, p.5];*

9. WHEREAS clause 35 of the said Instructions to the Resident Colonizing Commissioner required that –

'*the aborigines are* **not disturbed** *in the enjoyment of the lands over which they may possess proprietary rights, and of which they are not disposed to make a voluntary sale*' *and required* '*evidence of the faithful fulfillment of the bargains or* **treaties** *which you may effect with the aborigines for the cessation of lands*' *[op.cit.](Our Emphasis)*

… *Accordingly, as—*

THE NGARRINDJERI HAVE ALWAYS OCCUPIED THE TRADITIONAL LANDS OF THE NGARRINDJERI NATION and, NGARRINDJERI HAVE NEVER CEDED NOR SOLD OUR LANDS AND WATERS

We ambassadors of the Ngarrindjeri Nation, George Trevorrow, Rupelli of the Ngarrindjeri Tendi, Thomas Edwin Trevorrow, Chairperson of the Ngarrindjeri Heritage Committee, and Matt Rigney, Chairperson of the Ngarrindjeri Native Title Committee, having been properly authorized in the Ngarrindjeri way to make this proclamation on behalf of all Ngarrindjeri, do hereby: **declare and proclaim** our homeland as traditionally delineated, including all waters, foreshore and riverbed thereof, **is now and always has been occupied by Ngarrindjeri**.[21]

The Indigenous people of southern South Australia have been historically located in a particular place in relation to the story of settlement and Australian nationhood. Early in South Australia's history they were constructed as becoming rapidly 'extinct' in the face of British settlement—a settlement that was conceived of as part of the inevitable progress towards a British, white future.[22] In more recent times the Ngarrindjeri have been subjected to a Royal Commission into their traditions and spirituality.[23] Elders such as Darryl Sumner, Dr Doreen Kartineryi, Matt Rigney and Tom Trevorrow (all Ramindjeri descendants) unsuccessfully tried to protect their sacred lands and waters from desecration.[24] The story of cultural extinction is powerful in the settled, white space of southern South Australia.[25] Change is managed in this space through events and structures that memorialise the achievements of pioneer Australians, or the explorer heroes such as Matthew Flinders and Nicholas Baudin. As the 'proper' white foundations are reinforced, critical, disturbing histories are largely silenced.

A set of foundational myths are written into the landscape through developments such as the Hindmarsh Island bridge, the Goolwa jetty, the Victor Harbor monument to Flinders and Baudin and the Hindmarsh Island marina. They all represent the power of western technology to overwrite the 'natural landscape', land and seascapes in which Indigenous people and Indigenous interests have been traditionally located. It is assumed that the Indigenous place has been obliterated or covered over by the layers of progress. Time and progress are represented by built environs and the layering of the landscape—in southern South Australia archaeology underpins this story by scientifically authorising this reading of the progress of time, civilization and development.

Public artwork that fails to provide a serious challenge to the dominant white narratives of the Australian nation further colonises Indigenous space, displacing Indigenous traditions and negative stories of dispossession, imprisonment and death. The tourist and local see the place through the lens of the commemorative artwork—meaning must be brought to this space by the settlers. Its Indigenous significance is unexpected, ignored and defaced.[26] Through heritage legislation it is constructed as a threat to the security of the settler space.

Ramong, the Encounter Bay area, is also the cultural landscape of Ngurunderi, Kondoli and other Ngarrindjeri creation ancestors. Most South Australian school children, had until recently, seen the South Australian Museum's Ngurunderi film depicting creation stories from the Encounter Bay area. Some remember the Ngarrindjeri people's attempts to protect their sacred landscape from development in the Kumarangk (Hindmarsh Island) case (Bell 1998). If they remember, their understandings are framed by public accusations of 'fabricated' traditions—'secret women's business'. Both these stories are part of the ongoing colonial history of the Victor Harbor area.

Historian Tony Birch has written about the western districts of Victoria and the re-inscription of this landscape by the discourses of heritage and tourism with the myth of pioneers and progress. The physical remains of the white, historical landscape have begun to disappear through decay and depopulation. In their place are memorials and monuments that re-inscribe the landscape. The giant Koala is one of these. Birch argues that by 'identifying, naming and textualising such places, they remain "claimed by Europeans"'.[27] Steve Hemming has argued that in recent years colonialism has intensified in southern South Australia.[28] Even well-intentioned public artwork can have serious, colonising effects, particularly within a complex, white, modern cultural landscape.

Stories about the encounter between Flinders and Baudin and the silent Indigenous witnesses to these events of 'discovery' or dispossession are part of the broader historical landscape that includes debates such as the Stolen Children and the 'History Wars'. The South Australian Museum and the National Museum are key cultural sites in this contemporary story of the nation and its frontiers of authenticity. There is a clear intertextual relationship between exhibitions, publications and public pronouncements from these institutions and new nation-building sites such as the Flinders/Baudin memorial at Victor Harbor. In the ongoing 'History Wars' the authenticity of the settled south was earlier challenged through the 'revisionist' histories of Henry Reynolds, Lyndall Ryan and others.[29] This is the location of the 'Aussie backyards' that stand outside the claims of native title. This is the place that is beyond question, this is the normalised centre of Australia and any challenges to this space are fiercely contested. Alternative histories of this space are difficult to insert into the public space.

With the launch of the Flinders/Baudin public artwork in 2003, however, there has been perhaps the beginning of a new relationship between Ngarrindjeri and non-Indigenous people. This was not the intention of the Victor Harbor Council or the Encounter 2002 Committee; it was an unintended consequence of a poorly planned event (from a Ngarrindjeri perspective). Under the present Aboriginal Heritage regime the organisers should have planned their events in Victor Harbor with the Ngarrindjeri Heritage Committee.

On the day of the opening George Trevorrow, Rupelli (Head) of the Ngarrindjeri Nation gave an official speech and called for a minute's silence for the Ngarrindjeri people who have suffered under colonisation. He said this was a beginning and the first time that Ngarrindjeri have had the opportunity to formally welcome people to this part of their country. The Mayor of the City of Victor Harbor made a public apology to the Ngarrindjeri people (see Figure 1). Perhaps the most striking aspect of the Encounter 2002 ceremony was the exchange of flags between the Ngarrindjeri nation and the French and British representatives. This was organised by Tom Trevorrow, chair of the Ngarrindjeri Heritage Committee. He approached the two nations directly through proper diplomatic channels. The Australian government, however, would not participate in this symbolic flag exchange. Current member of the European Parliament and former French Prime Minister Michel Rocard and British Consul General Anthony Sprake as representatives of the two old imperial powers had no problem recognising the Ngarrindjeri nation through an exchange of flags. At the local level through apologies and KNY agreements new partnerships are being formed on the basis of a recognition of traditional owners. It seems only at the state and federal level that Australian governments have problems with recognising Indigenous First Nations.

Notes

1 The Ramindjeri are a local group of the Ngarrindjeri nation.
2 Even though the common knobby club rush is little-used by Ngarrindjeri people – it is not the more sought-after basketry rush, and the national colours of yellow and green are also not the colours of choice of Ngarrindjeri.
3 City of Victor Harbor, home-page, (http://www.victor.sa.gov.au/site/page.cfm?u=272, accessed 21st July 2006).
4 R. Simon, *Public Memory and the Ethical and Pedagogical Implications of Remembrance as a Social Practice, Centre for the Study of Historical Consciousness* (Vancouver, BC: University of British Columbia, 2001) 1. http://www.cshc.ubc.ca
5 *The Times* – Victor Harbour 'Hundreds at art opening', 2 April, 2003. http://www.thetimes.yourguide.com.au
6 D.A Gruenewald, 'The Best of Both Worlds: A Critical Pedagogy of Place', *Educational Researcher* 35:4 (2003a): 4.
7 See G. Worby & L-I. Rigney (eds) *Sharing Spaces: Indigenous and non-Indigenous Responses to Story, Country and Rights* (Perth: API Network, 2003) 305–328.
8 D. Gruenewald, 'Foundations of Place: A Multidisciplinary Framework for Place-Conscious Education', *American Educational Research Journal* 40:2 (2003b): 628.
9 City of Victor Harbor, *Annual Report of the City of Victor Harbor, 2002/2003*, Victor Harbor, SA, 2003: 2.
10 See for example S. Hemming & T. Trevorrow, 'Kungun Ngarrindjeri Yunnan: archaeology, colonialism and re-claiming the future', In C. Smith & M.H. Wobst (eds) *Indigenous Archaeologies: Decolonising Theory and Practice* (London: Routlege, 2005) 243–261.
11 See Ngarrindjeri Tendi (NT), Ngarrindjeri Heritage Committee (NHC) and Ngarrindjeri Native Title Management Committee (NNTMC) 2006 *Ngarrindjeri Nation Yarluwar-Ruwe Plan, Caring for Ngarrindjeri Sea Country and Culture*, Ngarrindjeri Land and Progress Association, Meningie, SA.
12 R. Walker 1938 'Rueben Walker's Life History', Manuscript in Norman B Tindale's *Journal of South East of South Australia*, vol 2, South Australian Museum Archives, 212–213.
13 See D. Rigney, S. Hemming & S. Berg, 'Letters Patent, Native Title and the Crown in South Australia' in *Indigenous Australians and the Law (2nd Edn)*, Eds Hinton, M., Johnston, E. (QC) & Rigney, D. (London: Routledge Cavendish Publishing, 2008).
14 R. Walker, *Up, Not Down, Mate! Thoughts From a Prison Cell* (Catholic Chaplaincy to Aborigines, 1981).
15 See K. Gelder & J. Jacobs, *Uncanny Australia: sacredness and identity in a postcolonial nation* (Carlton: Melbourne University Press, 1998); C. Mattingley & K. Hampton (eds), *Survival in Our Own Land: 'Aboriginal' experiences in 'South Australia' since 1836* (Adelaide: Wakefield Press, 1988); I. Watson 'Aboriginal Laws and the Sovereignty of Terra Nullius' in *borderlands* ejournal, 1(2) <http://www.borderlandsejournal.adelaide.edu.au/vol1no2_2002/watson_laws.html>, accessed online 2002; T. Trevorrow 'A shocking insult', *Overland* 171 (2003): 62–63; T. Trevorrow & S. Hemming, 'Conversation: Kunggun Ngarrindjeri Yunnan

– Listen to Ngarrindjeri People Talking', in *Sharing Spaces: Indigenous and Non-Indigenous Responses to Story, Country and Rights* (Curtin University of Technology, Perth: API Network Australia Research Institute, 2006) 295–304.

16 See S. Hemming, P. Jones & P. Clarke, *Ngurunderi: a Ngarrindjeri Dreaming* (Adelaide: South Australian Museum, 1989) 29. Photographs of the camp at Victor Harbor can be found in R. Berndt, C. Berndt & J. Stanton, *A World That Was: The Yaraldi of the Murray River and Lakes, South Australia* (Melbourne: Melbourne University Press, 1993).

17 See T. Trevorrow et al., *They took our land and then our children: Ngarrindjeri struggle for truth and justice* (Meningie, SA: Ngarrindjeri Lands and Progress Association, 2007).

18 R. Evans & B. Thorpe, 'Indigenocide and the Massacre of Aboriginal History', *Overland*, 163 (2001): 21–39; S. Hemming, 'The problem with Aboriginal heritage' in Worby & Rigney, *Sharing Spaces*.

19 On 13 February 2008, eighty-five years after the 1923 Ngarrindjeri petition to the South Australian government, the Commonwealth Government of Australia via Prime Minister Kevin Rudd apologised 'for the laws and policies of successive parliaments and governments that have inflicted profound grief, suffering and loss' upon the Indigenous people's of Australia (Rudd 2008:1). See K. Rudd, 13 February 2008, *Apology to Australia's Indigenous Peoples: Parliament House, Canberra*, at http://www.pm.gov.au/media/speech/2008/speech_0073. cfm accessed on line 25 March 2008. Aboriginal and Torres Strait Islander Social Justice Commissioner, Tom Calma stated 'by acknowledging and paying respect, Parliament has now laid the foundations for healing to take place and for a reconciled Australia' in which 'every single one of us [can] move forward together—with joint aspirations and a national story that contains a shared past and future' (Calma 2008:2) See T. Calma, *Response to government to the national apology to the Stolen Generations*, at http://www.hreoc.gov.au/about/media/speeches/social_justice/2008/20080213response_to_gov_to_the_national_apology_to_the_stolen_generations.html, accessed online 25 March 2008.

20 T. Trevorrow et al. *They took our land and then our children*.

21 Ngarrindjeri Tendi (NT), *Ngarrindjeri Nation Yarluwar-Ruwe Plan* 53–54.

22 See J.D. Woods, *The Native Tribes of South Australia* (Adelaide: Wigg & Son, 1879).

23 See for example I. Stevens, *Report of the Hindmarsh Island Royal Commission* (Adelaide: State Print, 1995); D. Bell, *Ngarrindjeri Wurruwarrin: A world that is was, and will be* (North Melbourne: Spinifex, 1998).

24 The Ngarrindjeri proponents of sacred women's knowledge associated with Kumarangk (Hindmarsh Island) and the surrounding waters were vindicated in a decision in the Federal court known as the Von Doussa decision (see J. Von Doussa, Chapmans vs Luminis & Ors, Federal Court of Australia, Summary of Judgement 21 August 2001).

25 See S. Hemming, 'The problem with Aboriginal heritage'.

26 See P. Carter, *Living in a New Country* (London: Faber, 1992); T. Birch, '"Come see the Giant Koala": Inscription and landscape in Western Victoria', *Meanjin* 3 (1999): 61–72.

27 T. Birch, 'Come see the Giant Koala' 64.

28 See S. Hemming & T. Trevorrow, 'Kungun Ngarrindjeri Yunnan'; Hemming, 'The problem with Aboriginal heritage'.

29 See for example H. Reynolds, *The other side of the frontier: Aboriginal resistance to the European invasion of Australia* (Ringwood, Vic.: Penguin, 1982); L. Ryan, *The Aboriginal Tasmanians* (St. Lucia, Queensland: University of Queensland Press, 1981); R. Evans & B. Thorpe, 'Indigenocide and the Massacre of Aboriginal History'.

Works cited

Bell, D. *Ngarrindjeri Wurruwarrin: A world that is was, and will be.* North Melbourne: Spinifex, 1998.

Berndt, R.M., Berndt, Catherine H. & Stanton, John. *A World That Was: The Yaraldi of the Murray River and Lakes, South Australia.* Melbourne: Melbourne University Press, 1993.

Birch, T. '"Come see the Giant Koala": Inscription and landscape in Western Victoria'. *Meanjin* 3 (1999): 61–72.

Calma, T. *Response to government to the national apology to the Stolen Generations,* 13 February accessed online 25 March 2008 at http://www.hreoc.gov.au/about/media/speeches/social_justice/2008/20080213response_to_gov_to_the_national_apology_to_the_stolen_generations.html

Carter, P. *Living in a New Country.* London: Faber, 1992.

City of Victor Harbor. *Annual Report of the City of Victor Harbor, 2002/2003,* Victor Harbor, SA, 2003.

City of Victor Harbor, home-page, (http://www.victor.sa.gov.au/site/page. cfm?u=272, accessed 21st July 2006)

Evans, R. & Thorpe, B. 'Indigenocide and the Massacre of Aboriginal History', *Overland* 163 (2001): 21–39.

Gelder, K. & Jacobs, J. *Uncanny Australia: sacredness and identity in a postcolonial nation.* Carlton: Melbourne University Press, 1998.

Gruenewald, D.A. 'The Best of Both Worlds: A Critical Pedagogy of Place'. *Educational Researcher* 35:4 (2003a): 3–12.

Gruenewald, D.A. 'Foundations of Place: A Multidisciplinary Framework for Place-Conscious Education'. *American Educational Research Journal,* 40:2 (2003b): 619–654.

Hemming, S. 'The problem with Aboriginal heritage' in G. Worby & L-I. Rigney (eds) *Sharing Spaces: Indigenous and non-Indigenous Responses to Story, Country and Rights.* Perth: API Network, 2006.

Hemming, S., Jones, P. & Clarke, P. *Ngurunderi: a Ngarrindjeri Dreaming.* Adelaide: South Australian Museum, 1989.

Hemming, S. & Trevorrow, T. 'Kungun Ngarrindjeri Yunnan: archaeology, colonialism and re-claiming the future', in Clare Smith & Martin H. Wobst (eds) *Indigenous Archaeologies: Decolonising Theory and Practice*. London: Routlege, 2005.

Kartinyeri, D. *Ngarrindjeri Anzacs*. Raukkan: Raukkan Council and South Australian Museum, 1996.

Mattingley, C. & Hampton, K. (eds). *Survival in Our Own Land: 'Aboriginal' experiences in 'South Australia' since 1836*. Adelaide: Wakefield Press, 1988.

Ngarrindjeri Tendi (NT), Ngarrindjeri Heritage Committee (NHC) and Ngarrindjeri Native Title Management Committee (NNTMC) *Ngarrindjeri Nation Yarluwar-Ruwe Plan, Caring for Ngarrindjeri Sea Country and Culture*. Meningie, SA: Ngarrindjeri Land and Progress Association, 2006.

Reynolds, H. *The other side of the frontier: Aboriginal resistance to the European invasion of Australia*. Ringwood, Vic: Penguin, 1982.

Rigney, D., Hemming, S. & Berg, S. 'Letters Patent, Native Title and the Crown in South Australia' in Hinton, M., Johnston, E. (QC) & Rigney, D. (Eds) *Indigenous Australians and the Law* (2nd Edn). London: Routledge Cavendish Publishing, 2008.

Rudd, K. 'Apology to Australia's Indigenous Peoples': Parliament House, Canberra, 13 February 2008 accessed on line 25 March 2008 at http://www. pm.gov.au/media/speech/2008/speech_0073.cfm

Ryan, L. *The Aboriginal Tasmanians*. St. Lucia, Queensland: University of Queensland Press, 1982.

Simon, R. *Public Memory and the Ethical and Pedagogical Implications of Rememberance as a Social Practice, Centre for the Study of Historical Consciousness*. Vancouver, BC: University of British Columbia, 2001 http://www.cshc.ubc.ca.

Stevens, I. *Report of the Hindmarsh Island Royal Commission*. Adelaide: State Print, 1995.

The Times – Victor Harbor 2003 'Hundreds at art opening', 2 April 2003. http:// www.thetimes.yourguide.com.au

Trevorrow, T. 'A shocking insult'. *Overland* 171 (2003) 62–63.

Trevorrow, T. & Hemming, S. 'Conversation: Kunggun Ngarrindjeri Yunnan – Listen to Ngarrindjeri People Talking' in *Sharing Spaces: Indigenous and Non-Indigenous Responses to Story, Country and Rights*. Curtin University of Technology, Perth: API Network Australia Research Institute, 2006.

Trevorrow, T., Finnimore, C., Hemming, S., Trevorrow, G., Rigney, M., Brodie, V. & Trevorrow, E. *They took our land and then our children: Ngarrindjeri struggle for truth and justice*. Meningie, SA: Ngarrindjeri Lands and Progress Association, 2007.

Von Doussa, J. Chapmans vs Luminis & Ors, Federal Court of Australia, Summary of Judgement 21 August 2001.

Walker, Robert *Up, Not Down, Mate! Thoughts From a Prison Cell*. Catholic Chaplaincy to Aborigines, 1981.

Walker, Rueben. 'Rueben Walker's Life History', in Norman B. Tindale's, *Journal of South East of South Australia*, vol 2. Adelaide: South Australian Museum Archives, 1938.

Watson, I. 'Aboriginal Laws and the Sovereignty of Terra Nullius' in borderlands ejournal, 1(2) 2002. Accessed online http://www.borderlandsejournal.adelaide.edu.au/vol1no2_2002/watson_laws.html

Woods, J.D. (ed.) *The Native Tribes of South Australia*. Adelaide: Wigg & Son, 1879.

The Saline Solution

PETER MANTHORPE

In primary school, in the 1960s, we were issued with a stencil made of pink plastic in the shape of Australia. This was to help our unsteady hands to draw the continent in to our social studies project books. The device had a number of design faults. Tasmania was missing. So was Kangaroo Island. I wondered if the islands had been withheld from us until we were older, and imagined an archipelago of tiny pieces of plastic in a drawer somewhere. Another problem was that, as I traced around the stencil, my unruly pencil would detach itself on every headland and take off on projects of its own across the sea: truncated legs of exploration into parts unknown. If I wanted to add colour to the continent, I had to lift the stencil to get to the subject, leaving no guide for the pencils at all. Australia would grow countless multicoloured legs to mingle with the others.

The solution to these problems would have been to issue children with a stencil the shape of the oceans *surrounding* Australia. Islands could then have been included without becoming a choking hazard, and pencil points would never escape the former penal colony again. This would be consistent with the advice given by art teachers that the best way to draw the outline of an object is not to concentrate on the object itself, but to look at the shape formed by the background surrounding it.

Given that islands are defined by the sea surrounding them, and Australia is the island continent, it is strange that the sea figures so little in the collective imagination of the Australian people. If we had a richer sense of the oceans surrounding us, with the wide horizons of metaphoric possibilities they make available, we might have a broader outlook; we might be less likely to find ourselves channelled into claustrophobic, xenophobic backwaters. If the sea were one of our national symbols in the same way that 'the Bush' is, we might have a better understanding of our place in the world.

Asserting that the sea figures little in our imaginations, that the ocean is not one of our defining national symbols, is likely to generate ripples of dissent. Don't most of us live on the coast? Don't we worship the beach? Aren't we a nation of surfers and fishers? Is it not true that we are prepared to pay a considerable premium for a house with 'sea-views', even if you can only catch a glimpse of blue by standing on the toilet in the upstairs bathroom?

But the beach is not the sea. Nor does the surf represent much of the ocean. Our culture loves the coast for all its transitional possibilities, but this littoral place is where the ocean ends. It is where the swells and waves that have travelled such epic distances, undulating and mingling in complex patterns, both rhythmic and chaotic in the manner of free verse, finally dissipate their energy and finish. A breaker is a wave in crisis. For tsunami or ripple, the beach is the graveyard of all waves. When we go to our beaches, we are celebrating not only the land's end, but also the end of the sea. We love our ocean views but, as a generalisation, Australian culture does not include an oceanic view—that is, a view *from* the ocean—to any sophisticated level at all. For a country surrounded by three oceans and four seas, this is extraordinary.

In 2005 I was sailing master on a reconstruction of a bronze age Majan boat, circa third century BCE, on a voyage from Oman on the eastern end of the Arabian Peninsula. Our destination was the coast of Gujarat in Western India. The boat and the voyage were part of an archaeological research project looking at the complex trading and cultural dynamics circulating around the Indian Ocean in ancient times.

Here is part of my journal entry on the day we put to sea:

> I am reeling with the horizontal vertigo of departure. I try to imagine the voyage and the rhythms of the ocean, but my thoughts have narrowed, focusing on the experience of the final moments alongside the wharf. I find myself concentrating on the minutiae of the departure rather than the future possibilities that it generates. In the familiar tasks of coiling lines and stowing for sea, and in the tactile reassurance of the boat, the familiar feel of rope and timber on my skin, I can sense only the present moment and the vague notion of a future arrival. In imagining the triumph of arrival, however vague and uncertain, the voyage becomes a blurry connection with the present triumph of departure, obscuring the doubts and dangers of the journey in between.[1]

'Vertigo' is a Latin word meaning a whirling or spinning movement. The noun *vertex* is a summit, but also a *vortex*, an eddy or whirlpool. The verb is *verto*: turn, turn upside down, transform, pass into a new frame of mind. This is a fine word for describing the dizziness of departure; it is the horizontal analogue of a fear of heights, the exhilaration of being in a high place and feeling the paradox of being terrified of the height while simultaneously having a strong urge to jump off. Jonathan Raban, in *Passage to Juneau*, describes these departure jitters as 'the nervous elation—half high hopes and half cold feet—that marks the start of a big adventure'.[2] His feet miss a step, hesitating between wanting to get wet and wanting to turn and run for his home on dry land. Later on that first night my journal reads:

> At the change of watch, Tom and I exchange congratulations on our good fortune. The crescent moon is low on the horizon, the stars are bright, the wind is fair and the boat is surging towards India. A populous pod of dolphins is playing under our bow and all about, leaving comet-trails of bioluminescence, until the sea is more luminous streaks than dark patches. They say that the souls of drowned sailors return as dolphins. If it is true, they are giving us a memorable send-off. From time to time the clew of the woven wool sail dips in the water with the roll of the boat and, on rising again, glows bright with stars as the water drips away. We feel as if nothing could go wrong.[3]

A short while later, things did go wrong. It turned out that our reconstruction was not as good as the boats that have sustained the Indian Ocean trade for millennia. Our boat was sinking.

> I checked that everyone was on board the life-raft. I must have counted the heads a dozen times. All eight of us were safely in, so I cut the rope joining the raft to the boat. We drifted slowly away, watching the boat settle so that she was now only just above the water. The dolphins were still making luminescent scribbles in the water underneath us. They were probably responding to our anxiety, sensing fellow mammals in trouble.
>
> In the darkness, our copious gear floated out to the limits of our close horizon. That, more than anything else, was making me sad. It was as if the sinking boat were too hard for me to comprehend, but the flotsam, the paradoxical symbol of a sinking boat, told the story. As the boat's elaborate rigging subsided into the waves, the bobbing oranges and watermelons surrounding her looked almost comical, like a tasteless joke.[4]

When you find yourself floating in the sea with nothing but your own buoyancy keeping you at the surface, you realise that the purpose of boats is to obviate the immediate necessity to swim. Sinking is generally an unusual event in a sailor's life and, until it happens, the ocean can feel like a safe place, where one can feel relaxed and comfortable. Captain Edward John Smith famously said:

> When anyone asks me how I can best describe my experience in nearly forty years at sea, I merely say, uneventful. Of course there have been winter gales, and storms and fog and the like. But in all my experience, I have never been in any accident … worth speaking about … nor was I ever in any predicament that threatened to end in disaster of any sort.[5]

Captain Smith's last command was the *Titanic*.

Those less at home on the ocean, passengers for example, are not as likely to be vulnerable to such hubris. The sea is a fearful place, as Shakespeare shows in the opening to *The Tempest*.[6] The play opens aboard a ship and with what many have described as an inversion of the social order. As the ship is threatened by the tempest, the lowly bosun asserts his authority over the kings, princes and councillors who are the ship's passengers, by virtue of his competence. He begins by asking them, bluntly, to return to their cabins because they are in the way. His only rudeness is to forget to preface his requests with polite gestures of reverence, which appear to have become irrelevant to him, if not to those whom he addresses. He remains patient; though they continue to ignore his requests, he never abuses his passengers.

Royalty, on the other hand, forget their manners entirely. 'A pox on your throat, you bawling, blasphemous, incharitable dog!' says Sebastian.[7] Hardly princely language, except that it echoes so many leaders who seek to silence others when they feel threatened. The bosun, who has not blasphemed, refuses to trade insults and offers to let the prince help work the ship. Sebastian declines. Antonio then joins in insulting the bosun: 'Hang, cur! Hang, you whoreson, insolent noisemaker! We are less afraid to be drowned than thou art.'[8]

Again, the bosun shows remarkable restraint, or perhaps he is just too preoccupied with his work to bother with the royal insults. He just gets on with the job of trying to save the ship, while the passengers continue to get in the way.

This is not an inversion of the social order. The bosun tells royalty what to do, but royalty takes no notice, as you would expect of superior beings. Only the register of manners is inverted: the bosun's plain eloquence makes him king of the deck, while the royal passengers swear and curse like a mob of sailors.

The reason for this inversion is that, while the bosun is in his element, surrounded by his ship-shaped domain and his loyal mariners, the royal passengers are in the opposite situation. The sea has separated them from the domains over which they reign, and their subjects are many miles away. They have nothing but their own resources, and these are shown to be scant. Isolated from the edifices of power, they are powerless.

To show us Antonio's and Sebastian's true characters, Shakespeare surrounds them with salt water. The sea threatens to overwhelm them so they are frightened, and it isolates them from their power-bases, but this same sea is also a unifying medium: the ship is on the return leg of a journey to marry a European princess to an African king. The journey will lead to other unions and reunions and, eventually, to another royal wedding.

The rest of the play takes place on an island, which is a good substitute for a boat: it shares many properties but none that involve sinking. Neither the island nor the ship has a name. They are both, in some senses, non-places; in particular, they are neither Naples nor Milan, which stand for the civilised world, the subject of the play. Shakespeare takes us out of a familiar European world and surrounds us by sea. This is not the equivalent of taking us to a field, a wood, a plain or a forest. Here on the island, or on the deck of the ship, all lines of communication with the rest of the world are closed. Whatever social order exists in the scene is a fabrication of the characters, the actors in the drama. The ship and the island represent a second order of theatricality. What happens on the stage is twice removed from normal reality. Perhaps a playwright resorts to sending the players to sea when the tricks of the art threaten to become too well known, too familiar, too much a part of normal life: when the bonds of their spell begin to loosen. As Hollywood shows us, for the disenchantment that success paradoxically entails, the dramatist's only remedy is special effects.

Despite the salty scene on the ship, it is clear that Shakespeare is not a mariner. For him the sea has rich metaphoric possibilities: the storm generates fear while a calm sea offers hope; the sea divides but it also unites; it invites the creative possibilities of dreaming but it also creates the bounds of an effective prison. The richness of these possibilities, though, is a result of the sea's strangeness. It is a space, not a place. The ship and the island are secluded, otherworldly stages where there can be play. They are only socialised to the extent that the castaways bring manners with them. Life is not fixed, so art can experiment. The island is a place where realities can be dreamed.

Robert Louis Stevenson's *Treasure Island* is another place of dreams surrounded by ocean.[9] However, it is no more a story of the sea than is *The Tempest*. The focus of the narrative is firmly on the land, where nearly all of the action occurs. The sea-passage of the *Hispaniola* from Bristol to the island is covered in one short chapter, all of which is observed from the inside of a barrel, a most uncomfortable vantage point for any young sailor. For the part of the narrative set on the island, the sea functions in the background only to quarantine the action from normal land-bound conventions of manners, as well as any chance of an easy rescue, as in *The Tempest*.

R M Ballantyne, in *The Coral Island*, calls the sea 'The great watery waste'.[10] In the beginning of the novel, which is an episode in the eternal struggle between the saccharine and the salty, Ballantyne uses the sea as an isolating medium, like the walls of a laboratory, so that he can conduct an experiment on the qualities of British imperialism. The island is his Petrie-dish of agar gel on which he smears three fit young Britons and watches and waits for the culture to grow in microcosm, thus proving the natural order: that muscular white Christians will always 'rise, naturally, to the top of affairs' over people of lesser morals, whether they be pirates or the 'savage' Indigenous inhabitants of the islands. Over the course of the novel, however, the ocean tends to subvert his purpose. By the close of the book, the reader has an unmistakable sense of the Pacific as a populated *place*: not only are there people scattered across it, but the lively traffic over its surface prohibits protracted isolation, as demonstrated by the rapid spread of the Gospels by Christian missionaries.

Ballantyne never visited the Pacific, but read reports and accounts of explorers, travellers and missionaries. These writings could not have avoided transmitting the notion that the Pacific Islanders consider themselves to belong to an oceanic community. Epeli Hau'ofa describes this sense in *Our Sea of Islands*. Of the peoples of Oceania, he says:

> Their universe comprised not only land surfaces, but the surrounding ocean as far as they could traverse and exploit it, the underworld with its fire-controlling and earth-shaking denizens, and the heavens above with their hierarchies of powerful gods and named stars and constellations that peoples could count on to guide their ways across the seas.[11]

Lord of the Flies, William Golding's rejoinder to *The Coral Island*, is set in the Indian Ocean, rather than the Pacific.[12] There is no sense of an oceanic community in the novel, nor any reference to the rich cultural traffic that has swirled around the Indian Ocean's rim, from East Africa to the Spice Islands, for millennia. *Lord of the Flies* is set in the age of aviation, in which journeys can end by 'dropping in' to a place, protected by a capsule, and in which the context of the journey is lost to another dimension. Once the boys are on the island and surrounded by sea, however, they climb the highest peak and survey what they consider now belongs to them:

> It was roughly boat shaped … The tide was running so that long streaks of foam trailed away from the reef and for a moment they felt that the boat was moving steadily astern.[13]

Another boat comes to rescue the boys from chaos: a 'trim cruiser'. As Ballantyne does in *The Coral Island*, Golding constructs a closed laboratory where he can conduct bizarre, sometimes deadly, experiments on humans in a sterile environment. The appearance of the floating war machine, the engine of chaos and death, in the final line of the novel, is Golding's most unambiguous signal that the behaviour of the young Britons on the island represents a wider world in microcosm. Golding's characterisation is more believable than Ballantyne's, simply because he allows the possibility of evil in everyone, even muscular young Britons. Ballantyne, however, is successful, probably by accident, in his portrayal of an oceanic outlook. His Anglocentric perspective, together with the fact that his understanding of the Pacific Islands is secondhand, make his success in this regard surprising.

In the original novel of a maroon on a deserted island, *Robinson Crusoe*, Defoe casts the island as a character.[14] It certainly plays a larger role than Crusoe's nameless wife, whose marriage to Crusoe, her bearing him three children, and her subsequent death, take up a half of one paragraph towards the end. The island, which is also never named, becomes an analogue for foreign lands, available and passively waiting for the colonial project to come and civilise them. As home to Crusoe's desperate loneliness, though, it also represents the social bankruptcy of personal endeavour in isolation. Crusoe begins the novel as a sailor, but the sea, which is his livelihood and the stage for his life's adventures, becomes a deadly moat, closing him off from contact with his beloved civilisation. The irony is that, although he can run the island by himself, sow crops, grind grain, bake bread, sharpen tools, build furniture and so on, he needs help if he is to build or sail a suitable boat. He literally needs community to escape his isolation. He is the original pattern for the Professor on *Gilligan's Island*, who, famously, can make a radio with coconut shells but cannot fix a hole in a boat. Even for Crusoe the expert sailor, the sea is a terrifying space, which menaces him with a kind of oblivion more complete than mere isolation.

The master of the ocean's metaphoric possibilities is Herman Melville. His masterpiece, *Moby Dick*, mobilises the ocean's paradoxes: its calms and its storms, its vastness and its claustrophobia: its simultaneous extremes. 'Yes, as every one knows, meditation and water are wedded for ever.' So asserts Ishmael the narrator, at once arrogant and charming.[15] This sea-drenched book is certainly a meditation, but it is, at the same time, a narrative detailing one man's fanaticism and single-minded, self-destructive passion. The sea isolates the ship, but it also makes a community of those on board. It creates as it destroys. It moves some, and holds others transfixed in thrall. Ahab is simultaneously mobile and fixed; as a captain in the whale fishery, he encompasses the globe, while he pivots on his ivory leg wedged in a hole bored in the deck of his ship. The whale might be Ahab's fatal obsession, but it swims in the same sea on which Ahab has spent his life. Melville's ocean is like the social stuff that laps and surges around us all, uniting us or isolating us, sustaining us or drowning us, we never quite know which.

I happened to be visiting friends in Scandinavia shortly after the federal government of the time refused to allow entry into Australia of a group of asylum seekers whose boat, the *Palapa 1*, sank and who were rescued by the Norwegian cargo ship the *Tampa*.

'What is going on in your country?' my seafaring friends would ask me. With characteristic straightforward courtesy they reminded me of one of the basic tenets of seamanship —the obligation to rescue those in distress—as if I needed reminding. 'I suppose it is not so surprising,' one of my friends told me. 'Australia is not a maritime nation.' As an Australian and a mariner I took exception to this remark, but, on reflection, I had to concede that it was true. I began to notice that being a sailor in Scandinavia, even a foreign sailor, I felt a less exotic creature than I do as a sailor in my own country. Scandinavians understand the sea and sailors. They are not only surrounded by sea, they are immersed in it.

If I am not actually *at* sea, I have to be overseas to find anything like what I have described as an oceanic outlook. Propping up the Strandlust Bar in Svendborg, or promenading along the Mutrah Corniche in Muscat, or sailing a New Zealand-registered schooner among the islands of Polynesia, I have a sense of living on an oceanic planet. As Raban says:

> For Odysseus, as for the Polynesian navigators … the ocean is a place, not a space; its mobile surface full of portents, clues, and meanings. It is as substantial and particular, as crowded with topographical features as, say, Oxfordshire.[16]

Returning to Australia, I find that the ocean is a view, not a viewpoint. *Strandlust* translates as a love of the beach. Australians can identify with that. But the maritime connotation of *strandlust*, which is a desire to see the beach *from the ocean*, as a signal of imminent homecoming, has no equivalent in our national vocabulary. Australian beaches are symbols of our insularity; in other places, they are a threshold to the rest of the planet.

Australia is girt by sea. We are constrained by it and, when our government treats it as a convenient moat, it becomes a border to protect our 'freedom', our mainly dry lifestyle. Our oceanic expertise seems anchored in that part of our history linked with using islands and ships as prisons. 'Girt' has a nautical meaning: a ship is girt when moored so tightly between two anchors that it will not swing with the tide. No turning. No whirling. Not going anywhere soon.

Australian writer Hai-Van Nguyen's essay, 'Journey to Freedom', is anthologised in *Dark Dreams: Australian Refugee Stories*. She came to Australia as a young child with her parents in a tiny, overcrowded boat. She describes the experience like this: 'The sea that encircled us promised everything and nothing at the same time. Our freedom was the deadly kind.'[17] Surrounded by the sea, Nguyen senses its profoundly paradoxical power. It is the medium for both her greatest hopes and her darkest fears. Her understanding of the nature of freedom is also profound: it can be deadly.

I do not believe that the Tampa crisis and the Pacific Solution would have been allowed to occur in a truly maritime nation, one in which the ocean—the deep, wide ocean beyond the surf line—were as much a part of our symbolic consciousness as, say, the beach, the Bush, the city, or even the desert. The ocean makes us an island, but it also connects us to the rest of the planet, and it is this unifying quality that we miss when we treat it merely as a protective moat, or a place to dunk the latest witch, or somewhere to pump our sewage, or even as no place at all.

I dream of the day Australia ungirts. I picture my stencil of Australia growing masts and sails and sliding from its moorings, released from its childish outline. The little vessel braves the whirlpool, finding itself on the big wide ocean, free to turn with the currents of the world, able to return with a new perspective. Then we can turn and look at ourselves from sea-level, see what other visitors have seen. When we return to the beach from out there, it is likely to be a new kind of arrival.

Australia is an island and, given that islands are made by the oceans that surround them, the Australian view of the sea is peculiarly thin. Australian writers about the sea are also thin on the ground. Whether we draw ourselves around a positive stencil or a negative one, the defining boundary always seems to be linear, lacking depth. Beyond the beach, beyond the surf-line, *there be sea-serpents*.

Notes

1   Peter Manthorpe (Unpublished journal, 2005).
2   Jonathan Raban, *Passage to Juneau* (London: Picador, 2000).
3   Peter Manthorpe (Unpublished journal, 2005).
4   Peter Manthorpe (Unpublished journal, 2005).
5   Captain Edward John Smith, cited from <http:www.uscgaux-danapoint.org> accessed 4 October 2006.
6   William Shakespeare, *The Tempest* (Harmondsworth: Penguin, 1987).
7   Shakespeare, *The Tempest* 39.
8   Shakespeare, *The Tempest* 39.
9   Robert Louis Stevenson, *Treasure Island* (London: Cassell, 1884).
10 Robert Ballantyne, *The Coral Island* (New York: Garland Publications, 1977).
11 Epeli Hau'ofa, 'Our Sea of Islands', from *A New Oceania: Rediscovering our Sea of Islands* (Suva: USP, 1993) cited from <http:www.pcf.org.nz> accessed 4 October 2006.
12 William Golding, *Lord of the Flies* (London: Faber, 1965).
13 Golding, *Lord of the Flies* 38.
14 Daniel Defoe, *The Life and Surprising Adventures of Robinson Crusoe of York, Mariner* (London: Andrew Dakers, undated).
15 Herman Melville, *Moby Dick* (London: Penguin, 2003) 4.

16 Raban, *Passage to Juneau* 95.
17 Hai-Van Nguyen, 'Journey to Freedom', anthologised in *Dark Dreams: Australian Refugee Stories* (Adelaide: Wakefield, 2004) 201.

Works cited

Ballantyne, Robert. *The Coral Island*. New York: Garland Publications, 1977.

Defoe, Daniel. *The Life and Surprising Adventures of Robinson Crusoe of York, Mariner*. London: Andrew Dakers, undated.

Golding, William. *Lord of the Flies*. London: Faber, 1965.

Hau'ofa, Epeli. 'Our Sea of Islands', from *A New Oceania: Rediscovering our Sea of Islands*. Suva: USP, 1993.

Manthorpe, Peter. Unpublished journal, 2005.

Melville, Herman. *Moby Dick*. London: Penguin, 2003.

Nguyen, Hai-Van. 'Journey to Freedom', anthologised in *Dark Dreams: Australian Refugee Stories*. Adelaide: Wakefield, 2004.

Raban, Jonathan. *Passage to Juneau*. London: Picador, 2000.

Shakespeare, William. *The Tempest*. Harmondsworth: Penguin, 1987.

Smith, Edward. Cited from <http:www.uscgaux–danapoint.org> accessed 4 October 2006.

Stevenson, Robert Louis. *Treasure Island*. London: Cassell, 1884.

At Home in Text on the Coast

MOYA COSTELLO

While historian Lyndall Ryan 'feels that she can never belong' to Australia because of its prior ownership, she still told Peter Read, for his book *Belonging*, that 'she is a saltwater person ... She prefers to live close to the coast because she was made by the sea and the shore ... Almost all her special places are seamarks ...'[1]

I grew up in Drummoyne, on the edge of the western suburbs of Sydney, just beyond the inner city. Drummoyne sits on the Parramatta River flowing into Sydney Harbour. Two of my father's drinking places were the Drummoyne Rowing Club and Drummoyne Sailing Club, both on the river. On many afternoons and evenings, the smell of salt water hung in the air, and that smell is inevitably nostalgic for me. To travel to the city centre by bus from Drummoyne, you cross three bridges over water: Iron Cove at Drummoyne, Anzac between Johnstons and Blackwattle Bay at Glebe, and Darling Harbour in the city at Cockle Bay.[2] On weekends in my childhood and adolescence, I went to the beach, sometimes alone, sometimes with family or friends: in the northern suburbs of Sydney, to Manly, Harbord, Collaroy, Dee Why, Narrabeen, Long Reef, Balgowlah, Whale and Palm; and in the eastern suburbs, to Bondi, Bronte, Tamarama, Maroubra and Coogee. My father, Frank, took us away to the beach every September school holidays. There was no one his equal for booking the absolutely best holiday bungalows. They were unglamorous, old-fashioned and right on the beach, at sleepy spots on the verge of discovery along the central and northern coast of New South Wales.

Later, I took myself with family members or friends, to the south coast, to the coasts of Queensland, Victoria, Tasmania and Western Australia. In Adelaide I live by the sea.

In the last two decades of the twentieth century, architect Philip Drew published his trilogy about an 'Australian spatial culture': *Leaves of Iron*, *Veranda* and *The Coast Dwellers*.[3] To describe and explain this spatial culture, Drew focuses on the topography of the coast, the buildings of architect Glenn Murcutt and the architectural space of the verandah. A fourth book, *Touch This Earth Lightly*, contains extracts from Drew's interviews with Murcutt. Drew notes that Australian spatial culture is characterised by the linear not the centripetal, and the expression of 'edges' as 'open boundaries'.[4]

Murcutt's hallmarks and concerns are: light, ventilation and breathing; the connection between outside and in; linking and continuum, horizontality and linearity; dynamic and quickened movement; minimalism and serenity; and freedom and security. The longitudinal, attenuated forms of his houses, reminiscent of coastal space, imply movement and a journey, a sense of the world outside.[5]

The boat-like nature of Murcutt's buildings has often been commented on. Beck and Cooper point out that he uses 'stainless steel yacht rigging to peg down flighty roof profiles'; and that he showed a client, Marie Short, how to operate her house 'like a yacht'. His Ball-Eastaway house 'is like a building that has docked, put out its bridge like a ship'.[6] Murcutt's Arthur and Yvonne Boyd Education Centre has been described as 'a ship progressing across the hillside'.[7] Richard Leplastrier, another Australian architect, has also been influenced by boats which he has described as 'delicate sanctuaries'.[8] Murcutt's own influence has spread; Nicola Bradley, James Grose and Peter Stutchbury are seen among his successors; he has also worked with Troppo in the Northern Territory, with Reg Lark, Wendy Lewin, his wife, and with Nick Murcutt, his son.[9]

In Polynesia, another Pacific setting, Greg Dening found that the boat was used by Indigenous people as a symbol of the in-between—in between land, sea and sky—and as a metaphor of transition.[10] Like the coast, the verandah is an in-between space. On my bedroom dresser is a photo of my father; he is seated on the front verandah of my childhood home in Drummoyne. He enjoyed the prospect—at the back verandah there were sunsets and a small view of the distant Parramatta River—and a space for thinking, meditating and dreaming. From him, I learned to love the verandah as an intermediary space. The best feature of the nondescript 1950s suburban house that belongs to my partner and me in Adelaide is the verandah and the enclosed verandah room.[11] What I note about being on the verandah is that I am comforted by not being in the landscape, fully exposed to the potential harshness of the elements—sun, wind, rain—yet still remaining in touch with it sensually. Frank Moorhouse has described the uneasiness which the Australian bush can induce as 'creeping hysteria and dread'.[12]

If we consider the inland spread of the outer suburbs in our major cities and a common view that the inland or centre is 'the spiritual heart of the country', Philip Drew may seem to have veered towards universalising and ignoring difference.[13] But he did state that though the paradigm he discussed 'may not always be the same everywhere, typical patterns do emerge'.[14]

Although Drew references Australia's literary and visual art culture to support his thesis, he does not mention Murray Bail, and though Bail has said he doesn't like sand or surf, the central section of his novel *Holden's Performance*—where its (anti)hero, Holden Shadbolt, is in Sydney—invoked the coastal life of Sydney through one of its seaside suburbs, Manly, in a way that is supportive of Drew's thesis [15]

In the novel, Manly is described as having a 'floating' population living at the 'effervescent edge of the continent'.[16] By way of contrast, we are regularly reminded that Australia has an ancient continental landscape: arid, flat, remote, empty, undifferentiated and predictable. All of this is embodied in Holden who is immutable and stolid. The fractal nature of Australia's coastal topography and Sydney's unruly layout are symbolised by a minor character, Harriet Chandler. Female, artist, with a crooked polio-stricken body and living at the beach in Manly, she is associated with mutability and potential: she was 'all flow and curve', 'all arches and pronounced crescents, a twisted attraction', 'a series of intricate promises'.[17]

In Sydney, the city of 'future possibilities', Holden has a brief period of potential blossoming, between Canberra and Adelaide which eventually win out in regimenting him.[18] The regular and regulating patterns, the circle and grid respectively, of Canberra and Adelaide, resonate with automation. Both cities reflect, in different ways, the arid interior of the country. Canberra is an inland city, and the desert penetrates Adelaide in hot winds and bright white light. In Sydney, according to Ross Gibson, the influences of the colonial maritime persist; the city's 'undulating, fugitive paths' remain disruptive of any attempted overlay of grids. Early white settlement on the foreshores of Sydney Harbour had to confront the liminal in its Pacific Ocean setting; 'doubtless patterns' and 'tight intentions' struggled against 'flux'; ratio, limits and grids against 'boundlessness' and the 'oceanic'; 'the fearful category of the sublime' against inconsistency and fluidity.[19]

While Adelaide is a coastal city and real estate by the sea is skyrocketing in popularity and price, few people go to the beach to swim; it has to be near forty degrees before there is a critical mass of people in the water. Admittedly, Adelaide's coastal water is affected by the cold Southern Ocean Current, only warming up in late summer; it is significantly colder than Sydney's warm East Australian current. But compared to the ever restless and populated Manly, and Sydney's other famous beaches such as Bondi, the bay in St Vincent's Gulf can look like a long, long stretch of empty beach—always with the noteworthy exception of a few iceberg elders and paddling, sand-bucketing, shell-gathering toddlers.

My migratory path mimicked in reverse that of Holden's, as if the parallel worlds of fact and fiction intersected. Helen Daniel recognises that '[i]nside contemporary Australian fiction there is a counterfeit history of Australia'.[20] While Holden was born and grew up in Adelaide and then later moved to Sydney and then Canberra, I grew up in Sydney, moved to Adelaide and had the opportunity to move to Canberra but passed it up. When Holden arrived in Manly in 1954, Glenn Murcutt was school captain at Manly Boys High.[21] While Holden threw himself into the surf at Manly, I imagine Harriet Chandler swam in a quiet corner. Harriet's and Holden's onetime employer, Alex Screech, drowned in the surf. Glenn Murcutt, however, was a strong, experienced swimmer, having developed under his father's disciplined training when he was a child, and able to read the water, particularly the rips in Sydney's beaches in high summer. My father was a beautiful body surfer; carried into the beach in the middle of a rolling wave, his torso jutting out ahead of the wave's fold, he was seemingly transformed into a sea creature.

I was not conscious of my dreams before my father's death. But after his death, and prompted by therapy for my depression following that event, I began to take note of them. They often concerned a search for housing and a home; establishing safety and rest, for family members; being able to comfortably carry my belongings and having a secure place to stow them. My overwhelming impression of my father before his death was his discomfort; he was tired and cold and couldn't cope with noise. His territory narrowed from the suburb, the street; he removed himself from the verandah to his room where he spent more and more of each day in bed.

A clay model of a spiral shell on my bedroom dresser is a symbol of housing and home. The shell is a space that you think of as already empty, but that you dream of inhabiting; although it looks small and cramped outside, you sense that inside it will open up into a spacious abode. It is a moveable house: you can carry safety, serenity and comfort with you as you go. And it is most often found at the shoreline, a site of movement and change. It was at the onset of depression that I was due to move to Canberra. But I couldn't move; I couldn't leave 'home'. What came acutely to the fore to prevent me leaving were my sense of loss of 'home'—and in that, safety, serenity, familiarity and comfort—and my heightened sense of unease at leaving the coast. I felt I had to remain where I was, at home, as a way of being grounded.

Paul Carter has written of an Indigenous way of inhabiting country and feeling home by walking through it, being lightly grounded. In contrast, the colonial practice was about settlement and staying in one place: 'for a culture that is ungrounded, movement, however integral to its survival, must always constitute a threat.' Because we are not at home, not grounded, we believe that the ground is 'treacherous, unstable, inclined to give way' and, as a consequence, we believe that movement is associated with 'the unstable, the unreliable, the wanton'. [22]

Everywhere along the coast in Adelaide, home-making consists of demolished bungalows being replaced by the mock Tuscan or Georgian: 'bald masonry (offering scant protection from dazzling sun)'.[23] Our homes, says Carter, are 'tumuli erected over the slaughtered body of the giant ground'.[24] Murcutt has called this being 'submerged' by developers; his way of designing and building by surveying the site, orienting the building to the topography, keeping the trees and maintaining the landform is rare in Australia because 'it costs the developer more, and requires care ...'.[25]

The alienation of such buildings from the landscape is expressed by Carter in his reference to our 'nervous decoration', our 'ornamented places' which grow 'out of the sacrifice of the ground'.[26] Murcutt also dismisses decorative items as 'a measure of how the building has very often failed'.[27] Embarrassingly, both Harriet Chandler and I, as home-makers, are unreconstructed consumers of ornamentation; we decorate with cushions, rugs, bowls, baskets and paintings. We live in 'failed' buildings. However, for Holden Shadbolt at least, who lived sequentially in a linoleum-floored bedroom, a boarding-house asbestos extension on the back of a laundry, an austere and brutal Canberra flat, and a youth-club Nissen hut, Harriet's place, with its 'many-layered softness' delivered through decorative items, was a comforting and welcoming space.[28]

Carter wants us to tread the earth 'lightly', so that we can live on and with the earth based on an 'environmentally-grounded poetics'.[29] Touching the earth lightly was associated with Murcutt who attributed it to Indigenous Australians.[30] I believe my father touched the earth lightly. 'What is your philosophy of life?' my eldest sister once asked him. 'Simplicity and humility,' he replied. Also on my bedroom dresser is a postcard he sent to me a year or two before his death. It advertised *Journeys through Landscapes*, an exhibition of the work of Conrad Martens. On the back he wrote 'Memories are all we really own'. He owned very little; he never owned a car, didn't drive and did a considerable amount of walking. As a family we travelled by public transport which included the ferry to Manly and boats to Christmas picnics on islands in Sydney Harbour.

Besides the clay shell, there is another symbol in my bedroom. On the back of the door is a Sydney Harbour Bridge coat hanger and on it hangs a small model of a sailboat made of stained glass in blue and green. The boat's swinging motion on the moving door has left marks that look like the wind written down. It's as if the boat is sailing under the bridge.

Two Australian visual artists, Kim Mahood and Julie Adams, have linked boats as a symbol with their respective fathers. A boat, like a shell, is a container or vessel, a travelling house. A boat enables you to be in water with relative safety and ease. It's a place for settling in a space, the sea, where you cannot settle.[31] It 'presents us with notions of exposure, but at the same time refuge'.[32] It represents the potential of falling into the 'trauma of the abyss', as well as entering a poetics of becoming.[33]

An empty rowboat is a symbol of desire, full of potential. In paintings such as Clarice Beckett's *The Boatsheds* and *The Red Boat*, the boats are empty and anchored or beached in a quiet spot. They're not out at sea. It's their potential and promise as housing for travel within the maritime—the oceanic, the fluid and shifting—that is so attractive.

Mahood took as an icon for her journey a boat the family once sailed, now marooned on a dry lake in the desert. The boat had become 'a craft for a dry lake, a vessel to carry the detritus of memory'.[34]

In her project 'Relics and Remnants of Desire', Adams painted a series of images that came out of a time when her father had cancer, and, when travelling herself and aware of 'a vastness of space, and elemental forces and energies', she needed to be alert to her own survival.[35] The images feature ritualistic containers or vessels, boats, basket boats, coracles, litters or coffins. While they are empty of visible, material objects and subjects, they are carry/contain desire. They are set within dark skies, water or land with illumination from the moon or sun. They are funereal or life-giving, sad or ecstatic, empty or full, still or mobile, frail or sturdy.

For years, a sailboat which my partner and I never sailed was beached on our verandah in Adelaide. It was a gift from friends who no longer sailed it. So we passed it on to neighbours in a similar fashion. This was only days before my partner's father died. We lost a container for safe travel, but we were no longer anchored; we were set loose from our moorings, floating free. While I want to continue to live by the sea, my partner wants a cooler, wetter climate than Adelaide can provide. He's worried generally about environmental degradation and climate change, and specifically about the lack of rainfall in South Australia and the diminishing quality of Adelaide's main source of water, the Murray River. He's attuned to the bush and the mountains. We talk about living in Middle Earth, New Zealand, where we imagine there is an abundance of water and wilderness, or about being at home on the south coast of New South Wales where bodies of water—lakes, rivers—are common and the bush meets the sea. I imagine we will get a little boat. And this time, even row or sail.

Notes

1 Peter Read, *Belonging: Australians, Place and Aboriginal Ownership* (Cambridge: Cambridge University Press, 2000) 191.

2 Moya Costello, *Small Ecstasies* (St Lucia: University Queensland Press, 1994) 84.

3 Philip Drew, *The Coast Dwellers: A Radical Reappraisal of Australian Identity* (Ringwood, Victoria: Penguin, 1994) 11.

4 Drew, *The Coast Dwellers* xiii. This latter view may be tempered by the Howard federal ministry's (1996+) international infamy for its treatment of refugees and asylum seekers breaching borders. It's the coast as a site of transgression and change that such governmental activity wants to control. It's worth noting here, given Indigenous Australian's intimate relationship to and knowledge of the land, that there is 'no known record of an Indigenous architecture graduate until the 1990s' (Davina Jackson and Chris Johnson, *Australian Architecture Now* 60). Haig Beck and Jackie Cooper, *Glenn Murcutt: A Singular Architectural Practice* (Mulgrave, Victoria: The Images Publishing Group, 2002) 133 have said of Murcutt's Marika-Alderton house that it was 'probably the first that is the outcome of a detailed investigation of Aboriginal culture and customs'.

5 Philip Drew, *Leaves of Iron: Glenn Murcutt: Pioneer of an Australian Architectural Form* (Pymble, New South Wales: Angus & Robertson, 1996) 57; Drew, *The Coast Dwellers* 141.

6 Haig Beck and Jackie Cooper, *Glenn Murcutt* 10, 49, 71.

7 Tim Fisher, 'Site for Dreams: Arthur Boyd and Glenn Murcutt Together at Riversdale', *Art and Australia,* 37.1 (1999): 55.

8 Richard Leplastrier, *An Attitude to Material,* Australian Broadcasting Corporation, 2000, http://www.abc.net.au/arts/headspace/special/materials/wood/at_pg2.htm, accessed 25 January 2006.

9 Davina Jackson and Chris Johnson, *Australian Architecture Now* (London: Thames & Hudson, 2000) 11, 243.

10 Ross Gibson, ed., 'Ocean Settlement', *Exchanges: Cross-Cultural Encounters in Australia and the Pacific* (Sydney, New South Wales: Historic Trust of New South Wales, 1996) 101.

11 Moya Costello, 'Lost in the Bush', *Picador New Writing 3*, eds Drusilla Modjeska and Beth Yahp (Sydney: Picador, 1995) 103.

12 Frank Moorhouse, 'From a Bush Log Book 1', *Forty-Seventeen* (Ringwood, Victoria: Viking, 1988) 24.

13 Drew, *The Coast Dwellers* 33.

14 Drew, *The Coast Dwellers* 11.

15 Paul Sheehan, 'Talking Turtle', *The Sydney Morning Herald,* 25 April (1998): Spectrum Books 10s.

16 Murray Bail, *Holden's Performance* (Ringwood, Victoria: Penguin, 1987) 136, 175.

17 Bail, *Holden's Performance* 168, 198, 329.

18 Bail, *Holden's Performance* 146.

19 Ross Gibson, 'Ocean Settlement' 95–101.

20 Helen Daniel, 'Counterfeit', *Australian Book Review,* 141, June (1992) 33: 32–41.

21 Drew, *Leaves of Iron* 15.

22 Paul Carter, *The Lie of the Land* (London: Faber and Faber, 1996) 2–3.
23 Davina Jackson and Chris Johnson, *Australian Architecture Now* 243.
24 Carter, *The Lie of the Land* 2.
25 Philip Drew, *Touch This Earth Lightly: Glenn Murcutt in His Own Words* (Potts Point, New South Wales: Duffy & Snellgrove, 2001) 83; George Seddon, *Landprints: Reflections on Place and Landscape* (Cambridge: Cambridge University Press, 1997) 149.
26 Carter, *The Lie of the Land* 2.
27 Drew, *Touch This Earth Lightly* 76.
28 Bail, *Holden's Performance* 305.
29 Carter, *The Lie of the Land* 5.
30 Drew, *Leaves of Iron* 8.
31 Paul Carter, *The Road to Botany Bay: An Essay in Spatial History* (London: Faber and Faber, 1987) 291.
32 Julie Adams, 'Relics and Remnants of Desire', Diss. (Monash University, 1995) 6.
33 Paul Carter, 'Translation', *Depth of Translation: The Book of Raft*, Paul Carter and Ruark Lewis (Burnley, Victoria: NMA Publications, 1999) 85, 55.
34 Kim Mahood, *Craft for a Dry Lake* (Sydney, New South Wales: Anchor, 2000) 59.
35 Julie Adams, 'Relics and Remnants of Desire' 19.

Works cited

Adams, Julie. 'Relics and Remnants of Desire'. Diss. Monash University, 1995.

Bail, Murray. *Holden's Performance*. Ringwood, Victoria: Penguin, 1987.

Beck, Haig, and Jackie Cooper. *Glenn Murcutt: A Singular Architectural Practice*. Mulgrave, Victoria: The Images Publishing Group, 2002.

Carter, Paul. *The Lie of the Land*. London: Faber and Faber, 1996.

Carter, Paul. *The Road to Botany Bay: An Essay in Spatial History*. London: Faber and Faber, 1987.

Carter, Paul. 'Translation'. *Depth of Translation: The Book of Raft*. Paul Carter and Ruark Lewis. Burnley, Victoria: NMA Publications, 1999, 22–109.

Costello, Moya . 'Lost in the Bush'. *Picador New Writing 3*. Eds. Drusilla Modjeska and Beth Yahp. Sydney: Picador, 1995, 95–105.

Costello, Moya. *Small Ecstasies*. St Lucia: UQP, 1994.

Daniel, Helen. 'Counterfeit', *Australian Book Review* 141 June (1992): 32–41.

Drew, Philip. *The Coast Dwellers: A Radical Reappraisal of Australian Identity*. Ringwood, Victoria: Penguin, 1994.

Drew, Philip. *Leaves of Iron: Glenn Murcutt: Pioneer of an Australian Architectural Form*. 1985. Pymble, New South Wales: Angus & Robertson, 1996.

Drew, Philip. *Touch This Earth Lightly: Glenn Murcutt in His Own Words*. Potts Point, New South Wales: Duffy & Snellgrove, 2001.

Drew, Philip. *Veranda: Embracing Place*. Pymble, New South Wales: Angus & Robertson, 1992.

Fisher, Tim. 'Site for Dreams: Arthur Boyd and Glenn Murcutt Together at Riversdale'. *Art and Australia,* 37.1 (1999).

Gibson, Ross. Ed. 'Ocean Settlement'. *Exchanges: Cross-Cultural Encounters in Australia and the Pacific.* Sydney, New South Wales: Historic Trust of New South Wales, 1996, 89–111.

Jackson, Davina and Chris Johnson. *Australian Architecture Now.* London: Thames & Hudson, 2000.

Leplastrier, Richard. *An Attitude to Material.* Australian Broadcasting Corporation, 2000. At <http://www.abc.net.au/arts/headspace/special/materials/wood/at_pg2.htm>. Accessed 25 January 2006.

Mahood, Kim. *Craft for a Dry Lake.* Sydney, New South Wales: Anchor, 2000.

Moorhouse, Frank. 'From a Bush Log Book 1'. *Forty-Seventeen.* Ringwood, Victoria: Viking, 1988, 23–31.

Read, Peter. *Belonging: Australians, Place and Aboriginal Ownership.* Cambridge: CUP, 2000.

Seddon, George. *Landprints: Reflections on Place and Landscape.* Cambridge, Cambridge: University Press, 1997.

Sheehan, Paul. 'Talking Turtle'. *The Sydney Morning Herald* 25 April 1998, Spectrum Books 10s.

Packin' Heat at Bojangles: Low Life and High Life on the St Kilda Littoral

BRIAN MATTHEWS

One hot January afternoon, when I was about eight or nine years old, I was breathlessly loitering on the corner of Fawkner and Grey Streets in St Kilda with my worldly-wise mate, Frank Darmody, while with a highly contrived pretence of uninterest and languour we tried to get a good look at gangster's moll, Pretty Dulcie Markham, who was sitting outside the pub. Dulcie had not long before, and very publicly, taken a bullet in the thigh, so she had one leg in a cast and propped up on a spare chair. Every now and then, one of her admirers would ferry a beer out to her, or join her for a yarn. In the same altercation that had left Dulcie with a broken leg, hoodlum ex-boxer, Gavan Walsh, was shot dead. All of this had been luridly reported in the famous scandal sheet of the time inaptly named *The Truth*. Just as, decades later, blokes said they read *Playboy* only for its superior political essays, so in those times more or less respectable working-class people owned to reading *Truth* but only for the racing guide. Somehow, anyway, Darmody always managed to read it undiscovered, and we were there that day because he was convinced that Pretty Dulcie, known as The Angel of Death because eight of her prostitution clients and two former lovers had died violently by the gun or the knife, would be taken out by the assassin who had left the job unfinished. As it happened, our elaborate show of being totally distracted was so obvious that she noticed and told us to 'Fuck off'.

A couple of hours later, and less than a mile away, I was wading knee deep in the water at St Kilda beach squinting in the hot summer sun and caressed every now and then by the welcome puff of sea breeze, brandishing the spear I had made myself, optimistically searching the rippled, sandy bottom for a snoozing flounder. It did not, needless to say, occur to me at the time, but within a couple of hours I had inhabited the two St Kildas, two worlds so different that they could scarcely be connected with each other by any conceivable common ground. Or could they?

St Kilda did not apparently derive its name from the storm bound, frowning cluster of inhospitable rocky islands at the edge of the world in the western

Hebrides; if it did, it was only by indirection. According to Edmund Finn's *The Chronicles of Early Melbourne 1835 to 1852*, the attribution was all the work of Governor La Trobe:

> ... there was a picnic [recalls Finn] in one of the then umbrageous nooks with which the beautiful [unnamed] suburb abounded ... Whilst the champagne corks were flying, someone said to Mr La Trobe, 'What name shall this place have?' and Mr La Trobe, at the moment looking over the water, saw a small yacht sailing like a swan before him ... 'Well, I don't think we can do better than name it after Captain ——'s yacht. The name of the little clipper was *St Kilda*, and so St Kilda came to be thenceforward known.

The champagne, the swan-like elegance of the yacht, the beauty of the coast, the vast benign bay are all part of one of the faces that St Kilda gradually developed and presented to the delighted colonial society of Melbourne. In a time when communications were neither swift nor reliable, its reputation nevertheless grew at an extraordinary rate.

To begin with, the split in St Kilda's personality was not immediately evident. In the settlement that became known as East St Kilda, fine colonial houses, wide boulevards and pleasant parks took rapid shape. As the novelist Martin Boyd remarks, through one of his characters in *The Cardboard Crown*, 'Most of the early colonists of the better sort ... lived in East St Kilda, which remained an "exclusive" neighbourhood until sometime in the 1920s'.

In his Langton series of novels he locates one of the families on the salubrious corner of Hotham and Inkerman Streets, in the heart of the eastern area. The heroine of Fergus Hume's *The Mystery of a Hansom Cab* lived in 'a magnificent town house down in St Kilda, which would have been not unworthy of Park Lane'.

This spot was, in fact, not far from Robe Street which ran down to Ackland Street, Luna Park and the beach and, as if gradually corrupted by its connection with the growing hedonism of the littoral, had become a focus for gangsters and prostitution by the 1930s and absolutely nothing at all like Park Lane.

At its other end, furthest away from the beach, Robe Street joined Grey Street and on that corner was the Sacred Heart School, my primary school, and a little up the hill, the Church of the Sacred Heart, where various members of my family were christened, confessed, communioned, confirmed, conjoined and coffined. In this sacred enclave, as if protected by a higher power, civilized behaviour reigned. But beyond it, down one way to the utterly infamous Fitzroy Street and down the other way to the bad end of Inkerman Street, near where Pretty Dulcie sat that day nursing her leg, corruption, violence and rag-taggery prevailed among a shifting population of down-and-outs, spivs, petty crooks, drunks, prostitutes and hit men.

So the terrain was like this: a thoroughly respectable eastern section shaded gradually into the more western depths of a precinct whose famous imperial street names—Barkly, Grey, Fawkner, Havelock (I lived in Havelock Street)—became metaphors for low life and gangland while, just a mile or so further, coming on to the littoral proper, seaside St Kilda began to develop along the lines of some English counterparts—like Brighton, under the influence of educated, affluent picnickers such as those with Governor La Trobe that day, and Blackpool for the workers who would come down by train to cool off. So, in the English manner, there was a pier with elaborate entertainments and a grand domed structure at its furthest end; there was, in due course, Luna Park. There was plenty of green parkland and, unlike the English models, plenty of bright white sand; there were sailing boats, and—also eventually—there was the St Kilda Baths.

Preceded by a number of eccentric privately run baths during the nineteenth century, the St Kilda Proprietary Baths, opened in 1906 and run by the municipality, was the wonder of the St Kilda littoral. This double-domed edifice was a cross between the Royal Pavilion in Brighton, England, and a Maharajah's palace —indeed its architectural style was often referred to as the Hindustan style, from which derived the fashion for towers and domes in seaside buildings. Replaced by the St Kilda City Baths in 1931, the structure retained its Moorish look and, in fact, many versions and manifestations later, it still does.

But the Baths—in whatever particular one of their several incarnations—became curiously focal in a way that was to connect the littoral with the dark labyrinthine streets and lanes and their shifty denizens further inland. This was because the idea of a structured bathing area raised moral problems and it was under the pressure of these moral problems that the Baths declined both physically and atmospherically. And that decline accompanied and somehow mirrored the decline of St Kilda itself. It happened like this.

The original attraction of the Baths was that the segregated sexes could indulge in sea bathing in reasonable privacy and within the law since any kind of mixed bathing in daylight in the open sea was still illegal at the turn of the century. Gradually, though, the innate democracy of the beach overwhelmed the local council's desperate attempts to rein in the swimmers. As Gillian Upton notes in her Exhibition catalogue, 'Splash: St Kilda Beach and Baths', the laws against so-called open bathing—men and women bathing together in the open sea—had been flouted with increasing abandon from around the mid 1890s.

The Council was on a hiding to nothing and its legislative edifice crumbled entirely in 1908. On the first day of that year the Bureau of Meteorology proudly opened for business; within a fortnight it was the centre of attention and interest as Melbourne embarked on what would be six successive days (15-20 January) of temperatures over the old 100°. Thousands of Melburnians flocked to the bayside, especially to St Kilda and mixed bathing became a *fait accompli*. But bathers still had to observe strict rules: there was a puritanical dress code; bathers had to 'walk in a straight line to the water'; they had to change back into their normal clothes immediately after swimming; and no one could sit on the beach in togs unless covered by an overcoat-like garment approved by the Council.

These irksome restrictions meant that, when not driven by extraordinary conditions, many people still found the baths preferable. This was especially the case for men who were allowed to swim and generally perambulate naked in their section of the St Kilda baths. Some natural events contributed to the Baths' fluctuating in the favour of bathers. From time to time, shark scares would thin the numbers on the open beach and a couple of actual attacks just off the St Kilda pier pretty well emptied the adjacent beaches for a week or two. And in the late 1940s, a stingray outbreak in the shallows terrified everyone and one man died as a result of stepping on one in shallow water and being lashed with the barbed tail. As a very small boy, I went one evening for a swim with my father at the height of this 'scare'.

As in the past, tremendous and constant heat had rapidly overcome fears and the beach was packed. My old man was standing in the shallows talking to a mate and having a smoke and, tired of waiting, I splashed my way out into the wavelets. When I was about thigh deep, I saw a stingray hurtling for the deeper water, his wings pulsing and his tail flicking puffs of sand from the bottom. Impossible to tell which of the two of us was the more scared, but I ran back to my father on literally wobbling legs—the first time I'd ever experienced such a phenomenon—and told my father.

'Stingray', I gasped, heaving terrified breaths, 'stingray, Dad!' He didn't believe me, but I can see it still.

The Man O'War jellyfish was another frequent invader—not a killer but it inflicted an excruciatingly painful sting. As a bloke explained to me and my mate in the men's section of the baths, any part of the anatomy stung by a Man O'War immediately went stiff. He carefully detailed each part and the degree of stiffness. Innocently I recounted the general outlines of this story to my mother and, reading between the lines, she banned me from going ever again to the men's baths.

Though unnoticed while it was happening, the St Kilda beach and littoral were the battleground for two sociological combatants. On the beach and in the surrounding esplanade and parks ever larger crowds—swollen by holidaymakers who could now arrive by tram as well as train, and soon would arrive by car—gradually but irresistibly eroded the Council's rules and barriers: a division of the beach with markers to segregate the sexes, injunctions against Sunday bathing, against the wearing of briefer swimming togs, against walking off the beach and into the streets in beach wear, all were inexorably eroded and abandoned under the benign democratic pressure of developing Australian attitudes to the rites and the rights of the beach and the littoral.

That was one side of the conflict. The other side was represented by the Baths and the pier with its entertainments. These more and more became rather wan hangovers of the English model of seaside resorts. In England, you needed to escape bad weather and often freezing summer seas; inhospitable or at best unpredictable conditions meant the provision of indoor entertainments on the pier and elsewhere was important to the life of the resort. But such amenities were redundant on Australia's suburban beaches during the long hot summers. It is an irony that St Kilda beach, where no one has ever glimpsed anything remotely reminiscent of surf, and where the sand and sea are the very epitome of domesticated coastal nature, was one of the places in Australia where Aussie attitudes to beach culture and beach behaviour were quietly fought for, won and established—though of course this was also going on elsewhere, and on more spectacular beaches.

And so the Baths and the pier entertainments declined. Oblivious, apparently, to social forces that were transforming beach behaviour and morality, the famously conservative Council opened new Baths in 1931, but these, as Gillian Upton observes, were 'almost obsolete when they opened'.

The idea of the Baths clung on during the 1930s, especially the naked bathing in the men's section; and mixed bathing permitted in the Ladies section produced a brief flare of interest. But essentially, from about 1930 to 1950 St Kilda was changing from being a resort to a suburb and the nature and direction of the transformation was profoundly influenced by an influx of refugees, gangland characters of varying degrees of notoriety and efficiency, and the invasion of the area by off-duty soldiers, especially Americans, during the Second World War.

St Kilda's rapid metamorphosis into a near-city holiday spot was attractive to the criminal element: it meant there were crowds with money to spend and their guard down; the police presence was not strong, at least to start with, and various kinds of other opportunities were beckoning, such as strong-arming growing businesses in the area, but above all gambling and prostitution—the mainstays of the criminal world until the flowering of the drug culture. The influx of soldiers enhanced all this but when military numbers waned after the war, the gangs stayed, the refugees increased and the holiday crowds grew.

After a resurgence driven by the large numbers of European refugees who came to live in St Kilda and for whom public spas and baths were familiar institutions, the St Kilda Baths, never really recovered the glories of the early century. Close to the infamous Fitzroy Street, where wannabe mafia figures—what Chopper Read contemptuously called 'Plastic Godfathers' whose 'idea of the mafia is to wear dark glasses in Lygon Street'—fought to control the stand-over scene, The Baths were enveloped by the general sleaze that took over the area. This came in various shapes: there was the Candy Corner, for example, which looked and sounded innocent but which my mother always hurried me past because it was in fact a big brothel operation; the Memorial Picture Theatre, which provided a lurid diet of as explicit sex and porn as was possible in those days; Robe Street, whose Park Lane pretensions degenerated into a string of brothels; and even the precincts of Luna Park became dangerous at night after it closed. All these were within a few drop kicks of each other and of the Baths and were all on the skids. The South Pacific, as the Baths was known in one of its manifestations, offered hot sea baths frequented by jockeys, but more importantly housed various swiftly produced and endlessly refurbished night clubs that were constantly closing and reopening under new, more forbidding management. Possibly the most notorious of these was Bojangles, which Chopper Read described like this:

> I went that night to Bojangles for a quiet drink, wearing a police bullet proof vest and carrying a handgun down the front of my strides and a sawn-off .410 shotgun down the back. Anyone who has been to Bojangles will know that if anything I was a bit light on for fire power when you consider the class of clientele that got there in the early hours of the morning.

Chopper's 'quiet drink', incidentally, ended with a confrontation with Sam The Turk, a dead set Plastic Godfather, in the car park:

> He's got the gun at my head going click, click. The cheeky bastard had my own gun at my head going click, click, click.
> But I carry two guns. I had the shotty down the back and the .32 at the front.
> So I've pulled out the shotty and gone bang and it's bye bye Turk.
> One hundred percent genuine self defence ... They were trying to kill a tiger snake with a feather duster.

And so, through the Baths and especially Bojangles and its clones, the gangs came to the beach. The destruction of the reputation of west St Kilda and the littoral—which had been gathering pace since the day Pretty Dulcie burst out of the Court House Hotel in her underwear wielding an axe and chasing a client who had quibbled at her price—seemed to be complete by the 1970s and 80s.

But in a way, St Kilda was indestructible because it was an idea as much as a place and a locality. The 'idea' of St Kilda began as a kind of colonial bonus—beauty, coastal exhilaration, peace where no one expected much at all. Only a few years after settlement, Charles Harpur—the first serious colonial poet and a *bush* poet at that—remarked of St Kilda that the 'beautiful shores of our bay have become a resort of numerous parties from town … a place far apart from the [city's] dust and bustle'.

The *idea* underwent, as we've seen, considerable metamorphosis, but it never lost its allure, even if the attraction became partly that of the forbidden, the exotic or the frankly sleazy. While Pretty Dulcie Markham's haunts fell into decay or were made over (the Court House Hotel is now the St Kilda Inn, for example), famous establishments like the Fitzroy Street George Hotel, of which Hal Porter was once the manager, and the Esplanade Hotel, which, with massive and vigorous community support, continues to survive corporate attempts to pull it down, live on into the twenty-first century, as does Leo's Spaghetti Bar and many other landmarks amid the rapidly gentrifying and ever more chic littoral. At the centre of which, incidentally, remain the Baths—no longer criminal, yet again rebuilt, still the focus of raging architectural, political, sociological and environmental argument.

But as well as being an 'idea' that entered the literature and culture of the country—a phenomenon which of course it shares with other city beaches and littorals, like Bondi and Cottesloe (I discount Coolangatta and Surfers as too recent)—the chequered history and many metamorphoses of the St Kilda littoral perhaps raise other questions and helps answer them.

In a country where the population from the start crowded to the coast and built coastal cities, how is it that our central myths derive so heavily from the interior? Why are the grim, saturnine bushman and the tough, heroic bushwoman and the thirsting outback at the heart of our national narrative and not the surfers and fishermen and sailors and the massive surrounding blue oceans and their bays and estuaries, where we float at the bottom of the world?

Well, look at the small but potent example of St Kilda and you find not the determination, the work ethic, the endurance, the moral fibre of the bush stereotype, but pleasure, hedonism, indulgence, *carpe diem*. And while St Kilda is a possibly special example—*sui generis*—the beach culture in Australia wherever encountered would present that general profile: not one, in short, to build your national myths on. Who wants a tradition polluted with human weaknesses and genuflections to temptation? A Latin temperament in the antipodes, banana republic laxness in the south? And so St Kilda and Bondi and the beach culture in general remain safely like the essays in *Playboy* and the racing guide in *Truth*: we love to take a look, but the tawdriness and vaguely forbidden images, the sheer, unaccountable pleasure in existence crowding at the edge of our glancing vision, has to be ignored as a candidate for national myth making. It's not really our thing.

Works cited

Splash! St Kilda Beach and Baths, an Exhibition curated by Gillian Upton with support from the City of Port Phillip's Art and Heritage Unit. It celebrated the reopening of the new St Kilda Sea Baths and aimed to place the enterprise in its historical context and to celebrate the rich history of bathing in St Kilda. *Splash* both celebrated and documented Australian's special love affair with St Kilda beach and baths.

Gillian Upton, *The George: St Kilda Life and Times*, St Kilda Historical Society

Edmund Finn, Maggie Weidenhofer, *Chronicles of Early Melbourne, 1835–1852.* (Melbourne, Nelson, 1967).

Martin Boyd, *The Cardboard Crown*, (Harmondsworth, Penguin, 1964).

Fergus Hume, *The Mystery of a Hansom Cab,* (Melbourne, Sun Books, 1971).

Mark Brandon ('Chopper') Read, *The Blowtorch Trilogy*, (Kilmore, Vic, Floradale/ Sly Ink, 2003a).

Colonial Coastlines: 'Unsettled' Settlements

One of the most significant beach side developments in Western Australia has been Port Bouvard. It is a development south of Perth, located on the border of the Mandurah and Peel regions, and is now one of the fastest growing regions in Australia. In one sense it represents the border between the southern most extension of the Perth conurbation (Mandurah) and northern most region of the south west rural areas. For the most part Port Bouvard sits on and around the northern embankment of the Peel inlet which is the mouth of the Murray River. The Peel inlet has been subject to extensive engineering with significant reinforcement of the embankments and dredging of the inlet to prevent the build up of silt and the build up of nutrients in the river system. In other words, Port Bouvard represents a development conundrum. On the one hand the engineering work indicates that Port Bouvard is located within a fragile ecological system; on the other hand it is a development that is the epitome of postmodern desirability and beachside lifestyle. And it is this contrast that suggests that at least in the case of Port Bouvard that the return to the beach is not without its anxieties.

The name Port Bouvard functions in two ways. It evokes the French exploration of the South West coast, notably from 1772 to 1801 with the voyages of St Allouran, D'Entrecasteaux and Baudin. Port Bouvard takes its name from Cape Bouvard named by Baudin after French astronomer Alexis Buvard. Port Bouvard then maintains its ties to Australia's European history. More than this, though, Port Bouvard maintains a tie to European culture through its promotion as a place whereby people can enjoy a Mediterranean lifestyle. It reaches out to the French Riviera.

Local histories inform us that:

[t]he first people known to have inhabited the area were people of the Bibbulmun tribe. These people lived well off the land, which abounded in fish, game, berries and fruits. The locality was known as Mandjar, which translates as 'meeting place.' After European settlement the name was adapted to Mandurah.[1]

Settlement began in the 1830s, following the establishment of the Swan

River settlement. From Perth, it was a day's journey by sea and a couple of days' journey overland. In the early years, provisioning came from outside and the settlement remained isolated until the 1850s. Nevertheless, the area developed a significant fishery with an accompanying cannery and later a timber mill that drew on the forests around Pinjarra. At the turn of the twentieth century Mandurah emerged as a holiday destination for people from the goldfields. By the 1920s the cannery and the timber mill had closed, and Mandurah settled into a small agricultural community boosted by a holiday season. In other words, it became a place to go for a holiday.

The current development can be read as a nexus between the colonial and the postmodern (or late-capitalism) and is marked by colonial erasure and postmodern celebration of lifestyle. Port Bouvard is divided into four precincts: Northport, Southport, Eastport and Bouvard Island. Northport is promoted as a place to relax or go surfing; Eastport as a place to relax or go boating; Southport as a place to relax or go golfing. The pressure is on; the overall promotion is ironically 'Do nothing and you could miss out'.

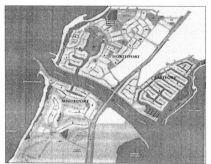

General Outline of Port Bouvard

The project is promoted by television and fishing identity Rex Hunt and, as expected, the beach and fishing are celebrated. However, the primary concern is the promotion of a lifestyle that erases the beach and the history of the site. As mentioned earlier, the developers want to sell Port Bouvard as a Mediterranean experience. Bouvard Island, a newly completed artificial island, is promoted as:

> a truly unique lifestyle opportunity—the chance to live on your own island, with a private, secure access way, and your own private jetty and water access … A variety of home styles are available, including elegant Mediterranean villas and studio apartments … with design suitable for singles, couples and families. Building covenants will ensure housing is of the highest standard, and in harmony with the exclusive island atmosphere.

Forming the hub of the development is the recently finished Piazza, more properly The Piazza. And, according to the developer the 'Mediterranean-style precinct' … 'generated total sales of over $8 million'. The nearby international standard golf course features an 'up-market restaurant … The Mediterranean'.[2]

View of Island

The Piazza

Port Bouvard is a very expensive, massive engineering exercise. It involves not only the creation of islands and canals, but also the optimisation of water flows in order to prevent a return mosquito-infested wetlands, given that the Mandurah-Peel region is estuarine. Overall, the development does not pretend to take advantage of natural contours of the landscape. Port Bouvard is not sold within the rhetorics of sixties and seventies suburban developments that led to the Australian experience of conurbation along the coast. While it gestures towards the idea of suburban village, it is sold as an up-to-the minute lifestyle and/or leisure precinct, home to the aspirational classes, living precariously on the credit boom, and to a semi-retired business community. It is seductive in a kind of high-end Macdonaldisation.

However, the excess surrounding Port Bouvard signifies 'unsettledness' and a lack of connectedness. It erases and writes over what has gone before. In reading

Douglas Sellicks *First Impressions of Albany, 1790–1900*, one can see the gradual disappearance of the Indigenous presence; they simply cease to exist in visitors' accounts. Similarly, the labour that went into making Albany is erased as visitors become more interested in what they can do there. In a sense, Port Bouvard does the same but in a much more compressed time period, and perhaps that is why it is unsettling. The beach almost disappears under the efforts to change the area into a lifestyle precinct.

Port Bouvard encapsulates a modern dilemma: the relation between work and leisure. From about 1840 onward in the West the beach has become a site of leisure; at Port Bouvard leisure has become lifestyle, ironically requiring a great deal of time, effort and labour. The beach compromises work and work compromises the beach.

How does the idea of the beach changes from the premodern to the modern? Alain Corbin, in the *Lure of the Sea*, reminds us that in premodernity, while Europe dwelled in a deistic universe in which the sea and the coastline were reminders of The Flood. Coastlines were the sublime ruins of the time before, and the beach was where the monsters of the deep, in their time of death, were cast ashore as a reminder of what dangers and evils lay beyond. The beach, then, often read positively as transitional space, has a longer and current history as a place of risk and perhaps a space of abjection. The beach may be a site of communication, whether of promise or threat—just what does that sail on the horizon mean? In its quotidian rhythms the beach is a site of arrival and departure, a gateway for the passage of people. But in the extreme, arrival is abandonment and departure is rescue, if one happens to be fortunate. In terms of colonial settlement the beach is unsettled in its purpose; it is a return or a reminder of the premodern. The colonial beach is a place of uncertainty.

To address these questions, we need to consider aspects of Daniel Defoe's *Robinson Crusoe*, the mythologisation of the Death(s) of James Cook, and Joseph Conrad's *Heart of Darkness*, invoking a cultural chronology in which Cook's death comes first. *Robinson Crusoe* may have been written earlier, but *Crusoe* can be read as a type of postfiguration in relation to Cook's death on the beach at Kealakekua Bay on the island of Hawai'i on 14 February 1779.

Roy Edmund reminds us that in the mythologising of Cook's death lies an event that, in its singularity, brings together the encounter between the premodern and the modern; it signals the convergence of modernity and colonialism in which the tragic but triumphalist celebration of bourgeois and national ideas of science and progress jostle with a pure expression of modest heroism. Little wonder Cook 'was presented as a role model to generations of Victorian schoolboys, particularly the younger sons of large middle-class Victorian families who had to leave home to better themselves'.[3] And in this regard Cook connects back to Crusoe and forward to Marlow.

Edmund makes three significant claims about Cook and his explorations. Cook's death 'became the founding event of colonial pacific history, that beginning which … is necessary if the European presence is to be justified and its usurping violence disavowed or suppressed'.[4] In the twentieth century his reputation was redeployed, 'particularly in the white settlements of Australia and New Zealand which adopted him as the founding father of their Anglo-Saxon nationhood'.[5]

In 1784 the Admiralty commissioned an extravagant account of Cook's third voyage, running to a cost of 4,000 pounds. Edmund notes that:

> [i]t was one of the earliest … examples of the state subsidizing publication of its discoveries. And to complete this assertion of national strength and identity through the launching of Cook as a national hero and prototype of the modern scientific explorer, the volumes were inscribed to the memory of 'The ablest and most renowned navigator this or any other country hath produced'.[6]

The significance of the Admiralty's action is that while it is clearly a celebration of Britain's colonial enterprise, it does so in modest fashion. What is important in this valorisation is the descriptor 'the ablest', pointing to the idea of work rather than conquest as the driving force behind British expansion. As a type of 'worker hero' drafted for the purposes of an expansionary bourgeois state, Cook through his life and death embodies the Aristotelian ideal of virtue expressed in the convergence of work and public service, which in turn acts as a disavowal of colonial usurpation and violence.

Edmund suggests that not only does Cook's death mark the beginning of colonial presence in the Pacific, but that also it breaks free from history. In general, it comes to mark colonial expansion expressed in the virtue of labour. It is this that allows us to consider Defoe, and Conrad and the Port Bouvard development in terms of the relationship between work and the beach. Paradoxically, while he may have been 'the ablest and most renowned navigator' and duly honoured for such work, as the cartographer of the colonial contact zone Cook is also something of a privileged beachcomber. The majesty of first landings gives way to the work of settlement in which case the contact zone, as Cook discovered on his return, is a precarious place. Work has to be done elsewhere. Part of this elsewhere is Crusoe's island.

Defoe's *Robinson Crusoe* is an ur-colonialist text, an ur- text because while it represents the beginning of an expansionist project Defoe's Crusoe inhabits a transitional space as mercantile transforms to the colonial proper. In comparison

Conrad is clearly aware that, some 180 years later, he is writing within a colonial space. However, an immediate concern is with Crusoe's relationship to his island and its beach. Robert P Marzec reminds us that when Crusoe first sights the island 'he codes the land "more frightful than the Sea"'.[7] This encoding refers to the shore, and even more precisely the unknown and unknowable shore. At the height of the storm we are told:

> [a]s to making sail, we had none … so we work'd at the oar towards the land, tho' with heavy hearts, like Men going to Execution; for all we knew, that when the Boat came nearer the Shore, she would be dash'd in a Thousand Pieces by the Breach of the Sea. However, we committed our souls to God in the most earnest manner … we hasten'd our own destruction with our own hands, pulling as well as we could towards Land. What the Shore was, whether Rock or Sand, whether Steep or Shoal we knew not; the only Hope that could rationally give us the least Shadow of Expectation, was, if we might happen into some bay or Gulph … But there was nothing of this appeared; but as we made nearer and nearer the Shore , the Land look'd more frightful than the Sea.[8]

Crusoe here evokes that pre-modern sense of the shore as a dangerous and forbidding place, where people labour at risk and as a site where the malevolent may be washed up. After the shipwreck, apart from the necessity of getting supplies ashore, Crusoe's priority is to vacate to the interior, not to the fringes of the beach but to the interior proper. He says: 'My next Work was to view the Country, and seek a proper Place for my Habitation, and where to stow my Goods to secure them from whatever may happen'.[9] He is successful in this, finding 'a little Plain on the Side of a rising Hill'.[10] This is important for a number of reasons. For Crusoe the understanding of the beach as a place of threat is underscored by the fact that the interior has a familiarity about it; it is the place that can be made knowable and it is a place where work can be done. Virginia Birdsall argues that 'Crusoe is always attempting to bring the wild, the threatening, the chaotic under rational control—that is subject to his own mastery'.[11] Birdsall is correct, but this refers to the interior of the island; this cannot be achieved on the beach, which is subject to too much change and the threat of unpredictable visitation. And regardless of Crusoe's ability through work to extend his dwelling to property to estate to colony, this does not extend in the final analysis to the shore. Without rehearsing the rescue of Friday (rescued to the interior) and others, it can be generally understood that the shore, for Crusoe, always remains unsettled and unsettling.

In Conrad's *Heart of Darkness* the concern is not so much with the heart but with Marlow's reaction to the beach head. Conrad's Marlow embodies modernity and colonialism. On the one hand, in being likened to a meditating Buddha, he literally embodies the colonial encounter; on the other hand he is driven by modernity's problematic assimilation of work, progress and civilisation. For Marlow, work and the colonial project are convergent if not coincident. And significantly, as with Crusoe, work can only take place and should only take place in the interior; Marlow tells us that his work begins some 200 miles inland from the shore. For a man of the sea, this sounds problematic but we see that Marlow indeed is unsettled by the colonial shore, for a number of reasons. First, because it is unknowable; and second because it is a place of trade, of exchange, which for Marlow does not appear to rate as work because trade does not mesh with progress and a civilising mission.

In terms of the shore, there are three significant events for Marlow pointing to the disturbing nature of the beach. In his encounter with the French man-of-war, Marlow provides a description pointing to Colonial indolence and purposelessness. There is a sense of an infectious incomprehensibility. The coast cannot be known and this leads to incomprehensible action—if you do not understand the space, how can what you do have any meaning? The lack of intent and the accompanying laziness is what disturbs Marlow:

> Once … we came upon a man-of-war anchored off the coast. There wasn't even a shed there and she was shelling the bush … Her ensign drooped limp like a rag, the muzzles of the long six-inch guns stuck out all over the low hull, the greasy slimy swell swung her up lazily and let her down, swaying her thin masts. In the empty immensity of earth, sky and water, there she was, incomprehensible, firing into a continent. Pop, would go one of the six-inch guns … and nothing happened. Nothing could happen.[12]

More tellingly Marlow's account invokes the post-Flood world that Courbin describes, and we feel a dread and a fear of the unknown and the unknowable. The shore is not somewhere one would wish to spend much time:

> We called at more places with farcical names where the merry dance of death and trade goes on in a still and earthy atmosphere as of an overheated catacomb; all along the formless coast bordered by dangerous surf, as if nature herself had tried to ward off intruders; in and out of rivers, streams of death in life, whose banks were rotting into mud, whose waters, thickened into slime, invaded the contorted mangroves that seemed to writhe at us in the extremity of an impotent despair. Nowhere did we stop long enough to get particularised impression, but the general sense of vague and oppressive wonder grew upon me. It was like a weary pilgrimage amongst hints for nightmares.[13]

Disturbingly, this unsettling contact zone projects thirty miles up river to the company station, marked, as we know, by pointless busyness, waste and brutal exploitation that reduces the local people to mere spectres haunting the colonial coast.

The point is that despite the ritualistic grandeur of the landing characterising the work of the explorer, thereafter the colonial coast is not necessarily a nice place to be. We might need to move on to consider the precariousness of the various settlements in Australia, long dependent on supplies until passage into the hinterland allowed for work to be truly undertaken.

However, at the same time the colonial coast was viewed with trepidation, the beach at home was undergoing a change. Courbin notes that from 1750 to 1845 pictorial representations of the beach shifted from representations of the people and the precarious work of the shore line to representations of aristocratic and bourgeois figures undertaking amateur collections and then to figures strolling along the promenade or perhaps walking the beach. He argues at the same time that we see the beach and the sea prescribed as places of healing and restoration. In the first instance, if one could afford it one would go to the beach resort or spa to take in the air, and, a little later in this process of transformation, perhaps take to the waters. Still later the beach becomes a place of leisure, entertainment and ultimately the emergence of the beach as a holiday place, a place distinct from and limited by work and domestic space. This transformation is exported later to the colonial settlements as they become imbricated in the relationship between work and leisure.

Thus, in modernity, the beach has various configurations. The first is the lingering but powerful pre-modern figure of the beach as a place of risk. However, by the mid-nineteenth century the beach enjoys a colonialist transformation, as it becomes a place for aristocratic rest and restoration as, for example, at Brighton, while in Blackpool or St Kilda or Manly it becomes a democratised and proletarian space. The key sense of the beach here is that it is the special place of the holiday. In our contemporary, postmodern times, often signalled in the memory 'we used to go to Christies Beach or Point Perron for a holiday', the beach has come adrift as a holiday place and become entangled, as seen in the Port Bouvard development, in the concept of lifestyle, but in so doing it appears to gesture back to the unease of the premodern. The aftermath of the Flood still marks the colonial shore, the phantasmic image of the flood that was and is colonialism. No matter the work done to transform, hide or disguise that feeling, the unsettledness remains.

Notes

1 http://www.Mandurah.wa.gov.au/council/history 5/12/2005
2 ttp://www.portbuvard.com.au/pbsite 5/12/2005
3 Roy Edmund, *Representing the South Pacific: Colonial Discourse from Cook to Gaugin* (Cambridge: Cambridge UP, 1997) 41.
4 Edmund, *Representing the South Pacific* 23.
5 Edmund, *Representing the South Pacific* 24.
6 Edmund, *Representing the South Pacific* 30.
7 Robert P. Marzec, 'Enclosures, Colonization, and the Robinson Crusoe Syndrome: A Genealogy of Land in a Global Context', *boundary 2*, 29.2 (2002): 129.
8 Daniel Defoe, *Robinson Crusoe*, ed. Michael Shinagel (New York: Norton, 1975) 27.
9 Defoe, *Robinson Crusoe* 43.
10 Defoe, *Robinson Crusoe* 48.
11 Virginia Birdsall, *Defoe's Perpetual Seekers* (London: Bucknell University Press, 1985) 27.
12 Joseph Conrad, *Heart of Darkness*, ed. Robert Kimbrough (NewYork: Norton, 1988) 17.
13 Conrad, *Heart of Darkness* 17.

Works cited

Birdsall, Virginia. *Defoe's Perpetual Seekers*. London: Bucknell University Press, 1985.

Corbin, Alian. *The Lure of the Sea: The Discovery of the Seaside in the Western World, 1750 – 1840*. Trans. Jocelyn Phelps. Harmondsworth: Penguin, 1995.

Conrad, Joseph. *Heart of Darkness*, ed. Robert Kimbrough. New York: Norton, 1988.

Defoe, Daniel. *Robinson Crusoe*, ed. Michael Shinagel. New York: Norton, 1975.

Edmund, Roy. *Representing the South Pacific: Colonial Discourse from Cook to Gaugin*. Cambridge: Cambridge UP, 1997.

Marzec, Robert P. 'Enclosures, Colonization, and the Robinson Crusoe Syndrome: A Genealogy of Land in a Global Context', *boundary 2*, 29.2 (2002) 129–156.

Sellick, Douglas. *First Impressions of Albany, 1790–1900*. Perth: Museum of Western Australia, 2001.

About the authors

Professor **Margaret Allen** teaches Gender Studies with a strong historical flavour at the University of Adelaide. She is interested in transnational, postcolonial and feminist histories and whiteness. Her current ARC funded research focuses upon relationships between India and Australia and Indians and Australians in the late 19th and early 20th centuries. She is working on Australian women missionaries in India as well as exploring the ways Indian men domiciled in Australia negotiated the White Australia Policy. Gender and notions of difference are central in her work. She has also researched 19th century Australian women writers and the making of a colonial culture. Professor Allen is working on a biography of the writer, Catharine E.M. Martin. She has long experience in oral history, and participated in a project on oral histories of older women of non-English speaking backgrounds. She is currently doing interviews as part of the Don Dunstan Oral History Project. She has been a Chief Investigator on the ARC funded Australian Women's Archives Project since 2003. See http://www.nfaw.org/women-s-history/

Ron Blaber is Head of Department of Communication and Cultural Studies in the School of Media Culture and Creative Arts at Curtin University. His research spans postcolonial studies, literary studies and cultural studies. His current research interests focus on the emergence of 'Post-civil' society and postnational identity. His path began doing Doctoral work at Flinders University under the supervision of Syd Harrex and Brian Matthews, for which he is deeply grateful.

Jonathan Bollen is co-author of *Men at Play: Masculinities in Australian Theatre since the 1950s* and co-editor of *What a Man's Gotta Do? Masculinities in Performance*. He trained in performance studies at the University of Sydney and the University of Western Sydney. In 2002 he received an Australian Research Council postdoctoral fellowship in theatre studies at the University of New England. His research on gender, sexuality and performance has been published in *The Drama Review, Australasian Drama Studies* and *Social Semiotics*. He now lectures in drama at Flinders University in Adelaide and reviews performance for *RealTime*.

Moya Costello has a PhD in Creative Writing from the University of Adelaide and she teaches Writing in the School of Arts and Social Sciences at Southern Cross University. Her three books are *Kites Jakarta* (Sea Cruise Books, 1985), *Small Ecstasies* (UQP, 1994) and *The Office as a Boat: A Chronicle* (Brandl & Schlesinger, 2000). She recently co-edited *Re-Placement* (SCU Press, 2008).

Dorothy Driver holds a half-time professorship in the Discipline of English, Adelaide University, and taught for many years at the University of Cape Town, South Africa, where she is now an honorary research associate. She has published journal articles and book chapters on aspects of South African literature and has edited books on South African women writers.

In 2007 **Caroline Ford** completed her Doctorate at the University of Sydney, which examined the development of a beach culture in Sydney between 1810 and 1920, with a particular emphasis on the creation of public spaces along the coast. This article has come out of that thesis. As a history researcher for Surf Life Saving Australia, Caroline was involved in the 2007 Year of the Surf Lifesaver celebrations, contributing to their centenary history book and the National Museum of Australia's travelling exhibition. Caroline is currently working as a cultural heritage researcher for the Department of Environment and Climate Change (NSW).

Lucy Frost is Professor of English at the University of Tasmania and Director of the multi-disciplinary Centre for Colonialism and its Aftermath. She has long been interested in the experiences of women in colonial Australia and her books in this area include *No Place for a Nervous Lady, A Face in the Glass, The Journal of Annie Baxter Dawbin 1858-1868,* and *Chain Letters: Narrating Convict Lives* (a collection of essays edited with historian Hamish Maxwell-Stewart). In collaboration with Susan Ballyn from the University of Barcelona, she has written about Spanish and lusaphone convicts transported to Australia, and they are the joint authors of *Adelaide de la Thoreza: A Convict Woman in Colonial Australia.* At present she is writing a collective biography of 78 women tried in Scotland and transported to Van Diemen's Land in 1838 aboard the *Atwick.*

Chad Habel completed his PhD in 2006, which has been published by VDM Verlag under the title *Ancestral Narratives: Irish-Australian Identities in History and Fiction*. His research interests include Australian, Irish and Asian Literature and History, Post-colonial Studies, Film Studies, Nationalism and Gender. His postdoctoral research applies Deleuze and Guattari's notion of the rhizome to ancestry and cultural identity. His career so far has been, in the words of one savvy commentator, 'more like a bus than a plane'.

Steve Hemming lectures in Australian Studies, Cultural Studies and Indigenous Studies at Flinders University. He was a long-time curator in the South Australian Museum's Anthropology Division and has been working with Indigenous nations in South Australia for twenty years. He has worked for a number of Indigenous organisations as a community researcher and native title anthropologist. More recently his research has focused on the colonial genealogies of cultural heritage management and traditionalist understandings of Indigenous culture.

Rick Hosking is an Associate Professor in English, Creative Writing, and Australian Studies at Flinders University where he teaches Australian Studies, colonial literary studies, historical fiction and travel writing. He co-authored with Robert Foster and Amanda Nettelbeck *Fatal Collisions: the South Australian Frontier and the Violence of Memory*.

Susan Hosking is a Senior Lecturer in English at the University of Adelaide. Her particular interests are contemporary Australian fiction, sources of historical fiction and literature that represents interactions between Indigenous and European cultures. She has published on Katharine Susannah Prichard, Mudrooroo (Colin Johnson), Archie Weller, South Australian Indigenous life narratives and literary and cultural representations of life in Australia.

John McLaren is former editor of *Overland* and *Australian Book Review*, and has recently published a memoir, *Not in Tranquillity*. His biography of Vincent Buckley was published in 2009.

Peter Manthorpe is a master mariner who has 'swallowed the anchor' and now lives in Tasmania, overlooking the sea.

Brian Matthews, who founded Australian literature courses at Flinders University, was Fulbright Scholar at the University of Oregon (1986), Professor of Australian Studies at London University (1993-96) and held Flinders' first Personal Chair in English. He won the Victorian, NSW and Queensland Premiers' Literary Awards, the Gold Medal of The Australian Literature Society, and, jointly, the John Hetherington Bicentennial Biography Prize. Well known as a columnist in *The Weekend Australian Magazine* and *Eureka Street*, he won the ARPA Award for best humorous column (2003 and 2008) and the ACPA Award for Best Columnist (2005). He is Professor of English at Flinders University. In 2008 Allen and Unwin published his biography, *Manning Clark A Life.*

Kay Merry is a PhD candidate in the Department of History at Flinders University. Soon after commencing her BA degree, in 1995, she discovered that one of her ancestors was an Indigenous woman from North East Tasmania who was abducted by a British sealer as an adolescent in 1810 and taken to Hunter Island in Bass Strait. This inspired her to study History, with an emphasis on contact between Indigenous and European people in the early colonial era.

Stephen Muecke is Professor of Writing at the University of NSW, his latest book is *Joe in the Andamans and Other Fictocritical Stories*, Sydney: Local Consumption Publications, 2008.

When **Maria Nugent** wrote her contribution to this volume, she held an ARC Postdoctoral Fellowship in the School of Historical Studies at Monash University in Melbourne. She is currently a Research Fellow in the Centre for Historical Research at the National Museum of Australia in Canberra. She is the author of *Botany Bay: Where Histories Meet* (Allen & Unwin, 2005) and *Captain Cook Was Here* (Cambridge University Press, 2009).

Rebecca Pannell has taught Australian Studies, Cultural Studies and Academic Professional Development at Flinders University and has written about spirituality in Australian performance texts. She is a graduate of the University of Adelaide BA (Hons) and is completing her PhD in Theology and Cultural Studies. Her research interests are broad and include Australian Film, Theology and the Arts, and Popular culture and Religion. Rebecca is also a graduate of the Adelaide Centre for the Performing Arts with a career in performance and dramaturgy. She is currently Head of Lincoln College, a residential college affiliated with the University of Adelaide where she lives with 230 residents from across the world.

Daryle Rigney is an Associate Professor of Indigenous Education and Indigenous Studies at the Yunggorendi, First Nations Centre for Higher Education and Research at Flinders University. Daryle as a representative of the Ngarrindjeri Nation Co-Chairs the Governing Board of the United League of Indigenous Nations Treaty.

Graham Rowlands is an Adelaide-based poet who has published widely in Australian magazines and newspapers since the late 1960s. In 2002 he was awarded the Barbara Hanrahan Fellowship.

Michael X. Savvas has completed a PhD at Flinders University and now works as an editor.

Susan Sheridan is Adjunct Professor of English and Womens Studies at Flinders University. She has published widely on womens writing, feminist cultural studies, Australian cultural history and womens studies. Her books include *Christina Stead* (Harvester (1988), *Along the Faultlines: Sex, Race and Nation in Australian womens writing 1880s to 1930s* (Allen & Unwin, 1995), and most recently *Who Was That Woman? The Australian Womens Weekly in the Postwar Years* (UNSW Press, 2002). As editor, she has recently published, with Paul Genoni, *Thea Astley's Fictional Worlds* (Cambridge Scholars Press, 2006). Current research project is a study of women writers and modernity in mid twentieth century Australia.

Heather Taylor Johnson moved from America to Australia in 1999. She holds a PhD in Creative Writing from the University of Adelaide, is a poetry editor for *Wet Ink* magazine and the author of a collection of poems published by Picaro Press, entitled *Exit Wounds*. She reviews poetry and other artforms regularly and is a sessional tutor in Media Studies at the University of Adelaide. She lives in Adelaide with her husband and three young children.

Helen Tiffin is Professor of English at the University of Tasmania. Her publications include (with Bill Ashcroft and Gareth Griffiths) *The Empire Writes Back: Theory & Practice in Post-Colonial Literatures* (1989, revised edition 2002), *Post-Colonial Studies: The Key Concepts* (1998, revised edition 2007) and *Post-Colonial Literatures: General, Theoretical & Comparative 1970–1993* (1997, with Alan Lawson et al.). Her most recent research is in the field of Animal Studies.

Annie Werner has completed a PhD in the school of English Literatures, Philosophy and Languages at the University of Wollongong. Her thesis is titled *Curating Inscription: The Legacy of Textual Exhibitions of Tattooing iin Colonial Literarture*. Like many English graduates, she currently works in the field of environmental education and conservation land management.

Richard White teaches Australian history and the history of travel and tourism at the University of Sydney. His publications include *Inventing Australia, The Oxford Book of Australian Travel Writing, Cultural History in Australia* and a collaborative monograph, *On Holidays: A History of Getting Away in Australia*. In 2007 he edited a special issue of *Studies in Travel Writing* on Australia, and *Symbols of Australia*, co-edited with Melissa Harper, will appear in 2009. He is currently writing a history of the cooee and working on Australian tourism in Britain and overland travel through Asia.

Wakefield Press is an independent publishing and
distribution company based in Adelaide, South Australia.
We love good stories and publish beautiful books.
To see our full range of titles, please visit our website at
www.wakefieldpress.com.au.